KU-201-204

The Polity Reader in *Social Theory*

Polity Press

Copyright © this collection and introductory material Polity Press 1994.

First published in 1994 by Polity Press
in association with Blackwell Publishers

Reprinted 1995

Editorial Office:
Polity Press
65 Bridge Street
Cambridge CB2 1UR, UK

Marketing and production:
Blackwell Publishers, the publishing imprint of Basil Blackwell Ltd
108 Cowley Road
Oxford OX4 1JF, UK

All rights reserved. Except for the quotation of short passages for the purposes of criticism and review, no part of this publication may be reproduced, stored in a retrieval system, or transmitted, in any form or by any means, electronic, mechanical, photocopying, recording or otherwise, without the prior permission of the publisher.

Except in the United States of America, this book is sold subject to the condition that it shall not, by way of trade or otherwise, be lent, re-sold, hired out, or otherwise circulated without the publisher's prior consent in any form of binding or cover other than that in which it is published and without a similar condition including this condition being imposed on the subsequent purchaser.

ISBN 0 7456 1205 9
ISBN 0 7456 1206 7 (pbk)

British Library Cataloguing-in-Publication Data

A CIP catalogue record for this book is available from the British Library.

Typeset in 10 on 12 pt Times
by Graphicraft Typesetters Ltd, Hong Kong
Printed in Great Britain by
Hartnolls Ltd, Bodmin, Cornwall

This book is printed on acid-free paper.

Contents

The extracts in this volume are taken from the following Polity Press books:

Michèle Barrett, *The Politics of Truth* (1991)
Michèle Barrett and Anne Phillips, *Destabilizing Theory* (1992)
Zygmunt Bauman, *Modernity and Ambivalence* (1991)
Zygmunt Bauman, *Modernity and the Holocaust* (1989)
Ulrich Beck, *Organized Irresponsibility* (1994)
Richard Bellamy, *Modern Italian Social Theory* (1987)
Richard Bernstein, *Habermas and Modernity* (1985)
Norberto Bobbio, *The Future of Democracy* (1987)
Pierre Bourdieu, *The Logic of Practice* (1990)
Pierre Bourdieu, *Language and Symbolic Power* (1991)
Alex Callinicos, *Against Postmodernism* (1989)
Nancy J. Chodorow, *Feminism and Psychoanalytic Theory* (1989)
Christopher Dandeker, *Surveillance, Power and Modernity* (1990)
Boris Frankel, *The Post-Industrial Utopians* (1987)
David Frisby, *Fragments of Modernity* (1985)
Harold Garfinkel, *Studies in Ethnomethodology* (1984)
Clifford Geertz, *Works and Lives* (1988)
Anthony Giddens, *The Constitution of Society* (1984)
Anthony Giddens, *The Consequences of Modernity* (1990)
Erving Goffman, *Exploring the Interaction Order* (1988)
Robert E. Goodin, *Green Political Theory* (1992)
Jürgen Habermas, *The Theory of Communicative Action*, Volume 2 (1987)
Jürgen Habermas, *The Philosophical Discourse of Modernity* (1987)
Susan J. Hekman, *Hermeneutics and the Sociology of Knowledge* (1986)
David Held, *Political Theory Today* (1991)
David Held, *Models of Democracy* (1987)
David Held, *Prospects for Democracy* (1993)
Agnes Heller, *Can Modernity Survive?* (1990)
Scott Lash and John Urry, *The End of Organized Capitalism* (1987)
Niklas Luhmann, *Ecological Communication* (1989)
Mary Lyndon Shanley and Carole Pateman, *Feminist Interpretations and Political Theory* (1991)
Lois McNay, *Foucault and Feminism* (1992)
Wolfgang J. Mommsen, *The Political and Social Theory of Max Weber* (1989)
Mark Poster, *Foucault, Marxism and History* (1984)
Mark Poster, *Jean Baudrillard* (1988)
John B. Thompson, *Ideology and Modern Culture* (1990)
Gianni Vattimo, *The Transparent Society* (1992)
Janet Wolff, *Feminine Sentences* (1990)

Acknowledgements

All the selections in this book are taken from works published by Polity Press. The choice of articles, Introduction and descriptive material at the opening of the sections was the result of a collaborative editorial enterprise. The following individuals were involved: Anthony Giddens, David Held, Don Hubert, Debbie Seymour and John Thompson.

We would like to thank the authors and, for sources that originally appeared in other languages, the publishers, for permission to reprint extracts as follows: 1, Wolfgang J. Mommsen; 2, David Frisby; 3, Richard Bellamy; 4, Stanford University Press; 5, Michèle Barrett; 6, Susan Hekman; 7, Prentice-Hall Inc.; 8, Randall Collins; 9, Anthony Giddens; 10, Anthony Giddens; 11, Pierre Bourdieu; 12, Pierre Bourdieu; 13, Jon Elster; 14, John Thompson; 15, Beacon Press; 16, MIT Press; 17, Richard Rorty; 18, Mark Poster; 19, Lois McNay; 20, Nancy Fraser; 21, Janet Wolff; 22, Sylvia Walby; 23, Nancy Chodorow; 24, Agnes Heller; 25, Scott Lash and John Urry; 26, Immanuel Wallerstein; 27, Christopher Dandeker; 28, Giulio Einaudi Editore; 29, David Held; 30, David Held; 31, Boris Frankel; 32, Westdeutscher Verlag GmbH; 33, Robert Goodin; 34, Suhrkamp Verlag; 35, Zygmunt Bauman; 36, Stanford University Press; 37, Garzanti Editore; 38, Alex Callinicos; 39, Zygmunt Bauman.

Every effort has been made to trace all copyright holders, but if any have been inadvertently overlooked, the publishers will be pleased to make the necessary arrangement at the first opportunity.

Introduction

The field of social theory is very wide, embracing as it does issues that span the whole of the social sciences and even the humanities. We can divide social theory into three major areas of concern – each of these covers a diversity of issues and problems.

The first domain of social theory is that of *methodology*. 'Methodology' here does not refer to concrete practices of research, but to the logical and philosophical questions that such practices presuppose. Since their inception, the social sciences have been riven by methodological debates. How should we best study human beings, their social and cultural products? What counts as appropriate 'evidence' in social science? How far does the logical form of the social sciences approximate to that of natural science? Can we expect to discover laws of human social behaviour similar to the laws of nature?

A second type of concern is *substantive*: the analysis of *modernity* and its impact on the world. Within two or three centuries, modern industrial capitalism, originating in the West, has swept all before it. All earlier civilizations have become either dissolved or altered beyond recognition by the impact of modern social forms. What explains the extraordinary dynamism of modernity and modernity's global spread? How should we best characterize modern institutions? In what sense, or senses, are they specifically 'Western'? What concepts should we use to characterize the nature of modernity?

The third set of issues concerns *critique*. For many social thinkers social theory should not only analyse social reality but should offer ways of transforming it in the interests of human betterment. But what guise should such a critical theory take? How can we be sure that the values involved in a given critique are not partial or one-sided? How should critical theory be connected to practice? For there is little point criticizing a given state of affairs if no practical means exist to change it.

Issues of methodology

For many years one of the main methodological divisions in social analysis was between those authors for whom the social sciences are close to natural science, on the one hand, and those who see a logical gulf between social and natural science on the other. Everyone recognizes that studying human social action and institutions cannot be exactly the same as studying objects in nature. Yet the dominant traditions in social theory, at least until the relatively recent period, tended to stress the affinities between them.

The tone was set in the nineteenth century by Auguste Comte's conception of 'positive philosophy'. Comte's positive philosophy, or, as he sometimes also called it, 'positivism', asserted the logical unity of all science. For Comte the sciences, including both the natural and the social sciences, exist in a hierarchy. The sciences of greatest generality, such as mathematics or physics, are at the foundation of the hierarchy: the phenomena they study include the domains of all the other scientific disciplines. Social science, or sociology, stands at the top of the hierarchy. It presumes the laws of all the other sciences but, like each of them, has its own autonomy and specific domain of analysis. Its objective is to discover laws of human behaviour and history comparable in character to the natural sciences which stand below it in the hierarchy.

Comte's ideas strongly influenced the writings of Emile Durkheim, and from there were conveyed into other schools of thought in twentieth-century social theory. Durkheim asserted that 'social facts' are as objective and 'given' as facts of nature; society pre-exists the individual and exerts a constraining effect upon his or her activities. He was critical of Comte's picture of the hierarchy of the sciences, but accepted the logical proximity of social science to the sciences of nature.

From the beginning others placed this type of view in question, particularly within the tradition of thought associated in Germany with the 'human sciences' (*Geisteswissenschaften*). According to authors in this tradition, human social action depends upon reasons, intentions and meanings; it has to be 'understood' in terms of its intelligibility and cannot be reduced to causal or law-like explanations. Max Weber was strongly influenced by this perspective, although he fashioned his own particular version of it. Human social life, he agreed, is indeed quite distinct from events in the realm of nature and has to be grasped in terms of its intelligibility; having 'understood' human behaviour, however, one can then go on to provide a causal account of it. Weber thus drew upon the hermeneutic tradition but in a somewhat novel and idiosyncratic fashion.

As in his studies of the development of modern capitalism, Max Weber set out his methodological views in specific opposition to those of Karl Marx. Marx was hostile to Comte's ideas, but nevertheless saw his 'materialist conception of history' as essentially an objective endeavour. Marx spoke of the 'iron laws' of capitalist development and believed that he was founding a more thorough-going science of society than had any of his predecessors or contemporaries. Marx's close associate, Friedrich Engels, regarded Marxism as what he called 'scientific socialism'. According to Engels, Marx showed that the transition from capitalism to socialism was inevitable – determined by causes as compelling as forces of nature.

At the same time, it should be noted, Marx's legacy was to some extent ambiguous. 'Scientific socialism' was the keynote of orthodox forms of Marxism, including those which became the official ideology of the Soviet Union, Eastern Europe and China. Other authors claiming to draw inspiration from Marx (such as those associated with the Frankfurt School), however, interpreted Marx differently. They saw Marxism less as a science than as a method stressing the historical and cultural character of human social organization.

Over the past half century or so this division between 'naturalistic' and 'interpretative' social science has become regarded by many with increasing scepticism. In some part this is because of changes in our understanding of natural science itself. The natural sciences used to be seen in terms akin to those Comte set out: as disciplines concerned above all with law-like explanation and causal analysis. During more recent years, however, this view has ceded place to one which holds that natural science has its own hermeneutic tasks and concerns. The natural sciences, in other words, develop frames of meaning that make the physical world intelligible to us in specific ways. It is not just the social sciences which concern themselves with issues of meaning.

At the same time, conceptions of meaning and human action have altered significantly, particularly in relation to new views about the nature of language. In the 'newer tradition' of hermeneutics, represented by authors such as Hans-Georg Gadamer and Paul Ricoeur, the intelligibility of human activity and institutions is associated less with what Weber called 'subjective meaning' than with linguistic frames of reference. The meaningful character of human action is given above all by its saturation with language; and language is not a property of the individual but of the social collectivity. The contrast between the 'subjective' character of the human sciences and the 'objective' form of natural science is thus to some degree transcended.

Diverse authors such as Jürgen Habermas, Pierre Bourdieu and Anthony Giddens have contributed to these trends. Although these writers differ in both their methodological and substantive views, in each case they place in question the old divisions in social theory. Habermas argues that the social sciences incorporate naturalistic as well as hermeneutic elements and these are often closely fused. Bourdieu and Giddens place a strong emphasis upon social practices. According to Bourdieu, social life is to be examined in relation to what he calls the *habitus*. The 'habitus' refers to the active dispositions which social agents employ in the course of social life. Social organization, in Bourdieu's eyes, neither expresses 'subjective meaning' nor is just 'given' as are states of nature; rather, social forms are actively created and re-created in the course of day-to-day social activity.

Giddens gives prominence to what he calls the 'duality of structure'. Groups, collectivities and societies have definite structural characteristics and these present themselves 'objectively' to the individual actor. On the other hand, such structural characteristics are not like objects in nature, because they are brought about only in and through human action. According to the theorem of the duality of structure, social agents draw upon structural properties of social wholes in the conduct of their everyday behaviour, but that behaviour at the same time constitutes or gives form to those structural qualities.

The analysis of modernity

Marxism was for many years the main focal point for debates about modernity and its impact on the world. For Marx modernity is bound up above all with the imperatives of capitalist development. Capitalism has an inner dynamism deriving from the need continually to generate the profit upon which investment in a competitive market economy depends. The capitalist economic order therefore, Marx argued, is a restlessly expanding one. It cannot be contained within the confines of the Western regions that were its point of origin. The economic drive of capitalist expansion fuelled the spread of Western institutions across the world, incorporating or eradicating other cultures wherever they were encountered.

Capitalism in Marx's eyes is a contradictory social order, containing tensions that will sooner or later lead to its downfall. Capitalist societies are class societies in which the normal tendency of the system is to produce a high degree of inequality of wealth and power. Those who control the means of production – wealth, or capital – are able effectively to monopolize power in the political and cultural sectors also. The class dynamics of capitalism, according to Marx, are at the origin of its tendency to transform itself from within; class conflict eventually leads to processes of revolutionary change, overthrowing the capitalist order and instituting a socialist society.

Max Weber, the so-called 'bourgeois Marx', drew upon Marx's work in a systematic way but in the end produced a very different interpretation of the modern social order. Weber spoke of modern society as 'capitalist society', yet what he meant by the term was in some key respects quite different from Marx. For Weber, modern capitalism is certainly a system of competitive enterprise, but its most distinctive characteristic is its promotion of 'rationalization', not only in economic life but in other social spheres also. Rationalization means essentially the co-ordination, standardization and increased predictability of economic and social relations. In the social arena, rationalization equals bureaucracy: a bureaucratic organization is one that is carefully and consciously ordered, having clear levels of authority and decision-making. Rationalization and bureaucracy cannot be transcended by any kind of economic or political revolution. In Weber's eyes a socialist society would mean more bureaucracy and more unequal power, not less.

The views of Marx and Weber on modern capitalist development have influenced a whole host of writers during the present century. Thus in his master work *The Philosophy of Money*, Georg Simmel developed an analysis of modernity that pursued the theme of rationalization, drawing upon ideas from both Marx and Weber. Gramsci, Althusser and other explicitly 'Marxist' authors forcefully rejected the lines of thought developed by authors such as Weber and Simmel; but in 'bringing Marxist ideas up to date' they also substantially modified and elaborated upon them.

The central importance of Marxism to debates about the nature of modernity has today become undermined. One reason is the collapse of socialism in the former Soviet Union and in Eastern Europe. Well before this time, however, even those who professed themselves followers of Marx in the West had come to distance themselves quite radically from Marx's classical writings.

Habermas is perhaps the most influential social thinker today with an explicit allegiance to Marxist thought. His ideas, however, diverge very substantially from Marx's picture of modern social development. Habermas substitutes his own theory of social evolution for Marx's historical materialism; and his theory of modernity draws just as heavily upon Weber as upon Marx himself. The movement of modern institutions, according to Habermas, is towards an 'uncoupling' of the dominant political and economic orders from their grounding in the practical world of everyday life. They invade day-to-day life and denude it of its symbolic and normative content. This process of the 'colonization of the life-world' creates new strains and tensions within modern capitalism, more significant than those associated with class division as such. Peace movements, ecological movements and the feminist movement represent various forms of engagement with these tensions and contradictions.

Other leading theorists of modernity have broken with Marx more completely. The French theorist Michel Foucault, for example, came to see Marxism as a flawed and limited doctrine steeped in its nineteenth-century origins. Although Foucault's methodological standpoint is very different from that of Weber, Foucault reiterates some Weberian themes in his writings on the modern era. For Foucault the rise of modern society is bound up with the intensifying of surveillance. 'Surveillance' means the use of direct supervision and the control of information to create what Foucault calls a 'disciplinary society'. Social discipline, based upon the control of the body as well as the mental outlook of individuals, is epitomized by the emergence of the prison and the mental hospital from the late eighteenth century onwards. In these organizations people's lives are confined, regulated and administered; such systems of control mirror wider processes in the economy and political order.

The body becomes not only the focus of discipline, but a site for the generation of what Foucault calls 'biopower': power produced through the co-ordination of bodily movements and energies. 'Sexuality', Foucault asserts, has been created through the very spread of biopower; modern societies display a fascination and absorption with sex unknown to most other civilizations.

Foucault avoids use of the term 'postmodernity' and was sceptical of some ideas associated with it. Yet his writings have influenced authors who claim that today we are at the 'end of modernity'. Modern industrial society, they say, has been supplanted not by socialism – which has become a lapsed and failed project – but by a new form of social order, a postmodern one. Many of the most intense debates in social theory today centre upon this thesis.

The word 'postmodern' is often applied in a vague way and there is little overall consistency in its usage among different authors. Many have been influenced, however, by the specific interpretation put forward by the French philosopher Jean-François Lyotard. Lyotard speaks of the end of 'grand narratives' – the end of attempts to make some kind of overall sense of 'history'. The theories of Hegel or Marx would be prime examples of such narratives. 'History', according to Lyotard, has no definite form; moreover, the kinds of generalizing knowledge stressed as both desirable and necessary within Enlightenment thought are declared to be incoherent or impossible. In postmodern thought, there are no universal criteria of truth and claims to knowledge are always contextual. The postmodern image of contemporary social institutions sees the emergence of a consumer society, replacing the old productivism. The consumer society has no fixed roots and everyday experience within it is influenced by a diversity of sources of communication, particularly by electronic communication; it is an inherently pluralistic order.

Social theory, critical theory and feminism

Critical theory over recent years has been revitalized by the impact of feminist thought – which has made a major impact in social theory in general over the past three or four decades (although feminism, of course, stretches back well beyond this period). Feminists have attacked the core traditions in social theory, pointing out that such traditions mostly had little to say either about the role of women in society or about issues of gender more broadly understood. As a result of the interventions of feminists, the study of patriarchy (the domination of men over women) now forms a central part of the social science agenda.

Some versions of feminist theory have been heavily indebted to Marxism. Others have from the beginning rejected Marx and have seen feminism as altogether more radical intellectually and politically. Postmodern theory has also in recent years heavily influenced some forms of feminist thinking. Postmodernism has seemed attractive to feminist theorists because it attacks conceptions of truth and scientific authority that might be seen as expressions of a 'masculine' orientation to the world and to knowledge. Since postmodernism embraces pluralism it tolerates the existence of many different voices, including those of women speaking out against male material and intellectual dominance. It should be noted, however, that many feminists are also critical of postmodernism and continue to draw their inspiration from other sources.

Feminism has made major contributions to the rethinking of critical theory that is proceeding today. The very idea of 'social science as critique' is now the subject of widespread discussion. For more than a century, even among those who rejected it, Marxism was of core importance for debates about critical social thought. Whether for it or against it, socialism seemed the main issue on the agenda when likely future transformations of the current social order were addressed.

Such is no longer the case. Ideals of socialism still persist and there are many who would wish to claim that socialist thought should continue to be defended today. Others, however, have abandoned Marx's idea of a 'union of theory and practice' altogether, or have come to re-cast critical theory in quite a different light from previous generations. We cannot say at the moment what is likely to emerge from a situation of some intellectual turmoil; but if new forms of critical practice emerge, they will certainly have to incorporate the issues raised by feminism, ecological movements and other groups that have stamped their mark on current debates.

An ellipsis has been used whenever material from the original has been omitted. Where more than a paragraph has been excluded, a line space appears above and below [. . .].

PART I

Some Schools of Social Theory: Marx and Weber to Gadamer and Ricoeur

MAX WEBER'S LIFELONG intellectual and political engagement with the residue of Marxist thought was one of the main formative influences upon the development of twentieth-century social theory. As Wolfgang Mommsen (Reading 1) points out, for Weber just as for Marx modern industrial capitalism is a revolutionary force, sweeping away the institutions of traditional culture. Whereas, however, Marx looked to the revolutionary overthrow of capitalism by socialism, for Weber it is capitalism itself that is vastly more transformative than any other society we could envisage for the future. Capitalism dissolves virtually all forms of pre-existing social order and in irreversible fashion.

Like Marx, Weber was critical of some of the consequences of capitalist industrial development, which he saw as crushing the scope of human potential. Weber sought to identify means whereby the autonomy of the human being, and human self-worth, could be protected from the standardizing influences of industrial production and bureaucracy. As Mommsen demonstrates, Weber's concern with individual autonomy and spontaneity in the end led him in a quite different direction from Marx. Weber did not substitute an 'idealism' for Marxist materialism, but rather sought to demonstrate the significance of the preservation of ultimate values; substantive values relevant to human self-worth, he concluded, could and should be defended against the extension of impersonal, 'formal' rationality into all spheres of social life.

A concern with individual autonomy in the face of the extraordinary social changes brought about by modernity was also a basic concern of Georg Simmel (see Frisby, Reading 2). In *The Philosophy of Money* Simmel sought to show that the 'totality' (modern society as a whole) could best be apprehended through its fragments, i.e. through the expression of larger structures within small-scale activities and transactions. Social life is in a constant process of creation and re-creation; we can grasp how this is so by showing how small-scale experiences and actions express larger social wholes, at the same time as those social wholes condition and influence local or contextual activities. This subtle and distinctive methodological standpoint today sounds very contemporary; Simmel anticipated some of the ideas now usually associated with the notion of postmodernity (see Readings 33 and 36 below).

Simmel was much concerned with cultural aspects of modern capitalism; even money, that apparently most sheerly economic phenomenon, has, he sought to demonstrate, aesthetic characteristics and influences forms of artistic production. Although he wrote from a more orthodox Marxist perspective than Simmel, Gramsci was similarly concerned with the cultural systems of modern societies (Bellamy, Reading 3). Gramsci, however, was interested in culture as ideology: as a means whereby the capitalist class system was stabilized. Pursuing this concern, he introduced his celebrated notion of 'hegemony', a concept which has later been used by many other authors, Marxist and non-Marxist.

Hegemony refers to the capability of the dominant or capitalistic class to secure the compliance of the rest of the population, not just by the direct use of power, but by securing their 'free' consent. Hegemony thus refers to the overall ideological ascendancy of a dominant group or class over the rest of society. In the context of Marxist thought, Gramsci's views were important because of his rejection of the notion that ideology is simply a 'reflection' of the wider economic system. For Gramsci ideology has a reality of its own; it is rooted in a number of substantive institutions whereby particular symbols and attitudes are spread through the population, particularly the educational system, religion and the media of communication.

Claude Lévi-Strauss (see Geertz, Reading 4) has also been preoccupied with questions of culture and symbolism throughout his intellectual career. It was Lévi-Strauss who popularized the term 'structuralism'; and he applied his own 'structuralist method' to the analysis of cultural codes. Structuralism has made a massive impact throughout the social sciences, but Lévi-Strauss's own particular concerns lie in the area of anthropology, particularly in the study of non-modern, oral cultures.

Just as the progression of industrial capitalism erodes tradition within the societies where it becomes dominant, so also, as modern institutions spread across the world, they tend to destroy the small-scale cultures in which human beings have lived for tens of thousands of years. Lévi-Strauss sees himself as the chronicler of this process of global destruction, a witness to, but also a defender of, a disappearing world. His autobiographical work, *Tristes Tropiques*, a bestseller in France when it was first published, both records his intellectual journey and charts out the triumph of modernity over cultural forms destined to disappear from the face of the earth. As Clifford Geertz indicates, *Tristes Tropiques* is a work of subtle textures, whose very style echoes the ambiguous brutality of the worldwide advance of Western civilization. *Tristes Tropiques* expresses the logic of structuralist method at the same time as it represents a dialogue between modern social thought, in the shape of anthropology, and traditional culture.

The writings of Louis Althusser (see Barrett, Reading 5) were strongly influenced by Lévi-Strauss's structuralism. Althusser drew upon Lévi-Strauss in an endeavour to reshape a framework of Marxist social thought. Althusser saw Marxism above all as a science and consequently made a clear distinction between science and ideology. Echoing to some degree Gramsci's conception of hegemony, Althusser argues that ideology is a form of 'lived experience': it is not just a set of beliefs but is incorporated in people's everyday actions and consciousness. Science, by contrast, provides a means of discerning the real social mechanisms which lie behind the appearance of things. As Michèle Barrett mentions, although it was once very influential, Althusser's conception of scientific Marxism has been very heavily criticized.

In the final Reading in Part I (Reading 6), Susan Hekman discusses a tradition of thought which stands at the opposite end of the spectrum from that represented by Althusser. The 'hermeneutic' tradition – 'hermeneutics' stands for the theory of interpretation – has consistently stressed that social life cannot be studied by the methods of natural science. There is a logical gulf between the concerns of the natural sciences, which are to do with causal relations between objects and events, and the objectives and methods of the social or 'human sciences', which are bound up with problems of meaning. Human action is intrinsically meaningful in a way that has no counterpart in the domain of nature.

The hermeneutic tradition influenced Max Weber among many others. The writings of Hans-Georg Gadamer form one of the leading contributions to hermeneutic philosophy. Gadamer's major work, *Truth and Method*, offers a comprehensive account of hermeneutics. Hermeneutics, Gadamer asserts, is not a 'method' which can be applied in the social sciences, but rather a universal framework which sees the understanding of meaning as at the core of all human experience. The meaning of human action can be read like a text: it can be deciphered by connecting individual acts to a narrative or 'story-line'.

Gadamer's version of hermeneutics can be complemented by considering the ideas of the French thinker Paul Ricoeur. For Ricoeur the parallel between human action and texts is a close one. In studying human action and in analysing texts, we can distinguish between subjective and objective meaning. Subjective meaning refers to the intentions an individual has in engaging in a particular act or an author has in writing a particular text. Just as the meaning to others of what an individual does or says might be different from what she or he intends, so texts develop objective meanings which escape the finite horizons of their individual authors. Social analysis, Ricoeur argues, can be methodical in character. However, the methodical character of social investigation can best be seen, not in terms of an extension of the methods of natural science, but in relation to linguistics.

1

Capitalism and Socialism: Weber's Dialogue with Marx

Wolfgang J. Mommsen

The advance of modern industrial capitalism and consequent social developments are the dominant themes of Max Weber's sociological work. As early as 1893, Weber predicted that, within a few generations, capitalism would destroy all tradition-bound social structures, and that this process was irreversible. He described modern capitalism as an essentially revolutionary force and believed that it was not possible to arrest, by any means, its triumphal march. Much of his scholarly work was concerned with investigating the societal and cultural effects of industrial capitalism from the standpoint of their meaning for the future of Western liberal societies. Consequently, it was inevitable that Max Weber would confront Karl Marx's analysis of modern capitalism and his ideas about a future socialist society. Weber's sociology can be viewed as an attempt to formulate an alternative position standing in harmony with his own bourgeois-liberal ideals, but one that does not simply dismiss the socialist critique of bourgeois society without foundation.

Weber belonged to a generation that stood midway between the generation of Marx and our own. His socio-political views were formed under the influence of the extraordinarily rapid growth of modern industrial capitalism in the last decades before 1914. The development of large industrial combinations, trusts and monopolies, all typical of a maturing capitalist system, took place before his eyes, and he could not but note how this new reality conflicted with classical political economy's ideal image of capitalism. Although Weber did not ignore these developments, he remained throughout his life a passionate champion of a liberal brand of dynamic capitalism. Weber was perhaps Marx's greatest theoretical opponent; given the range of his sociological work he has been rightly called a 'bourgeois Marx'.

Weber occasionally referred to himself as 'a member of the bourgeois class' who was 'educated in their views and ideals'. In 1907, in an argument about the German Social Democrats, he requested expressly that Roberto Michels simply regard him as a 'class-conscious bourgeois'. Nevertheless, one hesitates, in the light of Weber's constant striving for critical self-examination, to call him a bourgeois in the ordinary sense of the word. Rather, to use his own terminology, he is better located in the intelligentsia, a social group that cannot be assigned to any of the economic classes. Weber was less a 'bourgeois' than a liberal intellectual for whom the autonomy of the individual was an indispensable principle, and it was from this perspective that he approached the nature of capitalism and Marxism. As a result, Weber's attitude towards capitalism as a total societal configuration proved to be thoroughly ambivalent. Although he vigorously defended the capitalist system against its critics on the left (whether they were from the workers' movement or from those intellectuals whom he described as having succumbed to 'the romanticism of the general strike' or to 'revolutionary hope'), he did not hesitate to criticize the system's inhuman consequences.

The starting point of Weber's analysis of modern capitalism was not as far removed from Marx as Weber himself assumed. His concern for the preservation of human dignity under the social conditions created by and typical of mature capitalism (particularly, the severe discipline of work and exclusion of all principles of personal ethical responsibility from industrial labour) is entirely consistent with Marx's effort to find a way of overcoming the social alienation of the proletariat under industrial capitalism. But Weber's sociological analyses of industrial societies led him to conclusions that were, in many respects, opposed to those of Marx.

It is hardly necessary to point out that Weber always took Marx's theoretical work seriously. Weber labelled the *Communist Manifesto* 'a pathetic prophecy', but at the same time, despite his decidedly different views, he considered it 'a scholarly work of the highest order'.[1] Eduard Baumgarten reported that, in the last years of his life, Weber told one of his students:

> One can measure the integrity of a modern scholar, and especially of a modern philosopher, by how he sees his own relationship to Nietzsche and Marx. Whoever does not admit that he could not accomplish very important aspects of his own work without the work that these two have performed deceives both himself and others. The world in which we ourselves exist intellectually is largely a world stamped by Marx and Nietzsche.[2]

Weber achieved his own intellectual position through constant grappling with these two completely opposite thinkers. Weber's pronounced aristocratic individualism can be traced largely to Nietzsche. This was held in check, of course, not only by Weber's liberal convictions, but also by the insight that the fate of the individual is determined extensively by material and economic factors and to a very great degree is dependent upon anonymous socio-economic processes – an insight which is ultimately traceable to Marx.

Nevertheless, it seems that in his early writings Weber paid little attention to the original writings of Marx and Engels. We find, however, an extensive treatment of Marx and Marxism in his early lectures on national economics in Freiburg in the 1890s, but they seem not to have had a direct impact on his published work. Up to 1906 he referred primarily to vulgar Marxist interpretations; direct references to Marx were almost totally absent. During these years he confronted Marx and Marxism primarily in his methodological writings. There, Weber distanced himself sharply and repeatedly from what was then called 'historical materialism'. In principle, Weber rejected all material philosophies of history. He considered these and other approaches that claimed to discover objective historical laws or even an inner meaning to history 'charlatanism'. From his own standpoint, perhaps best characterized as a neo-Kantianism combined with Nietzschean principles, there could be no objective ordering of the historical process. In Weber's opinion the Marxist theory of history, which described historical change as a determinate sequence of social formations with each characterized by its respective mode of economic production and propelled by class conflict, lacked any scientific basis. For Weber, there were no objective laws of social reality. At best, it might be possible, with the aid of ideal types, to construct law-like theories of societal processes. These can serve as criteria for determining the degree to which certain segments of social reality depart from such nomological models.

Weber's radical position followed inevitably from the fundamental premise that history is meaningless in itself and that, at least from the standpoint of a random observer, it appears as more or less chaotic. Only when specific concepts and categories, formulated from the perspective of ultimate cultural values, are applied to a limited segment of reality (which in itself is limitless) does it become meaningful. Accordingly, Weber considered Marx's theory about the succession of different modes of production to be no more than a sociological hypothesis that provides essential insights into the nature and development of modern industrial societies, but on no account does Weber consider it as objectively valid scientific knowledge. In the former sense, namely as an ideal-typical construction, he regarded Marx's theory as extremely significant. On the other hand, he was not prepared to accept it as ontological truth. He expressed this in 'Objectivity in social science and social policy':

> Liberated as we are from the antiquated belief that all cultural phenomena can be *deduced* as a product or function of the constellation of 'material' interests, we believe nevertheless that the analysis of social and cultural phenomena with special reference to their economic conditioning and ramifications is a scientific principle of creative fruitfulness, and, if applied carefully and free from dogmatic restrictions, will remain so for a long time to come. However, the so-called 'materialistic conception of history' must be rejected most emphatically in so far as it is meant as a *Weltanschauung* or a formula for the causal explanation of historical reality.[3]

In these remarks Weber did not differentiate between Marx and Marxist theory in his own time. Marx's conception of a necessary and irreversible process, leading from feudalism to capitalism and eventually to socialism, was not a purely ontological statement; it was also a theory for practical orientation, requiring human action to become reality. Capitalist society comes into being only through the actions of the bourgeoisie, and without a socialist revolution carried out by the proletariat there can be no socialist society. This activist element in Marx's theory was obscured by the later interpretations by Engels and, finally, Kautsky. It was they who turned it into that rigid, mechanistic theory commonly called historical materialism.

When he wrote the above-quoted passages, Weber was apparently not fully aware of the substantial differences between Marx's theory and orthodox Marxist interpretations in his own time, even though it would appear that he discussed some of Marx's texts in his early academic lectures in the 1890s. A careful comparison of their methodological procedures shows that the two thinkers were actually not as antithetical as Weber himself claimed. Both Weber and Marx were concerned with extrapolating certain sequences of causal chains of events from the historical process. To be sure, unlike Marx, Weber emphasized that one could grasp only segments of social reality, never its totality. Weber thought it impossible, indeed dishonest, to go beyond the construction of ideal types: models that are used for describing particular historical sequences and for analysing their social effects and human consequences. In other words, from Weber's methodological perspective, claims about the objectivity of the historical process were fictitious.

It is no coincidence that he repeatedly took offence at precisely this element of Marx's teachings. Weber considered this view of history to be false not only on epistemological grounds but also in principle, or, if one prefers, for ethical reasons highly questionable. In his view it fatally weakened the responsibility of the autonomous individual, who is called upon constantly to decide between different ultimate values. The belief that history is determined by objective processes seduces individuals all too easily into adapting to the presumed objective course of things, rather than remaining faithful to their own ultimate convictions and value-positions.

[...]

A more detailed analysis of Weber's views of Marxism shows that Weber took exception, above all else, to the Marxist theory of 'superstructure'. Weber never accepted the thesis that all social phenomena could be explained sufficiently by relating them to economic causes: 'the common materialist view of history, that the "economic" is in some sense an "ultimate" in the chain of causation, is in my estimation totally worthless as a scientific statement.'[4] Weber ignored the fact that Marx and Engels's position on this matter was much more sophisticated.

Weber held that social phenomena could not, even in the final analysis, be explained by economic causes. However, he did not express an idealist counterposition. Weber's famous essays on *The Protestant Ethic and the Spirit of Capitalism* are commonly viewed as an attempt to prove that idealist, and especially religious, factors play an independent role in the historical process. In 1918 Weber presented the results of this study in a series of lectures at the University of Vienna under the title, 'A positive critique of the materialist view of history'. However, he did this with thoroughly ambivalent feelings. He never claimed that his 'Protestant ethic' thesis completely answered the question of how and why industrial capitalism arose. He pointed out repeatedly that he uncovered only one group of factors among others that had contributed to the rise of capitalism. Incidentally, Weber drew considerably closer to Marx when he indicated that mature capitalism no longer needed the Protestant ethic. In almost Marxian language, he described modern capitalism as a social power that forces people to subject themselves to the social conditions it has created, regardless of whether or not they are willing. They have no choice; they must be professionals (*Berufsmenschen*) because modern industrial capitalism does not permit otherwise. In almost apocalyptic terms he argued that capitalism is forging the conditions for a new 'iron cage of serfdom', which humanity will have to occupy as soon as the current phase of dynamic economic growth has reached its natural limits. In describing the capitalist system's almost mechanical domination of man, which in the long run threatens to become a modern form of slavery, Weber came close to Marx's conviction that capitalism is an inhuman social order that contains the propensity for self-destruction.

On the other hand, Weber refused to identify this immanent trend in the capitalist system (which he endeavoured to define precisely using sociological methods) with an objective developmental law. The universal–historical perspective of an approaching age of bureaucracy recurs repeatedly in Weber's scholarly writings; however, it is never hypostatized into an ontological statement of a philosophy of history. Here, the decisive difference between Weber's and Marx's conceptions of history becomes obvious. While Marx, in Hegelian fashion, framed his analysis in an almost apodictically conceived theory of history (although partly with political intentions), for Weber every holistic view of the historical process had only a hypothetical quality, serving orientation but not understood by itself as true and immutable. Accordingly, Weber was only being consistent when he gave particular attention to those forces and tendencies which were counteracting this process and sought to discover the conditions under which these can display their optimal effectiveness.

Weber's reaction to individual elements of Marxist theory also conforms to this fundamental attitude. He accepted the thesis that the material conditions of existence pervasively determine human action only as a nomological model for the definition of concrete social conduct, but not as conceptualized truth; and it was precisely the significant deviations from this model that he sought to establish. With respect to the role of material and particularly economic interests, Weber was fundamentally pluralistic. Weber found that, even under industrial capitalism, development is not determined exclusively by 'material interests'. Alongside their dynamics stand the dynamics of 'ideal interests'; every analysis must take both sets of factors into account. In his essays on the Protestant ethic and later studies of world religions, Weber was above all intent upon demonstrating that ideal interests can initiate social change of considerable magnitude; indeed, under certain circumstances they can have revolutionary effects although – or, better, precisely *because* – they have nothing in common with economic motivations.

On this point Weber perhaps stood furthest from Marx. In contrast to Marx, he was firmly convinced that individuals who are consciously guided by ultimate values of whatever sort – and the more these values stand in opposition to everyday reality, the more far-reaching their effects – can be an irreducible force that reshapes a given social reality so as to conform with their ultimate values. Naturally, the actual results of such individual actions are conditioned by the specific social situation. But the original motivation of action cannot be explained perfunctorily by referring to the social conditions, which significantly shape the eventual results.

[...]

In contrast to some recent neo-Marxist interpretations, Weber was in no way inclined to glorify capitalism, and certainly not a capitalist system with a maximum of formal rationality in all its social dimensions. Closer analysis reveals that the pure type of market economy, as Weber developed it in *Economy and Society*, is anything but attractive and is not at all identical with that form of capitalism which Weber favoured. This model postulates that a maximum of formal rationality is attainable only if the following conditions are met:

1 'constant struggle between autonomous groups in the market-place';
2 the rational calculation of prices under conditions of unrestricted competition in the market-place;
3 'formally free labour' (i.e. work performed on the basis of freely contracted wage agreements, as distinct from fixed salaries or the like);
4 'expropriation from workers of the means of production';
5 private ownership of the means of production.[5]

The majority of these conditions were no longer sufficiently met under the advanced capitalism of Weber's time (assuming, for the moment, that they had been present in early capitalism, which apparently served as Weber's model). Was he then describing a ghost that already belonged to the past? Such a questions fails to grasp the core of the issue. Weber intended to describe the specifics of capitalism in its pure form (a procedure which had methodological similarities to Marx). Thus Weber's process of concept formation must not be dismissed as a throwback to Manchester liberalism. As already mentioned, he conceded, indeed emphatically advocated, that under certain conditions deviations from the pure form of capitalist market economy would be necessary – deviations effected through appropriate state interventions and in some cases through a change in the legal and political parameters of economic activity. . . .

By stressing formal rationality as its basic characteristic, Weber never intended to immunize modern industrial capitalism against criticism. . . . Weber did not intend to elevate capitalism ontologically and thereby justify it ideologically, as Herbert Marcuse claimed. Marcuse's argument that Weber's emphasis on the formal rationality of all capitalist operations obscured capitalism's substantive irrationality is quite misleading. Weber discussed this very point repeatedly in *Economy and Society*, although not always without ambiguity. Weber distinguished explicitly between formal and substantive rationality, though perhaps not as consistently as the issue demanded. He was fully aware of the fact that a maximum of formal rationality was inseparably linked with substantive irrationalities, for example, 'the submission of workers to the domination of entrepreneurs'.[6] Likewise he never obscured the true nature of 'formally free labour contracts', which are fundamental to capitalism; he described them neutrally as a special form of domination. Weber proceeded from the premise that under the conditions of mature capitalism formal rationality and substantive rationality are always in conflict with each other, just as in other economic systems; it depended on the concrete situation what compromises had to be made in order to find a balance between these antagonistic principles.

In developing such a conceptualization Weber cleared the path for a critique of capitalism, a critique which rated substantive value-positions, regardless of their sort, more highly than the formal rationality of the system. He pleaded for practical measures of social reform rather than for radical remedies which would lead to the destruction of the capitalist market economy. He warned, however, that the implementation of substantive principles would bring an inevitable reduction in the efficiency and productivity of the economic system, or, to put it otherwise, they could be had only at a price. Proceeding from concrete substantive value-positions, he indicated that a large number of critical alternatives to the capitalist system were conceivable but in each case some reduction of the formal efficiency of the economic system must be accepted as part of the bargain.

Notes and References

1 *Zur Politik im Weltkrieg: Schriften und Reden 1914–18*, ed. Wolfgang J. Mommsen in collaboration with Gangolf Hübinger (Mohr, Tübingen, 1988), p. 616; Max Weber, 'Socialism', in *Max Weber, The Interpretation of Social Reality*, ed. J.E.T. Eldridge (Nelson, London, 1971), p. 205.

2 Eduard Baumgarten, *Max Weber: Werk und Person* (Mohr, Tübingen, 1964), pp. 554–5, n. 1.
3 Max Weber, *The Methodology of the Social Sciences*, tr. Edward A. Shils and Henry A. Finch (Free Press, Glencoe, Ill., 1949), p. 68.
4 Max Weber, *Gesammelte Aufsätze zur Soziologie und Sozialpolitik*, ed. Marianne Weber (Mohr, Tübingen, 1924), p. 456.
5 Max Weber, *Wirtschaft und Gesellschaft: Grundriss der verstehenden Soziologie*, 5th edn, ed. Johannes Winckelmann (Mohr, Tübingen, 1978), p. 87; Max Weber, *Economy and Society: An Outline of Interpretive Sociology*, ed. Günther Roth and Claus Wittich (California University Press, Berkeley, Calif., 1977), p. 151.
6 Weber, *Wirtschaft und Gesellschaft*, p. 44; Weber, *Economy and Society*, p. 84.

2

Georg Simmel: Modernity as an Eternal Present

David Frisby

Simmel's most sustained account of modernity is to be found in *The Philosophy of Money*. Here, from the very outset, Simmel rules out the possibility of some naive accumulation of empirical knowledge as an end in itself since

> the ever-fragmentary contents of positive knowledge seek to be augmented by definitive concepts into a world picture and to be related to the totality of life.[1]

Hence, 'the very standpoint of a single science, which is also based on the division of labour, never exhausts the totality of reality'. Yet in *The Philosophy of Money* at least, Simmel is in no doubt that this totality is apprehendable.

In turn, this totality is not an abstract postulate but is approachable from specific individual phenomena and problems. It is not the starting point of his analysis, rather its goal. Hence, in his investigation of money, Simmel maintains that he must 'regard the problem as restricted and small in order to do justice to it by extending it to the totality and the highest level of generality'.[2] In this respect, the specific object of study, money,

> is simply a means, a material or an example for the presentation of relations that exist between the most superficial, 'realistic' and fortuitous phenomena and the most idealised powers of existence, the most profound currents of individual life and history.[3]

Simmel's intention 'is simply to derive from the surface level of economic affairs a guideline that leads to the ultimate values and things of importance in all that is human'.

The starting point of his analysis is thus 'what is apparently most superficial and insubstantial'. Indeed, the unity of the whole study lies 'in the possibility . . . of finding in each of life's details the totality of its meaning'. In this respect, it follows the same method as art – in contrast to philosophy's concern with 'the totality of being' – which 'sets itself a single, narrowly defined problem every time: a person, a landscape, a mood'. It is Simmel's conviction that 'it is possible to relate the details and superficialities of life to its most profound and essential movements'.[4]

It follows from all this that empirical scientific research is restricted in the sense that it cannot approach the totality that alone gives meaning to 'each of life's details'. Hence,

> Science always finds itself on the path towards the absolute unity of the conception of the world but can never reach it; regardless of the point from which it starts, it always requires from that point a leap into another mode of thought – of a religious, metaphysical, moral or aesthetic nature – in order to expand and integrate the inevitably fragmentary nature of its results into a complete unity.[5]

Of these other modes of thought, it is the aesthetic perspective or '*Anschauungsweise*' to which Simmel himself most often has recourse.

Indeed, elsewhere, Simmel seems to suggest that the interactions between individuals and society as a whole constitute a totality that is only apprehendable aesthetically:

> The totality of the whole . . . stands in eternal conflict with the totality of the individual. The aesthetic expression of this struggle is particularly impressive because *the charm of beauty is always embedded in a whole,* no matter whether it has immediate distinctiveness or *a distinctiveness that is supplemented by fantasy as in the case of a fragment. The essential meaning of art lies in its being able to form an autonomous totality, a self-sufficient microcosm out of a fortuitous fragment of reality that is tied with a thousand threads to this reality.*[6]

Some fragments of our existence and, more especially, some modes of apprehension are more capable of grasping the totality. Simmel's sociological texts are richly populated with these fortuitous fragments of reality, with seemingly superficial social phenomena, with snapshots, with a myriad of social vignettes.

What this also suggests is that the aesthetic totality may itself exist as a fragment. Such a principle was later elevated into a universal principle in his later philosophy of life (*Lebensphilosophie*). In his study of

Rembrandt (1916), for example, Simmel maintains that 'each moment of life is the totality of life',[7]

> because life is thereby nothing other than continuous development by means of material oppositions, because it is not composed from individual pieces and its totality therefore does not exist outside of the individual element.[8]

However, at the time of publication of his *Philosophy of Money*, Simmel had not yet fully developed his philosophy of life and his interest in sociology was still much in evidence.

Nonetheless, there are passages in this work which suggest that Simmel's 'categories for interpreting the world' are already grounded in an essentialism that is far removed from an empiricist framework for the apprehension of social reality. Rather than viewing Simmel's philosophy as located within a neo-Kantian paradigm, certain crucial arguments suggest a very different alternative, as when Simmel maintains that

> If we describe the sum total of fragments that make up our knowledge at any one moment in relation to the goal we want to attain . . . then we can do so only by presupposing that which lies at the basis of the Platonic doctrine: that there is an ideal realm of theoretical values, of perfect intellectual meaning and coherence, that coincides neither with the objects . . . nor with the psychologically real knowledge that has been attained. On the contrary, this real knowledge only gradually and always imperfectly approximates to that realm which includes all possible truth.[9]

Yet it is not merely that our fragments of knowledge approximate imperfectly to the totality. Rather, Simmel views the human subject as playing an active role within this totality:

> the formula of our life as a whole, from the trivial practice of everyday to the highest peak of intellectuality, is this: in all that we do, we have a norm, a standard, an ideally preconceived totality before us, which we try to transpose into reality through our actions.[10]

Even more explicitly, Simmel sees an essential quality of our action as being that

> we follow some prefigured possibility and, as it were, carry out an ideal programme. *Our practical existence, though inadequate and fragmentary,*

> *gains a certain significance and coherence, as it were, by partaking in the realisation of a totality.*[11]

Precisely how that totality is realized is not clarified by Simmel.

Elsewhere, Simmel takes the problematic relationship between the universal and the particular to be a feature of modern times in so far as 'the evolution of the modern naturalistic spirit tends to dethrone universal concepts, and to emphasise singular instances as the only legitimate content of conceptions'.[12] Yet Simmel maintains that the importance of universals 'has not altogether disappeared'. Indeed, he asserts that

> we would attain a completely satisfying relation to the world only if every aspect of our world view reconciled the material reality of singular instances with the depth and scope of a formal universality. Historicism and a sociological world view are attempts to confirm universality and yet to deny its abstractedness, to transcend the singular instance, to derive the singular from the general without sacrificing its material reality; for society is universal but not abstract.[13]

By the time of writing this passage, Simmel had clearly moved away from his earlier psychologistic naturalism towards a preoccupation with social forms and 'a formal universality'. But although this passage is illustrative of his indebtedness to Platonism, it is in fact the reverse position which is his sociological starting point, namely the derivation of the essence of social phenomena from a particular instance. In other words, social reality is viewed *sub specie aeternitatis*.

It should already be evident that he sees some fragments of our existence and, more especially, some modes of apprehension as being more capable of apprehending a totality. We already know that, for Simmel, art forms 'an autonomous totality' out of fortuitous fragments of reality. In the preface to *Philosophy of Money*, Simmel emphasized that the empirical realm could never be capable of realizing this totality. The empirical needs to be located within a totality that it is itself incapable of creating. Hence, in a passage which unwittingly takes up a theme of Benjamin's later works, Simmel insists that

> even the empirical in its perfected state might no more replace philosophy as an interpretation, a colouring and an individually selective emphasis of what is real than would the perfection of the mechanical reproduction of phenomena make the visual arts superfluous.[14]

Indeed, Simmel maintains that the whole of his study of money is grounded in a world picture 'which I consider to be the most appropriate expression of the contemporary contents of science and emotional currents'.[15] Even from the preface we can surmise that Simmel favours a 'relativist interpretation' of social phenomena. This is confirmed in his theory of value as well as in the text as a whole. He also favours a perspective that we must term modernist.

Simmel is insistent in his *Philosophy of Money* that 'not a single line of these investigations is meant to be a statement about economics'. Almost as explicit is Simmel's lack of concern with 'the historical phenomena of money' even though this is his stated concern in the second part of his text. This becomes clear when we learn that this historical dimension has as its basis 'feelings of value', an analysis of 'praxis in relation to things and the reciprocal relationships between people'. Simmel's concern is, rather, with the effect of money 'upon the inner world – upon the vitality of individuals, upon the linking of their fates, upon culture in general'. The historical dimension is replaced by a phenomenology of human emotions.

Such preliminary remarks should suggest that the totality within which the fragments of social life are to be located or even the totality that they themselves are is not historical. Rather, this totality, this whole, rests upon the 'attitude' of the human observer. In seeking to demarcate Simmel's thought from the post-First World War generation, Margarete Susman points out that

> for Simmel, the philosophical perspective was always a view from the centre into the totality, which was only able to extract a single sector from the whole. This relationship of the individual to the totality Simmel termed the 'attitude' of the thinker. This attitude signifies for him the relationship of a mind to the totality of the world.[16]

Susman points out that this notion of attitude towards the world is fundamentally mystical and 'obtains a metaphysical justification only through the feelings'.

Though the notion of 'attitude' to the world belongs, more accurately, to Simmel's later philosophy, it also plays a subterranean role in his *Philosophy of Money*. We have already pointed out that Simmel did not view empirical knowledge as alone providing the key to the totality. In keeping with the later notion of our 'attitude' to the world, Simmel maintains that, psychologically, what we refer to as verification of empirical phenomena is merely a function of the creation of a specific 'feeling' for the object in question. He refers to

> the theory according to which everything held to be true is a certain *feeling* which accompanies a mental image; what we call proof is nothing

> other than the establishment of a psychological constellation which gives rise to such a feeling. No sense perception or logical derivations can directly assure us of a reality.[17]

Such intuitionism as the basis for grounding knowledge is hardly the firmest foundation for the development of a sociology of modernity. However, it could form the starting point for what we might term a sociological impressionism that is rooted in an aesthetic stance *vis-à-vis* social reality.

This brief examination of Simmel's emphasis upon the relationship between the aesthetic mode of apprehension and the totality should leave little doubt that Simmel viewed the aesthetic perspective as a legitimate one for acquiring insights into social reality. In evaluating Simmel's work, we should take this aesthetic dimension seriously and clearly distinguish it from a tendency towards the aestheticization of reality since the two are not synonymous. Indeed, in some respects, the aesthetic dimension in theorizing can be seen to be coterminous with modernity itself. Bubner, for instance, maintains that 'the *autonomous development of the arts* in fact dates from the middle of the previous century, which we have since become accustomed to characterise as modernity without an end to this development being perceived'.[18] Furthermore, Bubner highlights a tendency that is also apparent in Simmel's work, namely the tendency to see art as 'not so much an object' but rather that 'art serves as a medium in which philosophy seeks to make certain its own theoretical status'. In the context of Simmel's social theory of modernity, the aesthetic dimension also provides a degree of 'self-understanding' with regard to its own role in delineating modernity. One might even maintain that this aesthetic dimension makes Simmel's social theory of modernity possible.

If Simmel's social theory exhibits a somewhat problematic relationship towards the possibility of grasping the totality of existence, how does he view the role of the fragment in this context? More specifically, with the aim of understanding *modernité*, what is the justification for starting out from 'a fortuitous fragment' of reality, from 'each of life's details', from a 'snapshot' or 'fleeting image' of social interaction? Why not commence with 'the social structure' as a whole, with the 'social system' or with the central 'institutions' of society? In Simmel's case, the second of these questions is the easier to answer.

Concepts such as 'social structure', 'social system' and even 'social institution' play a very subordinate role in his sociology. From his early works onwards, Simmel was at pains to avoid the reification or hypostatization of 'society'. Already in 1890, Simmel was insisting that 'society is not an entity fully enclosed within itself, an absolute entity, any more than is the human individual. Compared with the real interactions of the parts, it is only secondary, only the result.'[19] Instead, Simmel commenced from 'a regulative world principle that everything interacts with everything else, that between every point in the world and every other force permanently moving relationships exist'.[20] This is not merely a heuristic principle but also a substantive feature of modernity since 'the dissolution of the societal soul into the sum of interactions of its participants lies in the direction of modern intellectual life itself'. Sociology should therefore not concern itself with a reified notion of society but with 'what is specifically societal; the form and forms of sociation as such are distinct from the particular interests and contents in and through which sociation is realised'.[21] Thus, from the outset, it is social interaction and forms of sociation and, later, 'the phenomenological structure of society' (1908) that constitute the key elements of sociology.

If one of the features of modernity is that social reality is felt to be in a state of ceaseless flux, then the concepts that can best express this fluid reality must be relational concepts. Interaction (*Wechselwirkung*) and sociation (*Vergesellschaftung*) are key concepts for Simmel and what interests him is relationships between phenomena. Society constitutes a social labyrinth within which individuals and groups intersect. This web or network of social relationships is itself symptomatic of what Kracauer describes as the 'core principle' of Simmel's social theory, namely 'the fundamental interrelatedness [*Wesenszusammengehörigkeit*] of the most diverse phenomena'. This implies that

> All expressions of cultural life . . . stand in an inexpressible plurality of relationships to one another, none is capable of being extracted from the contexts in which they find themselves associated with others.[22]

Each individual element is 'enmeshed' within this 'context of diversity'. The 'liberation of things from their individual isolation' takes place either through tracing real relationships between social phenomena or through revealing possible relationships by recourse to analogies.[23]

Since there exists, in principle at least, no hierarchy of significance in forms of interaction, we might expect that he would be equally interested in the fortuitous and seemingly insignificant social phenomena. In the first version of his 'Sociology of the senses' (1907), Simmel argues that just as 'the science of organic life' now concerns itself with 'the smallest agents, the cells' of human life, so too social science has recently come to concern itself with 'the beginnings of microscopic investigation'. It, too, originally started out from

> States and trade unions, priesthoods and forms of family structure, the nature of guilds and factories, class formation and the industrial division of labour – these and similar major organs and systems appear to constitute society and to form the sphere of science concerning it.[24]

Without denying the existence of these 'structures of a higher order', Simmel's interest lay not in these structured interactions but in 'countless others which, as it were, remain in a fluid, fleeting state but are no less agents of the connection of individuals to societal existence'.[25] The manner in which people look at one another, the fact that they write letters to one another, that they eat a midday meal together, that they are sympathetic or antithetical to one another, that they dress and adorn themselves for others are also momentary or persistent relations between people that go to make up society. Here Simmel's concern is quite explicitly with the 'fortuitous fragments' of social interaction:

> On every day, at every hour, such threads are spun, are allowed to fall, are taken up again, replaced by others, intertwined with others. Here lie the interactions – only accessible through psychological microscopy – between the atoms of society which bear the whole tenacity and elasticity, the whole colourfulness and unity of this so evident and so puzzling life of society.[26]

Simmel is convinced that their investigation produces a 'deeper and more accurate' understanding of society than does the study of society's major structures and institutions.

> We can no longer take to be unimportant consideration of the delicate, invisible threads that are woven between one person and another if we wish to grasp the web of society according to its productive, form-giving forces; hitherto, sociology has largely been concerned to describe this web only with regard to the finally created pattern of its highest manifest levels.[27]

Notes and References

1 G. Simmel, *Philosophy of Money*, T. Bottomore and D. Frisby (Routledge and Kegan Paul, London, 1978), p. 53.
2 Ibid., p. 56.

3 Ibid., p. 55.
4 Ibid., p. 56.
5 G. Simmel, *Kant und Goethe* (Marquardt, Berlin, 1906), p. 65.
6 Simmel, *Philosophy of Money*, pp. 494–5; my emphasis.
7 Simmel, *Rembrandt* (Kurt Wolff, Leipzig, 1919), p. 2.
8 Ibid., p. 51.
9 Simmel, *Philosophy of Money*, p. 450.
10 Ibid., p. 451.
11 Ibid.; my emphasis.
12 Ibid., p. 202.
13 Ibid.
14 Ibid., p. 53.
15 Ibid., p. 56.
16 M. Susman, *Die geistige Gestalt Georg Simmels* (Mohr, Tübingen, 1959), p. 36.
17 Simmel, *Philosophy of Money*, p. 452.
18 R. Bubner, 'Über einige Bedingungen gegenwärtiger Ästhetik', *Neue Hefte für Philosophie*, 5 (1973), pp. 38–73, esp. p. 38.
19 Simmel, *Über soziale Differenzierung* (Duncker Humblot, Leipzig, 1890), p. 13.
20 Ibid.
21 G. Simmel, 'Das Problem der Soziologie', *Jahrbuch für Gesetzgebung, Verwaltung und Volkswirtschaft*, 16 (1894), p. 272.
22 S. Kracauer, 'Georg Simmel', *Logos*, 9 (1920), p. 314.
23 Ibid., pp. 324f.
24 G. Simmel, 'Soziologie der Sinne', *Die Neue Rundschau*, 18 (2) (1907), p. 1025.
25 Ibid., p. 1026.
26 Ibid.
27 Ibid., p. 1035.

3

The Social and Political Thought of Antonio Gramsci

Richard Bellamy

The concept of hegemony was Gramsci's main contribution to political theory, and derived from his revision of orthodox Marxism. Gramsci did not reverse the traditional Marxist base–superstructure model. Instead he reinterpreted it in Crocean manner to mean that theory was the attempt to solve 'problems posed by the historical process'. Rational theories would be those which were adequate to the 'real' historical situation. This was not, as Croce argued, the product of a metaphysical entity, Spirit, but of the development of the forces of production.

This posed the question of why capitalism survived when, as Gramsci believed, the social and economic pre-conditions existed for the transition to communism. He attributed its survival to the interrelatedness of base and superstructure in determining social change. He divided the latter into two levels:

> the one that can be called 'civil society', that is the ensemble of organisms commonly called 'private', and that of 'political society' or 'the State'. These two levels correspond on the one hand to the function of 'hegemony', which the dominant group exercises throughout society, and on the other hand to that of 'direct domination' or command, expressed through the State and 'juridical' government.

The two functions were connected. The first set of institutions obtained 'the "spontaneous" consent given by the great masses of the population to the general direction imposed on social life by the dominant fundamental group, this consent derives "historically" from the prestige (and consequent confidence) which the dominant group enjoys because of its position and function in the world of production'. The organs of 'State coercive power . . . "legally" enforce discipline' when consent failed. Hegemony, therefore, referred to the ideological ascendency of one or more groups or classes over others in civil society. Capitalism continued to survive because the workers accepted its general outlook – the cultural dominance of the bourgeoisie made the resort to political force unnecessary to maintain their power. Thus the masses had to be freed from enthralment to the cultural hegemony of the capitalist classes before a successful challenge to the state could occur.

The importance Gramsci ascribed to cultural factors constituted a significant departure from the economism of classical Marxism. The ruling classes imposed their hegemonic vision through a whole variety of superstructural institutions, such as schools, the media, religion and the everyday practices people engaged in. People saw the world through ideologically distorted spectacles and thus a whole world view had to be challenged before a revolution would enlist mass support. As a result of this insight, he rejected the orthodox interpretation of ideology as an epiphenomenon of the base. He referred to Marx's assertion that 'men gain consciousness of their tasks on the ideological terrain of the superstructures', these being 'objective and operative.'[1] Whilst the economy was the motor of history, it could not itself produce radical political changes – 'the existence of the objective conditions is not in itself sufficient: one must "know them" and how to use them. And want to use them.'[2] Ideology fulfilled this function – it was 'the terrain on which men move, acquire consciousness of their position, struggle'.[3] Popular 'common sense' thinking always lagged behind economic changes. Revolt was easily contained because the masses were not fully conscious of what was wrong with their situation. Trade unions, for example, tended to demand a greater share of the capitalist cake, presenting workers' grievances in terms of the aspirations of the dominant group, rather than aiming at a new way of organizing productive activity. Change could not come about by waiting for economic laws to 'bring about palingenetic events'. Nor would simple intransigence work, since this was inchoate and unorganized and would simply result in a mindless Ludditism. . . . Gramsci insisted 'that there must be a conscious struggle predisposed to bring "understanding" of the exigencies of the economic position of the masses, which may conflict with the traditional leadership's policies'.[4] This involved Gramsci in three tasks: showing which properties rendered an ideology false, providing criteria for a true ideology; and developing a strategy for establishing it amongst the masses.

We have already examined one property of forms of false consciousness identified by Gramsci – their epistemology. They presented themselves 'as a dogmatic system of eternal and absolute truths'.[5] Agents suffered from this form of delusion when they regarded their acts as the products of some natural or metaphysical process outside their control. . . . A second identifying feature of erroneous ideologies was their function in upholding or legitimizing unjust social institutions and practices. The hegemony of the ruling class was maintained by a false representation of its customs and power as inevitable – as God's will, or the product of some natural law. Catholicism was Gramsci's favourite example and he was fascinated by the history and organization of the Roman Church. He regarded Croce's philosophy as serving a similar function in legitimizing Giolittean Italy, albeit only to fellow intellectuals.

Showing that an ideology functioned to support given power relations, rather than as an objective way of seeing the world, provided no reason for dropping it. This was the shortcoming of the Paretian, positivist critique of ideologies. Since, for positivists, all ideologies were more or less irrational or sham, and people simply acted as they did for more or less contingent reasons, there was no real benefit for the agent in revealing the illusion in the first place. Gramsci, on the other hand, wanted to demonstrate that the philosophy of praxis provided not only a more coherent way of looking at people's actions, but also a means of judging them, by providing knowledge of where their true interests lay. Marxism, as interpreted by Gramsci, 'is the historicist conception of reality which has liberated itself from every residue of transcendence and theology, even in their highest speculative incarnation, whilst Crocean idealist historicism still remains in the speculative theological phase'.[6] Historical materialism was the 'expression of real historical development' that is the underlying economic base. In accord with the Marxian preface, Gramsci argued that a true ideology promoted the development of the forces of production. This was in line with the productivism we noted in Gramsci's reflections on the factory councils, and his assertion that the proletariat's real interest was the maximization of output – something which could only be achieved by workers' control of the means of production. This suggests that the main aim was simply to increase productive efficiency. Yet this did not have to involve the liberation of people's intellectual and creative talents – a system could become more efficient if it made them desire less by reducing them to the level of machines.

Gramsci considered this possibility in the notes on Taylorism and Fordism. Taylor's *The Principles of Scientific Management* (1911) put forward just such a scheme for producing a pliant work force, suited to the requirements of modern industry. Gramsci believed it would never be successful in Europe because, unlike in America, the workers were less imbued with the ethic of work for work's sake. It was a means to other goals, producing resentment when the cost was too high. Nor did he think that dull routine labour would turn operatives into automatons. On the contrary, the repetitive nature of factory tasks would release their brains to consider their situation and appreciate the injustice of their exploitation by the capitalist.

However, this created more difficulties for Gramsci. The notion that human interests could be traced 'in the last analysis' to the requirements of the economy was appealing, because it seemed to provide an 'objective' standard for evaluating a given ideology. Unfortunately, for reasons Gramsci himself pointed out, the two could not be related in an unproblematic way. We cannot determine whether a society correctly or efficiently serves human interests without some idea of what they are, and the degree of satisfaction which is legitimate. A Christian, who subordinates everything to earning a place in heaven, will have different priorities from a capitalist, who measures success by the amount of money he has in the bank. Our interests depend upon the needs and wants we have. These are not immutable, but, as Gramsci showed, alter according to the particular theory we hold of them. Moreover, only the most naive utopian believes that all our desires can be satisfied. Some measure or procedure must therefore exist to adjudicate between conflicting or incompatible desires, even in a state of infinite material abundance. Gramsci recognized these problems, and for this reason stated that it was necessary first to decide what people's 'real' requirements were on the level of ideology. This made his argument somewhat circular, since the criteria for evaluating Marxist ideology were thus products of that same ideology.

Gramsci's dilemma was akin to Antonio Labriola's, whose work he admired and developed. Labriola had similarly argued that Marxism was only valid as praxis, but had failed to overcome his orthodox Marxist concern with the primacy of the economic factor. Gramsci developed this idea in a radical way. A doctrine proved its truth by its success, its ' "practical" efficacy'. The best philosophy was therefore one which provided a complete orientation for the lives of everybody – which was 'totalitarian'. This immediately gave rise to the worry that if a whole society could be completely deluded, then this 'delusion' would be true. Gramsci countered this objection by maintaining that no system could be totally successful unless it was in fact true to the prevailing historical conditions,

> Mass adhesion or non-adhesion to an ideology is the real critical test of the rationality and historicity of modes of thinking. Any arbitrary constructions are pretty rapidly eliminated by historical competition, even if sometimes, through a combination of immediately favourable

> circumstances, they succeed in enjoying a certain popularity, whilst constructions which correspond to the demands of a complex and organic period of history always end up by imposing themselves and prevail even if their affirmation only occurs in more or less bizarre and heterogeneous combinations.[7]

Gramsci drew the conclusion that even Marxism was 'an expression of historical contradictions' and hence 'perishable'. Christianity and vulgar Marxism were not wrong in the abstract sense – they had played a historical role, but this had passed. This defence appears problematic, for it relied on a base line – a set of objective historical conditions – which we, using Gramsci as our guide, have already condemned as inadequate. He denied that a situation could ever arise where a false ideology could combine with a set of extremely repressive social institutions in such a way that all critical discussion of its false world view would be prevented. But if a society were extraordinarily coercive, could it not enforce a distorted view of what counted as coercion, and hence be successful and 'true' in Gramsci's sense? The only way out of such a situation would be to hold to a view of eternal or transcendental truths, or pre-conditions for arriving at truth, such as he explicitly rejected.

Gramsci's response to the above problem was that criticism could only come from within, and that the criteria for evaluating repressive conditions were always present, albeit in 'embryonic form', in the experiences of the agents' frustration and suffering. This produced a contrast between thought and action which 'is the expression of profounder contrasts of a socio-historic order'. It meant that a social group 'manifests in its acts' a different conception of the world from that which, for reasons of 'intellectual subordination', it articulated in words. What was required was a 'critical' theory which would enable the masses to build on this dissatisfaction. For disaffection with the world did not provide the grounds for rejecting it and opting for an alternative. People might be at fault, and their dissent without foundation – some reason had to be given explaining why the current ideology was wrong. Gramsci's Marxian historicism claimed to provide this without falling into undue relativism: '[S]ince man is the ensemble of his conditions of life, one can quantitatively measure the difference between past and present, since one can measure the degree to which man dominates nature and chance.'[8]

The extent to which humanity could leave the realm of necessity and enter that of freedom made it possible to evaluate the options available at a given time. An ideology would be legitimate to the extent that it led to the maximum freedom for individuals. It was the capacity 'to transform the external world', that is, 'to potentiate oneself or develop oneself', which defined what human beings were. The truth of Marxism was thus one of degree. Its claim was that it represented the best guide to emancipation available to agents at any one time.

To recapitulate, Gramsci's argument was not that the economic base determined the superstructure, rather that it placed a constraint on what forms of consciousness were possible. Some ideologies were more restrictive than others, and did not allow individuals to become all they could be. The 'philosophy of praxis' was superior because it gave the masses 'the concrete means' to realize themselves:

> 1. by giving a determinate and concrete ('rational') direction to their own vital impulse or will; 2. by identifying the means which will make this will concrete and specific and not arbitrary; 3. by contributing to modify the ensemble of the concrete conditions for realising this will to the extent of one's own limits and capacities and in the most fruitful form.[9]

It created a new 'historical bloc' of structural and superstructural elements whereby individuals should achieve their potential through the conscious transformation of their relations with each other and nature. It presupposed that discontent with the present already existed, even if only exiguously, and that it had a 'real' basis in the 'material preconditions' for social change.

Notes and References

1 A. Gramsci, *Quaderni del Carcere*, Edizione critica dell' *Istituto Gramsci*, ed. Valentino Gerratana, 4 vols (Einaudi, Turin, 1975), vol. I, pp. 436–7; vol. II, p. 1319.
2 Ibid., II, pp. 1319, 1338.
3 Ibid., II, p. 869.
4 Ibid., III, p. 1612.
5 Ibid., II, p. 1489.
6 Ibid., I, pp. 454–5; II, p. 1492.
7 Ibid., II, pp. 1392–3.
8 Ibid., II, p. 1337.
9 Ibid.

4

The World in a Text: Lévi-Strauss's *Tristes Tropiques*

Clifford Geertz

For many interpreters of the work of Lévi-Strauss Tristes Tropiques *seems like a mere sport, even an embarrassment: a reflective, rather pointless pause in the long march toward intellective purity. But Geertz regards it as the key work, the center around which the whole pivots.*

From this perspective the first thing to be said about *Tristes Tropiques*, and in some ways the last as well, is that it is several books at once, several quite different sorts of texts superimposed one upon the other to bring out an overall pattern, rather like a moiré.

"Superimposed," however, is not exactly the right word. For what we have in *Tristes Tropiques* is not a hierarchical, surface-to-depth arrangement of texts, the one hidden beneath the other, so that interpretation consists in deeper penetration as one strips away the layers. What we have is co-occurring, competing, even sometimes mutually interfering texts existing at the same level.

The book is a virtual analog of Lévi-Strauss's kaleidoscope image of "concrete thought": a syntactic conjunction of discrete elements, played out horizontally along what Roman Jakobson called the plane of contiguity, rather than a paradigmatic hierarchy of continuate elements, played out vertically on what he called the plane of similarity. *Tristes Tropiques* is an ideal-typical Russian/Czech formalist poem: meaning constructed by projecting the analog axis of paradigmatic substitution, Jakobson's "metaphor," onto the digital one of syntactic combination, his "metonymy." It is, to put it more casually, and in a language less special, a manifold text *par excellence*: several books at once all jammed together to produce . . . well, we shall come back to what is produced later. First, it is necessary to look at the component elements, the thin books wildly signaling to get out inside this fat one.

In the first place, it is . . . a travel book in a very recognizable genre. I went here, I went there; I saw this strange thing and that; I was amazed, bored, excited, disappointed; I got boils on my behind, and once, in the Amazon . . . – all with the implicit undermessage: Don't you wish you had been there with me or could do the same?

[· · ·]

In any case, whatever the models, the image of the hardy traveler, sorely beset but terribly *interested*, never leaves the book, and it connects his account to a type of social consciousness – vulgar in the root, not the tendentious, sense of the word – that this almost classic *normalien* (even though he was, as he very carefully points out in *Tristes Tropiques*, by his own choice, not literally one) would never admit to and indeed has spent much of his career distancing himself from.

Second, the book is, however oddly looking a one, an ethnography.

[· · ·]

Unlike the travel text which is, as such texts are by nature, one damn thing after another, the ethnographic text has a thesis, the thesis in fact that Lévi-Strauss has pursued for the quarter century or so since: namely, "the ensemble of a people's customs has always its particular style; they form into systems." The "overture" and the "coda" to *Mythologiques* are perhaps more powerful statements, "The structural study of myth" a more systematic one, and the fourth chapter of *Totemism* a clearer one. But Lévi-Strauss has never been able to put capital-S Structuralism in so neat a nutshell as he was able to in *Tristes Tropiques*:

> The ensemble of a people's customs has always its particular style; they form into systems. I am convinced that the number of these systems is not unlimited and that human beings (at play, in their dreams, or in moments of delusion) never create *absolutely*; all they can do is to choose certain combinations from a repertory of ideas which it should be possible to reconstitute. For this one must make an inventory of all the customs which have been observed by oneself or others, the customs pictured in mythology, the customs invoked by both children and grown-ups in their games. The dreams of individuals, whether healthy or sick, should also be taken into account. With all this one could eventually establish a sort of periodical chart of chemical elements analogous to that devised by Mendelier. In this, all customs, whether real or merely possible, would be grouped by families and all that would remain for us to do would be to recognize those which societies had, in point of fact, adopted.[1]

Third, besides a travelogue and an ethnography, the book is a philosophical text. It is a philosophical text not simply in the man-in-the-street sense that it is flamboyantly reflective – the mute-exchanges-of-forgiveness-with-a-cat sort of thing – and full of dark sayings – "Marxism and Buddhism are doing the same thing, but at different levels." It is a philosophical text in the scholarly sense that it addresses itself, and with some resoluteness, to a central issue in Western thought: the natural foundations of human society. Not only does Lévi-Strauss hope to find Rousseau's Social Contract alive and well in deepest Amazon – and so counter such theories of the origins of sociality as Freud's primal parricide or Hume's conventionality – but he thinks that, among the Nambikwara, he has actually and literally done so:

> The evidence of the Nambikwara runs, to begin with, clean counter to the ancient sociological theory, now temporarily resurrected by the psychoanalysts, according to which the primitive chief derives from a symbolic father . . . . I should like to be able to show how markedly, in this regard, contemporary anthropology supports the thesis of the eighteenth century *philosophes*. Doubtless Rousseau's schema differs from the quasi-contractual relations which obtain between the chief and his companions. Rousseau had in mind a quite different phenomenon – the renunciation by the individual of his own autonomy in the interests of the collective will. It is nonetheless true, however, that Rousseau and his contemporaries displayed profound sociological intuition when they realized that attitudes and elements of culture such as are summed up in the words "contract" and "consent" are not secondary formations, as their adversaries (and Hume in particular) maintained: they are the primary materials of social life, and it is impossible to imagine a form of social organization in which they are not present.[2]

Lévi-Strauss does not merely think that he has found the Social Contract *in vivo* (a claim, a bit like saying one has discovered the country where Plato's Ideas or Kant's Noumena are stored). He wants to bring back to respectability Rousseau's *société naissante* model, which sees what we would now call the neolithic as, quoting from Rousseau, "un juste milieu entre l'indolence d'état primitif et la pétulante activité de notre amour propre" ("the middle ground between the indolence of the primitive state and the questing activity to which we are prompted by our *amour propre*"). Better we had never left that world, which we need now to reconstruct, and which we can reconstruct because Rousseau's model is eternal and universal. By knowing other societies, we can detach ourselves from our own and build, on the basis of an ideal beyond space and time, a rational social order, one, Lévi-Strauss says, in which man can live.

And this, in turn, leads to the fourth sort of text *Tristes Tropiques* is: a reformist tract. There has been an enormous number of indictments by now of the West for its impact on the non-West, but there are few, no matter how radical their authors, with the devastating bitterness and power of Lévi-Strauss's *Tristes Tropiques*. He makes Franz Fanon sound positively genial.

The passages are famous. The descriptions of the dilapidated "former savages" spoiling the view around São Paolo; the diatribes about empty beer bottles and discarded tin cans; and the intense hatred for industrial civilization that keeps breaking through: it is unnecessary to requote them here. What needs to be noted is that they connect with a distinctive strand in nineteenth- and early twentieth-century reformist thought – the one perhaps best represented in France by Flaubert, in Germany by Nietzsche, and by Arnold or Ruskin or Pater in England; one that reacted to much of modern life with an essentially aesthetic repugnance raised, or anyway transported, to a moral level. Distaste transmogrified.

[...]

And the crime, of course, is that it is we who have done this, whether out of greed and *pétulante activité* or mere fits of absentmindedness and callousness – we who have thrown, as he says somewhere in *Tristes Tropiques*, our filth in the faces of the rest of the world, which now proceeds to throw it back in ours.

As a reformist tract, *Tristes Tropiques* is an outburst, less of *moraliste* rage – which is one of the things that divides him from Sartre, who is rather more worried that people are dominated than that they are degraded – than of aesthetic repugnance. Like Swift's, Lévi-Strauss's deep social disgust seems to rise out of an even deeper disgust with the physical and the biological. His radicalism is not political. It is sensory.

Fifth, and finally, *Tristes Tropiques* is, and quite deliberately, a kind of symbolist literary text, . . . an application of *symboliste* views to primitive culture: Mallarmé in South America.

[...]

That Lévi-Strauss is concerned to place himself and his text in the literary tradition established by Baudelaire, Mallarmé, Rimbaud, and – though, as far as I can discover, he never mentions him in *Tristes Tropiques* – especially Proust, is clear from the way he writes, from what he writes, and from what he says he is concerned to do: decode, and, in decoding, recover the power to use the sensuous imagery of neolithic thought. *Tristes Tropiques* is, in one dimension, a record of a symbolist mentality, which Lévi-Strauss insists that not just his Indians but he himself has, at play in the forests and savannahs of the Amazon:

> Neither Brazil nor South America meant much to me at the time. But I can still see, in every detail, the images formed in my mind, in response to this unexpected suggestion [that is, that he go there]. Tropical countries, as it seemed to me, must be the exact opposite of our own, and the name of the antipodes has for me a sense at once richer and more ingenuous than its literal derivation. I should have been astonished to hear it said that any species, whether animal or vegetable, could have the same appearance on both sides of the globe. Every animal, every tree, every blade of grass, must be completely different and give immediate notice . . . of its tropical character. I imagined Brazil as a tangled mass of palm-leaves, with glimpses of strange architecture in the middle distance, and an all-permeating sense of burning perfume. This latter olfactory detail I owe, I think, to an unconscious awareness of the assonance between the words *Brésil* ("Brazil") and *grésiller* ("sizzle"). No amount of later experience . . . can prevent me from still thinking of Brazil in terms of burning scent.
>
> Now that I look back on them, these images no longer seem so arbitrary. I have learnt that the truth of any given situation does not yield so much to day-to-day observation as that patient and fractionated distillation which the equivocal notion of burning scent was perhaps already inviting me to put into practice. The scent brought with it, it may be, a symbolic lesson which I was not yet able to formulate clearly. Exploration is not so much a matter of covering ground as of digging beneath the surface: chance fragments of landscape, momentary snatches of life, reflections caught on the wing – such are the things that alone make it possible for us to understand and interpret horizons which would otherwise have nothing to offer us.[3]

[. . .]

So: a travel book, even a tourist guide, if, like the tropics, out of date. An ethnographic report, founding yet one more *scienza nuova.* A philosophical discourse, attempting to rehabilitate Rousseau, the Social Contract, and the virtues of the unpetulant life. A reformist tract, attacking European expansionism on aesthetic grounds. And a literary work, exemplifying and forwarding a literary cause. . . . All of these set next to one another, juxtaposed like pictures from an exhibition, producing in their interaction precisely what? What is the moiré that emerges?

To my mind what emerges, not altogether surprisingly I suppose, is a myth. The encompassing form of the book that all this syntactic, metonymic jostling of text-types produces is a Quest Story: the departure from familiar, boring, oddly threatening shores; the journey, with adventures, into another, darker world, full of various phantasms and odd revelations; the culminating mystery, the absolute other, sequestered and opaque, confronted deep down in the *sertão*; the return home to tell tales, a bit wistfully, a bit wearily, to the uncomprehending who have stayed unadventurously behind.

Notes and References

1 C. Lévi-Strauss, *A World on the Wane*, tr. John Russel (Criterion Books, New York, 1961), p. 160.
2 Ibid., p. 308.
3 Ibid., pp. 49–50.

5

Althusser and the Problem of Determinations

Michèle Barrett

Marx's warning to the prospective French readers of *Capital*, for whom he feared the book would prove a slow haul, has a bizarre ring for the modern reader who has discovered just how 'unscientific' much science has turned out to be. Marx writes: 'There is no royal road to science, and only those who do not dread the fatiguing climb of its steep paths have a chance of gaining its luminous summits.'[1] Here we have a kind of intellectual pilgrim's progress, in which hard work and perseverance in the manner of a nineteenth-century explorer will eventually pay off with the intrepid few arriving at 'the truth'; a somewhat moralistic approach to the pursuit of knowledge that is not uncommon in Marx. There are, however, many disagreements among philosophers of social science as to whether Marx formally held the position that a clear distinction can be drawn between ideology and science, as also there are disagreements about the epistemological claims and status of his own analyses. It is not necessary to go into detail here about these debates, although they are currently a focus of work among the new 'realist' philosophers. I want instead to go back a step, to the arguments within European Marxism and particularly those made by Louis Althusser in the 1960s on science and ideology in Marx's writings, since these have posed in a sharp, and highly contentious, way some of the key problems that need to be resolved in this area. In so far as Althusser has provided us with one of the strongest, most confident (verging on bombastic, as we shall see) statements of the claim that science and ideology can be disentangled, his work is a prime subject for scrutiny.

Althusser proposed that Marx's work should be read in terms of a fundamental divergence between the 'young' Marx – a left-Hegelian humanist and historicist, best known to us now for his theses on alienation – and the 'mature' Marx whose discovery of the operations of capitalist society was both structured and scientific. Althusser does not regard the young Marx as 'Marxist': 'Of course Marx's youth did *lead* to Marxism, but only at the price of a prodigious break with his origins, a heroic struggle against the illusions he had inherited from the Germany in which he was born, and an acute attention to the realities concealed by these illusions.'[2] It is not without interest that Althusser counterposes what he insists on calling Marx's scientific 'discoveries' about capitalism to the ideological character of the Hegelianism through which Marx had to make a gruelling theoretical 'long march': Althusser in practice often used the science/ideology distinction simply to indicate the general superiority of one discourse over another. Althusser concluded that the distance between the Hegelian and scientific Marxes was so great that we can reasonably speak of a break or rupture, often referred to (following Gaston Bachelard) as an 'epistemological rupture'.

[...]

Althusser's arguments about ideology and science, put forward in 1966 in *For Marx*, generated an extraordinary degree of enthusiasm among many left intellectuals. Looking at these immensely pretentious arguments now, it is difficult to keep a straight face: like the discovery that we had been talking prose all our lives, it was revealed that sitting thinking was really nothing less than *theoretical practice*. Althusser suggested that ideology could be firmly distinguished from science, or knowledge, on the following basis. Ideology, he wrote, 'is distinguished from science in that in it the practico-social function is more important than the theoretical function (function as knowledge)'.[3] Ideology, at this point in Althusser's thinking, is 'the *lived* relation between men and their world'.[4] This relation is both real, in the sense that it describes real historical social relations and how people are positioned in them, and imaginary, in the sense that it is in ideology that conservative or revolutionary *will* is expressed. So ideology is not restricted to the conscious level, it operates as images, concepts and, above all, as *structures* that impose themselves upon us. As a general system of representations, ideology for Althusser was an 'organic' or 'indispensable' part of the social totality and he maintained – he thought controversially – that ideology would always be present even in a future communist society.

Knowledge, on the other hand, was for Althusser quite different. He speaks of knowledge as a system of production, in which there are raw materials – received ideas – and a means of production – which he called a *problematic*, consisting of a set of related assumptions, methods and concepts. Althusser, in a flight of what psychoanalysts might call grandiosity, labels the raw materials *Generalities I*, the 'problematic' being used *Generalities II*, and the end result of applying II to I *Generalities III*, or 'knowledge'. Althusser's notion of a 'symptomatic reading' – the careful reading of a text in such a way as to disclose the theoretical 'silences' or absences that are often a better clue to the *problematic* being used than a text's overt declarations of intent – was in many ways a useful one, particularly in its applications to literary theory in the work of Pierre Macherey.

But in general Althusser's arguments have been widely and cogently criticized. Colin Sumner, for example, argues that the symptomatic reading is no more 'scientific' a technique than other forms of reading: 'it is simply the reading theorist's reflection on the differences between his grid and that of the object-text which he has comprehended and superseded'.[5] Terry Lovell, in a discussion of the weaknesses in Althusser's attempt to differentiate between ideology and science, suggests that each of the criteria he offers is inadequate to the task. His suggestions that ideology is 'obvious' and 'closed' and draws its problems from politics and practice rather than from theory, whereas science by contrast is 'counter-intuitive', 'open' and based on theoretically generated problems are, in Lovell's opinion, completely unsatisfactory. Although such criteria might well help with the relatively easy job of differentiating 'science' from what Gramsci called 'common sense' or 'folklore', they are of no help in the much more difficult task of separating knowledge from elaborated ideological systems of thought or philosophy. How, for example, could it be argued that neoclassical economics, or Parsonian sociology, is 'ideological', whereas Marxist political economy is 'scientific'? Lovell points out that the most thorny problem lies in distinguishing 'theoretical ideologies' from 'scientific theories', and this Althusser has not really touched.[6]

[. . .]

Jacques Rancière, a former colleague of Althusser, has decisively rejected the Althusserian approach to ideology and science. One point that he makes is fundamental. This is that Althusser's ideology/science distinction construes as separate two phenomena which are in fact integrally connected: 'Scientific theories are transmitted through a system of discourses, traditions and institutions which constitute the very existence of bourgeois ideology. . . . The dominant ideology is not the shadowy Other of the pure light of Science, it is the very space in which scientific knowledges are inscribed, and in which they are articulated as elements of a social formation's knowledge. It is in the forms of the dominant ideology that a scientific theory becomes an object of knowledge.'[7] Rancière's specific point is designed to show that Althusser fails in terms of a class analysis, since he does not understand the class character of scientific knowledge. More generally, the position from which Rancière is here taking issue with Althusser is one of philosophical 'conventionalism'. This leads into a set of related issues about science and epistemology. Is Marxism committed to a 'realist' epistemology or is this conventionalism equally compatible with Marxism? Does Marxism insist on the class character of all knowledge or does it allow forms of knowledge independent of the class affiliations of which Rancière speaks? The case of natural science is the one usually referred to here: Timpanaro has argued that Marxism has exaggerated the class contextualization of natural scientific knowledge, leaving too little room for an objective engagement with the substantive debates within natural scientific fields of enquiry.[8] What implications do these debates have for different definitions of ideology within Marxist theory?

Terry Lovell has taken a strong stand against 'conventionalism' – a term used to describe anti-empiricist arguments that insist on the theory-impregnated character of all languages of observation – on the general grounds that such positions inevitably lead to relativism and the abandonment of all claims to objective knowledge. Lovell writes that 'The limit position which all conventionalisms more or less approach is one in which the world is in effect constructed in and by theory. Given that there is no rational procedure for choosing between theories, relativism is the inevitable result. Epistemological relativism does not necessarily entail a denial that there is a real material world. But if our only access to it is via a succession of theories which describe it in mutually exclusive terms, then the concept of an independent reality ceases to have any force or function.'[9] Lovell, in common with many others, argues that Marxism tends towards the opposite of conventionalism – realism – in its epistemological position, and certainly there is little doubt that Marx himself believed in the possibility of objective knowledge. The case of Althusser, however, is more contentious. Terry Lovell suggests that Althusser fails to specify adequately the basis on which relativism might be avoided, but her imputation to him of an explicitly conventionalist position is more difficult to demonstrate other than in terms of contradictory or changing elements in his approach. As she points out, Althusser tried to solve (or duck) the realist/conventionalist problem by proposing a 'real-concrete' world that existed independently of the 'concrete-in-thought', but by which it could be apprehended. This formulation is clearly not satisfactory and, as Ted Benton has noted, does *not* resolve the problem anyway.[10] But to regard Althusser as systematically conventionalist goes against the general drift of many of his arguments – specifically on the ideology/science distinction. It is not hard, for instance, to find passages in Althusser that are as explicitly anti-conventionalist as the following: 'Marx never fell into the idealist illusion of believing that the knowledge of an object might ultimately replace the object or dissipate its existence.'[11]

Notes and References

1 Karl Marx, Preface to the French edn, *Capital* (Lawrence and Wishart, London, 1970), vol. 1, p. 21.
2 Louis Althusser, 'On the young Marx', *For Marx*, tr. Ben Brewster (Penguin Books, Harmondsworth, 1969), p. 84.
3 Althusser, *For Marx*, p. 231.
4 Ibid., p. 233.
5 Colin Sumner, *Reading Ideologies: An Investigation into the Marxist Theory of Ideology and Law* (Academic Press, London, 1979), p. 172.
6 Terry Lovell, *Pictures of Reality: Aesthetics, Politics and Pleasure* (British Film Institute, London, 1980), p. 36.
7 Jacques Rancière, 'On the theory of ideology – Althusser's politics', in *Radical Philosophy Reader*, ed. Roy Edgeley and Richard Osborne (Verso, London, 1985), p. 116.
8 See Sebastiano Timpanaro, *On Materialism* (Verso, London, 1980).
9 Lovell, *Pictures of Reality*, p. 15.
10 Ibid., pp. 32–43; Ted Benton, *The Rise and Fall of Structural Marxism: Althusser and His Influence* (Macmillan, London, 1984), p. 181.
11 Althusser, *For Marx*, p. 230.

6

Gadamer and Ricoeur on Hermeneutics

Susan Hekman

In *Truth and Method* as well as in his more recent works, Gadamer states unambiguously that he has no intention of providing a methodology for the social sciences. . . . Using his approach as a methodological 'tool' in the social sciences seriously distorts the meaning of the claim to universality that he posits for hermeneutical understanding. But arguing that hermeneutics is not a methodological tool for the social sciences on a par with, for example, statistical analysis does not preclude arguing that hermeneutics has methodological relevance for the social sciences. Gadamer's hermeneutics provides an understanding not merely of the social sciences but of the phenomenon of human understanding itself. His approach dictates that although hermeneutics cannot be employed as a method in the social sciences, it can and should be employed as a means of understanding what the social sciences are about. An examination of Gadamer's position leads to the following question: if Gadamer's philosophical hermeneutics is correct, what kind of methodological approach to the social sciences is entailed by his position?

The first problem that arises in the attempt to answer this question is the relationship between the analysis of action and the analysis of texts. In his extensive exploration of the nature of hermeneutical understanding Gadamer is concerned almost exclusively with the analysis of written texts. Although he clearly means to establish universal principles of human understanding through this analysis, it is nevertheless the case that the actual descriptions he provides involve texts, and, in *Truth and Method*, works of art. This creates a particular problem for the social sciences. What social scientists normally deal with in their analyses are not written texts or artistic creations but *actions*. Although Gadamer's claim of the universality of hermeneutical understanding entails the claim that anything, and this includes actions as well as texts, must be understood and interpreted according to the principles he establishes, it is nevertheless important for social scientific analysis to specify precisely how the analysis of texts can be translated into the analysis of action.

Unfortunately, Gadamer offers the social scientist little help in answering this question; in *Truth and Method* as well as in his later works he never confronts the issue directly. He has a good reason, however, for avoiding this question: he is not concerned with an essentially methodological problem because he has no intention of formulating a methodology. The most that can be gleaned from his works is that he assumes that action, like any other human phenomenon, is to be understood hermeneutically and that the model of textual interpretation that he presents is also applicable to the analysis of action. The first indication of this assumption can be found in his discussion of Ranke, Droysen and Dilthey in *Truth and Method*. Gadamer praises Dilthey for the innovation of interpreting historical reality as a text, a method that is repeated in the work of Ranke and Droysen. Gadamer quotes Dilthey with approval when he states that 'Life and history have meaning like the letters of a word.'[1] A second indication of this assumption is found in his discussion of style. In the course of making the point that style is a unity of expression he argues that actions can have a style that would be expressed in a series of events. His aim is to show that his analysis of style can also be applied to the study of political history. Finally, Gadamer's clearest statement of the link between actions and texts can be found in a discussion with Paul Ricoeur. Gadamer states:

> Consequently, by text-interpretation is implied the totality of our orientation of ourselves in the world, together with the assumption that deciphering and understanding a text is very much like encountering reality.[2]

But, as far as the social scientist is concerned, these brief comments are not sufficient, especially for a point so central to the social sciences. The connection between the analysis of texts and that of action must be made much more explicitly than Gadamer has done before a hermeneutically grounded methodology for the social sciences can be articulated. That philosophical grounding, however, has been provided by a contemporary social philosopher, Paul Ricoeur. In 'The model of the text'

Ricoeur supplies the link between actions and texts that is missing in Gadamer's work.

[...]

Ricoeur makes it clear at the outset that his purpose in developing a model of textual analysis that is applicable to the social sciences is to provide 'objective data' for those sciences. He argues that texts have an 'objective meaning' and that this meaning is distinct from the author's intention because it is fixed in the process of writing. It is the objective meaning of texts that, as Ricoeur sees it, constitutes the objective data of the social sciences. Thus when Ricoeur claims that the social sciences are hermeneutical, he means that they employ a methodology based in the exegesis of the objective meaning of texts. In another context he clarifies this point:

> The kind of hermeneutics which I now favor starts from the recognition of the objective meaning of the text as distinct from the subjective intention of the author. This objective meaning is not something hidden behind the text. Rather it is a requirement addressed to the reader. The interpretation accordingly is a kind of obedience to this injunction starting from the text.[3]

After establishing this point, Ricoeur goes on to make the distinction between written and spoken discourse that informs the main thesis of his analysis.

> The subjective intention of the speaking subject and the meaning of the discourse overlap each other in such a way that it is the same thing to understand what the speaker means and what his discourse means. . . . With written discourse, the author's intention and the meaning of the text cease to coincide. . . . But the text's career escapes the finite horizon lived by the author. What the text says now matters more than what the author intended to say. . . .[4]

Although neither speech nor writing is context-free, and thus there is a certain continuity between them, the distinction that Ricoeur wishes to emphasize here is that writing is fixed, that is, it becomes a text, while speech is an on-going event. Two aspects of this parallel between written discourse and accomplished actions on the one hand and spoken discourse and on-going events on the other are of central importance.

First, the essence of the parallel between an action and a text that Ricoeur is advancing lies in the fact that both are detached from their author–actor and, hence, can be 'read' apart from the author or actor's subjective meaning. Furthermore, the meaning of an action as well as a text is established by appealing to common (ordinary language) understandings. The contention here is that actions, like words, have meanings that are constitutive of everyday understandings and these meanings are, in both cases, fixed.

Secondly, by positing a parallel between actions and texts, Ricoeur is not arguing for an equivalence or an identity between them. What he is arguing is that because of the 'fixed' nature of both phenomena they can be analysed with a similar methodology. This becomes clear when Ricoeur attempts to sketch the methodological implications of the parallel between action and written discourse. To do so he returns to what he sees to be the central problematic of the human sciences: providing 'objective data' that would allow them to claim the status of a science. It now emerges that Ricoeur solves this problem by appealing to the objectification of action that, he asserts, parallels the objectification of meaning in texts. The objective data of the human sciences, he concludes, lies in the objective meaning of accomplished actions.

But for Ricoeur a further issue must be addressed before the human sciences can be securely established in the realm of the scientific: the problem of the logic of scientific analysis. Up to this point Ricoeur has shown in what sense the subject matter of the social sciences is objectified. He now asserts, along with the positivists, that if the social sciences are to be 'scientific' they must use the distinctive logic of scientific analysis. His argument differs from that of the positivists, however, in that he asserts that the model of objectivity which allows the human sciences to claim the status of 'science' can be derived not from the natural sciences but from one of the human sciences: linguistics. This point reveals the full relevance of Ricoeur's analysis of spoken discourse. He argues that recent advances in the science of linguistics provide, in a sense, a 'native' concept of objectivity and scientific method that offers a satisfactory answer to the question of the scientific status of the human sciences. As Ricoeur sees it, this solution, although it places the human sciences firmly in the scientific realm by providing them with a model of scientific method, does so by appealing not to a model of the natural sciences but to a model indigenous to the social sciences.

What Ricoeur has accomplished in 'The model of the text' is, without doubt, a significant achievement. He shows in concrete terms how the hermeneutical method of textual analysis can be extended to the analysis of social action in the human sciences.

Notes and References

1 Hans-Georg Gadamer, *Truth and Method* (Continuum, New York, 1975), p. 213.
2 Paul Ricoeur and Hans-Georg Gadamer, 'The conflict of interpretations', in *Phenomenology: Dialogues and Bridges*, ed. Ronald Bruzina and Bruce Wilshire (SUNY Press, Albany, N.Y., 1982), pp. 299–320.
3 Paul Ricoeur, *The Rule of Metaphor* (University of Toronto Press, Toronto, 1977), p. 319.
4 Paul Ricoeur, 'The Model of Text', in *Understanding and Social Inquiry,* ed. Dallmayr and McCarthy (University of Notre Dame Press, Notre Dame, Ind., 1977), p. 320.

PART II

Solidarity, Interaction and Social Practice

THIS PART PRESENTS an overview of some of the most distinctive theoretical perspectives in the social sciences today. In spite of the influence, from Max Weber onwards, of interpretative perspectives in social thought, for a long time social theory tended to be dominated by a combination of functionalism and naturalism. Functionalism offered a model of the social order according to which a social system can be analysed in terms of the functioning of its component parts, much in the same way as a physical organism. Naturalism sought to establish direct connections between the social and the natural sciences.

Over recent years, partly as a result of a resurgence of interest in hermeneutics, there has been a major break both with functionalism and with naturalism. On the level of method, as mentioned in the Introduction, there has been a movement towards emphasizing the centrality of social *practice* – together with that of *reproduction*. Each notion can be traced back to some of Marx's reflections about the nature of social *praxis*; but in many respects the new perspectives mark a break with the past. An emphasis upon the centrality of language is important, but not only upon language as means of communication; instead, language is understood as a complexity of situated practical activities and strategies. Social reproduction, in turn, is no longer treated as a mechanical process of social or cultural transmission, but is studied in relation to the active construction of social life by its participants.

Harold Garfinkel's conception of ethnomethodology represents a signal contribution to these trends. Ethnomethodology is both a programme of research in the social sciences and a direct contribution to social theory. Garfinkel (Reading 7) defines ethnomethodology as concerned with social life understood as a practical and ongoing accomplishment. Garfinkel places particular emphasis upon the significance of 'indexical expressions' in ethnomethodology. An indexical expression is an utterance, or act, whose meaning has to be understood in relation to the context of its production. Far from being unusual, indexicality is the preponderant characteristic of ordinary language and everyday action.

Social life has an intrinsic continuity and 'rationality'; Garfinkel stresses that these do not just 'happen', however, but are the result of continuous 'work' on the part of participants in interaction settings. In order to provide a down-to-earth illustration of the subject matter of ethnomethodology, Garfinkel studies the modes in which suicide is identified, and suicide statistics are constructed, by medical staff and coroners. He shows that deciding 'what really happened' in the case of a suspected suicide is not just a question of establishing 'the facts', but involves a complex process of sociological reasoning.

The idea that social reality is a 'collectively managed accomplishment' also crops up in the writings of Erving Goffman, whose ideas overlap in some important respects with those of Garfinkel. Goffman sometimes described his work as the study of the 'interaction order': the many forms of face-to-face interaction that are the 'basic stuff' of all larger forms of collectivity or social system.

As Randall Collins (Reading 8) shows, Goffman lays great stress upon the role of ritual in everyday life. Not just actions, but most conversations, have a ritual form. A conversation, however trivial, temporarily establishes a sort of shared reality that lasts as long as the exchange persists. The rituals of everyday life are far more than just a marginal aspect of it. They are the very core of the implicit 'social contract' which individuals, even strangers, ordinarily sustain as part and parcel of the routine continuance of their daily lives. The ritual aspects of interaction orders help organize self-identity, sustain a sense of personal security and at the same time contribute in a fundamental way to social reproduction; for the continuation of the larger institutions that compose social wholes depends upon the sustaining of a multiplicity of conventions.

These themes are taken up again in the selections from Giddens (Readings 9 and 10). Social systems, Giddens argues, are in a constant process of 'structuration': in other words, they are not merely given features of the social environments in which individuals exist, but are in a continuous way produced and reproduced by those very agents. A key notion of structuration theory is the idea of 'the duality of structure'. Giddens specifically opposes this notion to the emphases of functionalism and naturalism. Social reproduction must not be understood as a mechanical process, but as one geared to, and organized in terms of, the knowledgeable use of convention by actors in the interaction order.

The idea of the duality of structure implies that the concept of 'structure', as applied to social systems, should be distinguished from the usual uses of the notion in Anglo-Saxon social thought. Structure, for Giddens, should not be conceived of in analogy with, for example, the girders or walls of a building; social structure does not resemble physical structure in this way. Instead, structure is understood as being involved in, and brought about by, the knowledgeable use of rules and resources by actors engaging in the routine practices of social life. 'Rules' here should be understood as largely tacit conventions, which actors both draw upon and reproduce in the course of their day-to-day activities. The notion of 'duality of structure' refers to the fact that rules and resources are both drawn upon by actors, in a routine way, to produce their activities, yet are also reproduced by those activities, thereby giving continuity to social systems across time and space.

The notion of reflexivity is central to Giddens's thought. To be a human agent is *ipso facto* to reflexively monitor (as Garfinkel and Goffman both show) one's activities in a taken-for-granted, and chronic, fashion. Reflexivity in this sense is intrinsic to any sophisticated account of why the social sciences confront a subject matter distinct from that of natural science.

Yet reflexivity, in a different sense, also has a direct connection with the institutions of modern society. What Giddens calls 'institutional reflexivity' develops to the degree to which the conditions of social reproduction become infused with regularized and systematic knowledge about the conditions of social action, rather than being organized primarily in terms of tradition. In modern social circumstances tradition becomes swept away more thoroughly than ever before: or, to put things more precisely, traditions tend to persist only in so far as they themselves become 'detraditionalized' and therefore defended in a principled way like any other source of claimed social knowledge.

A society of developed institutional reflexivity is one subject to rapid, and to some extent unpredictable, social change. Indeed, the prevalence of institutional reflexivity is one of the main factors involved in that specific dynamism which separates modernity from prior types of human civilization. In modern social life, change tends to be far more rapid, bites more deeply into the tissue of daily life, and is much wider in scope, than is characteristic of pre-modern cultures.

Pierre Bourdieu also objects (Reading 11) to both naturalism (which he calls 'objectivism') and functionalism. Objectivism, he says, treats social structure from the point of view of an observer who sees it as a kind of theatrical play whose roles have already been written. Bourdieu's 'theory of practice' emphasizes that the scripts are never written in advance. Day-to-day social life, as well as larger social institutions, are structured in terms of a set of 'structuring dispositions' or *habitus*. The habitus is a set of dispositions which the individual brings to the conduct of day-to-day life, and which incline the individual to act and react in certain ways. The dispositions generate practices, perceptions and attitudes which are 'regular' without being consciously co-ordinated or governed by any rule. The habitus, Bourdieu argues, is the product of past experiences, but it always transmits these experiences in an active creative fashion. The idea of habitus, he claims, breaks away from dualisms which have long plagued social theory – for instance, those between subject and object, individual and society, determinism and freedom.

The habitus is the key concept with which Bourdieu seeks to grasp the ordered character of the practices, perceptions and attitudes which make up social life. But when individuals act, they always do so in contexts or settings which are structured in certain ways. The social world can be described as a series of positions in 'social space' (Reading 12) – so long as one remembers that these do not exist apart from the regularities induced by the habitus. Social space can be understood as a 'field of forces' – that is, as a set of relations of power not reducible to the interaction order as such.

Thus the possession of capital, whether this be economic wealth or the 'cultural capital' involved in the possession of cultural skills and educational qualifications, offers at any given moment power over those denied access to such capital. Social classes exist within such fields of power but do not exist, Bourdieu emphasizes, simply as givens: they are constructed through the active struggles of individuals and groups within social space. Unlike Marx, Bourdieu lays particular stress upon the symbolic ordering of social space. The differentiation of social space, and the power relations that go along with it, can be understood in terms of modes of 'distinction'. Individuals and groups claim distinction from others in terms of their symbolic identity and lifestyles; distinction is simultaneously a means of struggling for identity and a system of unequal power.

Rational choice theory (Reading 13), as developed by Jon Elster, has gained considerable influence in the social sciences today. It is represented first and foremost in the area of economics, but has been applied by Elster and others as part of a general theory of social behaviour. Rational choice theory places less emphasis upon the idea of social reproduction than do either Bourdieu or Giddens. However, there are some common emphases shared with these authors. In each case considerable weight is given to the 'knowledgeable agent': individuals in social theory are not to be thought of simply as the playthings of social forces but, in some sense or another, as rational agents pursuing definite goals in the course of their everyday actions.

Rational choice theory, as the term suggests, lays a great deal of stress upon the concept of rational action. The rationality of action is maximized where actors have consistent beliefs, weigh the evidence available to them in the light of those beliefs, and choose a course of conduct that realizes their known desires. Rational action thus conceived is always to some degree an ideal-typical model in Max Weber's sense. Irrational elements can affect action at various links in the chain. The information which an individual employs may be false or distorted; the person may be imperfectly aware of his or her desires; she or he might choose a course of action other than the optimum one in the light of the available evidence. The type-case of rational action is the maximizing of utility as understood in economic theory. Elster shows that applying such a model to other institutional domains, such as that of politics, can be very instructive, yet also has its pitfalls.

7

What is Ethnomethodology?

Harold Garfinkel

The earmark of practical sociological reasoning, wherever it occurs, is that it seeks to remedy the indexical properties of members' talk and conduct. Endless methodological studies are directed to the tasks of providing members a remedy for indexical expressions in members' abiding attempts, with rigorous uses of ideals to demonstrate the observability of organized activities in actual occasions with situated particulars of talk and conduct.

The properties of indexical expressions and indexical actions are ordered properties. These consist of organizationally demonstrable sense, or facticity, or methodic use, or agreement among "cultural colleagues." Their ordered properties consist of organizationally demonstrable rational properties of indexical expressions and indexical actions. Those ordered properties are ongoing achievements of the concerted commonplace activities of investigators. The demonstrable rationality of indexical expressions and indexical actions retains over the course of its managed production by members the character of ordinary, familiar, routinized practical circumstances. As process and attainment the produced rationality of indexical expressions consists of practical tasks subject to every exigency of organizationally situated conduct.

I use the term "ethnomethodology" to refer to the investigation of the rational properties of indexical expressions and other practical actions as contingent ongoing accomplishments of organized artful practices of everyday life.

[· · ·]

[Constructing suicide statistics is taken by Garfinkel as an illustration of practical sociological reasoning.] The Los Angeles Suicide Prevention

Center (SPC) and the Los Angeles Medical Examiner-Coroner's Office joined forces in 1957 to furnish Coroner's Death Certificates the warrant of scientific authority "within the limits of practical certainties imposed by the state of the art." Selected cases of "sudden, unnatural death" that were equivocal between "suicide" and other modes of death were referred by the Medical Examiner-Coroner to the SPC with the request that an inquiry, called a "psychological autopsy," be done.

The practices and concerns by SPC staff to accomplish their inquiries in common sense situations of choice repeated the features of practical inquiries that were encountered in other situations: studies of jury deliberations in negligence cases; clinic staff in selecting patients for out-patient psychiatric treatment; graduate students in sociology coding the contents of clinic folders into a coding sheet by following detailed coding instructions; and countless professional procedures in the conduct of anthropological, linguistic, social psychiatric, and sociological inquiry. The following features in the work at SPC were recognized by staff with frank acknowledgment as prevailing conditions of their work and as matters to consider when assessing the efficacy, efficiency, or intelligibility of their work – and added SPC testimony to that of jurors, survey researchers, and the rest:

1 an abiding concern on the part of all parties for the temporal concerting of activities;
2 a concern for the practical question *par excellence*: "What to do next?";
3 a concern on the inquirer's part to give evidence of his grasp of "what anyone knows" about how the settings work in which he had to accomplish his inquiries, and his concern to do so on the actual occasions in which the decisions were to be made by his exhibitable conduct in choosing;
4 matters which at the level of talk might be spoken of as "production programs," "laws of conduct," "rules of rational decision-making," "causes," "conditions," "hypothesis testing," "models," "rules of inductive and deductive inference" in the actual situation were taken for granted and were depended upon to consist of recipes, proverbs, slogans, and partially formulated plans of action;
5 inquirers were required to know and be skilled in dealing with situations "of the sort" for which "rules of rational decision-making" and the rest were intended in order to "see" or by what they did to insure the objective, effective, consistent, completely empirically adequate, *i.e.* rational character of recipes prophecies, proverbs, partial descriptions in an actual occasion of the use of rules;

6 for the practical decider the "actual occasion" as a phenomenon in its own right exercised overwhelming priority of relevance to which "decision rules" or theories of decision-making were without exception subordinated in order to assess their rational features rather than *vice versa*;
7 finally, and perhaps most characteristically, all of the foregoing features, together with an inquirer's "system" of alternatives, his "decision" methods, his information, his choices, and the rationality of his accounts and actions were constituent parts of the same practical circumstances in which inquirers did the work of inquiry – a feature that inquirers if they were to claim and recognize the practicality of their efforts knew of, required, counted on, took for granted, used, and glossed.

The work by SPC members of conducting their inquiries was part and parcel of the day's work. Recognized by staff members as constituent features of the day's work, their inquiries were thereby intimately connected to the terms of employment, to various internal and external chains of reportage, supervision, and review, and to similar organizationally supplied "priorities of relevances" for assessments of what "realistically," "practically," or "reasonably" needed to be done and could be done, how quickly, with what resources, seeing whom, talking about what, for how long, and so on. Such considerations furnished "We did what we could, and for all reasonable interests here is what we came out with," its features of organizationally appropriate sense, fact, impersonality, anonymity of authorship, purpose, reproducibility – *i.e.* of a *properly* and *visibly* rational account of the inquiry.

Members were required in their occupational capacities to formulate accounts of how a death *really*-for-all-practical-purposes-happened. "Really" made unavoidable reference to daily, ordinary, occupational workings. Members alone were entitled to invoke such workings as appropriate grounds for recommending the reasonable character of the result *without necessity for furnishing specifics*. On occasions of challenge, ordinary occupational workings would be cited explicitly, in "relevant part." Otherwise those features were disengaged from the product. In their place an account of how the inquiry was done made out the how-it-was-actually-done as appropriate to usual demands, usual attainments, usual practices, *and* to usual talk by SPC personnel talking as *bona fide* professional practitioners about usual demands, usual attainments, and usual practices.

One of several titles (relating to mode of death) had to be assigned to each case. The collection consisted of legally possible combinations of four elementary possibilities – natural death, accident, suicide, and homicide. *All* titles were so administered as not only to withstand the varieties of equivocation, ambiguity, and improvisation that arose in every actual occasion of their use, but to *invite* that ambiguity, equivocality, and improvisation. It was part of the work not *only* that equivocality is a trouble – is *perhaps* a trouble – but also the practitioners were directed to those circumstances in order to *invite* the ambiguity or the equivocality, to invite the improvisation, or to invite the temporizing, and the rest. It is not that the investigator, having a list of titles, performed an inquiry that proceeded stepwise to establish the grounds for electing among them. The formula was not, "Here is what we did, and among the titles as goals of our research *this* title finally interprets in a best fashion what we found out." Instead titles were continually postdicted and foretold. An inquiry was apt to be heavily guided by the inquirer's use of imagined settings in which the title will have been "used" by one or another interested party, including the deceased, and this was done by the inquirers in order to decide, using whatever "datum" might have been searched out, that *that* "datum" could be used to mask if masking needed to be done, or to equivocate, or gloss, or lead, or exemplify if they were needed. The prevailing feature of an inquiry was that nothing about it remained assured aside from the organized occasions of its uses. Thus a routine inquiry was one that the investigator used particular contingencies to accomplish, and depended upon particular contingencies to recognize and to recommend the practical adequacy of his work. When assessed by a member, *i.e.* viewed with respect to actual practices for making it happen, a routine inquiry is not one that is accomplished by rule, or according to rules. It seemed much more to consist of an inquiry that is openly recognized to have fallen short, but in the same ways it falls short its adequacy is acknowledged and for which no one is offering or calling particularly for explanations.

What members are *doing* in their inquiries is always somebody else's business in the sense that particular, organizationally located, locatable persons acquire an interest in light of the SPC member's account of whatever it is that will have been reported to have "really happened." Such considerations contributed heavily to the perceived feature of investigations that they were directed in their course by an account for which the claim will have been advanced that for all practical purposes it is correct. Thus over the path of his inquiry the investigator's task consisted of an account of how a particular person died in society that is adequately told, sufficiently detailed, clear, etc., for all practical purposes.

"What really happened," over the course of arriving at it, as well as after the "what really happened" has been inserted into the file and the title has been decided, may be chronically reviewed as well as chronically foretold in light of what might have been done, or what will have been done with those decisions. It is hardly news that on the way to a decision what a decision will have come to was reviewed and foretold in light of the anticipated consequences of a decision. *After* a recommendation had been made and the coroner had signed the death certificate the result can yet be, as they say, "revised." It can still be made a decision which needs to be reviewed "once more."

Inquirers wanted very much to be able to assure that they could come out at the end with an account of how the person died that would permit the coroner and his staff to withstand claims arguing that that account was incomplete or that the death happened differently than – or in contrast to or in contradiction of – what the members to the arrangement "claimed." The reference is neither only nor entirely to the complaints of the survivors. Those issues are dealt with as a succession of episodes, most being settled fairly quickly. The great contingencies consisted of enduring processes that lay in the fact that the coroner's office is a political office. The coroner's office activities produce continuing records of his office's activities. These records are subject to review as the products of the scientific work of the coroner, his staff, and his consultant. Office activities are methods for accomplishing reports that are scientific-for-all-practical-purposes. This involved "writing" as a warranting procedure in that a report, by reason of being written, is put into a file. That the investigator "does" a report is thereby made a matter for public record for the use of only partially identifiable other persons. Their interests in why or how or what the inquirer did would have in some relevant part to do with his skill and entitlement as a professional. But investigators know too that other interests will inform the "review," for the inquirer's work will be scrutinized to see its scientific-adequacy-for-all-practical-purposes as professionals' socially managed claims. Not only for investigators but on all sides there is the relevance of "What was really found out for-all-practical-purposes?" which consists unavoidably of how much can you find out, how much can you disclose, how much can you gloss, how much can you conceal, how much can you hold as none of the business of some important persons, *investigators* included. All of them acquired an interest by reason of the fact that investigators, as a matter of occupational duty, were coming up with written reports of how, for-all-practical-purposes persons-really-died-and-are-really-dead-*in*-the-society.

Decisions had an unavoidable consequentiality. By this is meant that investigators needed to say *in so many words*, "What really happened?" The important words were the titles that were assigned to a text to recover that text as the title's "explication." But what an assigned title consists of as an "explicated" title is at any particular time for no one to say with any finality even when it is proposed "in so many words." In fact, *that* it is proposed "in so many words," *that* for example a written text was inserted "into the file of the case," furnishes entitling grounds that can be invoked in order to make something of the "so many words" that will have been used as an account of the death. Viewed with respect to patterns of use, titles and their accompanying texts have an open set of consequences. Upon any occasion of the use of texts it can remain to be seen what can be done with them, or what they will have come to, or what remains done "for the time being" pending the ways in which the environment of that decision may organize itself to "reopen the case," or "issue a complaint," or "find an issue" and so on. Such ways for SPC'ers are, as patterns, certain; but as particular processes for making them happen are in every actual occasion indefinite.

SPC inquiries begin with a death that the coroner finds equivocal as to *mode* of death. That death they use as a precedent with which various ways of living in society that could have terminated with that death are searched out and read "in the remains"; in the scraps of this and that like the body and its trappings, medicine bottles, notes, bits and pieces of clothing, and other memorabilia – stuff that can be photographed, collected, and packaged. Other "remains" are collected too: rumors, passing remarks, and stories – materials in the "repertoires" of whosoever might be consulted via the common work of conversations. These *whatsoever* bits and pieces that a story or a rule or a proverb might make intelligible are used to formulate a recognizably coherent, standard, typical, cogent, uniform, planful, *i.e.* a professionally defensible, and thereby, for members, a *recognizably* rational account of how the society worked to produce those remains. This point will be easier to make if the reader will consult any standard textbook in forensic pathology. In it he will find the inevitable photograph of a victim with a slashed throat. Were the coroner to use that "sight" to recommend the equivocality of the mode of death he might say something like this: "In the case where a body looks like the one in that picture, you are looking at a suicidal death because the wound shows the 'hesitation cuts' that accompany the great wound. One can imagine these cuts are the remains of a procedure whereby the victim first made several preliminary trials of a hesitating sort and then performed the lethal slash. Other courses of action are imaginable, too, and so cuts that look like hesitation cuts can be produced by other mechanisms. One needs to start with the actual display and imagine how different courses of actions could have been organized such that *that* picture would be compatible with it. One might think of the photographed display as a phase-of-the-action. In any actual display is there a course of action with which that phase is uniquely compatible? *That* is the coroner's question."

The coroner (and SPC'ers) ask this with respect to each *particular* case, and thereby their work of achieving practical decidability seems almost unavoidably to display the following prevailing and important characteristic. SPC'ers must accomplish that decidability with respect to the "this's": they have to start with *this* much; *this* sight; *this* note; *this* collection of whatever is at hand. And *whatever* is there is good enough in the sense that *whatever* is there not only *will* do, but *does*. One makes whatever is there *do*. I do not mean by "making do" that an SPC investigator is too easily content, or that he does not look for more when he should. Instead, I mean: the *whatever* it is that he has to deal with, *that* is what will have been used to have found out, to have made decidable, the way in which the society operated to have produced *that* picture, to have come to *that* scene as its end result. In this way the remains on the slab serve not only as a precedent but as a goal of SPC inquiries. *Whatsoever* SPC members are faced with must serve as the precedent with which to read the remains so as to see how the society could have operated to have produced what it is that the inquirer has "in the end," "in the final analysis," and "in *any* case." What the inquiry can come to is what the death came to.

[. . .]

That practical actions are problematic in ways not so far seen; how they are problematical; how to make them accessible to study; what we might learn about them – these are proposed tasks. I use the term "ethnomethodology" to refer to the study of practical actions according to policies such as the following, and to the phenomena, issues, findings, and methods that accompany their use.

1 An indefinitely large domain of appropriate settings can be located if one uses a search policy that *any occasion whatsoever* be examined for the feature that "choice" among alternatives of sense, of facticity, of objectivity, of cause, of explanation, of communality *of practical actions* is a project of members' actions. Such a policy provides that inquiries of every imaginable kind, from divination to theoretical physics, claim our interest as socially organized artful practices. That the social structures of everyday activities furnish contexts, objects, resources,

justifications, problematic topics, etc. to practices and products of inquiries establishes the eligibility for our interest of every way of doing inquiries without exception.

No inquiries can be excluded no matter where or when they occur, no matter how vast or trivial their scope, organization, cost, duration, consequences, whatever their successes, whatever their repute, their practitioners, their claims, their philosophies or philosophers. Procedures and results of water witching, divination, mathematics, sociology – whether done by lay persons or professionals – are addressed according to the policy that every feature of sense, of fact, of method, for every particular case of inquiry without exception, is the managed accomplishment of organized settings of practical actions, and that particular determinations in members' practices of consistency, planfulness, relevance, or reproducibility of their practices and results – from witchcraft to topology – are acquired and assured only through particular, located organizations of artful practices.

2 Members of an organized arrangement are continually engaged in having to decide, recognize, persuade, or make evident the rational, *i.e.* the coherent, or consistent, or chosen, or planful, or effective, or methodical, or knowledgeable character of such activities of their inquiries as counting, graphing, interrogation, sampling, recording, reporting, planning, decision-making, and the rest. It is not satisfactory to describe how actual investigative procedures, as constituent features of members' ordinary and organized affairs, are accomplished by members as recognizedly rational actions *in actual occasions* of organizational circumstances by saying that members invoke some rule with which to define the coherent or consistent or planful, *i.e.* rational, character of their actual activities. Nor is it satisfactory to propose that the rational properties of members' inquiries are produced by members' compliance to rules of inquiry. Instead, "adequate demonstration," "adequate reporting," "sufficient evidence," "plain talk," "making too much of the record," "necessary inference," "frame of restricted alternatives," in short, every topic of "logic" and "methodology," including these two titles as well, are glosses for organizational phenomena. These phenomena are contingent achievements of organizations of common practices, and as contingent achievements they are variously available to members as norms, tasks, troubles. Only in these ways rather than as invariant categories or as general principles do they define "adequate inquiry and discourse."

3 Thus, a leading policy is to refuse serious consideration to the prevailing proposal that efficiency, efficacy, effectiveness, intelligibility,

consistency, planfulness, typicality, uniformity, reproducibility of activities – *i.e.* that rational properties of practical activities – be assessed, recognized, categorized, described by using a rule or a standard obtained outside actual settings within which such properties are recognized, used, produced, and talked about by settings' members. All procedures whereby logical and methodological properties of the practices and results of inquiries are assessed in their general characteristics by rule are of interest as *phenomena* for ethnomethodological study but not otherwise. Structurally differing organized practical activities of everyday life are to be sought out and examined for the production, origins, recognition, and representations of rational practices. All "logical" and "methodological" properties of action, every feature of an activity's sense, facticity, objectivity, accountability, communality is to be treated as a contingent accomplishment of socially organized common practices.

4 The policy is recommended that any social setting be viewed as self-organizing with respect to the intelligible character of its own appearances either as representations-of- or as evidences-of-a-social-order. Any setting organizes its activities to make its properties as an organized environment of practical activities detectable, countable, recordable, reportable, tell-a-story-aboutable, analyzable – in short, *accountable*.

8

Erving Goffman on Ritual and Solidarity in Social Life

Randall Collins

Goffman's work indicates that the entire structure of society, both work and private sociability, is upheld by rituals. Furthermore, it shows that this structure is ritually stratified. These implications are usually missed because Goffman tends to direct our attention to the individual self as one passes through these rituals. This is what has given the impression that Goffman is a symbolic interactionist. The basic model, though, is that the self is socially enacted through rituals on frontstages, supported by backstages. One's homes, and especially bedroom and bathroom, serve as backstage areas for hiding the less impressive aspects of self: for getting rid of dirt and garbage (literally), for putting on a frontstage self in the form of clothes, makeup, and hair styling. These same places also are psychological backstages, where one can plan, brood and complain about frontstage social relationships of past and present, as well as act spontaneously without concern for the proper impression one is making. Conversely, part of the frontstage self is the mood one tries to get into, the facial expressions that one wears, the style of one's talk.

This regionalization of the self has implications for social relationships. Interpersonal ties are more intimate to the extent that they take place on backstages rather than frontstages. Moreover (although Goffman does not go into this), one can readily see that there is a hierarchy of frontstages and backstages: workers out of sight of their boss are on one kind of backstage, while the same individual at home with family is on a more intimate backstage, and what transpires between husband and wife in bed is still more intimate. Nevertheless, the most intimate of situations still has a ritual structure to it, and Goffman comments that even sexual intercourse is in some sense a staged performance.

Goffman analyses situations as rituals centred on the self. Conversation is itself a ritual. 'Natural rituals' (my term rather than Goffman's) are found even in the most casual and ordinary interactions of everyday life. There is the assembly of the group (most commonly, two people); the shared focus of attention (the intention of doing the talking itself); and a shared mood, which builds up as the participants become drawn into the topic. Initially, the mood may be only a shared desire to be sociable; subsequently, if the conversation is successful and as people become engrossed in it, it is enhanced into whatever tone of humour, anger, interest or anything else which might emerge with the flow of talk.

The result of this conversational ritual is to create a little temporary cult, a shared reality consisting of whatever is being talked about. This is a major respect in which humans differ from other animals: we can take leave of our immediate physical surroundings and invoke a symbolic world of ideas referring to elsewhere, or to abstractions or fantasies which have no real physical locus. Goffman points out that once the conversational ritual is in full swing, it builds up its own pressures which control its participants. The topic has to be respected, at least temporarily believed in; it has become, for ever so short a time, a sacred object to be worshipped. Goffman describes this by saying that the conversation is a little social system with its own rules, which acts to protect its own boundaries, keeping the mundane surrounding world outside. Another way to put it would be to say that the circular reaction among attention and common mood builds up, so that the topic becomes more impelling as a focus, and the mood becomes successively stronger. A humorous conversation becomes funnier along the way, so that almost any remark, introduced with the right timing, becomes an occasion for laughter. Complaining about one's boss, one's job, political enemies, or the like becomes a ritual affirmation of the point of view shared by the talkers, so that sins are magnified and every detail becomes viewed in darkest perspective. The conversation as a ritual reality now demands that the individuals respect the mood that has built up. Its criterion is not whether what one has said is correct; in fact, one violates the ritual if one too bluntly questions a point, takes a joke literally, or fails to go along with the proper mood of sympathy in listening to someone's bragging or complaints. Goffman goes so far as to describe a conversation as a psychosis-like state, temporarily entered into, in which the only reality that counts is that which will keep the relationship going among the talkers: 'talk creates for the participant a world and a reality that has other participants in it. Joint spontaneous involvement is a *unio mystico*, a socialized trance. We must also see that a conversation has a life of its own and makes demands on its own behalf. It is a little social system with its own boundary-maintaining tendencies.'[1]

For Goffman, the self is not so much a private, individual attribute as a public reality, created by and having its primary existence in public interaction. His first important paper is 'On face-work: an analysis of ritual elements in social interaction'. The implications of the argument come out when this paper is seen in conjunction with his next article, 'The nature of deference and demeanor', which leads off by referring to Durkheim's theory of the soul. Most religions have a conception of the soul, a sacred part of the individual. The individual soul is regarded as akin to the gods or totems, or as created by them, and is spiritual or immortal and goes to join them after death. According to Durkheim, this represents the fact that the individual's consciousness (and especially his/her moral sentiments) is created by society, and that society is constantly within him/her. Goffman summarizes: 'the individual's personality can be seen as one apportionment of the collective *mana*, and . . . the rites performed to representations of the social collectivity will sometimes be performed to the individual himself.'[2] In modern society, these rituals centre especially around the 'worship' of the self. The 'line' one takes, the 'face' one presents, does not have to be realistic, but it has to be consistently maintained so that other people will be able to know what to expect and how to react to it. Hence ritual codes exist, requiring individuals to maintain a consistent face and also to help others in maintaining their own faces. Although there can be competitive and deceptive elements in interaction, these depend on a more basic *ritual co-operation* in upholding the enactment of a shared reality.

In other words, people accommodate to each other's constructions of their social selves. They tend to accept the way they define what they are. The politeness of everyday interaction is largely oriented towards protecting these self-definitions. The ritual code calls for people to avoid threatening topics in conversation, and to avoid questioning claims that people have made about themselves; to show tact in overlooking errors in what one's conversational partner has said. What Goffman calls 'face work' in conversation includes not insulting others, not getting into disagreements but rather covering up differences of opinion by polite assent or ambiguous expressions, and avoiding lulls or 'embarrassing pauses' which would reveal a lack of interest in the other person's line.

In 'The nature of deference and demeanor', Goffman uses evidence from a mental hospital to prove his point by comparison. What we consider to be mental illness, Goffman argues, is the violation of the ceremonial rules of everyday life. Extreme and consistent violation of these rules is what gets one committed to a mental hospital in the first place. The worst violators are put in the 'back wards', while those who are considered less 'ill', or on the road to recovery, are placed in a 'good ward', where the ceremonial rules of ordinary interaction are better observed. Moreover, the staff of the mental hospital defines the mental health or illness of its inmates according to what kind of *self* they have, although the actual behaviour they use to rate mental health is patients' adherence to ceremonial rules. This indicates that interaction is seen as an expression of one's self. Persons on the back wards, who tear off their clothes, defecate on the floor, drool, growl, curse or otherwise violate the ceremonial standards of polite society, are also showing no regard for the self-image they are expected to display. By this comparison, Goffman shows that the self depends on – one might also say, is created by – the acceptable use of the ritual of ordinary social etiquette.

Interaction is a process of exchange between ritually enacted selves. Each person defers to the other's demeanour self, and in return receives deference which helps them to uphold their own demeanour. One's personal self is partly based on other's reactions via deference to one's demeanour. Each individual relies on others to complete one's picture of one's self.

All this constitutes a ritual, non-utilitarian dimension of social behaviour. Goffman quotes Durkheim: 'The human personality is a sacred thing; one dare not violate it nor infringe its bounds, while at the same time the greatest good is in communion with others.'[3] The polite aspects of everyday interaction are rituals in the same sense as the religious ceremonies of the community, only on a smaller scale. Instead of worshipping the whole society or group, as symbolized by its gods and other public sacred objects, however, these everyday rituals express regard for each person's self as a sacred object. Goffman concludes:

> this secular world is not so irreligious as we might think. Many gods have been done away with, but the individual himself stubbornly remains as a deity of considerable importance. He walks with some dignity and is the recipient of many little offerings. He is jealous of the worship due him, yet approached in the right spirit, he is ready to forgive those who may have offended him. Because of their status relative to his, some persons will find him contaminating while others will find they contaminate him, in either case finding that they must treat him with ritual care.[4]

We may push the implication one step further. Durkheim's sacred objects, the gods of a society, do not really exist in themselves; they are merely symbols reflecting the structure. If the self is the central sacred object of modern society, it is correspondingly unreal. The self in Goffman is not something that individuals negotiate out of social interactions: it is, rather, the archetypal modern myth. We are *compelled* to have an individual self, not because we actually have one but because social interaction requires us to act as if we do. It is society that forces people to present a certain image of themselves, to appear to be truthful, self-consistent, and honourable. But the same social system, because it forces us to switch back and forth between many complicated roles, is also making us always somewhat untruthful, inconsistent, and dishonourable. The requirements of staging roles makes us actors rather than spontaneously the roles that we appear to be at any single moment. The self is real only as a symbol, a linguistic concept that we use to account for what we and other people do. It is an ideology of everyday life, used to attribute causality and moral responsibility in our society, just as in societies with a denser (e.g. tribal) structure, moral responsibility is not placed within the individual but attributed to spirits or gods.

I am suggesting that Goffman maintained this Durkheimian viewpoint from his early to his latest works. In what follows, I will discuss *Forms of Talk* which is the most generalized statement of Goffman's mature period. Goffman's vision is that conversation is always part of a larger frame of interaction. Only if the larger frame is properly handled can the conversation take place; and just how that larger frame is set will determine what kind of conversation can proceed within it. Most of the time we do not notice this larger frame, because it is routine and can be taken for granted; that is why Goffman is at pains to pick out instances when it is not quite routine, and hence intrudes in the form of 'byplay' and the like. But even when there is nothing disruptive about the larger frame, it has to be there to make the conversation possible. (An example would be the privacy and other situational appropriateness necessary for a casual chat.) Goffman is saying that talk needs to be analysed 'from the outside in', with the larger frame setting the conditions for what can emerge within it.

Now what determines the larger frame, with which the analysis should begin? There are several layers here, which (making more explicit what Goffman refers to only in passing) we can call (1) the physical world, (2) the social ecology, and (3) the institutional setting.

1 Often talk arises or takes on meaning from the relationship of participants to some event or task in the physical world around them. The talk which occurs when individuals are repairing a car ('There' – pointing to the problem; 'Hand me that') or playing cards ('Three spades')

is not understandable at all unless one knows what is being done physically, and often this requires being right there on the spot. This embedding in a *particularized* physical world is an instance of what the ethnomethodologists called 'indexicality': these statements have a meaning only in that context, which is not transferable or generalizable. Goffman concludes that the basis of language is not a primal intersubjectivity, a meeting of minds, but rather a common focus on a physical scene of action. The anchoring of the mind is outside ourselves, and communication at its most primitive derives from the way several people anchor themselves to the common physical world in which they are acting.

This does not mean that Goffman is a 'physical reductionist', with a purely external, behaviourist view of talk. Rather, he is saying that mental levels, are emergent from this most fundamental, physical frame, and are always anchored to it through one or more transformations. There is a mental level, but it is not a free-floating realm, and it is not the primary reality but a derived one.

2 The social ecology that Goffman takes as the social basis of any conversational situation comprises the physical bodies of the people who happen to be present, whether they are actually all talking to one another or not (i.e. bystanders must be included). This might be called an 'ecological' perspective, since Goffman is looking at human beings the way a biologist would look at birds or mammals who are in range of each other. Goffman asserts that people must always pay attention to other human beings in their presence; each one needs to check out the others, if only to see if it is safe to ignore them.

One piece of evidence Goffman brings to make this point is the kind of utterance that he calls 'self-talk'. These are the outcries, mutterings, and so forth that people utter in the presence of others but without being in conversation with them. For example, it is embarrassing to behave incompetently when there is someone else around. Hence one makes a 'ritual repair', implicitly directing it towards the other people. Talking to oneself (thinking out loud), and then suddenly discovering there are other people present, calls for just such a ritual repair. It violates the social demand that we should show ourselves as competent and self-controlled persons; hence one needs to do something to re-establish oneself, by communicating to the bystanders.

This might be referred to as a kind of 'ecological order'. As Goffman puts it, even 'when nothing eventful is occurring, persons in one another's presence are still nonetheless tracking one another and acting so as to make themselves trackable'.[5] Human beings, as sheer physical bodies, share an animal level of inter-awareness: each is potentially dangerous to another, as well as potentially someone who might be of aid (by calling out in common danger, for instance). Hence we are 'primed', perhaps even biologically, to pay attention to how each other is behaving. Whenever someone does something that is abnormal, they set up a flicker of attention among the people around them, because they are giving off a sign that they are not quite under control, and may in fact be dangerous. Hence, to reassure others and ward off their possible fear of our 'craziness', we communicate little ritual repairs disavowing our mistakes, and thereby rendering ourselves normal bodies walking down the street, whose behaviour can be taken for granted.

Goffman, like Wittgenstein, denies that private experience is primary; the social is always the centre of the action and of attention. Whenever something happens which takes us temporarily out of the social realm (e.g. when we are turned on sexually so that we pay no attention to anyone else) or when we fall short of expected competence (by feeling pain or muscular strain), the return to social awareness always triggers a need to re-establish contact, and to explain to other people why we have taken leave of them (if only for an instant). Hence these expressive cries, grunts, and groans. Goffman's theory depends on the empirical pattern that we make such noises mainly in the presence of other people, not when we are alone. But it does seem to be true that we also can make these noises in solitude. Goffman's argument implies that these solitary instances are derivatives of the social ones, that we can cry by ourselves, or grunt in muscular effort, because we are performing before an imaginary social audience. Presumably, if a person had never been socialized, they would not only be unable to talk: they would also be unable to make these kinds of 'non-linguistic' expressions.

3 The institutional setting is a frame which arises inside these two outermost frames: the physical world and the ecological co-presence of physical human bodies. We can see the significance of the institutional setting by looking at the variations in the kinds of micro-conversational events which can take place. In informal talk, the participants themselves must arrange, or negotiate, who takes which turn in a sequence of turns. But there are other kinds of interactions, organized by different turn-taking rules. There is the lecture, which not only gives one speaker a certain amount of time to talk, but also may have a chairperson who calls upon the persons who are allowed to ask questions. There is the theatre or the musical recital, which have their own ways of allotting turns. There are formal rituals, such as a church service or wedding, in which the turns (and for that matter what is said in them)

are rigidly programmed in advance. There are also situations of hierarchical authority (an army drill, a corporate board meeting, and so forth), in which there is a ranking according to who is allowed to initiate conversation, by giving orders, asking for reports, and so on. These institutional frames determine the kind of talk that can take place within them. Notice that a free, casual conversation does not escape the institutional model, but is itself constituted by certain institutional conditions: namely there must be a situation which is *away from* the more formal types; there are certain arrangements that call for informal talk – such as being invited to a party; there may also be prior sociable relationships among the persons involved, as when talk is called for when running into an acquaintance on the street.

Notes and References

1 Erving Goffman, *Interaction Ritual* (Doubleday Anchor, New York, 1967), p. 113.
2 Ibid., p. 47.
3 Ibid., p. 73.
4 Ibid., p. 95.
5 Erving Goffman, *Forms of Talk* (Blackwell, Oxford, 1981), p. 103.

9

Elements of the Theory of Structuration

Anthony Giddens

The core of structuration theory consists of the concepts of 'structure', 'system' and 'duality of structure'. The notion of structure (or 'social structure'), of course, is very prominent in the writings of most functionalist authors and has lent its name to the traditions of 'structuralism'. But in neither instance is this conceptualized in a fashion best suited to the demands of social theory. Functionalist authors and their critics have given much more attention to the idea of 'function' than to that of 'structure', and consequently the latter has tended to be used as a received notion. But there can be no doubt about how 'structure' is usually understood by functionalists and, indeed, by the vast majority of social analysts – as some kind of 'patterning' of social relations or social phenomena. This is often naively conceived of in terms of visual imagery, akin to the skeleton or morphology of an organism or to the girders of a building. Such conceptions are closely connected to the dualism of subject and social object: 'structure' here appears as 'external' to human action, as a source of constraint on the free initiative of the independently constituted subject. As conceptualized in structuralist and post-structuralist thought, on the other hand, the notion of structure is more interesting. Here it is characteristically thought of not as a patterning of presences but as an intersection of presence and absence; underlying codes have to be inferred from surface manifestations.

These two ideas of structure might seem at first sight to have nothing to do with one another, but in fact each relates to important aspects of the structuring of social relations, aspects which, in the theory of structuration, are grasped by recognizing a differentiation between the concepts of 'structure' and 'system'. In analysing social relations we have to acknowledge both a syntagmatic dimension, the patterning of social relations in time–space involving the reproduction of situated practices, and a paradigmatic dimension, involving a virtual order of 'modes of structuring' recursively implicated in such reproduction. In structuralist traditions there is usually ambiguity over whether structures refer to a matrix of admissible transformations within a set or to rules of transformation governing the matrix. I treat structure, in its most elemental meaning at least, as referring to such rules (and resources). It is misleading, however, to speak of 'rules of transformation' because all rules are inherently transformational. Structure thus refers, in social analysis, to the structuring properties allowing the 'binding' of time–space in social systems, the properties which make it possible for discernibly similar social practices to exist across varying spans of time and space and which lend them 'systemic' form. To say that structure is a 'virtual order' of transformative relations means that social systems, as reproduced social practices, do not have 'structures' but rather exhibit 'structural properties' and that structure exists, as time–space presence, only in its instantiations in such practices and as memory traces orienting the conduct of knowledgeable human agents. This does not prevent us from conceiving of structural properties as hierarchically organized in terms of the time–space extension of the practices they recursively organize. The most deeply embedded structural properties, implicated in the reproduction of societal totalities, I call *structural principles*. Those practices which have the greatest time–space extension within such totalities can be referred to as *institutions*.

To speak of structure as 'rules' and resources, and of structures as isolable sets of rules and resources, runs a distinct risk of misinterpretation because of certain dominant uses of 'rules' in the philosophical literature.

1. Rules are often thought of in connection with games, as formalized prescriptions. The rules implicated in the reproduction of social systems are not generally like this. Even those which are codified as laws are characteristically subject to a far greater diversity of contestations than the rules of games. Although the use of the rules of games such as chess etc. as prototypical of the rule-governed properties of social systems is frequently associated with Wittgenstein, more relevant is what Wittgenstein has to say about children's play as exemplifying the routines of social life.
2. Rules are frequently treated in the singular, as if they could be related to specific instances or pieces of conduct. But this is highly misleading if regarded as analogous to the operation of social life, in which practices are sustained in conjunction with more or less loosely organized sets.

3 Rules cannot be conceptualized apart from resources, which refer to the modes whereby transformative relations are actually incorporated into the production and reproduction of social practices. Structural properties thus express forms of *domination* and *power*.
4 Rules imply 'methodical procedures' of social interaction, as Garfinkel in particular has made clear. Rules typically intersect with practices in the contextuality of situated encounters: the range of *ad hoc* considerations which he identifies are chronically involved with the instantiation of rules and are fundamental to the form of those rules. Every competent social actor, it should be added, is *ipso facto* a social theorist on the level of discursive consciousness and a 'methodological specialist' on the levels of both discursive and practical consciousness.
5 Rules have two aspects to them, and it is essential to distinguish these conceptually, since a number of philosophical writers (such as Winch) have tended to conflate them. Rules relate on the one hand to the constitution of *meaning*, and on the other to the *sanctioning* of modes of social conduct.

I have introduced the above usage of 'structure' to help break with the fixed or mechanical character which the term tends to have in orthodox sociological usage. The concepts of system and structuration do much of the work that 'structure' is ordinarily called upon to perform. In proposing a usage of 'structure' that might appear at first sight to be remote from conventional interpretations of the term, I do not mean to hold that looser versions be abandoned altogether. 'Society', 'culture' and a range of other forms of sociological terminology can have double usages that are embarrassing only in contexts where a difference is made in the nature of the statements employing them. Similarly, I see no particular objection to speaking of 'class structure', 'the structure of the industrialized societies' and so on, where these terms are meant to indicate in a general way relevant institutional features of a society or range of societies.

One of the main propositions of structuration theory is that the rules and resources drawn upon in the production and reproduction of social action are at the same time the means of system reproduction (the duality of structure). But how is one to interpret such a claim? In what sense is it the case that when I go about my daily affairs my activities incorporate and reproduce, say, the overall institutions of modern capitalism? What rules are being invoked here in any case? Consider the following possible instances of what rules are:

1 'The rule defining checkmate in chess is . . .';
2 A formula: $a_n = n^2 + n - 1$;
3 'As a rule R gets up at 6.00 every day';
4 'It is a rule that all workers must clock in at 8.00 a.m.'

Many other examples could of course be offered, but these will serve in the present context. In usage (3) 'rule' is more or less equivalent to habit or routine. The sense of 'rule' here is fairly weak, since it does not usually presuppose some sort of underlying precept that the individual is following or any sanction which applies to back up that precept; it is simply something that the person habitually does. Habit is part of routine, and I strongly emphasize the importance of routine in social life. 'Rules', as I understand them, certainly impinge upon numerous aspects of routine practice, but a routine practice is not as such a rule.

Cases (1) and (4) have seemed to many to represent two types of rule, constitutive and regulative. To explain the rule governing checkmate in chess is to say something about what goes into the very making of chess as a game. The rule that workers must clock in at a certain hour, on the other hand, does not help define what work is; it specifies how work is to be carried on. As Searle puts it, regulative rules can usually be paraphrased in the form 'Do X', or 'If Y, do X'. Some constitutive rules will have this character, but most will have the form 'X counts as Y', or 'X counts as Y in context C'.[1] That there is something suspect in this distinction, as referring to two types of rule, is indicated by the etymological clumsiness of the term 'regulative rule'. After all, the word 'regulative' already implies 'rule': its dictionary definition is 'control by rules'. I would say of (1) and (4) that they express two aspects of rules rather than two variant types of rule. (1) is certainly part of what chess is, but for those who play chess it has sanctioning or 'regulative' properties; it refers to aspects of play that must be observed. But (4) also has constitutive aspects. It does not perhaps enter into the definition of what 'work' is, but it does enter into that of a concept like 'industrial bureaucracy'. What (1) and (4) direct our attention to are two aspects of rules: their role in the constitution of meaning, and their close connection with sanctions.

Usage (2) might seem the least promising as a way of conceptualizing 'rule' that has any relation to 'structure'. In fact, I shall argue, it is the most germane of all of them. I do not mean to say that social life can be reduced to a set of mathematical principles, which is very far from what I have in mind. I mean that it is in the nature of formulae that we can best discover what is the most analytically effective sense of 'rule' in social theory. The formula $a_n = n^2 + n - 1$ is from Wittgenstein's example of number games.[2] One person writes down a sequence of numbers; a second works out the formula supplying the numbers which follow. What is a formula of this kind, and what is it to understand one? To understand the formula is not to utter it. For someone could utter it and not understand the series; alternatively, it is possible to understand the series without being able to give verbal expression to the formula. Understanding is not a mental process accompanying the solving of the puzzle that the sequence of numbers presents – at least, it is not a mental process in the sense in which the hearing of a tune or a spoken sentence is. It is simply being able to apply the formula in the right context and way in order to continue the series.

A formula is a generalizable procedure – generalizable because it applies over a range of contexts and occasions, a procedure because it allows for the methodical continuation of an established sequence. Are linguistic rules like this? I think they are – much more than they are like the sorts of rule of which Chomsky speaks. And this seems also consonant with Wittgenstein's arguments, or a possible construal of them at any rate. Wittgenstein remarks, 'To understand a language means to be a master of a technique.'[3] This can be read to mean that language use is primarily methodological and that rules of language are methodically applied procedures implicated in the practical activities of day-to-day life. This aspect of language is very important, although not often given much prominence by most followers of Wittgenstein. Rules which are 'stated', as (1) and (4) above, are interpretations of activity as well as relating to specific sorts of activities: all codified rules take this form, since they give verbal expression to what is supposed to be done. But rules are procedures of action, aspects of *praxis*. It is by reference to this that Wittgenstein resolves what he first of all sets up as a 'paradox' of rules and rule-following. This is that no course of action can be said to be guided by a rule because every course of action can be made to accord with that rule. However, if such is the case, it is also true that every course of action can be made to conflict with it. There is a misunderstanding here, a confusing of the interpretation or verbal expression of a rule with following the rule.

Let us regard the rules of social life, then, as techniques or generalizable procedures applied in the enactment/reproduction of social practices. Formulated rules – those that are given verbal expression as canons of law, bureaucratic rules, rules of games and so on – are thus codified interpretations of rules rather than rules as such. They should be taken not as exemplifying rules in general but as specific types of formulated rule, which, by virtue of their overt formulation, take on various specific qualities.

So far these considerations offer only a preliminary approach to the problem. How do formulae relate to the practices in which social actors engage, and what kinds of formulae are we most interested in for general purposes of social analysis? As regards the first part of the question, we can say that awareness of social rules, expressed first and foremost in practical consciousness, is the very core of that 'knowledgeability' which specifically characterizes human agents. As social actors, all human beings are highly 'learned' in respect of knowledge which they possess, and apply, in the production and reproduction of day-to-day social encounters; the vast bulk of such knowledge is practical rather than theoretical in character. As Schutz and many others have pointed out, actors employ typified schemes (formulae) in the course of their daily activities to negotiate routinely the situations of social life. Knowledge of procedure, or mastery of the techniques of 'doing' social activity, is by definition methodological. That is to say, such knowledge does not specify all the situations which an actor might meet with, nor could it do so; rather, it provides for the generalized capacity to respond to and influence an indeterminate range of social circumstances.

Those types of rule which are of most significance for social theory are locked into the reproduction of institutionalized practices, that is, practices most deeply sedimented in time–space. The main characteristics of rules relevant to general questions of social analysis can be described as follows:

intensive		tacit		informal		weakly sanctioned
	:		:		:	
shallow		discursive		formalized		strongly sanctioned

By rules that are intensive in nature, I mean formulae that are constantly invoked in the course of day-do-day activities, that enter into the structuring of much of the texture of everyday life. Rules of language are of this character. But so also, for example, are the procedures utilized by actors in organizing turn-taking in conversations or in interaction. They may be contrasted with rules which, although perhaps wide in scope, have only a superficial impact upon much of the texture of social life. The contrast is an important one, if only because it is commonly taken for granted among social analysts that the more abstract rules – e.g. codified law – are the most influential in the structuring of social activity. I would propose, however, that many seemingly trivial procedures followed in daily life have a more profound influence upon the generality of social conduct. The remaining categories should be more or less self-explanatory. Most of the rules implicated in the production and reproduction of social practices are only tacitly grasped by actors: they know how to 'go on'. *The discursive formulation of a rule is already an interpretation of it*, and, as I have noted, may in and of itself alter the form of its application. Among rules that are not just discursively formulated but are formally codified, the type case is that of laws. Laws, of course, are among the most strongly sanctioned types of social rules and in modern societies have formally prescribed gradations of retribution. However, it would be a serious mistake to underestimate the strength of informally applied sanctions in respect of a variety of mundane daily practices. Whatever else Garfinkel's 'experiments with trust' might be thought to demonstrate, they do show the extraordinarily compelling force with which apparently minor features of conversational response are invested.

[. . .]

I distinguish 'structure' as a generic term from 'structures' in the plural and both from the 'structural properties of social systems'. 'Structure' refers not only to rules implicated in the production and reproduction of social systems but also to resources – the means material and symbolic, whereby actors make things happen. As ordinarily used in the social sciences, 'structure' tends to be employed with the more enduring aspects of social systems in mind, and I do not want to lose this connotation. The most important aspects of structure are rules and resources recursively involved in institutions. Institutions by definition are the more enduring features of social life. In speaking of the structural properties of social systems I mean their institutionalized features, giving 'solidity' across time and space. I use the concept of 'structures' to get at relations of transformation and mediation which are the 'circuit switches' underlying observed conditions of system reproduction.

Let me now answer the question I originally posed: in what manner can it be said that the conduct of individual actors reproduces the structural properties of larger collectivities? The question is both easier and more difficult to answer than it appears. On a logical level, the answer to it is nothing more than a truism. That is to say, while the continued existence of large collectivities or societies evidently does not depend upon the activities of any particular individual, such collectivities or societies manifestly would cease to be if all the agents involved disappeared. On a substantive level, the answer to the question depends upon issues yet to be broached – those concerning the mechanisms of integration of different types of societal totality. It is always the case that the day-to-day activity of social actors draws upon and reproduces structural features of wider social systems. But 'societies' – as I shall make clear – are not necessarily unified collectivities. 'Social reproduction' must not be equated with the consolidation of social cohesion. The location of actors and of collectivities in different sectors or regions of more encompassing social systems strongly influences the impact of even their habitual conduct upon the integration of societal totalities. Here we reach the limits of linguistic examples which might be used to illustrate the concept of the duality of structure. Considerable illumination of problems of social analysis can be derived from studying the recursive qualities of speech and language. When I produce a grammatical utterance, I draw upon the same syntactical rules as those that utterance helps to produce. But I speak the 'same' language as the other speakers in my language community; we all share the same rules and linguistic practices, give or take a range of relatively minor variations. Such is not necessarily the case with the structural properties of social systems in general. But this is not a problem to do with the concept of the duality of structure as such. It is to do with how social systems, especially 'societies', should be conceptualized.

Structure(s)	*System(s)*	*Structuration*
Rules and resources, or sets of transformation relations, organized as properties of social systems	Reproduced relations between actors or collectivities, organized as regular social practices	Conditions governing the continuity or transmutation of structures and therefore the reproduction of social systems

Let me summarize the argument thus far. Structure, as recursively organized sets of rules and resources, is out of time and space, save in its instantiations and co-ordination as memory traces, and is marked by an 'absence of the subject'. The social systems in which structure is recursively implicated, on the contrary, comprise the situated activities of human agents, reproduced across time and space. Analysing the structuration of social systems means studying the modes in which such systems, grounded in the knowledgeable activities of situated actors who draw upon rules and resources in the diversity of action contexts, are produced and reproduced in interaction. Crucial to the idea of structuration is the theorem of the duality of structure, which is logically implied in the arguments portrayed above. The constitution of agents and structures are not two independently given sets of phenomena, a dualism, but represent a duality. According to the notion of the duality of structure, the structural properties of social systems are both medium and outcome of the practices they recursively organize. Structure is not 'external' to individuals: as memory traces, and as instantiated in social practices, it is in a certain sense more 'internal' than exterior to their activities in a Durkheimian sense. Structure is not to be equated with constraint but is always both constraining and enabling. This, of course, does not prevent the structured properties of social systems from stretching away, in time and space, beyond the control of any individual actors. Nor does it compromise the possibility that actors' own theories of the social systems which they help to constitute and reconstitute in their activities may reify those systems. The reification of social relations, or the discursive 'naturalization' of the historically contingent circumstances and products of human action, is one of the main dimensions of ideology in social life.

Even the crudest forms of reified thought, however, leave untouched the fundamental significance of the knowledgeability of human actors. For knowledgeability is founded less upon discursive than practical consciousness. The knowledge of social conventions, of oneself and of other human beings, presumed in being able to 'go on' in the diversity of contexts of social life is detailed and dazzling. All competent members of society are vastly skilled in the practical accomplishments of social activities and are expert 'sociologists'. The knowledge they possess is not incidental to the persistent patterning of social life but is integral to it. This stress is absolutely essential if the mistakes of functionalism and structuralism are to be avoided, mistakes which, suppressing or discounting agents' reasons – the rationalization of action as chronically involved in the structuration of social practices – look for the origins of their activities in phenomena of which these agents are ignorant. But it is equally important to avoid tumbling into the opposing error of hermeneutic approaches and of various versions of phenomenology, which tend to regard society as the plastic creation of human subjects. Each of these is an illegitimate form of reduction, deriving from a failure adequately to conceptualize the duality of structure. According to structuration theory, the moment of the production of action is also one of reproduction in the contexts of the day-to-day enactment of social life. This is so even during the most violent upheavals or most radical forms of social change. It is not accurate to see the structural properties of social systems as 'social products' because this tends to imply that pre-constituted actors somehow come together to create them. In reproducing structural properties, agents also reproduce the conditions that make such action possible. Structure has no existence independent of the knowledge that agents have about what they do in their day-to-day activity. Human agents always know what they are doing on the level of discursive consciousness under some description. However, what they do may be quite unfamiliar under other descriptions, and they may know little of the ramified consequences of the activities in which they engage.

The duality of structure is always the main grounding of continuities in social reproduction across time–space. It in turn presupposes the reflexive monitoring of agents in, and as constituting, the *durée* of daily social activity. But human knowledgeability is always bounded. The flow of action continually produces consequences which are unintended by actors, and these unintended consequences also may form unacknowledged conditions of action in a feedback fashion. Human history is created by intentional activities but is not an intended project; it persistently eludes efforts to bring it under conscious direction. However, such attempts are continually made by human beings, who operate under the threat and the promise of the circumstance that they are the only creatures who make their 'history' in cognizance of that fact.

Notes and References

1 John R. Searle, *Speech Acts* (Cambridge University Press, Cambridge, 1969), pp. 34–5.
2 Ludwig Wittgenstein, *Philosophical Investigations* (Blackwell, Oxford, 1972), p. 59.
3 Ibid., p. 81.

10

Institutional Reflexivity and Modernity

Anthony Giddens

Inherent in the idea of modernity is a contrast with tradition. Many combinations of the modern and the traditional are to be found in concrete social settings. Indeed, some authors have argued that these are so tightly interlaced as to make any generalized comparison valueless. But such is surely not the case, as we can see by pursuing an enquiry into the relation between modernity and reflexivity.

There is a fundamental sense in which reflexivity is a defining characteristic of all human action. All human beings routinely 'keep in touch' with the grounds of what they do as an integral element of doing it. I have called this elsewhere the 'reflexive monitoring of action', using the phrase to draw attention to the chronic character of the processes involved. Human action does not incorporate chains of aggregate interactions and reasons, but a consistent – and, as Erving Goffman above all has shown us, never-to-be-relaxed – monitoring of behaviour and its contexts. This is not the sense of reflexivity which is specifically connected with modernity, although it is the necessary basis of it.

In traditional cultures, the past is honoured and symbols are valued because they contain and perpetuate the experience of generations. Tradition is a mode of integrating the reflexive monitoring of action with the time–space organization of the community. It is a means of handling time and space, which inserts any particular activity or experience within the continuity of past, present, and future, these in turn being structured by recurrent social practices. Tradition is not wholly static, because it has to be reinvented by each new generation as it takes over its cultural inheritance from those preceding it. Tradition does not so much resist change as pertain to a context in which there are few separated temporal and spatial markers in terms of which change can have any meaningful form.

In oral cultures, tradition is not known as such, even though these cultures are the most traditional of all. To understand tradition, as distinct from other modes of organizing action and experience, demands cutting into time–space in ways which are only possible with the invention of writing. Writing expands the level of time–space distanciation and creates a perspective of past, present, and future in which the reflexive appropriation of knowledge can be set off from designated tradition. However, in pre-modern civilizations reflexivity is still largely limited to the reinterpretation and clarification of tradition, such that in the scales of time the side of the 'past' is much more heavily weighed down than that of the 'future'. Moreover, since literacy is the monopoly of the few, the routinization of daily life remains bound up with tradition in the old sense.

With the advent of modernity, reflexivity takes on a different character. It is introduced into the very basis of system reproduction, such that thought and action are constantly refracted back upon one another. The routinization of daily life has no intrinsic connections with the past at all, save in so far as what 'was done before' happens to coincide with what can be defended in a principled way in the light of incoming knowledge. To sanction a practice because it is traditional will not do; tradition can be justified, but only in the light of knowledge which is not itself authenticated by tradition. Combined with the inertia of habit, this means that, even in the most modernized of modern societies, tradition continues to play a role. But this role is generally much less significant than is supposed by authors who focus attention upon the integration of tradition and modernity in the contemporary world. For justified tradition is tradition in sham clothing and receives its identity only from the reflexivity of the modern.

The reflexivity of modern social life consists in the fact that social practices are constantly examined and reformed in the light of incoming information about those very practices, thus constitutively altering their character. We should be clear about the nature of this phenomenon. All forms of social life are partly constituted by actors' knowledge of them. Knowing 'how to go on' in Wittgenstein's sense is intrinsic to the conventions which are drawn upon and reproduced by human activity. In all cultures, social practices are routinely altered in the light of ongoing discoveries which feed into them. But only in the era of modernity is the revision of convention radicalized to apply (in principle) to all aspects of human life, including technological intervention into the material world. It is often said that modernity is marked by an appetite for the new, but this is not perhaps completely accurate. What is characteristic of modernity is not an embracing of the new for its own sake, but the presumption of wholesale reflexivity – which of course includes reflection upon the nature of reflection itself.

Probably we are only now, in the late twentieth century, beginning to realize in a full sense how deeply unsettling this outlook is. For when the claims of reason replaced those of tradition, they appeared to offer a sense of certitude greater than that provided by pre-existing dogma. But this idea only appears persuasive so long as we do not see that the reflexivity of modernity actually subverts reason, at any rate where reason is understood as the gaining of certain knowledge. Modernity is constituted in and through reflexively applied knowledge, but the equation of knowledge with certitude has turned out to be misconceived. We are abroad in a world which is thoroughly constituted through reflexively applied knowledge, but where at the same time we can never be sure that any given element of that knowledge will not be revised.

Even philosophers who most staunchly defend the claims of science to certitude, such as Karl Popper, acknowledge that, as he expresses it, 'all science rests upon shifting sand'. In science, *nothing* is certain, and nothing can be proved, even if scientific endeavour provides us with the most dependable information about the world to which we can aspire. In the heart of the world of hard science, modernity floats free.

No knowledge under conditions of modernity *is* knowledge in the 'old' sense, where 'to know' is to be certain. This applies equally to the natural and the social sciences. In the case of social science, however, there are further considerations involved. We should recall at this point the observations made earlier about the reflexive components of sociology.

In the social sciences, to the unsettled character of all empirically based knowledge we have to add the 'subversion' which comes from the re-entry of social scientific discourse into the contexts it analyses. The reflection of which the social sciences are the formalized version (a specific genre of expert knowledge) is quite fundamental to the reflexivity of modernity as a whole.

Because of the close relation between the Enlightenment and advocacy of the claims of reason, natural science has usually been taken as the pre-eminent endeavour distinguishing the modern outlook from what went before. Even those who favour interpretative rather than naturalistic sociology have normally seen social science as the poor relation of the natural sciences, particularly given the scale of technological development consequent upon scientific discoveries. But the social sciences are actually more deeply implicated in modernity than is natural science, since the chronic revision of social practices in the light of knowledge about those practices is part of the very tissue of modern institutions.

All the social sciences participate in this reflexive relation, although sociology has an especially central place. Take as an example the discourse of economics. Concepts like 'capital', 'investment', 'markets', 'industry', and many others, in their modern senses, were elaborated as part of the early development of economics as a distinct discipline in the eighteenth and early nineteenth centuries. These concepts, and empirical conclusions linked to them, were formulated in order to analyse changes involved in the emergence of modern institutions. But they could not, and did not, remain separated from the activities and events to which they related. They have become integral to what 'modern economic life' actually is and inseparable from it. Modern economic activity would not be as it is were it not for the fact that all members of the population have mastered these concepts and an indefinite variety of others.

The lay individual cannot necessarily provide formal definitions of terms like 'capital' or 'investment', but everyone who, say, uses a savings account in a bank demonstrates an implicit and practical mastery of those notions. Concepts such as these, and the theories and empirical information linked to them, are not merely handy devices whereby agents are somehow more clearly able to understand their behaviour than they could do otherwise. They actively constitute what that behaviour is and inform the reasons for which it is undertaken. There cannot be a clear insulation between literature available to economists and that which is either read or filters through in other ways to interested parties in the population: business leaders, government officials, and members of the public. The economic environment is constantly being altered in the light of these inputs, thus creating a situation of continual mutual involvement between economic discourse and the activities to which it refers.

The pivotal position of sociology in the reflexivity of modernity comes from its role as the most generalized type of reflection upon modern social life. Let us consider an example at the 'hard edge' of naturalistic sociology. The official statistics published by governments concerning, for instance, population, marriage and divorce, crime and delinquency, and so forth, seem to provide a means of studying social life with precision. To the pioneers of naturalistic sociology, such as Durkheim, these statistics represented hard data, in terms of which the relevant aspects of modern societies can be analysed more accurately than where such figures are lacking. Yet official statistics are not just analytical characteristics of social activity, but again enter constitutively into the social universe from which they are taken or counted up. From its inception, the collation of official statistics has been constitutive of state power and of many other modes of social organization also. The co-ordinated administrative control achieved by modern governments is inseparable from the routine monitoring of 'official data' in which all contemporary states engage.

The assembling of official statistics is itself a reflexive endeavour, permeated by the very findings of the social sciences that have utilized them. The practical work of coroners, for example, is the basis for the collection of suicide statistics. In the interpretation of causes/motives for death, however, coroners are guided by concepts and theories which purport to illuminate the nature of suicide. It would not be at all unusual to find a coroner who had read Durkheim.

Nor is the reflexivity of official statistics confined to the sphere of the state. Anyone in a Western country who embarks upon marriage today, for instance, knows that divorce rates are high (and may also, however imperfectly or partially, know a great deal more about the demography of marriage and the family). Knowledge of the high rate of divorce might affect the very decision to marry, as well as decisions about related considerations – provisions about property and so forth. Awareness of levels of divorce, moreover, is normally much more than just consciousness of a brute fact. It is theorized by the lay agent in ways pervaded by sociological thinking. Thus virtually everyone contemplating marriage has some idea of how family institutions have been changing, changes in the relative social position and power of men and women, alterations in sexual mores, etc. – all of which enter into processes of further change which they reflexively inform. Marriage and the family would not be what they are today were they not thoroughly 'sociologized' and 'psychologized'.

The discourse of sociology and the concepts, theories, and findings of the other social sciences continually 'circulate in and out' of what it is that they are about. In so doing they reflexively restructure their subject matter, which itself has learned to think sociologically. *Modernity is itself deeply and intrinsically sociological.* Much that is problematic in the position of the professional sociologist, as the purveyor of expert knowledge about social life, derives from the fact that she or he is at most one step ahead of enlightened lay practitioners of the discipline.

Hence the thesis that more knowledge about social life (even if that knowledge is as well buttressed empirically as it could possibly be) equals greater control over our fate is false. It is (arguably) true about the physical world, but not about the universe of social events. Expanding our understanding of the social world might produce a progressively more illuminating grasp of human institutions and, hence, increasing 'technological' control over them, if it were the case either that social life were entirely separate from human knowledge about it or that knowledge could be filtered continuously into the reasons for social action, producing step-by-step increases in the 'rationality' of behaviour in relation to specific needs.

Both conditions do in fact apply to many circumstances and contexts of social activity. But each falls well short of that totalizing impact which the inheritance of Enlightenment thought holds out as a goal. This is so because of the influence of four sets of factors.

One – factually very important but logically the least interesting, or at any rate the least difficult to handle analytically – is differential power. The appropriation of knowledge does not happen in a homogeneous fashion, but is often differentially available to those in power positions, who are able to place it in the service of sectional interests.

A second influence concerns the role of values. Changes in value orders are not independent of innovations in cognitive orientation created by shifting perspectives on the social world. If new knowledge could be brought to bear upon a transcendental rational basis of values, this situation would not apply. But there is no such rational basis of values, and shifts in outlook deriving from inputs of knowledge have a mobile relation to changes in value orientations.

The third factor is the impact of unintended consequences. No amount of accumulated knowledge about social life could encompass all circumstances of its implementation, even if such knowledge were wholly distinct from the environment to which it applied. If our knowledge about the social world simply got better and better, the scope of unintended consequences might become more and more confined and unwanted consequences rare. However, the reflexivity of modern social life blocks off this possibility and is itself the fourth influence involved. Although least discussed in relation to the limits of Enlightenment reason, it is certainly as significant as any of the others. The point is not that there is no stable social world to know, but that knowledge of that world contributes to its unstable or mutable character.

The reflexivity of modernity, which is directly involved with the continual generating of systematic self-knowledge, does not stabilize the relation between expert knowledge and knowledge applied in lay actions. Knowledge claimed by expert observers (in some part, and in many varying ways) rejoins its subject matter, thus (in principle, but also normally in practice) altering it. There is no parallel to this process in the natural sciences; it is not at all the same as where, in the field of microphysics, the intervention of an observer changes what is being studied.

11

Structures, *Habitus* and Practices

Pierre Bourdieu

Objectivism constitutes the social world as a spectacle offered to an observer who takes up a 'point of view' on the action and who, putting into the object the principles of his relation to the object, proceeds as if it were intended solely for knowledge and as if all the interactions within it were purely symbolic exchanges. This viewpoint is the one taken from high positions in the social structure, from which the social world is seen as a representation (as the word is used in idealist philosophy, but also as in painting) or a performance (in the theatrical or musical sense), and practices are seen as no more than the acting-out of roles, the playing of scores or the implementation of plans. The theory of practice as practice insists, contrary to positivist materialism, that the objects of knowledge are constructed, not passively recorded, and, contrary to intellectualist idealism, that the principle of this construction is the system of structured, structuring dispositions, the *habitus*, which is constituted in practice and is always oriented towards practical functions. It is possible to step down from the sovereign viewpoint from which objectivist idealism orders the world, as Marx demands in the *Theses on Feuerbach*, but without having to abandon to it the 'active aspect' of apprehension of the world by reducing knowledge to a mere recording. To do this, one has to situate oneself *within* 'real activity as such', that is, in the practical relation to the world, the preoccupied, active presence in the world through which the world imposes its presence, with its urgencies, its things to be done and said, things made to be said, which directly govern words and deeds without ever unfolding as a spectacle. One has to escape from the realism of the structure, to which objectivism, a necessary stage in breaking with primary experience and constructing the objective relationships, necessarily leads when it hypostatizes these relations by treating them as realities already constituted outside of the history of the group – without falling back into subjectivism, which is quite incapable of giving an account of the necessity of the social world. To do this, one has to return to practice, the site of the dialectic of the *opus operatum* and the *modus operandi*; of the objectified products and the incorporated products of historical practice; of structures and *habitus*.

The bringing to light of the presuppositions inherent in objectivist construction has paradoxically been delayed by the efforts of all those who, in linguistics as in anthropology, have sought to 'correct' the structuralist model by appealing to 'context' or 'situation' to account for variations, exceptions and accidents (instead of making them simple variants, absorbed into the structure, as the structuralists do). They have thus avoided a radical questioning of the objectivist mode of thought, when, that is, they have not simply fallen back on to the free choice of a rootless, unattached, pure subject. Thus, the method known as 'situational analysis', which consists of 'observing people in a variety of social situations' in order to determine 'the way in which individuals are able to exercise choices within the limits of a specified social structure', remains locked within the framework of the rule and the exception, which Edmund Leach (often invoked by the exponents of this method) spells out explicitly: 'I postulate that structural systems in which all avenues of social action are narrowly institutionalized are impossible. In all viable systems, there must be an area where the individual is free to make choices so as to manipulate the system to his advantage.'[1]

The conditionings associated with a particular class of conditions of existence produce *habitus*, systems of durable, transposable dispositions, structured structures predisposed to function as structuring structures, that is, as principles which generate and organize practices and representations that can be objectively adapted to their outcomes without presupposing a conscious aiming at ends or an express mastery of the operations necessary in order to attain them. Objectively 'regulated' and 'regular' without being in any way the product of obedience to rules, they can be collectively orchestrated without being the product of the organizing action of a conductor.

It is never ruled out, of course, that the responses of the *habitus* may be accompanied by a strategic calculation tending to perform in a conscious mode the operation that the *habitus* performs quite differently, namely an estimation of chances presupposing transformation of the past effect into an expected objective. But these responses are first defined, without any calculation, in relation to objective potentialities, immediately inscribed in the present, things to do or not to do, things to say or not to say, in relation to a probable, 'upcoming' future (*un à venir*), which – in contrast to the future seen as 'absolute possibility' (*absolute Möglichkeit*) in Hegel's (or Sartre's) sense, projected by the pure project of a 'negative freedom' – puts itself forward with an urgency and a claim to existence that excludes all deliberation. Stimuli do not exist for practice in their objective truth, as conditional, conventional triggers, acting only on condition that they encounter agents conditioned to recognize them. The practical world that is constituted in the relationship with the *habitus*, acting as a system of cognitive and motivating structures, is a world of already realized ends – procedures to follow, paths to take – and of objects endowed with a 'permanent teleological character', in Husserl's phrase, tools or institutions. This is because the regularities inherent in an arbitrary condition ('arbitrary' in Saussure's and Mauss's sense) tend to appear as necessary, even natural, since they are the basis of the schemes of perception and appreciation through which they are apprehended.

If a very close correlation is regularly observed between the scientifically constructed objective probabilities (for example, the chances of access to a particular good) and agents' subjective aspirations ('motivations' and 'needs'), this is not because agents consciously adjust their aspirations to an exact evaluation of their chances of success, like a gambler organizing his stakes on the basis of perfect information about his chances of winning. In reality, the dispositions durably inculcated by the possibilities and impossibilities, freedoms and necessities, opportunities and prohibitions inscribed in the objective conditions (which science apprehends through statistical regularities such as the probabilities objectively attached to a group or class) generate dispositions objectively compatible with these conditions and in a sense pre-adapted to their demands. The most improbable practices are therefore excluded, as unthinkable, by a kind of immediate submission to order that inclines agents to make a virtue of necessity, that is, to refuse what is anyway denied and to will the inevitable. The very conditions of production of the *habitus*, a virtue made of necessity, mean that the anticipations it generates tend to ignore the restriction to which the validity of calculation of probabilities is subordinated, namely that the experimental conditions should not have been modified. Unlike scientific estimations, which are corrected after each experiment according to rigorous rules of calculation, the anticipations of the *habitus*, practical hypotheses based on past experience, give disproportionate weight to early experiences. Through the economic and social necessity that they bring to bear on the relatively autonomous world of the domestic economy and family relations, or more precisely, through the specifically familial manifestations of this external necessity (forms of the division of labour between the sexes, household objects, modes of consumption, parent–child relations, etc.), the structures characterizing a determinate class of conditions of existence produce the structures of the *habitus*, which in their turn are the basis of the perception and appreciation of all subsequent experiences.

The *habitus*, a product of history, produces individual and collective practices – more history – in accordance with the schemes generated by history. It ensures the active presence of past experiences, which, deposited in each organism in the form of schemes of perception, thought and action, tend to guarantee the 'correctness' of practices and their constancy over time, more reliably than all formal rules and explicit norms. This system of dispositions – a present past that tends to perpetuate itself into the future by reactivation in similarly structured practices, an internal law through which the law of external necessities, irreducible to immediate constraints, is constantly exerted – is the principle of the continuity and regularity which objectivism sees in social practices without being able to account for it; and also of the regulated transformations that cannot be explained either by the extrinsic, instantaneous determinisms of mechanistic sociologism or by the purely internal but equally instantaneous determination of spontaneist subjectivism. Overriding the spurious opposition between the forces inscribed in an earlier state of the system, outside the body, and the internal forces arising instantaneously as motivations springing from free will, the internal dispositions – the internalization of externality – enable the external forces to exert themselves, but in accordance with the specific logic of the organisms in which they are incorporated, i.e. in a durable, systematic and non-mechanical way. As an acquired system of generative schemes, the *habitus* makes possible the free production of all the thoughts, perceptions and actions inherent in the particular conditions of its production – and only those. Through the *habitus*, the structure of which it is the product governs practice, not along the paths of a mechanical determinism, but within the constraints and limits initially set on its inventions. This infinite yet strictly limited generative capacity is difficult to understand only so long as one remains locked in the usual antinomies – which the concept of the *habitus* aims to transcend – of determinism and freedom, conditioning and creativity, consciousness and the unconscious, or the individual and society. Because the *habitus* is an infinite capacity for generating products – thoughts, perceptions, expressions and actions – whose limits are set by the historically and socially situated conditions of its production, the conditioned and conditional freedom it provides is as remote from creation of unpredictable novelty as it is from simple mechanical reproduction of the original conditioning.

Nothing is more misleading than the illusion created by hindsight in which all the traces of a life, such as the works of an artist or the events in a biography, appear as the realization of an essence that seems to pre-exist them. Just as a mature artistic style is not contained, like a seed, in an original inspiration but is continuously defined and redefined in the dialectic between the objectifying intention and the already objectified intention, so too the unity of meaning which, after the event, may seem to have preceded the acts and works announcing the final significance, retrospectively transforming the various stages of the temporal series into mere preparatory sketches, is constituted through the confrontation between questions that only exist in and for a mind armed with a particular type of schemes and the solutions obtained through application of these same schemes. The genesis of a system of works or practices generated by the same *habitus* (or homologous *habitus*, such as those that underlie the unity of the lifestyle of a group or a class) cannot be described either as the autonomous development of a unique and always self-identical essence, or as a continuous creation of novelty, because it arises from the necessary yet unpredictable confrontation between the *habitus* and an event that can exercise a pertinent incitement on the *habitus* only if the latter snatches it from the contingency of the accidental and constitutes it as a problem by applying to it the very principles of its solution; and also because the *habitus*, like every 'art of inventing', is what makes it possible to produce an infinite number of practices that are relatively unpredictable (like the corresponding situations) but also limited in their diversity. In short, being the product of a particular class of objective regularities, the *habitus* tends to generate all the 'reasonable', 'common-sense', behaviours (and only these) which are possible within the limits of these regularities, and which are likely to be positively sanctioned because they are objectively adjusted to the logic characteristic of a particular field, whose objective future they anticipate. At the same time, 'without violence, art or argument', it tends to exclude all 'extravagances' ('not for the likes of us'), that is, all the behaviours that would be negatively sanctioned because they are incompatible with the objective conditions.

Because they tend to reproduce the regularities immanent in the conditions in which their generative principle was produced while adjusting to the demands inscribed as objective potentialities in the situation as defined by the cognitive and motivating structures that constitute the *habitus*, practices cannot be deduced either from the present conditions which may seem to have provoked them or from the past conditions which have produced the *habitus*, the durable principle of their production. They can therefore only be accounted for by relating the social conditions in which the *habitus* that generated them was constituted to the social conditions in which it is implemented, that is, through the scientific work of performing the interrelationship of these two states of the social world that the *habitus* performs, while concealing it, in and through practice. The 'unconscious', which enables one to dispense with this interrelating, is never anything other than the forgetting of history which history itself produces by realizing the objective structures that it generates in the quasi-natures of *habitus*. As Durkheim puts it:

> In each one of us, in differing degrees, is contained the person we were yesterday, and indeed, in the nature of things it is even true that our past *personae* predominate in us, since the present is necessarily insignificant when compared with the long period of the past because of which we have emerged in the form we have today. It is just that we don't directly feel the influence of these past selves precisely because they are so deeply rooted within us. They constitute the unconscious part of ourselves. Consequently we have a strong tendency not to recognize their existence and to ignore their legitimate demands. By contrast, with the most recent acquisitions of civilization we are vividly aware of them just because they are recent and consequently have not had time to be assimilated into our collective unconscious.[2]

The *habitus* – embodied history, internalized as a second nature and so forgotten as history – is the active presence of the whole past of which it is the product. As such, it is what gives practices their relative autonomy with respect to external determinations of the immediate present. This autonomy is that of the past, enacted and acting, which, functioning as accumulated capital, produces history on the basis of history and so ensures the permanence in change that makes the individual agent a world within the world. The *habitus* is a spontaneity without consciousness or will, opposed as much to the mechanical necessity of things without history in mechanistic theories as it is to the reflexive freedom of subjects 'without inertia' in rationalist theories.

Thus the dualistic vision that recognizes only the self-transparent act of consciousness or the externally determined thing has to give way to the real logic of action, which brings together two objectifications of history, objectification in bodies and objectification in institutions or, which amounts to the same thing, two states of capital, objectified and incorporated, through which a distance is set up from necessity and its urgencies. This logic is seen in paradigmatic form in the dialectic of expressive dispositions and instituted means of expression (morphological, syntactic and lexical instruments, literary genres, etc.) which is observed in the intentionless invention of regulated improvisation. Endlessly overtaken by his own words, with which he maintains a relation of 'carry and be carried', as Nicolai Hartmann put it, the virtuoso finds in his discourse the triggers for his discourse, which goes along like a train laying its own rails. In other words, being produced by a *modus operandi* which is not consciously mastered, the discourse contains an 'objective intention', as the Scholastics put it, which outruns the conscious intentions of its apparent author and constantly offers new pertinent stimuli to the *modus operandi* of which it is the product and which functions as a kind of 'spiritual automaton'. If witticisms strike as much by their unpredictability as by their retrospective necessity, the reason is that the *trouvaille* that brings to light long buried resources presupposes a *habitus* that so perfectly possesses the objectively available means of expression that it is possessed by them, so much so that it asserts its freedom from them by realizing the rarest of the possibilities that they necessarily imply. The dialectic of the meaning of the language and the 'sayings of the tribe' is a particular and particularly significant case of the dialectic between *habitus* and institutions, that is, between two modes of objectification of past history, in which there is constantly created a history that inevitably appears, like witticisms, as both original and inevitable.

This durably installed generative principle of regulated improvisations is a practical sense which reactivates the sense objectified in institutions. Produced by the work of inculcation and appropriation that is needed in order for objective structures, the products of collective history, to be reproduced in the form of the durable, adjusted dispositions that are the condition of their functioning, the *habitus*, which is constituted in the course of an individual history, imposing its particular logic on incorporation, and through which agents partake of the history objectified in institutions, is what makes it possible to inhabit institutions, to appropriate them practically, and so to keep them in activity, continuously pulling them from the state of dead letters, reviving the sense deposited in them, but at the same time imposing the revisions and transformations that reactivation entails. Or rather, the *habitus* is what enables the institution to attain full realization: it is through the capacity for incorporation, which exploits the body's readiness to take seriously the performative magic of the social, that the king, the banker or the priest are hereditary monarchy, financial capitalism or the Church made flesh. Property appropriates its owner, embodying itself in the form of a structure generating practices perfectly conforming with its logic and its demands. If one is justified in saying, with Marx, that 'the lord of an entailed estate, the first-born son, belongs to the land', that 'it inherits him', or that the 'persons' of capitalists are the 'personification' of capital, this is because the purely social and quasi-magical process of socialization, which is inaugurated by the act of marking that institutes an individual as an eldest son, an heir, a successor, a Christian, or simply as a man (as opposed to a woman), with all the corresponding privileges and obligations, and which is prolonged, strengthened and confirmed by social treatments that tend to transform instituted difference into natural distinction, produces quite real effects, durably inscribed in the body and in belief. An institution, even an economy, is complete and fully viable only if it is durably objectified not only in things, that is, in the logic, transcending individual agents, of a particular field, but also in bodies, in durable dispositions to recognize and comply with the demands immanent in the field.

In so far – and only in so far – as *habitus* are the incorporation of the same history, or more concretely, of the same history objectified in *habitus* and structures, the practices they generate are mutually intelligible and immediately adjusted to the structures, and also objectively concerted and endowed with an objective meaning that is at once unitary and systematic, transcending subjective intentions and conscious projects, whether individual or collective. One of the fundamental effects of the harmony between practical sense and objectified meaning (*sens*) is the production of a common-sense world, whose immediate self-evidence is accompanied by the objectivity provided by consensus on the meaning of practices and the world, in other words the harmonization of the agents' experiences and the constant reinforcement each of them receives from expression – individual or collective (in festivals, for example), improvised or programmed (commonplaces, sayings) – of similar or identical experiences.

The homogeneity of *habitus* that is observed within the limits of a class of conditions of existence and social conditionings is what causes practices and works to be immediately intelligible and foreseeable, and hence taken for granted. The *habitus* makes questions of intention superfluous, not only in the production but also in the deciphering of practices and works. Automatic and impersonal, significant without a signifying intention, ordinary practices lend themselves to an understanding that is no less automatic and impersonal. The picking up of the objective intention they express requires neither 'reactivation' of the 'lived' intention of their originator, nor the 'intentional transfer into the Other' cherished by the phenomenologists and all advocates of a 'participationist' conception of history or sociology, nor tacit or explicit inquiry ('What do you *mean*?') as to other people's intentions. 'Communication of consciousnesses' presupposes community of 'unconsciouses' (that is, of linguistic and cultural competences). Deciphering the objective intention of practices and works has nothing to do with 'reproduction' (*Nachbildung*, as the early Dilthey puts it) of lived experiences and the unnecessary and uncertain reconstitution of an 'intention' which is not their real origin.

The objective homogenizing of group or class *habitus* that results from homogeneity of conditions of existence is what enables practices to be objectively harmonized without any calculation or conscious reference to a norm and mutually adjusted in the absence of any direct interaction or, *a fortiori*, explicit co-ordination. The interaction itself owes its form to the objective structures that have produced the dispositions of the interacting agents, which continue to assign them their relative positions in the interaction and elsewhere. 'Imagine', Leibniz suggests,[3] 'two clocks or watches in perfect agreement as to the time. This may occur in one of three ways. The first consists in mutual influence; the second is to appoint a skilful workman to correct them and synchronize constantly; the third is to construct these two clocks with such art and precision that one can be assured of their subsequent agreement.' So long as one ignores the true principle of the conductorless orchestration which gives regularity, unity and systematicity to practices even in the absence of any spontaneous or imposed organization of individual projects, one is condemned to the naive artificialism that recognizes no other unifying principle than conscious co-ordination. The practices of the members of the same group or, in a differentiated society, the same class, are always more and better harmonized than the agents know or wish, because, as Leibniz again says, 'following only (his) own laws', each 'nonetheless agrees with the other'. The habitus is precisely this immanent law, *lex insita*, inscribed in bodies by identical histories, which is the precondition not only for the co-ordination of practices but also for practices of co-ordination. The corrections and adjustments the agents themselves consciously carry out presuppose mastery of a common code; and undertakings of collective mobilization cannot succeed without a minimum of concordance between the *habitus* of the mobilizing agents (prophet, leader, etc.) and the dispositions of those who recognize themselves in their practices or words, and, above all, without the inclination towards grouping that springs from the spontaneous orchestration of dispositions.

It is certain that every effort at mobilization aimed at organizing collective action has to reckon with the dialectic of dispositions and occasions that takes place in every agent, whether he mobilizes or is mobilized (the hysteresis of *habitus* is doubtless one explanation of the structural lag between opportunities and the dispositions to grasp them which is the cause of missed opportunities and, in particular, of the frequently observed incapacity to think historical crises in categories of perception and thought other than those of the past, however revolutionary). It is also certain that it must take account of the objective orchestration established among dispositions that are objectively co-ordinated because they are ordered by more or less identical objective necessities. It is, however, extremely dangerous to conceive collective action by analogy with individual action, ignoring all that the former owes to the relatively autonomous logic of the institutions of mobilization (with their own history, their specific organization, etc.) and to the situations, institutionalized or not, in which it occurs.

Sociology treats as identical all biological individuals who, being the products of the same objective conditions, have the same *habitus*. A social class (in-itself) – a class of identical or similar conditions of existence and conditionings – is at the same time a class of biological individuals having the same *habitus*, understood as a system of dispositions common to all products of the same conditionings. Though it is impossible for all (or even two) members of the same class to have had the same experiences, in the same order, it is certain that each member of the same class is more likely than any member of another class to have been confronted with the situations most frequent for members of that class. Through the always convergent experiences that give a social environment its physiognomy, with its 'closed doors', 'dead ends' and 'limited prospects', the objective structures that sociology apprehends in the form of probabilities of access to goods, services and powers inculcate the 'art of assessing likelihoods', as Leibniz put it, of anticipating the objective future, in short, the 'sense of reality', or realities, which is perhaps the best-concealed principle of their efficacy.

To define the relationship between class *habitus* and individual *habitus* (which is inseparable from the organic individuality that is immediately given to immediate perception – *intuitus personae* – and socially designated and recognized – name, legal identity, etc.), class (or group) *habitus*, that is, the individual *habitus* in so far as it expresses or reflects the class (or group), could be regarded as a subjective but non-individual system of internalized structures, common schemes of perception, conception and action, which are the precondition of all objectification and apperception; and the objective co-ordination of practices and the sharing of a world-view could be founded on the perfect impersonality and interchangeability of singular practices and views. But this would amount to regarding all the practices or representations produced in accordance with identical schemes as impersonal and interchangeable, like individual intuitions of space which, according to Kant, reflect none of the particularities of the empirical ego. In fact, the singular *habitus* of members of the same class are united in a relationship of homology, that is, of diversity within homogeneity reflecting the diversity within homogeneity characteristic of their social conditions of production. Each individual system of dispositions is a structural variant of the others, expressing the singularity of its position within the class and its trajectory. 'Personal' style, the particular stamp marking all the products of the same *habitus*, whether practices or works, is never more than a deviation in relation to the style of a period or class, so that it relates back to the common style not only by its conformity – like Phidias, who, for Hegel, had no 'manner' – but also by the difference that makes the 'manner'.

The principle of the differences between individual *habitus* lies in the singularity of their social trajectories, to which there correspond series of chronologically ordered determinations that are mutually irreducible to one another. The *habitus* which, at every moment, structures new experiences in accordance with the structures produced by past experiences, which are modified by the new experiences within the limits defined by their power of selection, brings about a unique integration, dominated by the earliest experiences, of the experiences statistically common to members of the same class. Early experiences have particular weight because the *habitus* tends to ensure its own constancy and its defence against change through the selection it makes within new information by rejecting information capable of calling into question its accumulated information, if exposed to it accidentally or by force, and especially by avoiding exposure to such information. One only has to think, for example, of homogamy, the paradigm of all the 'choices' through which the *habitus* tends to favour experiences likely to reinforce it (or the empirically confirmed fact that people tend to talk about politics with those who have the same opinions). Through the systematic 'choices' it makes among the places, events and people that might be frequented, the *habitus* tends to protect itself from crises and critical challenges by providing itself with a milieu to which it is as pre-adapted as possible, that is, a relatively constant universe of situations tending to reinforce its dispositions by offering the market most favourable to its products. And once again it is the most paradoxical property of the *habitus*, the unchosen principle of all 'choices', that yields the solution to the paradox of the information needed in order to avoid information. The schemes of perception and appreciation of the *habitus* which are the basis of all the avoidance strategies are largely the product of a non-conscious, unwilled avoidance, whether it results automatically from the conditions of existence (for example, spatial segregation) or has been produced by a strategic intention (such as avoidance of 'bad company' or 'unsuitable books') originating from adults themselves formed in the same conditions.

Even when they look like the realization of explicit ends, the strategies produced by the *habitus* and enabling agents to cope with unforeseen and constantly changing situations are only apparently determined by the future. If they seem to be oriented by anticipation of their own consequences, thereby encouraging the finalist illusion, this is because, always tending to reproduce the objective structures that produced them, they are determined by the past conditions of production of their principle of production, that is, by the already realized outcome of identical or interchangeable past practices, which coincides with their own outcome only to the extent that the structures within which they function are identical to or homologous with the objective structures of which they are the product. Thus, for example, in the interaction between two agents or groups of agents endowed with the same *habitus* (say A and B), everything takes place as if the actions of each of them (say a_1 for A) were organized by reference to the reactions which they call forth from any agent possessing the same *habitus* (say b_1 for B). They therefore objectively imply anticipation of the reaction which these reactions in turn call forth (a_2, A's reaction to b_1). But the teleological description, the only one appropriate to a 'rational actor' possessing perfect information as to the preferences and competences of the other actors, in which each action has the purpose of making possible the reaction to the reaction it induces (individual A performs an action a_1, a gift for example, in order to make individual B produce action b_1, so that he can then perform action a_1, a stepped-up gift), is quite as naive as the mechanistic description that presents the action and the riposte as so many steps in a sequence of programmed actions produced by a mechanical apparatus.

To have an idea of the difficulties that would be encountered by a mechanistic theory of practice as mechanical reaction, directly determined by the antecedent conditions and entirely reducible to the mechanical functioning of pre-established devices – which would have to be assumed to exist in infinite number, like the chance configurations of stimuli capable of triggering them from outside – one only has to mention the grandiose, desperate undertaking of the anthropologist, fired with positivist ardour, who recorded 480 elementary units of behaviour in 20 minutes' observation of his wife in the kitchen: 'Here we confront the distressing fact that

> the sample episode chain under analysis is a fragment of a larger segment of behavior which in the complete record contains some 480 separate episodes. Moreover, it took only twenty minutes for these 480 behavior stream events to occur. If my wife's rate of behavior is roughly representative of that of other actors, we must be prepared to deal with an inventory of episodes produced at the rate of some 20,000 per sixteen-hour day per actor. . . . In a population consisting of several hundred actor-types, the number of different episodes in the total repertory must amount to many millions in the course of an annual cycle.'[4]

The *habitus* contains the solution to the paradoxes of objective meaning without subjective intention. It is the source of these strings of 'moves' which are objectively organized as strategies without being the product of a genuine strategic intention – which would presuppose at least that they be apprehended as one among other possible strategies. If each stage in the sequence of ordered and oriented actions that constitute objective strategies can appear to be determined by anticipation of the future, and in particular, of its own consequences (which is what justifies the use of the concept of strategy), it is because the practices that are generated by the *habitus* and are governed by the past conditions of production of their generative principle are adapted in advance to the objective conditions whenever the conditions in which the *habitus* functions have remained identical, or similar, to the conditions in which it was constituted. Perfectly and immediately successful adjustment to the objective conditions provides the most complete illusion of finality, or – which amounts to the same thing – of self-regulating mechanism.

The presence of the past in this kind of false anticipation of the future performed by the *habitus* is, paradoxically, most clearly seen when the sense of the probable future is belied and when dispositions ill-adjusted to the objective chances because of a hysteresis effect (Marx's favourite example of this was Don Quixote) are negatively sanctioned because the environment they actually encounter is too different from the one to which they are objectively adjusted. In fact the persistence of the effects of primary conditioning, in the form of the *habitus*, accounts equally well for cases in which dispositions function out of phase and practices are objectively ill-adapted to the present conditions because they are objectively adjusted to conditions that no longer obtain. The tendency of groups to persist in their ways, due *inter alia* to the fact that they are composed of individuals with durable dispositions that can outlive the economic and social conditions in which they were produced, can be the source of misadaptation as well as adaptation, revolt as well as resignation.

One only has to consider other possible forms of the relationship between dispositions and conditions to see that the pre-adjustment of the *habitus* to the objective conditions is a 'particular case of the possible' and so avoid unconsciously universalizing the model of the near-circular relationship of near-perfect reproduction, which is completely valid only when the conditions of production of the *habitus* and the conditions of its functioning are identical or homothetic. In this particular case, the dispositions durably inculcated by the objective conditions and by a pedagogic action that is tendentially adjusted to these conditions tend to generate practices objectively compatible with these conditions and expectations pre-adapted to their objective demands (*amor fati*). As a consequence, they tend, without any rational calculation or conscious estimation of the chances of success, to ensure immediate correspondence between the *a priori* or *ex ante* probability conferred on an event (whether or not accompanied by subjective experiences such as hopes, expectations, fears, etc.) and the *a posteriori* or *ex post* probability that can be established on the basis of past experience. They thus make it possible to understand why economic models based on the (tacit) premise of a 'relationship of intelligible causality', as Max Weber calls it, between generic ('typical') chances 'objectively existing as an average' and 'subjective expectations', or, for example, between investment or the propensity to invest and the rate of return expected or really obtained in the past, fairly exactly account for practices which do not arise from knowledge of the objective chances.

By pointing out that rational action, 'judiciously' oriented according to what is 'objectively valid', is what 'would have happened if the actors had had knowledge of all the circumstances and all the participants' intentions',[5] that is, of what is 'valid in the eyes of the scientist', who alone is able to calculate the system of objective chances to which perfectly informed action would have to be adjusted, Weber shows clearly that the pure model of rational action cannot be regarded as an anthropological description of practice. This is not only because real agents only very exceptionally possess the complete information, and the skill to appreciate it, that rational action would presuppose. Apart from rare cases which bring together the economic and cultural conditions for rational action oriented by knowledge of the profits that can be obtained in the different markets, practices depend not on the average chances of profit, an abstract and unreal notion, but on the specific chances that a singular agent or class of agents possesses by virtue of its capital, this being understood, in this respect, as a means of appropriation of the chances theoretically available to all.

> Economic theory which acknowledges only the rational 'responses' of an indeterminate, interchangeable agent to 'potential opportunities', or more precisely to average chances (like the 'average rates of profit' offered by the different markets), converts the immanent law of the economy into a universal norm of proper economic behaviour. In so doing, it conceals the fact that the 'rational' *habitus* which is the precondition for appropriate economic behaviour is the product of a particular economic condition, the one defined by possession of the economic and cultural capital required in order to seize the 'potential opportunities' theoretically available to all; and also that the same dispositions, by adapting the economically most deprived to the specific condition of which they are the product and thereby helping to make their adaptation to the generic demands of the economic cosmos (as regards calculation, forecasting, etc.), lead them to accept the negative sanctions resulting from this lack of adaptation, that is, their deprivation. In short, the art of estimating and seizing chances, the capacity to anticipate the future by a kind of practical induction or even to take a calculated gamble on the possible against the probable, are dispositions that can only be acquired in certain social conditions, that is, certain social conditions. Like the entrepreneurial spirit or the propensity to invest, economic information is a function of one's power over the economy. This is, on the one hand, because the propensity to acquire it depends on the chances of using it successfully, and the chances of acquiring it depend on the chances of successfully using it; and also because economic competence, like all competence (linguistic, political, etc.), far from being a simple technical capacity acquired in certain conditions, is a power tacitly conferred on those who have power over the economy or (as the very ambiguity of the word 'competence' indicates) an attribute of status.

Only in imaginary experience (in the folk tale, for example), which neutralizes the sense of social realities, does the social world take the form of a universe of possibles equally possible for any possible subject. Agents shape their aspirations according to concrete indices of the accessible and the inaccessible, of what is and is not 'for us', a division as fundamental and as fundamentally recognized as that between the sacred and the profane. The pre-emptive rights on the future that are defined by law and by the monopolistic right to certain possibles that it confers are merely the explicitly guaranteed form of the whole set of appropriated chances through which the power relations of the present project themselves into the future, from where they govern present dispositions, especially those towards the future. In fact, a given agent's practical relation to the future, which governs his present practice, is defined in the relationship between, on the one hand, his *habitus* with its temporal structures and dispositions towards the future, constituted in the course of a particular relationship to a particular universe of probabilities, and on the other hand a certain state of the chances objectively offered to him by the social world. The relation to what is possible is a relation to power; and the sense of the probable future is constituted in the prolonged relationship with a world structured according to the categories of the possible (for us) and the impossible (for us), of what is appropriated in advance by and for others and what one can reasonably expect for oneself. The *habitus* is the principle of a selective perception of the indices tending to confirm and reinforce it rather than transform it, a matrix generating responses adapted in advance to all objective conditions identical to or homologous with the (past) conditions of its production; it adjusts itself to a probable future which it anticipates and helps to bring about because it reads it directly in the present of the presumed world, the only one it can ever know. It is thus the basis of what Marx calls 'effective demand' (as opposed to 'demand without effect', based on need and desire), a realistic relation to what is possible, founded on and therefore limited by power. This disposition, always marked by its (social) conditions of acquisition and realization, tends to adjust to the objective chances of satisfying need or desire, inclining agents to 'cut their coats according to their cloth', and so to become the accomplices of the processes that tend to make the probable a reality.

Notes and References

1 E. Leach, 'On certain unconsidered aspects of double descent systems', *Man* (1962), p. 133.
2 E. Durkheim, *The Evolution of Educational Thought* (Routledge and Kegan Paul, London, 1977), p. 11.
3 G.W. Leibniz, *Second éclaircissement du système de la communication des substances*, in his *Œuvres philosophiques*, vol. II, ed. P. Janet (Landrange, Paris, 1866), p. 548.
4 M. Harris, *The Nature of Cultural Things* (Random House, New York, 1964), pp. 74–5.
5 M. Weber, *Economy and Society* (Bedminster, New York, 1968), vol. I, p. 6.

12

Social Space and Symbolic Power

Pierre Bourdieu

The construction of a theory of the social space presupposes a series of breaks with Marxist theory. It presupposes a break with the tendency to emphasize substances – here, real groups whose number, limits, members, etc. one claims to be able to define – at the expense of *relations* and with the intellectualist illusion which leads one to consider the theoretical class, constructed by the social scientist, as a real class, an effectively mobilized group; a break with economics, which leads one to reduce the social field, a multi-dimensional space, to the economic field alone, to the relations of economic production, which are thus established as the co-ordinates of social position; and a break, finally, with objectivism, which goes hand in hand with intellectualism, and which leads one to overlook the symbolic struggles that take place in different fields, and where what is at stake is the very representation of the social world, and in particular the hierarchy within each of the fields and between the different fields.

To begin with, sociology presents itself as a *social topology*. Accordingly, the social world can be represented in the form of a (multi-dimensional) space constructed on the basis of principles of differentiation or distribution constituted by the set of properties active in the social universe under consideration, that is, able to confer force or power on their possessor in that universe. Agents and groups of agents are thus defined by their *relative positions* in this space. Each of them is confined to a position or a precise class of neighbouring positions (i.e. to a given region of this space), and one cannot in fact occupy – even if one can do so in thought – two opposite regions of the space. In so far as the properties chosen to construct this space are active properties, the space can also be described as a field of forces: in other words, as a set of objective power relations imposed on all those who enter this field, relations which are not reducible to the intentions of individual agents or even to direct *interactions* between agents.

The active properties that are chosen as principles of construction of the social space are the different kinds of power or capital that are current in the different fields. Capital, which can exist in objectified form – in the form of material properties – or, in the case of cultural capital, in an incorporated form, one which can be legally guaranteed, represents power over a field (at a given moment) and, more precisely, over the accumulated product of past labour (and in particular over the set of instruments of production) and thereby over the mechanisms which tend to ensure the production of a particular category of goods and thus over a set of revenues and profits. The kinds of capital, like trumps in a game of cards, are powers which define the chances of profit in a given field (in fact, to every field or sub-field there corresponds a particular kind of capital, which is current, as a power or stake, in that field). For example, the volume of cultural capital (the same would be true, *mutatis mutandis*, of economic capital) determines the aggregate chances of profit in all games in which cultural capital is effective, thereby helping to determine position in the social space (in so far as this position is determined by success in the cultural field).

The position of a given agent in the social space can thus be defined by the position he occupies in the different fields, that is, in the distribution of the powers that are active in each of them. These are, principally, economic capital (in its different kinds), cultural capital and social capital, as well as symbolic capital, commonly called prestige, reputation, fame, etc., which is the form assumed by these different kinds of capital when they are perceived and recognized as legitimate. One can thus construct a simplified model of the social field as a whole, a model which allows one to plot each agent's position in all possible spaces of the game (it being understood that, while each field has its own logic and its own hierarchy, the hierarchy which is established between the kinds of capital and the statistical relation between different assets mean that the economic field tends to impose its structure on other fields).

The social field can be described as a multi-dimensional space of positions such that each actual position can be defined in terms of a multi-dimensional system of co-ordinates whose values correspond to the values of the different pertinent variables. Agents are thus distributed, in the first dimension, according to the overall volume of the capital they possess and, in the second dimension, according to the composition of their capital – in other words, according to the relative weight of the different kinds of capital in the total set of their assets.

The form assumed, at each moment, in each social field, by the set of the distributions of the different kinds of capital (whether incorporated or materialized), as instruments for the appropriation of the objectified product of accumulated social labour, defines the state of the relations of power, institutionalized in durable social statuses that are socially recognized or legally guaranteed, between agents who are objectively defined by their position within these relations; this form determines the actual or potential powers in different fields and the chances of access to the specific profits they procure.

Knowledge of the position occupied in this space contains information on the intrinsic properties (i.e. condition) and the relational properties (i.e. position) of agents. This is particularly clear in the case of those who occupy intermediate or middle positions – those which, apart from the middle or median values of their properties, owe a certain number of their most typical characteristics to the fact that they are situated *between* the two poles of the field, in the *neutral* point of the space, and are balanced between the two extreme positions.

Classes on paper

On the basis of knowledge of the space of positions, one can carve out *classes* in the logical sense of the word, i.e. sets of agents who occupy similar positions and who, being placed in similar conditions and submitted to similar types of conditioning, have every chance of having similar dispositions and interests, and thus of producing similar practices and adopting similar stances. This 'class on paper' has the *theoretical* existence which belongs to all theories: as the product of an explanatory classification, one which is altogether similar to that of zoologists or botanists, it allows one to *explain* and predict the practices and properties of the things classified – including their propensity to constitute groups. It is not really a class, an actual class, in the sense of being a group, a group mobilized for struggle; at most one could say that it is a *probable class*, in so far as it is a set of agents which will place fewer objective obstacles in the way of efforts of mobilization than any other set of agents.

Thus, contrary to the *nominalist relativism* which cancels out social differences by reducing them to pure theoretical artefacts, we have to affirm the existence of an objective space determining compatibilities and incompatibilities, proximities and distances. Contrary to the *realism of the intelligible* (or the reification of concepts), we have to affirm that the classes which can be carved out of the social space (for instance, for the purposes of statistical analysis, which is the sole means of demonstrating the structure of the social space) do not exist as real groups, although they explain the probability of individuals constituting themselves as practical groups, families (homogamy), clubs, associations and even trade-union or political 'movements'. What exists is a *space of relations* which is just as real as a geographical space, in which movements have to be paid for by labour, by effort and especially by time (to move upwards is to raise oneself, to climb and to bear the traces or the stigmata of that effort). Distances can also be measures in time (the time of ascent or of the reconversion of capital, for example). And the probability of mobilization into organized movements, endowed with an apparatus and a spokesperson, etc. (the very thing which leads us to talk of a 'class'), will be inversely proportional to distance in this space. While the probability of bringing together, really or nominally, a set of agents – by virtue of the delegate – is greater when they are closer together in the social space and belong to a more restricted and thus more homogeneous constructed class, nevertheless the alliance of the closest agents is never *necessary* or inevitable (because the effects of immediate competition may get in the way), and the alliance of the agents that are most separated from one another is never *impossible*. Although there is more chance of mobilizing in the same real group the set of workers than the set of bosses and workers, it is possible, in the context, for example, of an international crisis, to provoke a grouping on the basis of links of national identity. (This is in part because, due to its specific history, each of the national social spaces has its own structure – for instance, as regards hierarchical divergences in the economic field.)

Like 'being' according to Aristotle, the social world can be uttered and constructed in different ways: it can be practically perceived, uttered, constructed, in accordance with different principles of vision and division (for instance, ethnic divisions), it being understood that groupings founded in the struggle of the space constructed on the basis of the distribution of capital have a greater chance of being stable and durable and that other forms of grouping will always be threatened by splits and oppositions linked to distances in the social space. To speak of a social space means that one cannot group together just anyone with anyone else while ignoring the fundamental differences, particularly economic and cultural differences, between them. But this never completely excludes a possible organization of agents in accordance with other principles of division – ethnic, national, etc. – though it should be remembered that these are generally linked to the fundamental principles, since ethnic groups are themselves at least roughly hierarchized in the social space, for instance, in the United States (by the criterion of how long it has been since one's family first immigrated – blacks excepted).

This marks a first break with the Marxist tradition: this tradition either identifies, without further ado, the constructed class with the real class (i.e. as Marx himself reproached Hegel with doing, it confuses the things of logic with the logic of things); or else, when the tradition does draw the distinction, opposing the 'class-in-itself', defined on the basis of a set of objective conditions, to the 'class-for-itself', based on subjective factors, it describes the movement from the one to the other, a movement which is always celebrated as a real ontological advance, in accordance with a logic which is either totally determinist or on the contrary fully voluntarist. In the former case, the transition appears as a logical, mechanical or organic necessity (the transformation of the proletariat from a class-in-itself to a class-for-itself being presented as an inevitable effect of time, of the 'maturing of the objective conditions'); in the latter case, it is presented as the effect of an 'awakening of consciousness', conceived as a 'taking cognizance' of the theory which occurs under the enlightened leadership of the party. In both cases nothing is said about the mysterious alchemy by which a 'group in struggle', as a personalized collective, a historical agent setting its own aims, arises from the objective economic conditions.

By a sort of sleight of hand, the most essential questions are spirited away: first, the very question of the political, of the specific action of agents who, in the name of a theoretical definition of 'class', assign to the members of that class the aims which officially conform most closely to their 'objective' (i.e. theoretical) interests, and of the labour through which they succeed in producing, if not the mobilized class, a belief in the existence of the class, which is the basis of the authority of its spokespersons; and second, the question of the relations between the supposedly objective classifications produced by the social scientist, similar in that respect to the zoologist, and the classifications which agents themselves continually produce in their ordinary existence, and through which they seek to modify their position in the objective classifications or to modify the very principles in accordance with which these classifications are produced.

The most resolutely objectivist theory must take account of agents' representation of the social world and, more precisely, of the contribution they make to the construction of the vision of this world, and thereby to the very construction of this world, via the *labour of representation* (in all senses of the term) that they continually perform in order to impose their own vision of the world or the vision of their own position in this world, that is, their social identity. The perception of the social world is the product of a double social structuring: on the 'objective' side, this perception is socially structured because the properties attached to agents or institutions do not make themselves available to perception independently, but in combinations whose probability varies widely (and just as feathered animals have a greater chance of having wings than furry animals, so the possessors of a substantial cultural capital are more likely to be museum visitors than those who lack such capital); on the 'subjective' side, it is structured because the schemes of perception and evaluation susceptible of being brought into operation at a given moment, including all those which are laid down in language, are the product of previous symbolic struggles and express, in a more or less transformed form, the state of symbolic relations of power. The fact remains, none the less, that the objects of the social world can be perceived and expressed in different ways because, like the objects of the natural world, they always include a certain indeterminacy and vagueness – because, for example, the most constant combinations of properties are never founded on anything other than statistical connections between interchangeable features; and also because, as historical objects, they are subject to variations in time and their meaning, in so far as it depends on the future, is itself in suspense, in a pending and deferred state, and is thus relatively indeterminate. This element of risk, of uncertainty, is what provides a basis for the plurality of world views, a plurality which is itself linked to the plurality of points of view, and to all the symbolic struggles for the production and imposition of the legitimate vision of the world and, more precisely, to all the cognitive strategies of *fulfilment* which produce the meaning of the objects of the social world by going beyond the directly visible attributes by reference to the future or the past. This reference may be implicit and tacit, through what Husserl calls protension and retention, practical forms of prospection or retrospection excluding the positioning of past and future as such; or it may be explicit, as in political struggles in which the past, with the retrospective reconstruction of a past adjusted to the needs of the present . . . , and especially the future, with the creative foresight associated with it, are continually invoked, in order to determine, delimit, and define the ever-open meaning of the present.

To point out that perception of the social world implies an act of construction is not in the least to accept an intellectualist theory of knowledge: the essential part of one's experience of the social world and of the labour of construction it implies takes place in practice, without reaching the level of explicit representation and verbal expression. Closer to a class unconscious than to a 'class consciousness' in the

Marxist sense, the sense of the position one occupies in the social space (what Goffman calls the 'sense of one's place') is the practical mastery of the social structure as a whole which reveals itself through the sense of the position occupied in that structure. The categories of perception of the social world are essentially the product of the incorporation of the objective structures of the social space. Consequently, they incline agents to accept the social world as it is, to take it for granted, rather than to rebel against it, to put forward opposed and even antagonistic possibilities. The sense of one's place, as the sense of what one can or cannot 'allow oneself', implies a tacit acceptance of one's position, a sense of limits ('that's not meant for us') or – what amounts to the same thing – a sense of distances, to be marked and maintained, respected, and expected of others. And this is doubtless all the more true when the conditions of existence are more rigorous and the reality principle is more rigorously imposed. (Hence the profound realism which most often characterizes the world view of the dominated and which, functioning as a sort of socially constituted instinct of conservation, can appear conservative only with reference to an external and thus normative representation of the 'objective interest' of those whom it helps to live or to survive.)

If the objective relations of power tend to reproduce themselves in visions of the social world which contribute to the permanence of those relations, this is therefore because the structuring principles of the world view are rooted in the objective structures of the social world and because the relations of power are also present in people's minds in the form of the categories of perception of those relations. But the degree of indeterminacy and vagueness characteristic of the objects of the social world, together with the practical, pre-reflexive and implicit character of the patterns of perception and evaluation which are applied to them, is the Archimedean point which is objectively made available to truly political action. Knowledge of the social world and, more precisely, the categories which make it possible are the stakes *par excellence* of the political struggle, a struggle which is inseparably theoretical and practical, over the power of preserving or transforming the social world by preserving or transforming the categories of perception of that world.

The capacity for bringing into existence in an explicit state, of publishing, of making public (i.e. objectified, visible, sayable, and even official) that which, not yet having attained objective and collective existence, remained in a state of individual or serial existence – people's disquiet, anxiety, expectation, worry – represents a formidable social power, that of bringing into existence groups by establishing the *common sense*, the explicit consensus, of the whole group. In fact, this labour of categorization, of making things explicit and classifying them, is continually being performed, at every moment of ordinary existence, in the struggles in which agents clash over the meaning of the social world and their position in it, the meaning of their social identity, through all the forms of speaking well or badly of someone or something, of blessing or cursing and of malicious gossip, eulogy, congratulations, praise, compliments, or insults, rebukes, criticism, accusations, slanders, etc.

It is easy to understand why one of the elementary forms of political power should have consisted, in many archaic societies, in the almost magical power of *naming* and bringing into existence by virtue of naming. Thus in traditional Kabylia, the function of making things explicit and the labour of symbolic production that poets performed, particularly in crisis situations, when the meaning of the world was no longer clear, conferred on them major political functions, those of the war-lord or ambassador. But with the growing differentiation of the social world and the constitution of relatively autonomous fields, the labour of the production and imposition of meaning is performed in and through struggles in the field of cultural production (and especially in the political sub-field); it becomes the particular concern, the specific interest, of the professional producers of objectified representations of the social world, or, more precisely, of the methods of objectification.

If the legitimate mode of perception is such an important stake in different struggles, this is because on the one hand the movement from the implicit to the explicit is in no way automatic, the same experience of the social being recognizable in very different expressions, and on the other hand, the most marked objective differences may be hidden behind more immediately visible differences (such as, for example, those which separate ethnic groups). It is true that perceptual configurations, social *Gestalten*, exist objectively, and that the proximity of conditions and thus of dispositions tends to be re-translated into durable links and groupings, immediately perceptible social units such as socially distinct regions or districts (with spatial segregation), or sets of agents possessing altogether similar visible properties, such as Weber's *Stände*. But the fact remains that socially known and recognized differences exist only for a subject capable not only of perceiving the differences but of recognizing them as significant and interesting, i.e. exists only for a subject endowed with the aptitude and the inclination to *establish* the differences which are held to be significant in the social world under consideration.

In this way, the social world, particularly through properties and their distribution, attains, in the objective world itself, the status of a *symbolic system* which, like a system of phonemes, is organized in accordance with the logic of difference, of differential deviation, which is thus constituted as significant *distinction*. The social space, and the differences that 'spontaneously' emerge within it, tend to function symbolically as *a space of lifestyles* or as a set of *Stände*, of groups characterized by different lifestyles.

Distinction does not necessarily imply, as is often supposed, following Veblen and his theory of conspicuous consumption, a quest for distinction. All consumption and, more generally, all practice, is *conspicuous*, visible, whether or not it was performed *in order to be seen*: it is distinctive, whether or not it was inspired by the desire to get oneself noticed, to make oneself conspicuous, to distinguish oneself or to act with distinction. Hence, every practice is bound to function as a *distinctive sign* and, when the difference is recognized, legitimate and approved, as a *sign of distinction* (in all senses of the term). The fact remains that social agents, being capable of perceiving as significant distinctions the 'spontaneous' differences that their categories of perception lead them to consider as pertinent, are also capable of intentionally underscoring these spontaneous differences in life-style by what Weber calls 'the stylization of life' (*Stilisierung des Lebens*). The pursuit of distinction – which may be expressed in ways of speaking or in a refusal to countenance marrying beneath one's station – produces separations which are meant to be perceived or, more precisely, known and recognized as legitimate differences – most frequently as differences of nature (in French we speak of 'natural distinction').

Distinction – in the ordinary sense of the word – is the difference written into the very structure of the social space when it is perceived in accordance with the categories adapted to that structure; and the Weberian *Stand*, which people so often like to contrast with the Marxist class, is the class adequately constructed when it is perceived through the categories of perception derived from the structure of that space. Symbolic capital – another name for distinction – is nothing other than capital, of whatever kind, when it is perceived by an agent endowed with categories of perception arising from the incorporation of the structure of its distribution, i.e. when it is known and recognized as self-evident. Distinctions, as symbolic transformations of *de facto* differences, and, more generally, the ranks, orders, grades and all the other symbolic hierarchies, are the product of the application of schemes of construction which – as in the case, for instance, of the pairs of adjectives used to express most social judgements – are the product of the incorporation of the very structures to which they are applied; and recognition of the most absolute legitimacy is nothing other than an apprehension of the everyday social world as taken for granted, an apprehension which results from the almost perfect coincidence of objective structures and incorporated structures.

It follows, among other consequences, that symbolic capital is attracted to symbolic capital and that the – real – autonomy of the field of symbolic production does not prevent this field from remaining dominated, in its functioning, by the constraints which dominate the social field as a whole. It also follows that objective relations of power tend to reproduce themselves in symbolic relations of power, in visions of the social world which contribute to ensuring the permanence of those relations of power. In the struggle for the imposition of the legitimate vision of the social world, in which science itself is inevitably involved, agents wield a power which is proportional to their symbolic capital, that is, to the recognition they receive from a group. The authority which underlies the performative effectiveness of discourse about the social world, the symbolic force of visions and pre-visions aimed at imposing the principles of vision and division of this world, is a *percipi*, a being known and recognized (*nobilis*), which allows a *percipere* to be imposed. It is the most *visible* agents, from the point of view of the prevailing categories of perception, who are the best placed to change the vision by changing the categories of perception. But they are also, with a few exceptions, the least inclined to do so.

13

Rational Choice Theory

Jon Elster

Rational choice theory is first and foremost normative. It tells us what we ought to do in order to achieve our aims as closely as possible. It does not, in the standard version, tell us what our aims ought to be. From the normative account we can derive an explanatory theory, by assuming that people are rational in the normatively appropriate sense.

The central *explananda* of rational choice theory are *actions*. To explain an action, we must first verify that it stands in an optimizing relationship to the desires and beliefs of the agent. The action should be the best way of satisfying the agent's desires, given his beliefs. Moreover, we must demand that these desires and beliefs themselves be rational. At the very least, they must be internally consistent. With respect to beliefs we must also impose a more substantive requirement of rationality: they should be optimally related to the evidence available to the agent. In forming their beliefs, the agents should consider all and only the relevant evidence, with no element being unduly weighted. As a logical extension of this requirement, we also demand that the collection of evidence itself be subject to the canons of rationality. The efficacy of action may be destroyed both by gathering too little evidence and by gathering too much. The optimal amount of evidence is partly determined by our desires. (In the case of more important decisions it is rational to collect more evidence.) Partly it is determined by our prior beliefs about the likely cost, quality and relevance of various types of evidence.

Rational action, then, involves three optimizing operations: finding the best action, for given beliefs and desires; forming the best-grounded belief, for given evidence; and collecting the right amount of evidence, for given desires and prior beliefs. Here, desires are the unmoved movers, reflecting Hume's dictum that 'Reason is, and ought only to be the slave of the passions.' In saying this, he did not mean that reason ought to obey every whim and fancy of the passions. In particular, he would not have endorsed the direct shaping of reason by passion found in wishful thinking. To serve his master well, a slave must have some independence of execution: beliefs born of passion serve passion badly.

It follows that irrationality can arise at several links in the causal chain that leads up to action. The processes of evidence collection and of belief formation may be distorted by motivational bias or skewed by erroneous cognition. More importantly for the present purpose, people may fail to act rationally on given beliefs and desires. On the one hand, there is weakness of will: acting against one's better judgement, failing to resist temptation, and the like. On the other hand, there is excess of will: trying to bring about by instrumental action states that – like sleep, self-respect or spontaneity – can come about only as the by-product of actions undertaken for other ends.

On one conception, politics is like individual choice writ large. First, political preferences – goals, trade-offs and priorities – are defined by the democratic political process. Next, government agencies gather information about factual matters and about ends–means relationships, to form an opinion about which policies will best realize those goals. Finally, other agencies implement these optimal policies. Parliament, the central bureau of statistics and government form, on this conception, a unified system for making rational political decisions.

My concern is not with those (if any) who believe that this view of the political process is literally true, i.e. that political choice can be understood in terms of the desires, beliefs and actions of a supra-individual entity, 'society'. Rather my concern is with those who, while accepting the canons of methodological individualism, assume that we may proceed *as if* the view were correct. They assume, in other words, that little harm is done by treating the polity as a unitary actor, with coherent and stable values, well-grounded beliefs and a capacity to carry out its decisions. The assumption has been most prominent in the study of international relations and in the theory of economic planning. For obvious reasons, it has been less pronounced in the study of domestic politics in pluralist democracies. Yet even here, the temptation to use the convenient 'actor' language can be strong. In this section I survey some reasons why this language, while tempting, can also be treacherous and misleading.

Opportunism provides a general reason why polities differ from individuals. It is easier for an individual to deceive others than to deceive himself. When individuals engage in self-serving deception or opportunism, there is no certainty that the aggregate outcome of their behaviour will correspond to the unitary-actor model of political rationality. Let me explain what this means in the three dimensions of choice that concern us here: preferences, information and action.

Let us first define the problem more carefully, as a difficulty for *democratic* politics. Specifically, the method for aggregating individual preferences should not be dictatorial. In addition, we want the method to be invulnerable to opportunism: the individual should not be able, by misrepresenting his preferences, to bring about an outcome which is better according to his true preferences than that which would have resulted had he expressed these true preferences. Finally, we would want the mechanism to ensure that outcomes are Pareto optimal. It so happens that the only method satisfying these requirements is some form of lottery voting, which, however, has too many other drawbacks to be seriously considered. Although strategy-proof mechanisms for preference revelation can be devised for special cases, one cannot in general assume that people can be induced to be honest out of self-interest.

The problem of incentive compatibility extends to that of gathering information about factual matters. When economic agents are asked to provide information which is easily available to them, but would be available to others only at some cost (if at all), one may assume that they will ask themselves whether it is in their interest to do so. It is well known, for instance, that the only non-distorting form of taxation is to impose a lump-sum tax on individuals according to their estimated productive capacity rather than according to their actual production. But it would rarely be in the interest of the individuals to give correct information about their capacity. Similarly, it may not be in the interest of individuals to report truthfully how much they are willing to pay for the provision of public goods. Soviet-type economies are well known for the perverse incentives they create against truthful reporting. Sometimes the fear of being punished as the bearer of bad tidings creates an incentive to present things as better than they really are. At other times, self-interest leads one to present the situation as worse than it actually is, as when a manager under-reports production in order to avoid an increase in his quota. Essentially similar problems can be expected to arise in any system that depends on the collection of information from decentralized sources. Again, while the problem may be overcome in special cases, there is no general recipe for inducing truthful reporting.

Finally, incentive problems arise at the level of implementation. For the individual there is usually no distance between making a decision and carrying it out, barring weakness of will or physical inability. In typical cases, the unity of the individual ensures that decisions, once made, are also executed. The lack of unity of the polity makes this a much more problematic assumption. The agents who are charged with implementing the decisions cannot in general be trusted to disregard their self-interest or their personal conception of the general interest. Nor can their principal always effectively monitor their activities, if only for the reason that the monitoring agents may themselves be corrupt.

One need not, however, rest one's case on the dangers of opportunism. Indeed, one should not. While there is always a risk of self-serving behaviour, the extent to which it is actually present varies widely. Much of the social choice and public choice literature, with its assumption of universally opportunistic behaviour, simply seems out of touch with the real world, in which there is a great deal of honesty and sense of duty. If people always engaged in opportunistic behaviour when they could get away with it, civilization as we know it would not exist. We should not assume that the only task of politics is to devise institutions that can harness opportunistic self-interest to socially useful purposes. An equally important task is to create institutions that embody a valid conception of justice. If people do not feel they are being taken advantage of, the temptation to take advantage of society will be much reduced.

We must ask, therefore, whether a just society, with effective norms of honesty and trust, would be a good approximation to the unitary-actor model of rational politics. The short answer is that while it would surely be a better approximation than a society in which opportunism was rampant, serious difficulties would remain. Although the implementation problem would disappear, problems of aggregating preferences and centralizing information would not. Even when preferences are sincerely expressed, the notion of the 'popular will' is incoherent. Even if individuals tried to report their preferences and abilities as truthfully as possible, and even if we disregard the opportunity costs of writing the reports and the risk that the information might be out of date when finally used, the centre would not find it very useful. The individual's knowledge about his mental states and productive capacities is largely tacit, embodied and personal, rather than explicit, verbal and abstract. Firms do not have access to the whole production function on which they are operating. They have to know what they are doing, but they have no incentive to know what they could do, until forced to by circumstances. Consumers may be quite unable to tell what purchases they plan to make over the next year or years. These familiar objections to central planning remain, I believe, irrefutable.

In conclusion, we may note that the analogy between individual and social choice could also be made from the converse perspective. Instead of arguing that society is to be understood on the model of the unitary individual actor, one might argue that the individual should be understood on the model of the fragmented polity. First, there are intrapersonal problems of preference aggregation; second, there is self-deception and other forms of cognitive compartmentalization; third, there is weakness of will and other obstacles to the execution of decisions. Individuals, like polities, often do not know what they want; or do not know what they know; or fail to do what they have decided to do. I believe, however, that the analogy breaks down in a crucial respect: individuals, unlike polities, have an organizing centre – variously referred to as the will or the ego – that is constantly trying to integrate these fragmented parts. Societies, by contrast, have no centre.

PART III

Critical Theory of Modernity

IN THE OPENING Reading of this part (Reading 14), John Thompson discusses one of the concepts which has played a central role in the critical analysis of social phenomena – the notion of ideology. In recent years the notion of ideology has itself been subjected to criticism from various quarters. But Thompson argues that this concept, if carefully reformulated, remains a valuable tool for a critical theory of modern societies.

Thompson distinguishes two approaches to the study of ideology. The 'neutral conception' of ideology sees ideology as sets of ideas involved in any aspect of social life. In this conception, ideology is simply part of the make-up of society; it has no particular connection with illusory beliefs or with sectional power. For Thompson, however, ideology is best seen as a critical concept. Analysing ideology means studying the ways in which ideas or idea-systems are utilized to sustain modes of exploitative domination. What makes a set of ideas ideological is not so much their content, but whether or not they operate in the service of differential power.

Thompson identifies several forms of ideological mechanism. Symbol systems may act to 'legitimate' – that is, justify – inequalities of power by declaring them to be right and proper. 'Dissimilation' is a second mechanism of ideology where relations of domination are concealed or denied by prevalent symbol systems. A third mechanism of ideology is 'unification': here ideology appeals to collective interests in such a way as to override differences of power within a given group or state. Nationalism may be ideological in this sense. Ideology also operates through an opposing tendency: 'fragmentation'. Here symbolic constructions serve to disaggregate individuals or groups who might otherwise have course to contest a given social order. Finally there is 'reification': transitory historical circumstances are represented symbolically as though they were eternal or unchanging.

Over a period of several decades the German social thinker Jürgen Habermas has sought to take over where Marx left off – to develop a critical theory of modern society relevant to social life today. He has sought to do so methodologically as well as substantively. In both areas for Habermas the notion of 'communication' plays a pivotal role. A normative framework for critical theory (Reading 15), Habermas argues, can be discerned in the nature of language. Every instance of linguistic communication presupposes the possibility of interaction free from constraint and free from distortion. Language raises the possibility of what Habermas calls an 'ideal speech situation', which in turn implies a particular form of communicative community.

In an ideal speech situation, individuals are autonomous and equal;

communication between them is governed by the 'force of the better argument' rather than by constraint and power. An ideal speech situation thus provides a model against which the reality of power divided or exploitative social systems can be assessed.

How much room a society allows for public discussion and debate is thus of vital significance. In modern societies, opportunity for open discussion of problems and policies depends upon the development of a 'public sphere'. The public sphere has become expanded in conjunction with the rise of modern media of communication; but a variety of factors also serve to constrain and limit it. Habermas is critical of the idea that television, radio, newspapers and other media create a stereotypical mass culture which deprives the ordinary member of the population of the opportunity to reflect upon public issues. The development of modern communications media frees communication processes, Habermas says, from the provinciality of local context, and this is a positive advance. On the other hand, in so far as the media flow in a 'one-way' direction, from central organizations to the public, they tend to become hierarchical and authoritarian.

The media here participate in what Habermas calls the 'colonization of the lifeworld' – the invasion of local cultures and habits by more abstract and centralized forms of social and economic organization. The main conflicts and tensions to which a critical theory of society must give attention arise not primarily in the arena of material production but in cultural systems and socialization processes. Groups and movements, such as ecological and feminist organizations, which criticize the 'productivism' of modern society become much more subversive than those, such as labour movements, which are mainly concerned with distributing the fruits of economic growth.

In Reading 16 Habermas amplifies this argument. The colonization of the lifeworld is part of an extended process of rationalization, which Habermas analyses in a way indebted to Max Weber. In contemporary society the welfare state is at the centre of various important conflicts. Defended for the most part by Leftists and Liberals, it is attacked by those on the political Right, who tend to see it as a bureaucratic monolith. A more important question, however, in Habermas's view, is how far 'post-material values', which tend to reassert the primacy of social solidarity and communication, stimulate a demand for more radical changes in the socio-economic order.

Habermas is critical of the systems theory of Niklas Luhmann (see Reading 32 below), which sees rationalization as producing a social system separated into distinct and autonomous 'subsystems'. According to such a conception, there would neither be a role for the public sphere in the way in which Habermas wishes to understand it, nor would the 'lifeworld' of shared communication continue to exist. In fact, Habermas says, we become today more and more conscious of the limitations of a social order dominated solely by rationalized systems. Social solidarity and meaning cannot be achieved through the development of technically efficient modes of administration. Crises in the lifeworld therefore fuel a range of oppositional tendencies whose long-term implications may well be very profound.

In Reading 17 Richard Rorty compares Habermas, as a defender both of critical theory and the emancipatory potential of modernity, with ideas of a quite different kind. Like many thinkers associated with the versions of postmodernism and postmodernity, Jean-François Lyotard argues that critical theory today is a lapsed and incoherent project. Postmodernity, in Lyotard's conception, is marked by an 'incredulity towards meta-narratives' – a rejection of any view which identifies avenues of progress in history, or indeed which supposes that 'history' has any intrinsic coherence at all. For Lyotard, Habermas's ideas are as irrelevant to contemporary social circumstances as are those of Marx. There is no 'independent perspective' through which history can be 'corrected' or 'set on the right tract'.

Habermas, on the other hand, regards Lyotard and Foucault (see Reading 18 below) as 'neo-Conservatives' who are forced to acquiesce in the status quo because they have relinquished any means of providing a critical appraisal of it. Critique for them, according to Habermas, can be no more than *ad hoc* negation. 'Context-dependent criticism', in his view, by abandoning the 'force of the better argument', also abandons the aspirations that have always been at the core of all forms of non-Conservative politics.

Besides outlining the respective views of the two antagonists, Rorty seeks to steer a way between them. Neither Habermas nor Lyotard has properly grasped what is at issue in concentrating their attention upon whether or not historical metanarratives can be defended. Habermas is mistaken in supposing that there has to be a universalizing speech community, or ideal speech situation, which is the litmus paper of critical theory. We do not need, nor could we satisfactorily defend, the universal knowledge claims so central to Habermas's intellectual and political project. Yet recognition that this is so condemns social theory neither to irrationalism nor to neo-Conservatism.

Thinkers like Lyotard and Foucault, according to Rorty, are wrong to reject a critical engagement with society because of their fear of succumbing to metanarratives; they fall into this position only because they accept too much of the sort of story which Habermas tells, even if in the end only to reject it. In Rorty's view we can accept that modernity has generated conditions under which human communities are prepared to value 'undistorted communication' and struggle to achieve it; we do not need to take the further step of asserting that this phenomenon somehow corresponds to universal needs or universal knowledge claims. The sorts of studies developed by Foucault are valuable precisely because they are historically located narratives. These narratives do not unmask power in the name of something which could be called 'universal emancipation'; they do, however, contrary to what Foucault himself seems to propose, allow us to understand how specific forms of domination associated with modern institutions might be translated into more liberal and enlightened modes of life.

Foucault's writings are discussed from two further perspectives in Readings 18 and 19. In Reading 18 Mark Poster concentrates upon the complex relation between Foucault and Marxism as represented in the writings of Sartre and others. Foucault developed some of his basic ideas in explicit opposition to Sartre and to Sartre's version of Marxism. However, whereas Sartre took as his starting point the intrinsic freedom of the human individual or subject, Foucault, drawing on Lévi-Strauss and structuralism, rejected such 'subjectivism'.

Foucault's announcement that 'man is dead' was in some substantial part aimed specifically at Sartre. Yet Foucault was also led to champion some of Sartre's ideas, although he tried to place them in a different intellectual and political context. Foucault discovered a common ancestry with Sartre in respect of the influence of Nietzsche and became drawn to forms of political activism close to those which Sartre had championed. Poster therefore sees a greater distinction between the views of Lyotard and Foucault than is acknowledged by Rorty. Foucault disavows the notion of universal truth, but does not discard the notion of truth altogether; there is no 'truth', but there are many truths and the identifying of these can have radical political implications.

14

Ideology and Modern Culture

John Thompson

Let me begin by distinguishing between two general *types* of conception of ideology. This distinction will enable us to classify the various conceptions of ideology into two basic categories and it will serve as a springboard for the development of an alternative view. One general type is what I shall call 'neutral conceptions of ideology'. Neutral conceptions are those which purport to characterize phenomena as ideology or ideological without implying that these phenomena are necessarily misleading, illusory or aligned with the interests of any particular group. Ideology, according to the neutral conceptions, is one aspect of social life (or form of social inquiry) among others, and is no more nor any less attractive or problematic than any other. Ideology may be present, for example, in every political programme, irrespective of whether it is oriented towards revolution, restoration or reform, irrespective of whether it aspires to the transformation or the preservation of the social order. Ideology may be as necessary to subordinate groups in their struggle against the social order as it is to dominant groups in their defence of the status quo. Like military hardware or tactical know-how, ideology may be a weapon which is oriented towards victory but towards no particular victor, since it is in principle available to any combatant who has the resources and skills to acquire and employ it.

We can distinguish neutral conceptions of ideology from a second general type, which I shall describe as 'critical conceptions of ideology'. Critical conceptions are those which convey a negative, critical or pejorative sense. Unlike neutral conceptions, critical conceptions imply that the phenomena characterized as ideology or ideological are misleading, illusory or one-sided; and the very characterization of phenomena as ideology carries with it an implicit criticism or condemnation of them. Critical conceptions of ideology differ in terms of the bases upon which they imply a negative sense. We may describe these differing bases as the *criteria of negativity* associated with particular conceptions of ideology. . . .

The criteria of negativity, by virtue of which the different critical conceptions convey a negative sense, vary from one conception to another. In Napoleon's use of the term, 'ideology' conveyed a negative sense by suggesting that the ideas concerned were both erroneous and impractical, both misleading and divorced from the practical realities of political life. Marx's polemical conception of ideology retained these two criteria of negativity, while shifting the target of attack from de Tracy's science of ideas to the philosophical speculation of the Young Hegelians. With the transition to Marx's epiphenomenal conception, the criteria of negativity change: the ideas which constitute ideology are still illusory, but they are also regarded as ideas which express the interests of the dominant class. The latter criterion is replaced by another in what I described as the latent conception of ideology in Marx. Ideology, according to the latent conception, is a system of representations which conceal and mislead and which, in so doing, serve to sustain relations of domination. With the subsequent formulation of Mannheim's restricted conception, the criteria of negativity revert to those which were characteristic of Napoleon's use of the term and Marx's polemical conception.

This schema could be extended to encompass more recent contributions to the theory and analysis of ideology. I shall not, however, undertake to extend this schema here. I have considered some recent contributions elsewhere, but have done so with a slightly different aim in mind: I have been less concerned with the specific conceptions of ideology employed by contemporary authors, and more concerned with their general accounts of the nature and role of ideology in modern societies. Nevertheless, most contemporary authors who write on ideology – from Martin Seliger to Clifford Geertz, from Alvin Gouldner to Louis Althusser – employ some version of what I have described as a neutral conception of ideology. Ideology is conceived of, in a general way, as systems of beliefs or symbolic forms and practices; and in some cases these authors – like Mannheim several decades ago – seek explicitly to distance themselves from what they regard as a 'restrictive' or 'evaluative' conception of ideology. In developing an alternative approach to the analysis of ideology, my aim will be quite different. I shall seek to counter what I have described as the neutralization of the concept of ideology. I shall attempt to formulate a critical conception of ideology, drawing on some of the themes implicit in earlier conceptions while abandoning others; and I shall attempt to show that this conception can provide a basis for a fruitful and defensible approach to the analysis of ideology, an approach which is oriented towards the concrete analysis of social–historical phenomena but which, at the same time, preserves the critical character bequeathed to us by the history of the concept.

The analysis of ideology, according to the conception which I shall propose, is primarily concerned with the ways in which symbolic forms intersect with relations of power. It is concerned with the ways in which meaning is mobilized in the social world and serves thereby to bolster up individuals and groups who occupy positions of power. Let me define this focus more sharply: *to study ideology is to study the ways in which meaning serves to establish and sustain relations of domination.* Ideological phenomena are meaningful symbolic phenomena *in so far as* they serve, in particular social–historical circumstances, to establish and sustain relations of domination. *In so far as*: it is crucial to stress that symbolic phenomena, or certain symbolic phenomena, are not ideological as such, but are ideological only in so far as they serve, in particular circumstances, to maintain relations of domination. We cannot read the ideological character of symbolic phenomena off the symbolic phenomena themselves. We can grasp symbolic phenomena as ideological, hence we can analyse ideology, only by situating symbolic phenomena in the social–historical contexts within which these phenomena may, or may not, serve to establish and sustain relations of domination. Whether symbolic phenomena do or do not serve to establish and sustain relations of domination is a question which can be answered only by examining the interplay of meaning and power in particular circumstances, only by examining the ways in which symbolic forms are employed, circulated and understood by individuals situated in structured social contexts.

[...]

In order to develop my proposed reformulation of the concept of ideology, there are three aspects which require elaboration: the notion of meaning, the concept of domination, and the ways in which meaning may serve to establish and sustain relations of domination. In studying the ways in which meaning serves to establish and sustain relations of domination, the meaning with which we are concerned is the meaning of symbolic forms which are embedded in social contexts and circulating in the social world. By 'symbolic forms' I understand a broad range of actions and utterances, images and texts, which are produced by subjects and recognized by them and others as meaningful constructs.

Linguistic utterances and expressions, whether spoken or inscribed, are crucial in this regard, but symbolic forms can also be non-linguistic or quasi-linguistic in nature (e.g. a visual image, or a construct which combines images and words). We can analyse the meaningful character of symbolic forms in terms of four typical aspects – what I shall call the 'intentional', 'conventional', 'structural' and 'referential' aspects of symbolic forms. There is a fifth aspect of symbolic forms, what I shall call the 'contextual' aspect, which indicates that symbolic forms are always embedded in socially structured contexts and processes. To describe these contexts and processes as 'socially structured' is to say that there are systematic differentials in terms of the distribution of, and access to, resources of various kinds. Individuals situated within socially structured contexts have, by virtue of their location, different quantities of, and different degrees of access to, available resources. The social location of individuals, and the entitlements associated with their positions in a social field or institution, endow them with varying degrees of 'power', understood at this level as a socially or institutionally endowed capacity which enables or empowers some individuals to make decisions, pursue ends or realize interests. We can speak of 'domination' when established relations of power are 'systematically asymmetrical', that is, when particular agents or groups of agents are endowed with power in a durable way which excludes, and to some significant degree remains inaccessible to, other agents or groups of agents, irrespective of the basis upon which such exclusion is carried out.

These initial characterizations of meaning and domination provide the backcloth against which we may pursue the third issue raised by the proposed reformulation of the concept of ideology: in what ways can meaning serve to establish and sustain relations of domination? There are innumerable ways in which meaning may serve, in particular social–historical conditions, to maintain relations of domination, and we can answer this question properly only by attending carefully to the interplay of meaning and power in the actual circumstances of social life. It may be helpful to identify certain general *modes of operation* of ideology and to indicate some of the ways in which they may be linked, in particular circumstances, with *strategies of symbolic construction*. In distinguishing these modes and developing these connections, my aim is not to provide a comprehensive account of the ways in which meaning may serve to establish and sustain relations of domination. Rather, my aim is simply to stake out, in a preliminary manner, a rich field of analysis.

I shall distinguish five general modes through which ideology can operate: 'legitimation', 'dissimulation', 'unification', 'fragmentation' and

Table 14.1 Modes of operation of ideology

General modes	*Some typical strategies of symbolic construction*
Legitimation	Rationalization Universalization Narrativization
Dissimulation	Displacement Euphemization Trope (e.g. synecdoche, metonymy, metaphor)
Unification	Standardization Symbolization of unity
Fragmentation	Differentiation Expurgation of the other
Reification	Naturalization Eternalization Nominalization/passivization

'reification'. Table 14.1 indicates some of the ways in which these modes can be linked with various strategies of symbolic construction.

[...]

Let me begin by considering *legitimation*. Relations of domination may be established and sustained, as Max Weber observed, by being represented as legitimate, that is, as just and worthy of support. The representation of relations of domination as legitimate may be regarded as a *claim to legitimacy* which is based on certain grounds, expressed in certain symbolic forms and which may, in given circumstances, be more or less effective. Weber distinguished three types of grounds on which claims to legitimacy may be based: rational grounds (appealing to the legality of enacted rules), traditional grounds (appealing to the sanctity of immemorial traditions) and charismatic grounds (appealing to the exceptional character of an individual person who exercises authority).

Claims based on such grounds may be expressed in symbolic forms by means of certain typical strategies of symbolic construction. One typical strategy is what we could call *rationalization*, whereby the producer of a symbolic form constructs a chain of reasoning which seeks to defend or justify a set of social relations or institutions, and thereby to persuade an audience that it is worthy of support. Another typical strategy is *universalization*. By means of this strategy, institutional arrangements which serve the interests of some individuals are represented as serving the interests of all, and these arrangements are regarded as being open in principle to anyone who has the ability and the inclination to succeed within them. Claims to legitimacy may also be expressed by means of the strategy of *narrativization*: claims are embedded in stories which recount the past and treat the present as part of a timeless and cherished tradition. Indeed traditions are sometimes *invented* in order to create a sense of belonging to a community and to a history which transcends the experience of conflict, difference and division.

[...]

A second *modus operandi* of ideology is *dissimulation*. Relations of domination may be established and sustained by being concealed, denied or obscured, or by being represented in a way which deflects attention from or glosses over existing relations or processes. Ideology *qua* dissimulation may be expressed in symbolic forms by means of a variety of different strategies. One such strategy is *displacement*: a term customarily used when one object or individual is used to refer to another, and thereby the positive or negative connotations of the term are transferred to the other object or individual. . . . Another strategy which facilitates the dissimulation of social relations is *euphemization*: actions, institutions or social relations are described or redescribed in terms which elicit a positive valuation. There are many well-known examples of this process: the violent suppression of protest is described as the 'restoration of order'; a prison or concentration camp is described as a 'rehabilitation centre'; institutionalized inequalities based on ethnic divisions are described as 'separate development'; foreign labourers deprived of citizenship rights are described as 'guest workers'.

[...]

Ideology *qua* dissimulation may be expressed through another strategy, or cluster of strategies, which we may subsume under the general label of *trope*. By trope I mean the figurative use of language or, more generally, of symbolic forms. The study of trope is generally confined to the domain of literature, but the figurative use of language is much more widespread than this disciplinary specialization would suggest. . . . Thus the former British Prime Minister Margaret Thatcher was often described as 'the Iron Lady', a metaphor which endowed her with a super-human determination and firmness of will. Or consider this comment by Margaret Thatcher herself, made in an interview with the Press Association in 1988 and reported in the British daily the *Guardian*: reflecting on her first eight years in office and on her perception of the changing status of Britain among the Western industrial nations, she observes that 'They used, when I first came in, to talk about us in terms of the British disease. Now they talk about us and say "Look, Britain has got the cure." ' The metaphor of disease and cure, combined with the language of 'us' and 'them', gives this comment a vivid and evocative character; it shrouds the process of social and economic development in the imagery of illness and health, while neglecting or glossing over the actual circumstances underlying and affecting this process.

[· · ·]

A third *modus operandi* of ideology is *unification*. Relations of domination may be established and sustained by constructing, at the symbolic level, a form of unity which embraces individuals in a collective identity, irrespective of the differences and divisions that may separate them. A typical strategy by means of which this mode is expressed in symbolic forms is the strategy of *standardization*. Symbolic forms are adapted to a standard framework which is promoted as the shared and acceptable basis of symbolic exchange. . . . Another strategy of symbolic construction by means of which unification can be achieved is what we may describe as the *symbolization of unity*. This strategy involves the construction of symbols of unity, of collective identity and identification, which are diffused throughout a group or plurality of groups. Here again, the construction of symbols of national unity, such as flags, national anthems, emblems and inscriptions of various kinds, are evident examples.

[· · ·]

A fourth mode through which ideology may operate is *fragmentation*. Relations of domination may be maintained, not by unifying individuals in a collectivity, but by fragmenting those individuals and groups that might be capable of mounting an effective challenge to dominant groups, or by orienting forces of potential opposition towards a target which is projected as evil, harmful or threatening. Here a typical strategy of symbolic construction is *differentiation* – that is, emphasizing the distinctions, differences and divisions between individuals and groups, the characteristics which *dis*unite them and prevent them from constituting an effective challenge to existing relations or an effective participant in the exercise of power. Another pertinent strategy may be described as the *expurgation of the other*. This involves the construction of an enemy, either within or without, which is portrayed as evil, harmful or threatening and which individuals are called upon collectively to resist or expurgate.

[. . .]

A fifth *modus operandi* of ideology is *reification*: relations of domination may be established and sustained by representing a transitory, historical state of affairs as if it were permanent, natural, outside of time. Processes are portrayed as things or as events of a quasi-natural kind, in such a way that their social and historical character is eclipsed. . . . This mode may be expressed in symbolic forms by means of the strategy of *naturalization*. A state of affairs which is a social and historical creation may be treated as a natural event or as the inevitable outcome of natural characteristics, in the way, for example, that the socially instituted division of labour between men and women may be portrayed as the product of the physiological characteristics of and differences between the sexes. A similar strategy is what may be described as *eternalization*: social–historical phenomena are deprived of their historical character by being portrayed as permanent, unchanging and ever-recurring.

[. . .]

Ideology *qua* reification may also be expressed by means of various grammatical and syntactic devices, such as *nominalization* and *passivization*. Nominalization occurs when sentences or parts of sentences, descriptions of action and the participants involved in them, are turned into nouns, as when we say 'the banning of imports' instead of 'the Prime Minister has decided to ban imports'. Passivization occurs when verbs are rendered in the passive form, as when we say 'the suspect is being investigated' instead of 'police officers are investigating the suspect'. Nominalization and passivization focus the attention of the hearer or reader on certain themes at the expense of others. They delete actors and agency and they tend to represent processes as things or events which take place in the absence of a subject who produces them. They also tend to elide references to specific spatial and temporal contexts by eliminating verbal constructions or converting them into the continuous tense. These and other grammatical or syntactic devices may, in particular circumstances, serve to establish and sustain relations of domination by reifying social–historical phenomena. Representing processes as things, deleting actors and agency, constituting time as an eternal extension of the present tense: these are so many ways of re-establishing the dimension of society 'without history' at the heart of historical society.

By identifying these various modes of operation of ideology and some of the typical strategies of symbolic construction with which they may be associated and through which they may be expressed, I have called attention to some of the ways in which we can begin to think about the interplay of meaning and power in social life. I have called attention to some of the strategies and devices by virtue of which meaning can be constructed and conveyed in the social world, and some of the ways in which the meaning thus conveyed can serve to establish and sustain relations of power. . . . Particular strategies of symbolic construction, or particular kinds of symbolic forms, are not ideological as such: whether the meaning generated by symbolic strategies, or conveyed by symbolic forms, serves to establish and sustain relations of domination is a question that can be answered only by examining the specific contexts within which symbolic forms are produced and received, only by examining the specific mechanisms by which they are transmitted from producers to receivers, and only by examining the sense which these symbolic forms have for the subjects who produce and receive them.

15

The Tasks of a Critical Theory

Jürgen Habermas

With its distinction between system and lifeworld, the theory of communicative action brings out the independent logic of socializatory interaction; the corresponding distinction between two contrary types of communication media makes us sensitive to the ambivalent potential of mass communications. The theory makes us skeptical of the thesis that the essence of the public sphere has been liquidated in postliberal societies. According to Horkheimer and Adorno, the communication flows steered via mass media *take the place of* those communication structures that had once made possible public discussion and self-understanding by citizens and private individuals. With the shift from writing to images and sounds, the electronic media – first film and radio, later television – present themselves as an apparatus that completely permeates and dominates the language of everyday communication. On the one hand, it transforms the authentic content of modern culture into the sterilized and ideologically effective stereotypes of a mass culture that merely replicates what exists; on the other hand, it uses up a culture cleansed of all subversive and transcending elements for an encompassing system of social controls, which is spread over individuals, in part reinforcing their weakened internal behavioral controls, in part replacing them. The mode of functioning of the culture industry is said to be a mirror image of the psychic apparatus, which, as long as the internalization of paternal authority was still functioning, had subjected instinctual nature to the control of the superego in the way that technology had subjected outer nature to its domination.

Against this theory we can raise the empirical objections that can always be brought against stylizing oversimplifications – that it proceeds ahistorically and does not take into consideration the structural change in the bourgeois public sphere; that it is not complex enough to take account of the marked national differences – from differences between private, public–legal, and state-controlled organizational structures of broadcasting agencies, to differences in programming, viewing practices, political culture, and so forth. But there is an even more serious objection.

I distinguished two sorts of media that can ease the burden of the (risky and demanding) coordinating mechanism of reaching understanding: on the one hand, steering media, via which subsystems are differentiated out of the lifeworld; on the other hand, generalized forms of communication, which do not replace reaching agreement in language but merely condense it, and thus remain tied to lifeworld contexts. Steering media uncouple the coordination of action from building consensus in language altogether and neutralize it in regard to the alternative of coming to an agreement or failing to do so. In the other case we are dealing with a specialization of linguistic processes of consensus formation that remains dependent on recourse to the resources of the lifeworld background. The mass media belong to these generalized forms of communication. They free communication processes from the provinciality of spatiotemporally restricted contexts and permit public spheres to emerge, through establishing the abstract simultaneity of a virtually present network of communication contents far removed in space and time and through keeping messages available for manifold contexts.

These media publics hierarchize and at the same time remove restrictions on the horizon of possible communication. The one aspect cannot be separated from the other – and therein lies their ambivalent potential. Insofar as mass media one-sidedly channel communication flows in a centralized network – from the center to the periphery or from above to below – they considerably strengthen the efficacy of social controls. But tapping this authoritarian potential is always precarious because there is a counterweight of emancipatory potential built into communication structures themselves. Mass media can simultaneously contextualize and concentrate processes of reaching understanding, but it is only in the first instance that they relieve interaction from yes/no responses to criticizable validity claims. Abstracted and clustered though they are, these communications cannot be reliably shielded from the possibility of opposition by responsible actors.

When communications research is not abridged in an empiricist manner and allows for dimensions of reification in communicative everyday practice, it confirms this ambivalence. Again and again reception research and program analysis have provided illustrations of the theses in culture criticism that Adorno, above all, developed with a certain overstatement. In the meantime, the same energy has been put into working out the contradictions resulting from the facts that

1 the broadcasting networks are exposed to competing interests; they are not able to integrate economic, political and ideological, professional and aesthetic viewpoints smoothly;
2 normally the mass media cannot, without generating conflict, avoid the obligations that accrue to them from their journalistic mission and the professional code of journalism;
3 the programs do not only, or even for the most part, reflect the standards of mass culture; even when they take the trivial forms of popular entertainment, they may contain critical messages – "popular culture as popular revenge";
4 ideological messages miss their audience because the intended meaning is turned into its opposite under conditions of being received against a certain subcultural background;
5 the inner logic of everyday communicative practice sets up defenses against the direct manipulative intervention of the mass media; and
6 the technical development of electronic media does not necessarily move in the direction of centralizing networks, even though "video pluralism" and "television democracy" are at the moment not much more than anarchist visions.

My thesis concerning the colonization of the lifeworld, for which Weber's theory of societal rationalization served as a point of departure, is based on a critique of functionalist reason, which agrees with the critique of instrumental reason only in its intention and in its ironic use of the word "reason". One major difference is that the theory of communicative action conceives of the lifeworld as a sphere in which processes of reification do not appear as mere reflexes – as manifestations of a repressive integration emanating from an oligopolistic economy and an authoritarian state. In this respect, the earlier critical theory merely repeated the errors of Marxist functionalism. My references to the socializatory relevance of the uncoupling of system and lifeworld and my remarks on the ambivalent potentials of mass media and mass culture show the private and public spheres in the light of a rationalized lifeworld in which system imperatives *clash with* independent communication structures. The transposition of communicative action to media-steered interactions and the deformation of the structures of a damaged intersubjectivity are by no means predecided processes that might be distilled from a few global concepts. The analysis of lifeworld pathologies calls for an (unbiased) investigation of tendencies *and* contradictions. The fact that in welfare-state mass democracies class conflict has been institutionalized and thereby pacified does not mean that protest potential has been altogether laid to rest. But the potentials for protest emerge now along different lines of conflict – just where we would expect them to emerge if the thesis of the colonization of the lifeworld were correct.

In the past decade or two, conflicts have developed in advanced Western societies that deviate in various ways from the welfare-state pattern of institutionalized conflict over distribution. They no longer flare up in domains of material reproduction; they are no longer channeled through parties and associations; and they can no longer be allayed by compensations. Rather, these new conflicts arise in domains of cultural reproduction, social integration, and socialization; they are carried out in subinstitutional – or at least extraparliamentary – forms of protest; and the underlying deficits reflect a reification of communicatively structured domains of action that will not respond to the media of money and power. The issue is not primarily one of compensations that the welfare state can provide, but of defending and restoring endangered ways of life. In short, the new conflicts are not ignited by distribution problems but by questions having to do with the grammar of forms of life.

This new type of conflict is an expression of the "silent revolution" in values and attitudes that R. Inglehart has observed in entire populations. Studies by Hildebrandt and Dalton, and by Barnes and Kaase, confirm the change in themes from the "old politics" (which turns on questions of economic and social security, internal and military security) to a "new politics." The new problems have to do with quality of life, equal rights, individual self-realization, participation, and human rights. In terms of social statistics, the "old politics" is more strongly supported by employers, workers, and middle-class tradesmen, whereas the new politics finds stronger support in the new middle classes, among the younger generation, and in groups with more formal education. These phenomena tally with my thesis regarding internal colonization.

If we take the view that the growth of the economic–administrative complex sets off processes of erosion in the lifeworld, then we would expect old conflicts to be overlaid with new ones. A line of conflict forms between, on the one hand, a center composed of strata *directly* involved in the production process and interested in maintaining capitalist growth as the basis of the welfare-state compromise, and, on the other hand, a periphery composed of a variegated array of groups that are lumped together. Among the latter are those groups that are further removed from the "productivist core of performance" in late capitalist societies, that have been more strongly sensitized to the self-destructive consequences of the growth in complexity or have been more strongly affected by them. The bond that unites these heterogeneous groups is the critique of growth. Neither the bourgeois emancipation movements nor the struggles of the organized labor movement can serve as a model for this protest. Historical parallels are more likely to be found in the social–romantic movements of the early industrial period, which were supported by craftsmen, plebians, and workers, in the defensive movements of the populist middle class, in the escapist movements (nourished by bourgeois critiques of civilization) undertaken by reformers, the *Wandervögel*, and the like.

The current potentials for protest are very difficult to classify, because scenes, groupings, and topics change very rapidly. To the extent that organizational nuclei are formed at the level of parties or associations, members are recruited from the same diffuse reservoir. The following catchphrases serve at the moment to identify the various currents in the Federal Republic of Germany: the antinuclear and environmental movements; the peace movement (including the theme of north–south conflict); single-issue and local movements; the alternative movement (which encompasses the urban "scene," with its squatters and alternative projects, as well as the rural communes); the minorities (the elderly, gays, handicapped, and so forth); the psychoscene, with support groups and youth sects; religious fundamentalism; the tax-protest movement, school protest by parents' associations, resistance to "modernist" reforms; and, finally, the women's movement. Of international significance are the autonomy movements struggling for regional, linguistic, cultural, and also religious independence.

In this spectrum I will differentiate emancipatory potentials from potentials for resistance and withdrawal. After the American civil rights movement – which has since issued in a particularistic self-affirmation of black subcultures – only the feminist movement stands in the tradition of bourgeois-socialist liberation movements. The struggle against patriarchal oppression and for the redemption of a promise that has long been anchored in the acknowledged universalistic foundations of morality and law gives feminism the impetus of an offensive movement, whereas the other movements have a more defensive character. The resistance and withdrawal movements aim at stemming formally organized domains of action for the sake of communicatively structured domains, and not at conquering new territory. There is an element of particularism that connects feminism with these movements; the emancipation of women means not only establishing formal equality and eliminating male privilege, but overturning concrete forms of life marked by male monopolies. Furthermore, the historical legacy of the sexual division of labor to which women were subjected in the bourgeois nuclear family has given them access to contrasting virtues, to a register of values complementary to those of the male world and opposed to a one-sidedly rationalized everyday practice.

Within resistance movements we can distinguish further between the defense of traditional and social rank (based on property) and a defense that already operates on the basis of a rationalized lifeworld and tries out new ways of cooperating and living together. This criterion makes it possible to demarcate the protest of the traditional middle classes against threats to neighborhoods by large technical projects, the protest of parents against comprehensive schools, the protest against taxes (patterned after the movement in support of Proposition 13 in California), and most of the movements for autonomy, on the one side, from the core of a new conflict potential, on the other: youth and alternative movements for which a critique of growth sparked by themes of ecology and peace is the common focus. It is possible to conceive of these conflicts in terms of resistance to tendencies toward a colonization of the lifeworld, as I hope now to indicate, at least in a cursory way. The objectives, attitudes, and ways of acting prevalent in youth protest groups can be understood, to begin with, as reactions to certain problem situations that are perceived with great sensitivity.

The intervention of large-scale industry into ecological balances, the growing scarcity of nonrenewable natural resources, as well as demographic developments present industrially developed societies with major problems; but these challenges are abstract at first and call for technical and economic solutions, which must in turn be globally planned and implemented by administrative means. What sets off the protest is rather the tangible destruction of the urban environment; the despoliation of the countryside through housing developments, industrialization, and pollution; the impairment of health through the ravages of civilization, pharmaceutical side-effects, and the like – that is, developments that noticeably affect the organic foundations of the lifeworld and make us drastically aware of standards of livability, of inflexible limits to the deprivation of sensual-aesthetic background needs.

There are certainly good reasons to fear military potentials for destruction, nuclear power plants, atomic waste, genetic engineering, the storage and central utilization of private data, and the like. These real anxieties are combined, however, with the terror of a new category of risks that are literally invisible and are comprehensible only from the perspective of the system. These risks invade the lifeworld and at the same time burst its dimensions. The anxieties function as catalysts for a feeling of being overwhelmed in view of the possible consequences of processes for which we are morally accountable – since we do set them in motion technically and politically – and yet for which we can no longer take moral responsibility – since their scale has put them beyond our control. Here resistance is directed against abstractions that are forced upon the lifeworld, although they go beyond the spatial, temporal, and social limits of complexity of even highly differentiated lifeworlds, centered as these are around the senses.

Something that is expressed rather blatantly in the manifestations of the psychomovement and renewed religious fundamentalism is also a motivating force behind most alternative projects and many citizens' action groups – the painful manifestations of deprivation in a culturally impoverished and one-sidedly rationalized practice of everyday life. For this reason, ascriptive characteristics such as gender, age, skin color, neighborhood or locality, and religious affiliation serve to build up and separate off communities, to establish subculturally protected communities supportive of the search for personal and collective identity. The revaluation of the particular, the natural, the provincial, of social spaces that are small enough to be familiar, of decentralized forms of commerce and despecialized activities, of segmented pubs, simple interactions and dedifferentiated public spheres – all this is meant to foster the revitalization of possibilities for expression and communication that have been buried alive. Resistance to reformist interventions that turn into their opposite, because the means by which they are implemented run counter to the declared aims of social integration, also belongs in this context.

The new conflicts arise along the seams between system and lifeworld. The interchange between the private and public spheres, on the one hand, and the economic and administrative action systems, on the other, takes place via the media of money and power, and how it is institutionalized in the roles of employees and consumers, citizens and clients of the state. It is just these roles that are the targets of protest. Alternative practice is directed against the profit-dependent instrumentalization of work in one's vocation, the market-dependent mobilization of labor power, against the extension of pressures of competition and performance all the way down into elementary school. It also takes aim at the monetarization of services, relationships, and time, at the consumerist redefinition of private spheres of life and personal lifestyles. Furthermore, the relation of clients to public service agencies is to be opened up and reorganized in a participatory mode, along the lines of self-help organizations. It is above all in the domains of social policy and health policy (e.g. in connection with psychiatric care) that models of reform point in this direction. Finally, certain forms of protest negate the definitions of the role of citizen and the routines for pursuing interests in a purposive-rational manner – forms ranging from the undirected explosion of disturbances by youth ("Zurich is burning!"), through calculated or surrealistic violations of rules (after the pattern of the American civil rights movement and student protests), to violent provocation and intimidation.

According to the programmatic conceptions of some theoreticians, a partial disintegration of the social roles of employees and consumers, of clients and citizens of the state, is supposed to clear the way for counter-institutions that develop from within the lifeworld in order to set limits to the inner dynamics of the economic and political–administrative action systems. These institutions are supposed, on the one hand, to divert out of the economic system a second, informal sector that is no longer oriented to profit and, on the other hand, to oppose to the party system new forms of a "politics in the first person," a politics that is expressive and at the same time has a democratic base. Such institutions would reverse just those abstractions and neutralizations by which in modern societies labor and political will-formation have been tied to media-steered interaction. The capitalist enterprise and the mass party (as an "ideology-neutral organization for acquiring power") generalize their points of social entry via labor markets and manufactured public spheres; they treat their employees and voters as abstract labor power and voting subjects; and they keep at a distance – as environments of the system – those spheres in which personal and collective identities can alone take shape. By contrast, the counter-institutions are intended to dedifferentiate some parts of the formally organized domains of action, remove them from the clutches of the steering media, and return these "liberated areas" to the action-coordinating mechanism of reaching understanding.

However unrealistic these ideas may be, they are important for the polemical significance of the new resistance and withdrawal movements reacting to the colonization of the lifeworld. This significance is obscured, both in the self-understanding of those involved and in the ideological imputations of their opponents, if the communicative rationality of cultural modernity is rashly equated with the functionalist rationality of self-maintaining economic and administrative action systems – that is, whenever the rationalization of the lifeworld is not carefully distinguished from the increasing complexity of the social system. This confusion explains the fronts – which are out of place and obscure the real political oppositions – between the antimodernism of the Young Conservatives and the neoconservative defense of postmodernity that robs a modernity at variance with itself of its rational content and its perspectives on the future.

16

The Normative Content of Modernity

Jürgen Habermas

The paradoxes of societal rationalization may be summarized in an oversimplified way as follows. The rationalization of the lifeworld had to reach a certain maturity before the media of money and power could be legally institutionalized in it. The two functional systems of the market economy and the administrative state, which grew beyond the horizon of the political orders of stratified class societies, destroyed the traditional life forms of old European society to begin with. The internal dynamic of these two functionally intermeshed subsystems, however, also reacts back upon the rationalized life forms of modern society that made them possible, to the extent that processes of monetarization and bureaucratization penetrate the core domains of cultural reproduction, social integration, and socialization. Forms of interaction shaped by these media cannot encroach upon realms of life that by their function are dependent on action oriented to mutual understanding without the appearance of pathological side-effects. In the political systems of advanced capitalist societies, we find compromise structures that, historically considered, can be conceived of as reactions on the part of the lifeworld to the independent systemic logic and growth in complexity proper to the capitalist economic process and a state apparatus with a monopoly on force. These origins have left their traces on the options that remain open to us in a social-welfare state in crisis.

The options are determined by the logic of a politics adjusted to the system imperatives of economy and state. The two media-steered subsystems, which constitute environments for one another, are supposed to be intelligently attuned to one another – and not simply to reciprocally externalize their costs so as to burden a total system incapable of self-reflection. Within the scope of such a politics, only the correctly dosed distribution of problems as between the subsystems of state and economy is in dispute. One side sees the causes of crisis in the unleashing of the dynamics proper to the economy; the other side, in the bureaucratic fetters imposed on the former. The corresponding therapies are a social subduing of capitalism or a displacement of problems from administrative planning back to the market. The one side sees the source of the systemically induced disturbances of everyday life in monetarized labor power; the other, in the bureaucratic crippling of personal initiative. But both sides agree in assigning a merely passive role to the vulnerable domains of lifeworld interaction as against the motors of societal modernization: state and economy.

Meanwhile, the legitimists of the social-welfare state are everywhere in retreat, while the neoconservatives complacently undertake to terminate the social-welfare-state compromise – or at least to redefine its conditions. In return for an energetic improvement of the valorization conditions of capital, neoconservatives accept in the bargain costs that can be shifted in the short term to the lifeworld of the underprivileged and marginalized, but also risks that rebound upon society as a whole. There arise the new class structures of a society segmented on its ever widening margins. Economic growth is kept going by innovations that for the first time are *intentionally* tied to an armaments spiral that has gone out of control. At the same time, the intrinsic normative logic of rationalized lifeworlds now finds expression, however selectively, not only in the classical demands for more distributive justice, but in the wide spectrum of so-called postmaterial values, in the interest in conserving the natural bases of human life and in preserving the internal communicative structures of highly differentiated life forms. So it is that system imperatives and lifeworld imperatives form new frictional surfaces that spark new conflicts which cannot be dealt with in the existing compromise structures. The question posed today is whether a new compromise can be arranged in accord with the old rules of system-oriented politics – or whether the crisis management attuned to crises that are systemically caused and perceived as systemic will be undermined by social movements no longer oriented to the system's steering needs, but to the *processes at the boundaries* between system and lifeworld.

With this question we touch upon the other moment – the possibility of mastering crises in grand format, for which praxis philosophy once offered the means of revolutionary praxis. If society as a whole is no longer thought of as a higher-level subject that knows itself, determines itself, and realizes itself, there are no paths of relation-to-self upon which the revolutionaries could enter in order to work with, for, and on the crippled macrosubject. Without a self-relating macrosubject, anything like a self-reflective knowledge on the part of the social totality is just as *inconceivable* as society's having an influence upon itself. As soon as the higher-level intersubjectivity of public processes of opinion and consensus formation takes the place of the higher-level subject of society as a whole, relationships-to-self of this kind lose their meaning. It is questionable whether under these changed premises it still makes any sense to speak of a "society exercising influence upon itself."

For a society to influence itself in this sense it must have, on the one hand, a reflexive center, where it builds up a knowledge of itself in a process of self-understanding, and, on the other hand, an executive system that, as a part, can act for the whole and influence the whole. Can modern societies meet these conditions? Systems theory projects a picture of them as acentric societies "without central organs." On this account, the lifeworld has disintegrated without remainder into the functionally specialized subsystems such as economy, state, education, science, etc. These systemic monads, which have replaced withered intersubjective relationships with functional connections, are symmetrically related to one another, but their precarious equilibrium is not susceptible of being regulated for society as a whole. They must reciprocally balance one another, since none of the total societal functions that come to the fore with them attains a *primacy* for society as a whole. None of the subsystems could occupy the top of a hierarchy and represent the whole the way the emperor could once do for the empire in stratified societies. Modern societies no longer have at their disposal an authoritative center for self-reflection and steering.

From the viewpoint of systems theory, only the subsystems develop anything like a *self-consciousness*, and they do so only in view of their *own* function. The whole is reflected in the partial system's self-consciousness only from the perspective of that system, as its respective social *environment*: "Hence, a consensus functional for society as a whole about what is and what is valid is difficult, in fact impossible; what is used as a consensus functions in the form of a recognized provisional arrangement. In addition to this, there are the really productive syntheses of reality that are functionally specific at the levels of complexity that individual functional systems can achieve for themselves but can no longer add up to a comprehensive world view in the sense of a *congregatio corporum*, or a *universitas rerum*."[1] Luhmann elaborates on this "provisional arrangement" in a footnote as follows: "It was a peculiar decision of Husserlian philosophy, with considerable ramifications for sociological discussions, to endow this provisional arrangement with the status of an ultimately valid basis of a concrete *a priori* by giving it the title of 'lifeworld.'" It is sociologically untenable to postulate for the lifeworld any kind of "primacy in being."

The legacy of Husserlian apriorism may mean a burden for various versions of social phenomenology; but the communications-theoretic concept of the lifeworld has been freed from the mortgages of transcendental philosophy. If one is to take the basic fact of *linguistic* socialization into account, one will be hard put to do without this notion. Participants in interaction cannot carry out speech acts that are effective for coordination unless they impute to everyone involved an intersubjectively shared lifeworld that is angled toward the situation of discourse and anchored in bodily centers. For those acting in the first person singular or plural with an orientation to mutual understanding, each lifeworld constitutes a totality of meaning relations and referential connections with a zero point in the coordinate system shaped by historical time, social space, and semantic field. Moreover, the different lifeworlds that collide with one another do not stand *next to each other* without any mutual understanding. As totalities, they follow the pull of their claims to universality and work out their differences until their horizons of understanding "fuse" with one another, as Gadamer puts it. Consequently, even modern, largely decentered societies maintain in their everyday communicative action a virtual center of self-understanding, from which even functionally specified systems of action remain within intuitive reach, as long as they do not outgrow the horizon of the lifeworld. This center is, of course, a projection, but it is an effective one. The polycentric projections of the totality – which anticipate, outdo, and incorporate one another – generate competing centers. Even collective identities dance back and forth in the flux of interpretations, and are actually more suited to the image of a fragile network than to that of a stable center of self-reflection.

Nevertheless, everyday practice affords a locus for spontaneous processes of self-understanding and identity formation, even in nonstratified societies that no longer have a knowledge of themselves available in the traditional forms of representative self-presentation. Even in modern societies, a diffuse common consciousness takes shape from the polyphonous and obscure projections of the totality. This common consciousness can be concentrated and more clearly articulated around specific themes and ordered contributions; it achieves greater clarity in the higher-level, concentrated communicative processes of a public sphere. Technologies of communication – such as book publishing and the press, first of all, and then radio and television – make utterances available for practically any context, and make possible a highly differentiated network of public spheres – local and transregional, literary, scientific, and political, within parties or associations, media-dependent or subcultural. Within these public spheres, processes of opinion and consensus formation, which depend upon diffusion and mutual interpenetration no matter how specialized they are, get institutionalized. The boundaries are porous; each public sphere is open to other public spheres. To their discursive structures they owe a universalist tendency that is hardly concealed. All partial public spheres point to a comprehensive public sphere in which society as a whole fashions a knowledge of itself. The European Enlightenment elaborated this experience and took it up into its programmatic formulas.

What Luhmann calls "the consensus functioning for the whole of society" is context-dependent and fallible – provisional in fact. But this reflexive knowledge on the part of society as a whole *exists*. Only now it is due to the higher-level intersubjectivity of public spheres and hence can no longer satisfy the sharp criteria of self-reflection by a higher-level subject. Of course, such a center of self-understanding is insufficient for a society to exercise influence over itself; for this, it would also require a central steering authority that could receive and translate into action the knowledge and the impulses from the public sphere.

According to the normative ideas of our political tradition, the democratically legitimated apparatus of state – having been shifted from the sovereignty of princes to the sovereignty of the people – is supposed to be able to put into effect the opinion and will of the citizenry as a public. The citizens themselves participate in the formation of collective consciousness, but they cannot act collectively. Can the government do so? "Collective action" would mean that the government would transpose the intersubjectively constituted self-knowledge of society organizationally into the self-determination of society. And yet, even on systems-theoretic grounds, one has to doubt this possibility. As a matter of fact, today politics has become an affair of a functionally specialized subsystem; and the latter does not dispose over the measure of autonomy relative to the other subsystems that would be required for central steering, that is, for an influence of society as a totality upon itself, an influence that comes from it and goes back to it.

In modern societies, there obviously exists an asymmetry between the (weak) capacities for intersubjective self-understanding and the (missing) capacities for the self-organization of society as a whole. Under these changed premises, there is no equivalent for the philosophy of the subject's model of self-influence in general and for the Hegelian–Marxist understanding of revolutionary action in particular.

This insight has come into broad effect, carried along by a specific experience that labor parties and unions have had, above all, in their attempts to realize the social-welfare-state project since the end of the Second World War. I am talking neither about the economic problems that cropped up as a result of successful social-welfare legislation during the period of reconstruction, nor about the limits upon the power and the ability of planning administrations to intervene, nor about problems of *steering* at all. I mean, rather, a characteristic transformation in the perception of the democratically legitimated state power that had to be brought to bear in pursuing the goal of "socially taming" the naturelike capitalist economic system, and especially the goal of neutralizing the destructive side effects of its crisis-filled expansion on the existence and lifeworld of dependent workers. Advocates of the social-welfare state regarded it as unproblematic that an active government should intervene not only in the economic cycle but also in the life cycle of its citizens – the goal indeed was to reform the living conditions of the citizens by way of reforming the conditions of labor and employment. Underlying this was the democratic tradition's idea that society could exercise an influence over itself by the neutral means of political–administrative power. Just this expectation has been disappointed.

In the meantime, an increasingly dense network of legal norms, of governmental and paragovernmental bureaucracies, has been drawn over the everyday life of its actual and potential clients. Extensive discussions about legal regulation and bureaucratization in general, about the counterproductive effects of government welfare policies in particular, about the professionalization and scientization of social services have drawn attention to circumstances that make one thing clear: the legal–administrative means of translating social-welfare programs into action are not some passive, as it were, propertyless medium. They are connected, rather, with a praxis that involves isolation of facts, normalization, and surveillance, the reifying and subjectivating violence of which Foucault has traced right down into the most delicate capillary tributaries of everyday communication. The deformations of a lifeworld that is regulated, fragmented, monitored, and looked after are surely more subtle than the palpable forms of material exploitation and impoverishment; but internalized social conflicts that have shifted from the corporeal to the psychic are not therefore less destructive.

Today one sees the contradiction inherent in the social-welfare-state project as such. Its substantive goal was to set free life forms structured in an egalitarian way, which were supposed at the same time to open up space for individual self-realization and spontaneity; but too great a demand was placed upon the medium of power in expecting it to call forth new forms of life. Once the state has been differentiated out as one among many media-steered functional systems, it should no longer be regarded as the central steering authority in which society brings together its capabilities for organizing itself. A functional system that has grown beyond the horizon of the lifeworld and become independent, that shuts itself off from perspectives of society as a whole, and that can perceive society as a whole only from the perspective of a subsystem, stands over against processes of opinion and will formation in a general public sphere, which, however diffuse, are still directed to society as a whole.

A new, as it were, stereoscopically sharpened view of "the political" emerges from the historical disillusionment with a bureaucratically coagulated social-welfare-state project. In addition to the independent systemic logic of a power medium that only seems to be usable in a purposive-rational manner, another dimension becomes visible. The public sphere as political, in which complex societies can acquire normative distance from themselves and work out experiences of crisis collectively, takes on a remoteness from the political system similar to the remoteness it previously had from the economic system. The political system has acquired a similarly problematic character, or at least one with two battlefronts. Now it is itself perceived as a source of steering problems, and not simply as a means for the solution of problems. Thus, we have become conscious of *the difference between steering problems and problems of mutual understanding.* We can see the difference between systemic disequilibria and lifeworld pathologies, between disturbances of material reproduction and deficiencies in the symbolic reproduction of the lifeworld. We come to recognize the distinction between the deficits that inflexible structures of the lifeworld can cause in the maintenance of the systems of employment and domination (via the withdrawal of motivation or legitimation), on the one hand, and manifestations of a colonization of the lifeworld by the imperatives of functional systems that externalize their costs on the other. Such phenomena demonstrate once more that the achievements of steering and those of mutual understanding are resources that cannot be freely substituted for one another. Money and power can neither buy nor compel solidarity and meaning. In brief, the result of the process of disillusionment is a new state of consciousness in which the social-welfare-state project becomes reflexive to a certain extent and aims at taming not just the capitalist economy, but the state itself.

However, if not only capitalism but also the interventionist state itself is to be "socially tamed," the task has to be defined anew. The welfare-state project entrusted the planning capacity of public administrations with having a stimulating influence upon the self-steering mechanism of a *different* subsystem. If this "regulation," applied so very indirectly, is now supposed to extend to the organizational performances of the state, the mode of influence may not be specified again as indirect steering, for a new *steering* potential could only be furnished by *another* subsystem.

Even if we could come up with a supplementary system of this sort, after a further round of disappointment and distantiation we would again face the problem that *perceptions of crises in the lifeworld* cannot be translated without remainder into *systems-related problems of steering*.

Instead, it is a question of building up restraining barriers for the exchanges between system and lifeworld and of building in sensors for the exchanges between lifeworld and system. At any rate, limit problems of this sort are posed as soon as a highly rationalized lifeworld is to be shielded against the intolerable imperatives of the occupational system or against the penetrating side-effects of the administrative provision for life. The systemic spell cast by the capitalist labor market over the life histories of those able to work, by the network of responsible, regulating, and supervising public authorities over the life forms of their clients, and by the now autonomous nuclear arms race over the life expectancy of peoples, cannot be broken by systems learning to function better. Rather, impulses from the lifeworld must be able to enter into the self-steering of functional systems. Of course, this would require altering the relationship between autonomous, self-organized public spheres, on the one hand, and realms of action steered by money and power, on the other, or in other words: a new division of powers within the dimension of social integration. The socially integrating power of solidarity would have to be in a position to assert itself against the systemically integrating steering media of money and power.

I call those public spheres autonomous which are neither bred nor kept by a political system for purposes of creating legitimation. Centers of concentrated communication that arise spontaneously out of microdomains of everyday practice can develop into autonomous public spheres and consolidate as self-supporting higher-level intersubjectivities only to the degree that the lifeworld potential for self-organization and for the self-organized use of the means of communication are utilized. Forms of self-organization strengthen the collective capacity for action. Grassroots organizations, however, may not cross the threshold to the formal organization of independent systems. Otherwise they will pay for the indisputable gain in complexity by having organizational goals detached from the orientations and attitudes of their members and dependent instead upon imperatives of maintaining and expanding organizational power. The lack of symmetry between capacities for self-reflection and for self-organization that we have ascribed to modern societies as a whole is repeated on the level of the self-organization of processes of opinion and will formation.

This need not be an obstacle, if one considers that the indirect influence of functionally differentiated subsystems on the individual mechanisms of self-steering means something altogether different from the goal-oriented influence of society upon itself. Their self-referential closedness renders the functional systems of politics and economics immune against attempts at intervention in the sense of *direct* interventions. Yet this same characteristic also renders systems sensitive to stimuli aimed at increasing their capacity for self-reflection, that is, their sensitivity to the reactions of the environment to their own activities. Self-organized public spheres must develop the prudent combination of power and intelligent self-restraint that is needed to sensitize the self-steering mechanisms of the state and the economy to the goal-oriented outcomes of radical democratic will formation. In place of the model of society influencing itself, we have the model of boundary conflicts – which are held in check by the lifeworld – between the lifeworld and two subsystems that are superior to it in complexity and can be influenced by it only indirectly, but on whose performances it at the same time depends.

Autonomous public spheres can draw their strength only from the resources of largely rationalized lifeworlds. This holds true especially for culture, that is to say, for science's and philosophy's potential for interpretations of self and world, for the enlightenment potential of strictly universalistic legal and moral representations, and, not last, for the radical experiential contents of aesthetic modernity. It is no accident that social movements today take on cultural–revolutionary traits. Nonetheless, a structural weakness can be noticed here that is indigenous to all modern lifeworlds. Social movements get their thrust-power from threats to well-defined collective identities. Although such identities always remain tied to the particularism of a special form of life, they have to assimilate the normative content of modernity – the fallibilism, universalism, and subjectivism that undermine the force and concrete shape of any given particularity. Until now, the democratic, constitutional nation-state that emerged from the French Revolution was the only identity formation successful on a world-historical scale that could unite these two moments of the universal and the particular without coercion. . . . If not in the nation, in what other soil can universalistic value orientations today take root? The Atlantic community of values crystallized around NATO is hardly more than a propaganda formula for ministers of defense. The Europe of de Gaulle and Adenauer merely furnishes the superstructure for the basis of trade relations. Quite recently, Left intellectuals have been projecting a completely different design as a counter-image to the Europe of the Common Market.

The dream of such a completely different European identity, which assimilates in a decisive way the legacy of Occidental rationalism, is taking shape at a time when the United States is getting ready to fall back into the illusions of the early modern period under the banner of a "second American Revolution." In the utopias painted in the old romances about the state, rational forms of life entered into a deceptive symbiosis with the technological mastery of nature and the ruthless mobilization of social labor power. This equation of happiness and emancipation with power and production has been a source of irritation for the self-understanding of modernity from the start – and it has called forth two centuries of criticism of modernity.

But the same utopian (in the bad sense) gestures of mastery are living on now in a caricature that moves the masses. The science fiction of Star Wars is just good enough for the ideology planners to spark – with the macabre vision of a militarized space – an innovative thrust that would give the colossus of worldwide capitalism sufficient footing for its next round of technological development. Old Europe could only find its way clear to a new identity if it opposed to this short circuit of economic growth, arms race, and "traditional values" the vision of breaking out of these self-inflicted systemic constraints, if it put an end to the confused idea that the normative content of modernity that is stored in rationalized lifeworlds could be set free only by means of ever more complex systems. The idea that the capacity to compete on an international scale – whether in markets or in outer space – is indispensable for our very survival is one of those everyday certitudes in which systemic constraints are condensed. Each one justifies the expansion and intensification of its own forces by the expansion and intensification of the forces of the others, as if it were not the ground rules of social Darwinism that are at the bottom of the play of forces. Modern Europe has created the spiritual presuppositions and the material foundations for a world in which this mentality has taken the place of reason. That is the real heart of the critique of reason since Nietzsche. Who else but Europe could draw from *its own* traditions the insight, the energy, the courage of vision – everything that would be necessary to strip from the (no longer metaphysical, but metabiological) premises of a blind compulsion to system maintenance and system expansion their power to shape our mentality.

Reference

1 Niklas Luhmann, *Gesellschaftsstruktur und Semantik* (Suhrkamp, Frankfurt, 1980), vol. 1, p. 33.

17

Habermas and Lyotard

Richard Rorty

In *Knowledge and Human Interests* Habermas tried to generalize what Marx and Freud had accomplished by grounding their projects of "unmasking" in a more comprehensive theory. The strand in contemporary French thought which Habermas criticizes as "neoconservative" starts off from suspicion of Marx and Freud, suspicion of the masters of suspicion, suspicion of "unmasking." Lyotard, for example, says that he will

> use the term "modern" to designate any science that legitimates itself with reference to a metadiscourse of this kind [i.e. "a discourse of legitimation with respect to its own status, a discourse called philosophy"] making an explicit appeal to some grand narrative, such as the dialectics of the Spirit, the hermeneutics of meaning, the emancipation of the rational or working subject, or the creation of wealth.[1]

He goes on to define "postmodern" as "incredulous towards metanarratives," and to ask "Where, after the metanarratives, can legitimacy reside?"[2] From Lyotard's point of view, Habermas is offering one more metanarrative, a more general and abstract "narrative of emancipation" than the Freudian and Marxian metanarratives.

For Habermas, the problem posed by "incredulity towards metanarratives" is that unmasking only makes sense if we "preserve at least one standard for [the] explanation of the corruption of *all* reasonable standards."[3] If we have no such standard, one which escapes a "totalizing self-referential critique," then distinctions between the naked and the masked, or between theory and ideology, lose their force. If we do not have these distinctions, then we have to give up the Enlightenment notion of "rational criticism of existing institutions," for "rational" drops out. We can still, of course, have criticism, but it will be of the sort which Habermas ascribes to Horkheimer and Adorno: "they abandoned any theoretical approach and practiced *ad hoc* determinate negation. . . . The praxis of negation is what remains of the 'spirit of . . . unremitting theory.' "[4] Anything that Habermas will count as retaining a "theoretical approach" will be counted by an incredulous Lyotard as a "metanarrative." Anything that abandons such an approach will be counted by Habermas as "neoconservative," because it drops the notions which have been used to justify the various reforms which have marked the history of the Western democracies since the Enlightenment, and which are still being used to criticize the socio-economic institutions of both the Free and the Communist worlds. Abandoning a standpoint which is, if not transcendental, at least "universalistic," seems to Habermas to betray the social hopes which have been central to liberal politics.

So we find French critics of Habermas ready to abandon liberal politics in order to avoid universalistic philosophy, and Habermas trying to hang on to universalistic philosophy, with all its problems, in order to support liberal politics. To put the opposition in another way, the French writers whom Habermas criticizes are willing to drop the opposition between "true consensus" and "false consensus," or between "validity" and "power," in order not to have to tell a metanarrative in order to explicate "true" or "valid." But Habermas thinks that if we drop the idea of "the better argument" as opposed to "the argument which convinces a given audience at a given time," we shall have only a "context-dependent" sort of social criticism. He thinks that falling back on such criticism will betray "the elements of reason in cultural modernity which are contained in . . . bourgeois ideals," e.g. "the internal theoretical dynamic which constantly propels the sciences – and the self-reflexion of the sciences as well – *beyond* the creation of merely technologically exploitable knowledge."[5]

Lyotard would respond to this last point by saying that Habermas misunderstands the character of modern science. The discussion of "the pragmatics of science" in *The Postmodern Condition* is intended to "destroy a belief that still underlies Habermas's research, namely that humanity as a collective (universal) subject seeks its common emancipation through the regularization of the 'moves' permitted in all language games, and that the legitimacy of any statement resides in its contribution to that emancipation." Lyotard claims to have shown that "consensus is only a particular state of discussion [in the sciences], not its end. Its end, on the contrary, is paralogy."[6] Part of his argument for this odd suggestion is that "Postmodern science – by concerning itself with such things as undecidables, the limits of precise control, conflicts characterized by incomplete information, '*fracta*', catastrophes, and pragmatic paradoxes – is theorizing its own evolution as discontinuous, catastrophic, non-rectifiable and paradoxical."[7]

I do not think that such examples of matters of current scientific concern do anything to support the claim that "consensus is not the end of discussion." Lyotard argues invalidly from the current concerns of various scientific disciplines to the claim that science is somehow discovering that it should aim at permanent revolution, rather than at the alternation between normality and revolution made familiar by Kuhn. To say that "science aims" at piling paralogy on paralogy is like saying that "politics aims" at piling revolution on revolution. No inspection of the concerns of contemporary science or contemporary politics could show anything of the sort. The most that could be shown is that talk of the aims of either is not particularly useful.

[...]

If one ignores this notion of a recent change in the nature of science (which Lyotard makes only casual and anecdotal attempts to justify), and focuses instead on Lyotard's contrast between "scientific knowledge" and "narrative", that turns out to be pretty much the traditional positivist contrast between "applying the scientific method" and "unscientific" political or religious or common-sensical discourse. Thus Lyotard says that a "scientific statement is subject to the rule that a statement must fulfill a given set of conditions in order to be accepted as scientific."[8] He contrasts this with "narrative knowledge" as the sort which "does not give priority to the question of its own legitimation, and . . . certifies itself in the pragmatics of its own transmission without having recourse to argumentation and proof." He describes "the scientist" as classifying narrative knowledge as "a different mentality: savage, primitive, under-developed, backward, alienated, composed of opinions, customs, authority, prejudice, ignorance, ideology."[9] Lyotard, like Hesse, wants to soften this contrast and to assert the rights of "narrative knowledge." In particular, he wants to answer his initial question by saying that once we get rid of the *meta*narratives, legitimacy resides where it always has, in the first-order narratives:

> There is, then, an incommensurability between popular narrative pragmatics, which provides immediate legitimation, and the language game known as the question of legitimacy. . . . Narratives . . . determine criteria of competence and/or illustrate how they are to be applied. They thus

define what has the right to be said and done in the culture in question, and since they are themselves a part of that culture, they are legitimated by the simple fact that they do what they do.[10]

This last quotation suggests that we read Lyotard as saying: the trouble with Habermas is not so much that he provides a metanarrative of emancipation as that he feels the need to legitimize, that he is not content to let the narratives which hold our culture together do their stuff. He is scratching where it does not itch.

[. . .]

What Habermas calls "the internal theoretical dynamic which constantly propels the sciences . . . beyond the creation of technologically exploitable knowledge" should be seen not as a *theoretical* dynamic, but as a social practice. One will see the reason why modern science is more than engineering not as an ahistorical teleology – e.g. an evolutionary drive towards correspondence with reality, or the nature of language – but as a particularly good example of the social virtues of the European bourgeoisie. The reason will simply be the increasing self-confidence of a community dedicated to (in Blumenberg's phrase) "theoretical curiosity." Modern science will look like something which a certain group of human beings invented in the same sense in which these same people can be said to have invented Protestantism, parliamentary government, and Romantic poetry. What Habermas calls the "self-reflection of the sciences" will thus consist not in the attempt to "ground" scientists' practices (e.g. free exchange of information, normal problem-solving, and revolutionary paradigm creation) in something larger or broader, but rather of attempts to show how these practices link up with, or contrast with, other practices of the same group or of other groups. When such attempts have a critical function, they will take the form of what Habermas calls "*ad hoc* determinate negation."

Habermas thinks that we need not be restricted, as Horkheimer and Adorno were, to such merely socio-historical forms of social criticism. He views Horkheimer, Adorno, Heidegger, and Foucault as working out new versions of "the end of philosophy":

no matter what name it [philosophy] appears under now – whether as fundamental ontology, as critique, as negative dialectic, or genealogy – these pseudonyms are by no means disguises under which the traditional [i.e. Hegelian] form of philosophy lies hidden; the drapery of philosophical concepts more likely serves as the cloak for a scantily concealed end of philosophy.[11]

Habermas's account of such "end of philosophy" movements is offered as part of a more sweeping history of philosophy since Kant. He thinks that Kant was right to split high culture up into science, morality, and art and that Hegel was right in accepting this as "the standard [*massgeblich*] interpretation of modernity."[12] He thinks that "The dignity specific to cultural modernism consists in what Max Weber has called the stubborn differentiation of value-spheres."[13] He also thinks that Hegel was right in believing that "Kant does not perceive the . . . formal divisions within culture . . . as diremptions. Hence he ignores the need for unification that emerges with the separations evoked by the principle of subjectivity."[14] He takes as seriously as Hegel did the question "How can an intrinsic ideal form be constructed from the spirit of modernity, that neither just imitates the historical forms of modernity nor is imposed upon them from the outside?"[15]

From the historicist point of view I share with Geuss, there is no reason to look for an intrinsic ideal that avoids "just imitating the historical forms of modernity." All that social thought can hope to do is to play the various historical forms of modernity off against one another in the way in which, for example, Blumenberg plays "self-assertion" off against "self-grounding." But because Habermas agrees with Hegel that there is a "need for unification" in order to "regenerate the devastated power of religion in the medium of reason,"[16] he wants to go back to Hegel and start again. He thinks that in order to avoid the disillusionment with "the philosophy of subjectivity" which produced Nietzsche and the two strands of post-Nietzschean thought which he distinguishes and dislikes (the one leading to Foucault, and the other to Heidegger), we need to go back to the place where the young Hegel took the wrong turn. That was the place where he still "held open the option of using the idea of uncoerced will formation in a communication community existing under constraints of cooperation as a model for the reconciliation of a bifurcated civil society."[17] He thus suggests that it was the lack of a sense of rationality as *social* that was missing from "the philosophy of the subject" which the older Hegel exemplified (and from which he believes the "end-of-philosophy" thinkers have never really escaped).

But whereas Habermas thinks that the cultural need which "the philosophy of the subject" gratified was and is real, and can perhaps be fulfilled by his own focus on a "communication community," I would urge that it is an artificial problem created by taking Kant too seriously. On this view, the wrong turn was taken when Kant's split between science, morals, and art was accepted as a *donnée*, as *die massgebliche Selbstauslegung der Moderne*. Once that split is taken seriously, then the *Selbstvergewisserung der Moderne*, which Hegel and Habermas both take to the "fundamental philosophical problem," will indeed seem urgent. For once the philosophers swallow Kant's "stubborn differentiation," then they are condemned to an endless series of reductionist and antireductionist moves. Reductionists will try to make everything scientific, or political (Lenin), or aesthetic (Baudelaire, Nietzsche). Antireductionists will show what such attempts leave out. To be a philosopher of the "modern" sort is precisely to be unwilling either to let these spheres simply coexist uncompetitively, or to reduce the other two to the remaining one. Modern philosophy has consisted in forever realigning them, squeezing them together, and forcing them apart again. But it is not clear that these efforts have done the modern age much good (or, for that matter, harm).

Habermas thinks that the older Hegel "solves the problem of the self-reassurance of modernity too well," because the philosophy of Absolute Spirit "removes all importance from its own present age . . . and deprives it of its calling to self-critical renewal."[18] He sees the popularity of "end-of-philosophy" thought as an over-reaction to this over-success. But surely part of the motivation for this kind of thought is the belief that Hegel too was scratching where it did not really itch. Whereas Habermas thinks that it is with Hegel's own over-success that philosophy becomes what Hegel himself called "an isolated sanctuary" whose ministers "form an isolated order of priests . . . untroubled by how it goes with the word," it is surely possible to see this development as having been Kant's fault, if anybody's, and precisely the fault of his "three-sphere" picture of culture. On the latter view, Kant's attempt to deny knowledge to make room for faith (by inventing "transcendental subjectivity" to serve as a fulcrum for the Copernican revolution) was provoked by an unnecessary worry about the spiritual significance, or insignificance, of modern science. Like Habermas, Kant thinks that modern science has a "theoretical dynamic," one which can be identified with (at least a portion of) "the nature of rationality." Both think that by isolating and exhibiting this dynamic, but distinguishing it from other dynamics (e.g. "practical reason" or "the emancipatory interest"), one can keep the results of science without thereby disenchanting the world. Kant suggested that we need not let our knowledge of the world *qua* matter in motion get in the way of our moral sense. The same suggestion was also made by Hume and Reid, but unlike these pragmatical Scottish men, Kant thought that he had to back up this suggestion with a story which would differentiate and "place" the three great spheres into which culture must be divided. From the point of view common to Hume and Reid (who disagreed on so much else) no such metanarrative is needed. What is needed is a sort of intellectual analog of civic virtue – tolerance, irony, and a willingness to let spheres of culture flourish without worrying too much about their "common ground," their unification, the "intrinsic ideals" they suggest, or what picture of man they "presuppose."

In short, by telling a story about Kant as the beginning of modern philosophy (and by emphasizing the difference between modern and pre-modern philosophy) one might make the kind of fervent end-of-philosophy writing Habermas deplores look both more plausible and less interesting. What links Habermas to the French thinkers he criticizes is the conviction that the story of modern philosophy (as successive reactions to Kant's diremptions) is an important part of the story of the democratic societies' attempts at self-reassurance. But it may be that most of the latter story could be told as the history of reformist politics, without much reference to the kinds of theoretical backup which philosophers have provided for such politics. It is, after all, things like the formation of trade unions, the meritocratization of education, the expansion of the franchise, and cheap newspapers which have figured most largely in the willingness of the citizens of the democracies to see themselves as part of a "communicative community" – their continued willingness to say "us" rather than "them" when they speak of their respective countries. This sort of willingness has made religion progressively less important in the self-image of that citizenry. One's sense of relation to a power beyond the community becomes less important as one becomes able to think of oneself as part of a body of public opinion, capable of making a difference to the public fate. That ability has been substantially increased by the various "progressive" changes I have listed.

Weber was of course right in saying that some of these changes have also worked the other way (to increase our sense of being controlled by "them"). But Habermas is so preoccupied with the "alienating" effects of such changes that he allows himself to be distracted from the concomitant increase in people's sense of themselves as free citizens of free countries. The typical German story of the self-consciousness of the modern age (the one which runs from Hegel through Marx, Weber, and Nietzsche) focuses on figures who were preoccupied with the world we lost when we lost the religion of our ancestors. But this story may be both too pessimistic and too exclusively German. If so, then a story about the history of modern thought which took Kant and Hegel less seriously and, for example, the relatively untheoretical socialists more seriously might lead us to a kind of "end-of-philosophy" thinking which would escape Habermas's strictures on Deleuze and Foucault. For these French writers buy in on the usual German story, and thus tend to share Habermas's assumption that the story of the realignment, assimilation, and expansion of the three "value-spheres" is essential to the story of the *Selbstvergewisserung* of modern society, and not just to that of the modern intellectuals.

In order to interpret this problem of the three spheres as a problem only for an increasingly "isolated order of priests," one has to see the "principle of the modern" as something other than that famous "subjectivity" which post-Kantian historians of philosophy, anxious to link Kant with Descartes, took as their guiding thread. One can instead attribute Descartes's role as "founder of modern philosophy" to his development of what I earlier called "an overzealous philosophy of science" – the sort of philosophy of science which saw Galilean mechanics, analytic geometry, mathematical optics, and the like, as having more spiritual significance than they in fact have. By taking the ability to do such science as a mark of something deep and essential to human nature, as the place where we got closest to our true selves, Descartes preserved just those themes in ancient thought which Bacon had tried to obliterate. The preservation of the Platonic idea that our most distinctively human faculty was our ability to manipulate "clear and distinct ideas," rather than to accomplish feats of social engineering, was Descartes's most important and most unfortunate contribution to what we now think of as "modern philosophy." Had Bacon – the prophet of self-assertion, as opposed to self-grounding – been taken more seriously, we might not have been stuck with a canon of "great modern philosophers" who took "subjectivity" as their theme. We might, as J. B. Schneewind puts it, have been less inclined to assume that epistemology (i.e. reflection on the nature and status of natural science) was the "independent variable" in philosophical thought and moral and social philosophy the "dependent variable." We might thereby see what Blumenberg calls "self-assertion" – the willingness to center our hopes on the future of the race, on the unpredictable successes of our descendants – as the "principle of the modern." Such a principle would let us think of the modern age as defined by successive attempts to shake off the sort of ahistorical structure exemplified by Kant's division of culture into three "value-spheres."

On this sort of account, the point I claimed Lyotard shared with Feyerabend and Hesse – the point that there are no interesting epistemological differences between the aims and procedures of scientists and those of politicians – is absolutely fundamental. The recovery of a Baconian, non-Cartesian attitude towards science would permit us to dispense with the idea of "an internal theoretical dynamic" in science, a dynamic which is something more than the "anything goes that works" spirit which unites Bacon and Feyerabend. It would break down the opposition between what Habermas calls "merely technologically exploitable knowledge" and "emancipation," by seeing both as manifestations of what Blumenberg calls "theoretical curiosity." It would free us from preoccupation with the purported tensions between the three "value-spheres" distinguished by Kant and Weber, and between the three sorts of "interests" distinguished by Habermas.

In the present space, I cannot do more than gesture towards the various rosy prospects which appear once one suggests that working through "the principle of subjectivity" (and out the other side) was just a side-show, something which an isolated order of priests devoted themselves to for a few hundred years, something which did not make much difference to the successes and failures of the European countries in realizing the hopes formulated by the Enlightenment. So I shall conclude by turning from the one issue on which I think Lyotard has a point against Habermas to the many issues about which Habermas seems to me in the right.

The thrust of Habermas's claim that thinkers like Foucault, Deleuze, and Lyotard are "neoconservative" is that they offer us no "theoretical" reason to move in one social direction rather than another. They take away the dynamic which liberal social thought (of the sort represented by Rawls in America and Habermas himself in Germany) has traditionally relied upon, namely, the need to be in touch with a reality obscured by "ideology" and disclosed by "theory." Habermas says of Foucault's later work that it

> replaced the model of repression and emancipation developed by Marx and Freud with a pluralism of power/discourse formations. These formations intersect and succeed one another and can be differentiated according to their style and intensity. They cannot, however, be judged in terms of validity, which was possible in the case of the repression and emancipation of conscious as opposed to unconscious conflict resolutions.[19]

This description is, I think, quite accurate, as is his remark that "the shock" which Foucault's books produce "is not caused by the flash of *insight* into a confusion which threatens identity" but instead by "the affirmed de-differentiation and by the affirmed collapse of those categories which alone can account for category mistakes of existential relevance." Foucault affects to write from a point of view light-years away from the problems of contemporary society. His own efforts at social reform (e.g. of prisons) seem to have no connection with his exhibition of the way in which the "humane" approach to penal reform tied in with the needs of the modern state. It takes no more than a squint of the inner eye to read Foucault as a stoic, a dispassionate observer of the present social order, rather than its concerned critic. Because the rhetoric of emancipation – the notion of a kind of truth which is *not* one more production of power – is absent from his work, he can easily be thought of as reinventing American "functionalist" sociology. The extraordinary *dryness* of Foucault's work is a counterpart of the dryness which Iris Murdoch once objected to in the writing of British analytic philosophers. It is a dryness produced by a lack of identification with any social context, any communication. Foucault once said that he would like to write "so as to have no face." He forbids himself the tone of the liberal sort of thinker who says to his fellow-citizens: "*We* know that there must be a better way to do things than this; let us look for it together." There is no "we" to be found in Foucault's writings, nor in those of many of his French contemporaries.

It is this remoteness which reminds one of the conservative who pours cold water on hopes for reform, who affects to look at the problems of the fellow-citizens with the eye of the future historian. Writing "the history of the present," rather than suggestions about how our children might inhabit a better world in the future, gives up not just on the notion of a common human nature, and on that of "the subject," but on our untheoretical sense of social solidarity. It is as if thinkers like Foucault and Lyotard were so afraid of being caught up in one more metanarrative about the fortunes of "the subject" that they cannot bring themselves to say "we" long enough to identify with the culture of the generation to which they belong. Lyotard's contempt for "the philosophy of subjectivity" is such as to make him abstain from anything that smacks of the "metanarrative of emancipation" which Habermas shares with Blumenberg and Bacon. Habermas's socialization of subjectivity, his philosophy of consensus, seems to Lyotard just one more pointless variation on a theme which has been heard too often.

But although disconnecting "philosophy" from social reform – a disconnection previously performed by analytic philosophers who were "emotivist" in metaethics while being fiercely partisan in politics – is one way of expressing exasperation with the philosophical tradition, it is not the only way. Another would be to minimize the importance of that tradition, rather than seeing it as something which urgently needs to be overcome, unmasked, or genealogized. Suppose, as I suggested above, one sees the wrong turn as having been taken with Kant (or better yet, with Descartes) rather than (like Habermas) with the young Hegel or the young Marx. Then one might see the canonical sequence of philosophers from Descartes to Nietzsche as a distraction from the history of concrete social engineering which made the contemporary North Atlantic culture what it is now, with all its glories and all its dangers. One could try to create a new canon – one in which the mark of a "great philosopher" was awareness of new social and religious and institutional possibilities, as opposed to developing a new dialectical twist in metaphysics or epistemology. That would be a way of splitting the difference between Habermas and Lyotard, of having things both ways. We could agree with Lyotard that we need no more metanarratives, but with Habermas that we need less dryness. We could agree with Lyotard that studies of the communicative competence of a transhistorical subject are of little use in reinforcing our sense of identification with our community, while still insisting on the importance of that sense.

If one had such a de-theoreticized sense of community, one could accept the claim that valuing "undistorted communication" was of the essence of liberal politics without needing a theory of communicative competence as backup. Attention would be turned instead to some concrete examples of what was presently distorting our communication – e.g. to the sort of "shock" we get when, reading Foucault, we realize that the jargon we liberal intellectuals developed has played into the hands of the bureaucrats. Detailed historical narratives of the sort Foucault offers us would take the place of philosophical metanarratives. Such narratives would not unmask something created by power called "ideology" in the name of something not created by power called "validity" or "emancipation." They would just explain who was currently getting and using power for what purposes, and then (unlike Foucault) suggest how some other people might get it and use it for other purposes. The resulting attitude would be neither incredulous and horrified realization that truth and power are inseparable nor Nietzschean *Schadenfreude*, but rather a recognition that it was only the false lead which Descartes gave us (and the resulting over-valuation of scientific theory which, in Kant, produce "the philosophy of subjectivity") that made us think truth and power *were* separable. We could thus take the Baconian maxim that "knowledge is power" with redoubled seriousness. We might also be made to take seriously Dewey's suggestion that the way to re-enchant the world, to bring back what religion gave our forefathers, is to stick to the concrete. Much of what I have been saying is an attempt to follow up on the following passage from Dewey:

> We are weak today in ideal matters because intelligence is divorced from aspiration. . . . When philosophy shall have cooperated with the force of events and made clear and coherent the meaning of the daily detail, science and emotion will interpenetrate, practice and imagination will embrace. Poetry and religious feeling will be the unforced flowers of life.[20]

Notes and References

1 Jean-François Lyotard, *The Postmodern Condition: A Report on Knowledge*, tr. Geoff Bennington and Brian Massumi (University of Minnesota Press, Minneapolis, Minn., 1984), p. xxiii.
2 Ibid., pp. xxiv–xxv.
3 Jürgen Habermas, "The entwinement of myth and Enlightenment: re-reading *Dialectic of Enlightenment*," *New German Critique*, 26 (1982), p. 28.
4 Ibid., p. 29.
5 Ibid., p. 18.
6 Lyotard, *The Postmodern Condition*, pp. 65–6.
7 Ibid., p. 60.
8 Lyotard, *The Postmodern Condition*, p. 8.
9 Ibid., p. 27.
10 Ibid., p. 23.
11 Jürgen Habermas, *The Philosophical Discourse of Modernity* (Polity, Cambridge, 1987), p. 53.
12 Ibid., I, p. 17.
13 Habermas, "Entwinement," p. 18.
14 Habermas, *Philosophical Discourse*, p. 19.
15 Ibid., p. 20.
16 Ibid., p. 20.
17 Ibid., p. 63.
18 Ibid., p. 42.
19 Habermas, "Entwinement," p. 29.
20 John Dewey, *Reconstruction in Philosophy* (Beacon Press, Boston, Mass., 1957), p. 164.

18

Foucault and Marxism

Mark Poster

In the English-speaking world Foucault is often considered a post-structuralist. His ideas are examined in relation to those of Derrida and Lacan. Although there are good reasons for setting Foucault in the post-structuralist context, a compelling case can be made for an alternative strategy, one which depicts Foucault as a continuation of and departure from the Marxist tradition. In this discussion I shall consider only 'Western' Marxism. The juxtaposition of Foucault and Western Marxism is especially fruitful when one is considering Foucault's recent works, where the question of political commitment is in the forefront. *Discipline and Punish* and *The History of Sexuality* can be interpreted as Foucault's response to the events of May 1968 in France, exploring a new Leftist political position in which the traditional critique of capitalism and advocacy of the working class were held in suspense. If Western Marxism emerged as the theoretical response to the impasses of classical Marxism confronting the events from the First Word War to the Cold War, Foucault's books may be seen as a theoretical response to the difficulties of Western Marxism in confronting the upheavals of the 1960s and the new social formation emerging thereafter.

Western Marxism, a term coined by Merleau-Ponty in the postwar period, is defined most often as a response to the theoretical limitations of Leninism and the Social Democracy of the Second International. Its origins go back to Georg Lukács and Antonio Gramsci, but its chief manifestations were the work of the Frankfurt School in Germany and the existential Marxists in France after the Second World War. Broadly speaking, the Western Marxists sought to redefine the place of the subject in Marxist theory by confronting Marx's positions with recent intellectual developments such as psychoanalysis and existentialism. They also examined the epistemological difficulties in the Marxist dialectic by reassessing its Hegelian roots and restricting more than Marx had done the metaphysical scope of dialectical thought. Finally, they shifted the attention of critical theory away from the means and relations of production toward issues of everyday life and culture. At every point a disturbing question pursued them: were they still Marxists or simply disgruntled intellectuals? In general, their political allegiance to Marxist political organizations was tenuous or non-existent. Theoretically, their position as Marxists was at best ambiguous. It was rarely clear if their work was supplementary to the classical Marxist concept of the mode of production, or a thorough-going revision of Marxist doctrine which adhered only to the general spirit of the critique of political economy. These issues were especially difficult to clarify in a political context where the Western Marxists had no organic contact with class struggles. The events of May 1968 changed everything, because in these events a radical movement emerged outside the parameters of the Marxist parties, providing a political basis for a new critical theory. In this conjuncture the Western Marxists could at last tabulate the balance sheet of their relations to Marxism.

Foucault's intellectual trajectory kept him separate from the Western Marxists until after May 1968. He complains that his teachers never so much as uttered the words 'Frankfurt School', so that he was denied the opportunity of confronting a body of theory that he now thinks might have been of great assistance to him then and continues to interest him. The relation of Foucault to the French Western Marxists is more complicated however. Although a generation younger than Merleau-Ponty and Sartre, he was, like them, influenced by the Hegelian revival in the postwar years, since he studied with Jean Hyppolite, one of its chief representatives. He was also, like them, exposed to and attracted by German existentialism. His early work *Mental Illness and Psychology* (1954) was indebted to Ludwig Binzwanger, a psychologist who himself owed much to Martin Heidegger. Furthermore, Foucault's first major work, *Madness and Civilization* (1961), was animated by a critique of Western reason that was not entirely at odds with the anti-scientism of Sartre and Merleau-Ponty. Finally, like the existential Marxists, Foucault moved in and around the French Communist Party in the early postwar years. And yet, by the early 1960s, Foucault was much taken with structuralist currents of thought, tendencies which Sartre found so repellent.

Foucault's intellectual course thus ran somewhat parallel to that of the existential Marxists until the early 1960s. At that point he diverged radically from Sartre, considering his own position the antithesis of all philosophies of consciousness, including Sartrean existential Marxism.

In this way the books of this period, *The Birth of the Clinic* (1963, though published in 1969), *The Order of Things* (1966) and *The Archeology of Knowledge* (written before May 1968), are ostensibly opposed to positions like Sartre's which rely on a theory of the subject. That much is certainly true. Yet even at this point of extreme opposition, I would maintain that it is possible to suggest certain similarities between Foucault and Sartre. Even though Parisian intellectuals understood Sartre as the antithesis of the new structuralist currents, both Sartre and the structuralists defined themselves in opposition to what has come to be called the Western metaphysical tradition. Sartre, after all, disputed the Cartesian concept of the rational subject as the epistemological and ontological ground of reality. While it is true, as the structuralists charged, that Sartre relied on what they saw as an idealist notion of the subject, it remains the case that the explicit intention of Sartre's thought, especially in the *Critique of Dialectical Reason*, was to undermine the metaphysical grounds of Cartesian reason, an intellectual direction akin to that of Foucault. It is also true that Foucault and others associated with structuralism denied the success of Sartre at this task. Yet during the 1970s, after the structuralist movement had passed its heyday, Foucault reconsidered the question of the subject, recognizing that, whatever the dangers it involved of a relapse into metaphysics, the question of the subject was impossible to avoid for critical theory. Without some theory of the subject (or subjects) it was not possible to account for resistance to authority. What had to be avoided for Foucault was a notion of the subject as transcendental and unchanging over time, traces of which were still to be found in Sartre's later work.

In the 1960s Foucault was openly hostile to all forms of humanism and philosophies of consciousness, a hostility that was also directed against Western Marxism in general and Sartre in particular. When Foucault trumpeted the call 'man is dead', he would no doubt have included Sartre among the humanists he was defying. After 1968, however, Foucault's icy hostility to Sartre and Western Marxism melted away. He began to acknowledge the importance of their standpoint and to many observers Foucault, more than anyone else, had taken up Sartre's position in the Parisian intellectual and political world.

Until he became ill in the mid-1970s, Sartre had been the twentieth-century version of Voltaire, an intellectual of diverse talents who championed under the banner of justice the causes of the oppressed and, without party or organization, did battle with the established order. Sartre, like Voltaire before him, enjoyed broad popularity and was therefore relatively immune from retribution by the authorities. It is clear that Foucault has never attained the celebrity status of Sartre, but in the early 1970s he began to champion the causes of several oppositional groups and to write political pieces for *Le Nouvel observateur*. He spoke on behalf of prison reform, and the rights of homosexuals; he supported the anti-psychiatry movement and the women's movement; he analysed the importance of the revolution that overthrew the Shah in Iran. During these years Foucault was perhaps the most eminent and widely acknowledged intellectual who participated in Leftist politics. Ironically, Foucault was at that time criticizing the role and function of the traditional intellectual.

Without understanding Foucault's new political status in the 1970s, his praise of Sartre in articles and interviews would be perplexing. Back in the 1960s a polite exchange of sorts took place between the two men in the pages of *La Quinzaine littéraire*. Sartre acknowledged the achievement of Foucault's *Les Mots et les choses*, but repeated a complaint he had registered against Lévi-Strauss: Foucault avoided the question of history, how one episteme is supplanted by another. A few months earlier in the same journal, Foucault dismissed Sartre and Merleau-Ponty as 'courageous and generous' men of an earlier era, animated by a spirit that had passed from the intellectual scene. Again in the same journal, in March 1968, only two months before the events of May, Foucault politely dismissed the 'enterprise of totalization' in philosophy from Hegel to Sartre, an enterprise no longer on the agenda. Foucault continued with a statement of characteristic modesty: 'I think the immense work and political action of Sartre defines an era. . . . I would never accept a comparison – even for the sake of contrast – of the minor work of historical and methodological spade work that I do with a body of work like his.'[1] Yet the intellectual generation gap revealed in *La Quinzaine littéraire* was shortly to be bridged as both men worked together in the 1970s for the journal *Libération*.

After 1968 Foucault's attitude to Sartre and Western Marxism began to change. Sartre was no longer simply the philosophical enemy, as Foucault began to discover points of agreement and convergence of thought. In one interview Foucault praised the role that Sartre played in raising the intellectual and political consciousness of the French public: 'from the end of the war onwards . . . we have seen ideas of profoundly academic origins, or roots . . . addressed to a much broader public than that of the universities. Now, even though there is nobody of Sartre's stature to continue it, this phenomenon has become democratized. Only Sartre – or perhaps Sartre and Merleau-Ponty – could do it. . . . The public's cultural level, on average, has really risen considerably.'[2]

Or here again Sartre is alluded to as a kind of Leftist that Foucault identifies with: 'if the Left exists in France . . . I think an important factor has been the existence of a Left thought and a Left reflection . . . of political choices made on the Left since at least 1960, which have been made outside the parties. . . . It is because, through the Algerian War for example, in a whole sector of intellectual life also . . . there was an extraordinarily lively Left thought.'[3] Foucault's reference here is clearly to Sartre, Francis Jeanson and *Les Temps modernes*, which was a centre for opposition to the Algerian War at a time when the French Communist Party supported it. Foucault now sees himself as an heir to the existential Marxists who developed their Leftist critique outside the Communist Party. Speaking of his own debt to Nietzsche, Foucault is almost proud to find in Sartre a similar interest in Nietzsche. 'Did you know that Sartre's first text – written when he was a young student – was Nietzschean? "The History of Truth," a little paper first published in a *Lycée* review around 1925. He began with the same problem [as Foucault?] and it is very odd that his approach should have shifted from the history of truth to phenomenology, while for the next generation – ours – the reverse was true.'[4] Foucault imagines Sartre and himself as children of Nietzsche, with the difference that Sartre strayed from the paternal heritage. Foucault identifies with Sartre as a brother and even regrets ('it is very odd that') their differences.

After May 1968 Foucault carried out a reorientation and clarification of ideas that substantially altered the direction of his work. I am not so much interested in the question of the unity or inconsistency of Foucault's thought, but rather in the theoretical direction of his work after 1968. I will argue that at this time Foucault came to grips with issues that were central to Western Marxism and that the positions he took, while in some cases resembling those of Western Marxists, generally went beyond their positions toward a new formulation of critical theory. In short, Foucault both came to terms with the problematic of Western Marxism and carried it to a new level.

The events of May 1968 signified that an oppositional stance toward existing society was possible beyond the confines of contemporary Marxist orientations. During the month of May new groups participated in the protest movement, groups not traditionally associated with the proletariat. The events were sparked by students, continued by professional and technical workers, and supported by younger factory workers who were not the mainstays of the Marxist organizations. These groups relied on new methods of action, such as the tactic of provocation which served to reveal the weaknesses of the established order rather than to overthrow authority and take power. They developed new organizational forms, notably the Action Committee which was radically democratic and was oriented toward the enactment of new kinds of social relations rather than toward mobilizing the strength of the revolt. And finally they formulated a set of demands in their wall posters that constituted a post-Marxist critique of society. The ideology contained in the wall posters spoke not only against capitalism, but also against bureaucracy and all non-democratic forms of social organization. It contested not so much exploitation, but alienation. Its focus was not simply the factory, but all sectors of everyday life. It demanded not so much an equal share for all in the spoils of capitalism, but an active participation (*autogestion*) and creative role in all social action.

For most Leftist intellectuals, May 1968 constituted a break in the traditions of revolution. It became apparent that a new social formation was being born and that a new critical theory would be required to account for it and formulate an opposition to it. . . .

In Foucault's case, the themes of domination and power came to the fore. It has often been noted that, starting with his inaugural address at the Collège de France in 1970, Foucault began to stress the connection between reason and power. The *Discourse on Language* spoke of 'the institutional support' for 'the will to truth' and emphasized 'the manner in which knowledge is employed in society'.[5] More to the point, Foucault defined his future studies as genealogies of discourse in which discourse was to be understood as forms of power. 'The genealogical side of discourse . . . attempts to grasp it in its power of affirmation, by which I do not mean a power opposed to that of negation, but the power of constituting domains of objects.'[6] No longer would Foucault study only systems of exclusion, that which reason repressed; he would henceforth elucidate the mechanisms by which reason constituted and shaped forms of action. Power was no longer a negative, exclusionary function, but a positive formative one. In the 1970s Foucault's books on prisons and sexuality did just that.

Associated with the new concern with power and its new 'positive' definition was a tendency to associate reason with practice, a tendency that became more and more prominent after 1968. The structuralist concern with language and its autonomy that was prominent in *The Order of Things* (1966) gave way to an ill-defined but suggestive category of discourse/practice in which the reciprocal interplay of reason and action was presumed. Reason, manifested in discourse, was always already present in history. . . . This subtle yet ill-defined sense of the interplay of truth and power, theory and practice, became the central theme of Foucault's investigations. It characterizes his effort to go beyond structuralism and leads him into direct confrontation with the traditions of Western Marxism.

The purpose of presenting these indicators of change in Foucault's thought is not to prepare a brief for a detailed intellectual history. Instead, I have noted the new directions of his work after 1968 as a prelude to a systematic treatment of the relation of Foucault's work to that of Western Marxism. It should by now be clear that such a comparison is apposite and indeed crucial to current theoretical work. Foucault, finding support in Nietzsche, elaborated a new formulation of the thesis that reason is within history, a thesis that is central to Western Marxism. Whereas figures such as Sartre and Marcuse presented this thesis in a Hegel–Marx form, Foucault did so by resort to Nietzsche. The differences in their formulations are no less decisive than their similarities.

The Western Marxists argued that reason was shaped by class-bound history. Both the positions of the theorist and those of any ideologies found in the world are regulated by class. For the later Sartre, to take one case, the situation of the thinker, his being-in-the-world, is in the last analysis a class situation, with the mode of production providing the final horizon of thought. The reason-in-history thesis effectively undercut the pretence of reason as arbiter of reality; it served as a kind of Kantian condition of possibility for thought that protected the thinker against the idealist tendency to ontologize reason.

[...]

Foucault ironically defends the reason-in-history thesis by giving it up. Foucault's Nietzschean scepticism about truth enables him to take a radical stance with respect to reason; there is not truth, only truths, and there is no epistemological ground upon which one can stand to ontologize reason, to grasp the totality and claim it all leads to this or that. But Foucault's radical scepticism does not lead to nihilism, because it enables him to search for the close connection between manifestations of reason and patterns of domination. The couplet discourse/practice presumes this connection as a condition for studying it, a hermeneutic circle that is unavoidable, though full of logical contradiction. Foucault can study the ways in which discourse is not innocent, but shaped by practice – without privileging any form of practice, such as class struggle. He can also study how discourse in turn shapes practice without privileging any form of discourse. Thus he writes a history of prisons in which Benthamite doctrine, responding to the Enlightenment reformer's horror at Old Regime punishment practices, in part leads to incarcerating institutions which develop their own system of power to manage inmate populations, and this in turn leads to new discourses (criminology) that study 'scientifically' and finally influence the administration of prisons. The interpenetration of discourse and practice goes on interminably because they imply each other's existence from the beginning. In studying discourse it is not a question of perfect truth; in studying practice it is not a question of determining discourse. Both ontologizing tendencies are thus cut off from the start.

But Foucault's project would finally lead to nihilism unless a further dimension is given full recognition: the political dimension. For the couplet discourse/practice operates for the theorist as well as for the object studied. Foucault's discourse is also connected with politics. His own political motivation and situation shapes his discourse. He has recognized this explicitly:

> I would like to write the history of this prison, with all the political investments of the body that it gathers together in its closed architecture. Why? Simply because I am interested in the past? No, if one means by that writing a history of the past in terms of the present. Yes, if one means writing the history of the present.[7]

The important point is the following. Foucault's own situation is one in which discourses, like the ones he writes, are institutionalized as the human sciences and play a decisive role in the formation of practice (policy studies). In other words, Foucault has been able to develop the position that discourse and practice are intertwined in a world where domination takes the form of disciplines and discourse is organized into disciplines. In short, reason has become, in history, a form of power in a way that it perhaps was not before the eighteenth century. Foucault has come to terms with his situation, a world where the human sciences are organized and play a political role, by arguing for a position that looks at the human sciences only by de-ontologizing the concept of reason.

Notes and References

1 *La Quinzaine littéraire*, 46 (1 March 1968), p. 21.
2 Georges Raulet, 'Interview with Michel Foucault', *Telos*, 55 (Spring 1983), p. 210.
3 Ibid., p. 209.
4 Ibid., p. 204.

5 Michel Foucault, *The Archeology of Knowledge and the Discourse on Language*, tr. M. Sheridan Smith (Pantheon, New York, 1972), p. 219.
6 Ibid., p. 234.
7 Michel Foucault, *Discipline and Punish*, tr. Alan Sheridan (Pantheon, New York, 1977; original edition 1975), p. 31.

PART IV

Feminism, Gender and Subjectivity

FEMINIST THOUGHT HAS made a major impact upon social theory, and the social sciences more generally, over the past quarter of a century or so. Feminist theory is in an important sense a subject matter in its own right, concerned with addressing the 'invisibility' of women in social theoretical thinking and with theorizing gender. Yet it also has implications for some of the most basic problems of social theory as such. In this part some of the contributions address feminist issues in relation to the works of male authors influential in social theory, including both Foucault and Habermas; others are more concerned with exploring the character of feminism as a body of thought and as a social movement.

Foucault's writings have been extensively drawn upon by feminist thinkers, albeit normally in a partial or selective way. Foucault's work on the body, and more specifically on sexuality, has been especially important. In his work on the rise of the asylum and the prison, Foucault shows that the body was the focus of new disciplinary procedures integral to the establishing of the modern state. In the 'disciplinary society' of modernity the body is rigorously controlled and ordered through the imposition of forms of 'surveillance'. Surveillance means the use of information, or direct supervision, to co-ordinate the activities of individuals within the regularized settings of modern organizations.

The body here appears as relatively passive: indeed, in his study of the rise of the prison, *Discipline and Punish*, Foucault speaks of the new administrative orders as producing 'docile bodies'. In his later writings, particularly when he moved to consider the nature of sexuality, Foucault came to place more emphasis upon the body as a medium of action and a source of pleasure. His multi-volume work on *The History of Sexuality* attempts to demonstrate that the body in modern societies becomes a site of 'biopower': it is disciplined on the one hand, but on the other becomes a focus of a search for fulfilment and self-understanding.

As Lois McNay (Reading 19) points out, many feminists have objected to Foucault's treatment of the body as non-gendered. His discussion of prisons, for example, concentrates almost wholly upon an implicit model of male experience, rather than considering the specific ways in which the disciplining of women differed from that affecting men. Yet the force of this criticism, as McNay points out, can also be exaggerated. Foucault's writings provide major insights into how the body is 'worked upon' by gender constructions, because in some key ways the 'inscription' of social influences upon the body is actually the means of the very production of gender differences. The rendering 'visible' of women's history should not lead us to infer that it is a separate and insulated experience which bears no relation to other aspects of social organization and change.

In McNay's view, rather than criticizing Foucault for neglecting gender, we should look to produce a critical appraisal of Foucault's conception of the relation between power and the body. Foucault correctly sees power not just as negative, 'the ability to say no', but as a generative phenomenon. The idea that Foucault's studies of the 'disciplinary society' provide no basis for analysing resistance to power, McNay argues, is wrong. Foucault's theory, in fact, problematizes resistance and sees that it takes as many different forms as there are contexts in which power is wielded. Nevertheless, Foucault fails adequately to see that 'biopower' is a contradictory and tensionful force. Biopower can under some circumstances provide a means of liberation and is not just to be connected to processes of administrative regulation.

Nancy Fraser (Reading 20) concentrates her attention on Habermas. Like Foucault, although he quite often refers to the struggles of women's movements Habermas rarely discusses issues of gender in a systematic fashion.

In his most detailed statement of his social theory, *The Theory of Communicative Action*, Habermas distinguishes between the symbolic and material reproduction of societies. To survive over time, a society must provide for economic interchange with the material environment, and it must also create and sustain symbolic values and norms that provide a framework for communication between its members. In Habermas's view, in modern societies paid employment is part of the system of material reproduction, while unpaid activities carried on by women in the domestic sphere, including childbearing and childrearing, belong to the domain of symbolic reproduction. Fraser finds this view inadequate. The bearing and rearing of children is a material as well as a symbolic phenomenon; after all, it is the very means of the physical survival of the species.

Yet so is the sphere of paid work: work is never just a series of economic transactions, but involves symbolic meanings and norms. Fraser also questions Habermas's thesis that the domestic sphere belongs to the realm of 'social integration' – linking individuals in direct communication – whereas economic relations are bound up with system 'integration' – the integration of large-scale institutions. Habermas's conceptual distinctions, because they are not informed by a satisfactory interpretation of gender, in fact easily serve to reinforce ideological distinctions which they are supposed precisely to uncover and criticize. Habermas's theory of the 'colonization of the lifeworld' is flawed for similar reasons. In the conclusion of her discussion Fraser indicates how Habermas's ideas might be modified if they are connected, as they have to be, with an account of gender.

Janet Wolff (Reading 21) considers the implications of taking gender seriously for the analysis of modernism as a cultural phenomenon. She begins with a brief discussion of some of the views of her namesake, Virginia Woolf. Virginia Woolf was a champion of modernism and a defender of the break with tradition which modernity installs. Woolf was sympathetic to feminism and saw the new movements in literature of her time as a means of breaking with what she called 'the sentence made by men' – heavy, long-winded contorted writing styles. Women might be able to make use of new modes of linguistic expression to give voice to their own specific experiences in a world dominated by men. Woolf's views about the relation between modernism and feminism have since been echoed by a variety of other feminist authors.

Modernism, Janet Wolff points out (like postmodernism), is difficult to define. It is usually located at the period from 1890 to 1930, but covers a variety of different literary and artistic forms. Following Eugene Lunn, Wolff defines modernism as a revolt against realism and romanticism, characterized by aesthetic self-consciousness, simultaneity, ambiguity and the disappearance of the 'integrated personality'. She notes, nevertheless, that these traits are actually remarkably parallel to those often associated with postmodernism!

Understood in this way at any rate, modernism appears as a history of male achievement. The usual accounts of the development of modernism, as she puts it, consist of 'a long list of the names of men'. At issue here is more than a failure to recognize the role of women writers and artists. Modernism is in fact primarily a masculine phenomenon. Looking specifically at the work of women writers, it is possible to see that modernism, as Virginia Woolf suggests, quite often depicted the mechanisms of a patriarchal society.

If women have on occasion turned modernism to critical ends, feminist authors today have sought widely to make use of conceptions of 'postmodernism' in their interpretations of the experience of women and of gender. Theories of 'postmodernism' or 'postmodernity' (sometimes these terms are treated as equivalent, sometimes authors differentiate between them) have tended to follow the views set out by Lyotard, noted previously. Feminists influenced by conceptions of postmodernism have argued that there can be no universalizing theories of male domination, patriarchy or sexual difference. They have distanced themselves from what they see as a misplaced 'essentialism': the view that there are some characteristics or experiences which differentiate virtually all women from virtually all men. Gender categories, like other social categories, are fragmented and contextual.

Thus it is asserted, for example, that the life of a poor black woman living in an inner city ghetto may differ more from that of an affluent suburban white woman than it does from the experience of a poor black male. There is no intrinsic unity to being a 'woman' apart from the anatomical similarity of sex. This sort of standpoint has a substantive as well as theoretical thrust. For in postmodern conditions, it is held, social life itself has become fragmented and decentred.

Sylvia Walby (Reading 22) accepts the importance of these points but rejects the basic position underlying them. The concept of 'patriarchy', she notes, has come under particular criticism on the part of those worried about essentialism. Yet the generalizing relevance of patriarchy needs to be defended; there are some quite generic ways in which women's experience, in a variety of different societies, differs from that typical of men. The concept of patriarchy is capable of general application as long as it is not treated in a monolithic way. Patriarchy, Walby argues, consists of several major structural characteristics, found in various combinations in all societies. The nature of patriarchal power has changed very substantially with the advent of modern industrial capitalism; but we cannot even analyse such changes if we do not recognize that they involve factors of a very general nature.

If patriarchy is indeed more or less universal, it probably has psychological as well as social roots. In searching for these Freud's writings have an obvious relevance. Yet as Nancy Chodorow (Reading 23) recognizes, the relation between feminism and psychoanalytic theory has been a charged and ambivalent one. Many feminists have found Freud's theory wanting. For although it is largely based upon clinical case histories of women, it places prime emphasis upon male psychosexual development. The idea of 'penis envy', seen by Freud to be central to women's experience, has been thought by many to be sexist in the extreme. For Chodorow, however, Freud's ideas provide fundamental insights into both female and male development – if these insights are substantially modified in certain ways. Freud's writings, in her view, contain several breakthroughs relevant to the understanding of gender difference. Freud showed that there is no biological connection between gender and sexuality; femininity and masculinity are not innate. He demonstrated that there is no specific connection between gender and heterosexuality either: all sexual activity is on a continuum. In addition, Freud made clear the degree to which gender and sexual identity are developed around early relations to parental figures. Freud's theory was certainly sexist. He treats as something entirely natural, for instance, that little girls find their genitals inferior to those of little boys. Yet Freud's own ideas often cross-cut, and in fact largely subvert, his own misogyny. Psychoanalytic theory can be used to explore how it comes about that male dominance is reproduced from generation to generation.

Psychoanalytic theory shows that the human individual or 'subject' is socially constructed. It is partly because of the very influence of psychoanalysis that so many authors, both within the domain of feminist thought and outside, have spoken of the 'end of the subject' in modern social theory. Agnes Heller (Reading 24) takes up this issue. She does not discuss it specifically in relation to feminism, or even gender, but the alert reader will easily be able to apply her arguments back to points raised by previous selections within this part.

The 'death of the subject' is particularly associated with postmodernism, but, as she shows, has a prior ancestry in social theory and philosophy. Yet who precisely is it that is supposed to have died? Those critical of essentialism would say that it is the category of a 'unitary person' that today has no relevance in social analysis. Yet such a category was from the beginning a constructed one and in some part such critics are attacking a position that few, if any, have ever held.

We can see that this is so by taking the concrete example of autobiography. A person who writes an autobiography is both the author of the text and the author of his or her own life. The writer presents herself or himself as a subject and at the same time authorizes a 'world' in which that subject exists. The subject (the human individual) and the world (the natural and social environment) are never in fact separate entities which simply 'act upon' one another; they are mutually constructed in the course of history. Individuals have existed in all societies; 'the subject' is a creation of modernity. In conditions of modern social life in which, as has been stressed before, tradition is largely stripped away, the individual inherits no pre-given map for her or his self-understanding. Women and men in modern societies have contingent identities and are aware of this contingency; it is precisely this which makes for the constitution of 'the subject'. Rather than speaking of the death of the subject, therefore, we should see that the 'openness' of experience associated with socially constructed identity has been bound up with modernity since its inception.

19

Foucault, Feminism and the Body

Lois McNay

Whilst Foucault's work on the body has contributed significantly to feminist theories of the body and sexual identity, it must be recognized that the trade-off has not been simply one way. Feminists have also drawn attention to certain inadequacies in Foucault's treatment of gender issues. One important criticism has been that Foucault's analysis does not pay enough attention to the gendered nature of disciplinary techniques on the body and that this oversight perpetuates a 'gender blindness' that has always predominated in social theory.

In her article on disciplinary power and the female subject, Sandra Lee Bartky argues that Foucault's treatment of the body as an undifferentiated or neutral gender is inadequate because it fails to explain how men and women relate differently to the institutions of modern life. If, as Foucault claims, there is no such thing as a 'natural' body and it is therefore impossible to posit a pre-given natural sex difference, then he needs to elaborate on how the systematic effect of sexual division is perpetuated by the techniques of gender that are applied to the body. By analysing various practices and discourses aimed specifically at women and the different aspects of the 'feminine' body image, Bartky shows how the female body is ordered and controlled within what she calls a 'disciplinary regime of femininity'. Bartky follows a well-known criticism of the concept of disciplinary power: that it is generalized from an analysis of the practices of 'total' institutions – the prison, asylum, etc. – to other social institutions which do not operate in such a closed way. Accordingly, Bartky argues that the discipline of the feminine body is hard to locate in so far as it is 'institutionally unbound'. This absence of a formal institutional structure creates the impression that the assumption of femininity by female subjects is either natural or voluntary:

> Feminine bodily discipline has this dual character: on the one hand, no one is marched off for electrolysis at gunpoint, nor can we fail to appreciate the initiative and ingenuity displayed by countless women in an attempt to master the rituals of beauty. Nevertheless, in so far as the disciplinary practices of femininity produce a 'subjected and practiced', an inferiorised, body, they must be understood as aspects of a far larger discipline, an oppressive and inegalitarian system of sexual subordination. This system aims at turning women into the docile and compliant companions of men just as surely as the army aims to turn its raw recruits into soldiers.[1]

Bartky is undoubtedly right to criticize Foucault for neglecting to consider in what distinct ways disciplinary techniques operate on the female body inscribing physical effects, such as restricted and hesitant body movement and posture, that compound the secondary position or object status that dominant conceptions of femininity ascribe to women. For Foucault, the female body seems to possess no specificity apart from the male norm. Ultimately, Bartky argues that this silence on the question of the production of female bodies reproduces, regardless of authorial intention, a sexism endemic in supposedly gender-neutral social theory. Foucault is 'blind to those disciplines that produce a modality of embodiment that is peculiarly feminine. To overlook the forms of subjection that engender the feminine body is to perpetuate the silence and powerlessness of those upon whom these disciplines have been imposed.'[2]

Other feminists have made similar criticisms about the gender blindness of Foucault's work. Patricia O'Brien claims that the problem with Foucault's analysis of prison regimes in *Discipline and Punish* is that he does not consider how the treatment of male and female prisoners differed and how these differences related to dominant constructions of masculinity and femininity. For Foucault, the prisoner's body, indeed the disciplined body in general, is often implicitly assumed to be male. O'Brien acknowledges that, in certain respects, there was a close congruence in age, social background and occupation between prisoners of different sexes. Women were in prison mostly for the same categories of crime as men – the predominant category being thieving. However, in other respects O'Brien shows that there were substantial differences in the social perceptions of male and female criminality. Female criminality was perceived solely through the grid of what was regarded as the inferior biological make-up of women. It was explicitly linked to what were understood as fundamental traits of the feminine physiology – delicacy, nervousness, susceptibility. O'Brien shows how diverse categories of crime were labelled as 'menstrual psychoses'. Suicides and homicides amongst women were seen as 'organic maladies of the uterus'.

Informing these attitudes towards the female criminal was an understanding of female sexuality as inherently pathological and regressive. As O'Brien puts it: 'The argument at its most extreme was that all menstruating, lactating, ovulating, pregnant, newly delivered, newly sexually initiated and menopausal women were prone to crime. Most women, therefore, could become criminally deviant during any portion of their adult lives.'[3]

The female criminal, then, was at the end of the spectrum of an inherently regressive, biologically limited female sexuality. This widespread notion that women were not greatly influenced by socialization but were biologically determined meant that female criminals were perceived as less receptive to rehabilitation than male criminals whose crimes were perceived, in stark contrast, in terms of social rather than natural deviance. To a large extent, penal institutions were seen as being absolved of any useful role in the rehabilitation of women.

O'Brien's account of the fundamental differences in the social perceptions of female and male criminality reinforces Foucault's identification of the process of hysterization of the female body as a dominant form of social control in the nineteenth century. However, in *The History of Sexuality*, where it is introduced, this concept remains unelaborated and no attempt is made in *Discipline and Punish* to explore how the regulation of the body of the female prisoner intersects with conceptions of female sexuality dominant in other realms. To put it another way, it is necessary to explore how meanings, particularly representations of gender, are mobilized within the operations of power to produce asymmetrical relations amongst subjects. In the analysis of institutional regimes, such as the prison, it is important to show how and why women do not relate to these institutions in the same way as men.

Along with the prison, Foucault also identifies military training as one of the principal sites from which arose techniques for regulating the body, not by external threat or coercion, but by acquired, internalized modes of operation:

> Politics, as a technique of internal peace and order, sought to implement the mechanism of the perfect army, of the disciplined mass, of the docile, useful troop, of the regiment in camp and in the field. . . . The classical age saw the birth of . . . meticulous military and political tactics by which the control of bodies and individual forces was exercised within states.[4]

Here, too, Foucault's historical analysis does not account for the different ways the female body may be positioned in relation to the generalization of a military technology of the body, to a wider form of social control. With regard to dominant conceptions of masculinity, there is a continuity, on many levels, between the notion of the soldier and that of the citizen/worker. As Nancy Fraser points out, the concept of citizenship encompasses a strong soldiering aspect, the idea of the citizen as the defender of the polity and protector of those – women, children, the elderly – who allegedly cannot protect themselves. In terms of Foucault's schema, this soldiering aspect of citizenship can be interpreted as a residual trace of the military origins of disciplinary power which invests the male body as a productive and obedient citizen/worker. The soldiering element in citizenship is an indication of how the role is implicitly masculine and it also means that women can occupy the role of citizen only with some conceptual uneasiness; 'this division between male protectors and female protected introduces further dissonance into woman's relation to citizenship'.[5]

Whilst it is undoubtedly right to criticize Foucault for failing to pursue the implications of his theory of the body and power in relation to the issue of sexual difference, there are, however, theoretical problems arising from too great an insistence on the specificity of female bodies. There is a danger that, by placing too much emphasis on the different strategies by which women's bodies are disciplined, one ends by positing a separate history of repression for women, thereby perpetuating an artificial polarization between the experiences of men and women. As a consequence, women are placed outside, or in a position of innocence, *vis-à-vis* the male-defined social realm. For example, at various points in her article, Bartky seems to make the problematic assumption that women are simply passive victims of systems of patriarchal domination. She argues that the disciplinary techniques which invade the female body are 'total', 'perpetual' and 'exhaustive'. At times, women have offered resistance to this system of domination, but resistance has always failed and this very failure further strengthens the inexorable hold of disciplinary techniques upon the body: 'As women (albeit a small minority of women) begin to realise an unprecedented political, economic, and sexual self-determination, they fall ever more completely under the dominating gaze of patriarchy.'[6] The implicit assumption Bartky makes is that under the 'ensemble of systematically duplicitous practices' which control the female body, there is a 'true' female body, undetermined by social constraints, that has yet to be expressed. Added to the well-documented difficulties of a notion of liberation defined in terms of an 'extra' social essence, Bartky reduces the complex ways in which feminine identity has been and is constructed in social relations to a long history of repression in which women have always masochistically complied. Consequently, this reduces the historically realized experiences and desires of women to a case of false consciousness or misrecognition.

An analysis of disciplinary techniques must undoubtedly take account of the distinct ways that the female body is operated upon, but care must be taken not to elide this distinction into an absolute separation or polarization. The development of the female body does not constitute a separate history of an unchanging, constant repression. Rather, just like the category of 'woman' in which it is caught up, the female body is socially and discursively constructed and therefore a historically variable construct. It follows from this that the history of the female body is not completely separate from that of the male body. Whilst the body is worked upon by gender constructions, it is also inscribed by other formations: class, race, the system of commodity fetishism. These formations may, to varying degrees, be internally gendered but they also work across gender distinctions, breaking down the absolute polarity between the male and the female body. Thus, to use an obvious example, conceptions of the black body cut across and problematize in a fundamental manner any homogeneous category of woman's body. Similarly, in *Distinction*, Pierre Bourdieu illustrates how the marks of class are inscribed upon the body in a manner as fundamental as those of gender.[7] Thus, in many respects, the female body is worked upon and inscribed by the same institutional mechanisms that inscribe the male body. The sexed body is caught up with the different ways in which the body, as a general category, is conceived in relation to concepts such as the unconscious, society, the person, etc. As Denise Riley puts it:

> If it's taken for granted that the category of women simply refers, over time, to a rather different content, a sort of Women Through the Ages approach, then the full historicity of what is at stake becomes lost. We would miss seeing the alterations in what 'women' are posed against, as well as established by – Nature, Class, Reason, Humanity and other concepts – which by no means form a passive backdrop to changing conceptions of gender.[8]

This is not to deny the differences in the way in which the male and female bodies are constructed, but rather to accept that female bodies are worked upon in socially and historically specific ways, rather than in terms of an eternal, undifferentiated opposition between the sexes. To borrow Winship's terms, the history of the female body is simultaneously included and set apart in the history of the male body. As Denise Riley explains, it is necessary to abandon 'the ambition to retrieve women's bodies from their immersions beneath "male categories, values and norms". The body circulates inexorably among the other categories which sometimes arrange it in sexed ranks, sometimes not. For the concept "women's bodies" is opaque, and like "women" it is always in some juxtaposition to "human" and to "men".'[9] An analysis of the female body, therefore, needs not just to examine the disciplinary techniques exclusive to the female body – for example, Foucault's idea of hysterization – but also to show how the history of the female body is caught up with the history of the male body and how, in turn, both are related to changes within the social realm. This may seem an obvious point, but some feminists given the impression that women's history constitutes a catalogue of separate experiences of oppression which have little connection to other changes occurring within society.

Ultimately, then, whilst criticisms about a certain level of gender insensitivity in Foucault's work are correct, they draw attention to lacunae rather than major theoretical difficulties with his theory of the body. Furthermore, these lacunae have, to a large extent, been filled by subsequent feminist studies of the 'feminine' body which have employed a Foucauldian approach. I believe, however, that there are more serious problems, connected to the monolithic, unidirectional notion of power with which Foucault works and which has problematic implications for an understanding of the relation between the body and gender identity. This criticism of the one-dimensional nature of Foucault's theory of power has been made by some social theorists but has not been developed much by feminists in relation to the question of gender. These issues will be considered in the following sections.

One of the most innovative aspects of Foucault's theory of power was the insistence on power as a productive and positive force, rather than as a purely negative, repressive entity. In relation to the body, power does not simply repress its unruly forces; rather it incites, instils and produces effects in the body. There is therefore no such thing as the 'natural' or 'pre-social' body; it is impossible to know the body outside of the meaning of its cultural significations. Such a conception of power problematizes oversimplified notions of the 'feminine' body – used by both traditionalists and some radical feminists – which tend to equate the biological capacities of women with their social capabilities.

However, despite Foucault's theoretical assertion that power is a diffuse, heterogeneous and productive phenomenon, his historical analyses tend to depict power as a centralized, monolithic force with an inexorable and repressive grip on its subjects. This negative definition of power arises, in part, from the fact that Foucault's examination of power is one-sided; power relations are only examined from the perspective of how they are installed in institutions and they are not considered from the point of view of those subject to power. Peter Dews has pointed out that Foucault's analysis of the disciplinary techniques within the penal system is skewed towards the official representatives of the institutions – the governors, the architects, etc. – and not towards the voices and bodies of those being controlled. Failure to take into account any 'other' knowledges – such as a prison subculture or customs inherited from the past – which those in control may have encountered and come into conflict with means that Foucault significantly overestimates the effectivity of disciplinary forms of control.[10]

In reply to this charge of limiting his view of disciplinary power to its 'official' representations, Foucault could refer to his idea of resistance which he sees arising at the points where power relations are at their most rigid and intense. The category of resistance is closely linked, therefore, to the idea of power as productive. For Foucault, repression and resistance are not ontologically distinct; rather repression produces its own resistance: 'there are no relations of power without resistances; the latter are all the more real and effective because they are formed right at the point where relations of power are exercised.'[11] In this way, Foucault gets round the problematic tendency to posit resistance as an 'extra-social' force.

From this understanding of resistance, it follows that the sexed body is to be understood not only as the primary target of the techniques of disciplinary power, but also as the point where these techniques are resisted and thwarted. The sexed body may have been 'driven out of hiding and constrained to lead a discursive existence',[12] but at the same time, 'discourse transmits and produces power; it reinforces it, but also undermines and exposes it, renders it fragile and makes it possible to thwart it'.[13] Thus, on the one hand, the 'perverse implantation' of the nineteenth century – the massive proliferation of discourses on 'deviant' sexualities – served to reinforce social controls in the area of 'perversity' and to legitimate a notion of 'normal' heterosexuality. Yet on the other hand, this very multiplication of controlling discourses created a counter-vocabulary or 'reverse discourse' which could be used by those labelled deviant to establish their own identity and to demand certain rights: 'homosexuality began to speak in its own behalf, to demand that its legitimacy or "naturality" be acknowledged, often in the same vocabulary, using the same categories by which it was medically disqualified.'[14]

Yet despite Foucault's assertions about the nature of resistance, on the whole, this idea remains theoretically undeveloped and, in practice, Foucault's historical studies give the impression that the body presents no material resistance to the operations of power. In *The History of Sexuality*, bodies are 'saturated' with disciplinary techniques, sex is 'administered' by a controlling power that 'wrapped the sexual body in its embrace'. Individuals live 'under the spell' of telling the truth about sex, they cannot resist the 'imperious compulsion' to confess: 'We have . . . become a singularly confessing society. . . . One confesses – or is forced to confess . . . The obligation to confess is now relayed through so many different points, is so deeply ingrained in us, that we no longer perceive it as the effect of a power that constrains us.'[15] Despite his assertions to the contrary, Foucault in fact produces a vision of power as a unidirectional, dominatory force which individuals are unable to resist. This tendency of Foucault to elide power with domination is apparent in *Discipline and Punish*, where Foucault sees disciplinary methods as producing 'subjected and practised bodies, "docile bodies" '.[16]

Without elaborating how resistance to the insidious workings of modern 'biopower' may be developed from the libidinal forces of the body, the body is, in effect, deprived of any salience or oppositional force. In this respect, there is a tension in Foucault's work between his explicit statements about not wishing to deny the materiality of the body and his failure to show in what way such a materiality manifests itself. The result of this annulment of the materiality of the body is that power 'loses all explanatory content and becomes a ubiquitous metaphysical principle' because it has nothing determinate against which it operates.[17] For the concept of power to have some critical force, it is necessary to produce a counterfactual which would show how a situation would change if an operation of power were cancelled or resisted. Although the body is the principal site of the operations of power, it poses no such resistance and power becomes a unidirectional monolithic force.

A consequence of Foucault's definition of power exclusively in terms of its disciplinary effects on passive bodies is that other aspects of individuals' existence are effaced. This is to say that Foucault tends to understand subjects as 'docile' bodies, rather than as individuals or persons. However, some critics have rightly argued that the construction of the subject cannot simply be explained through reference to bodily experiences, but must be understood as a complex and often contradictory amalgam of legal, social and psychological constructs. Foucault emphasizes too heavily the effects of a corporeally centred disciplinary power at the expense of considering how other forms of power – such as legal definitions of the person – contribute to the construction of the modern individual. As a result, Foucault simplifies the process through which hegemonic social relations are maintained and also effaces the different types of experiences of individuals in modern society. Thus, as we have seen, Foucault argues that the female body was subjected in the nineteenth century to a process of hysterization. By representing the female body as 'thoroughly saturated with sexuality' and inherently pathological, a certain knowledge was established which allowed the regulation of desire and sexual relations with the ultimate aim of discipline and control of family populations.

Although, during the nineteenth century, there was undoubtedly an intensified feminization of the female body, the implication of Foucault's monolithic conception of power and passive account of the body is that the experiences of women were completely circumscribed by this notion of a pathological and hysterical feminine sexuality. What Foucault's account of power does not explain is how, even within the intensified process of the hysterization of female bodies, women did not slip easily and passively into socially prescribed feminine roles. Foucauldian 'biopower' provides no understanding of how the presence of power dynamics within sexuality cannot be equated with 'a simple consolidation or augmentation of a heterosexist or phallogocentric power regime'.[18] Although the unity of gender is the effect of a regulatory practice that seeks to render gender identity uniform through a compulsory heterosexuality, this effect of unity is never fully installed. The rigid dualism of masculine/feminine is constantly being disrupted and undermined by gender discontinuities that run through the heterosexual, gay and bisexual communities in which gender does not necessarily follow from sex.

[...]

For feminists, Foucault's emphasis on the body, at the expense of a more rounded notion of individuality, is particularly difficult given the stress that is placed on the re-discovery and revalorization of women's experiences. Thus, without wanting to underestimate the effects of the apparatus of regulatory practices brought to bear on women in the nineteenth century, feminist historians have attempted to show how, within the oppressive constraints that operate around ideas of femininity, there are contradictions and instabilities which, at times, have provided women with a base from which to undermine the very system which constricts them. As Ellen Willis comments:

> Power is not a monolithic system but a system of overlapping contradictions. Women have always struggled against their situation both individually and collectively. They have seized on contradictions in the system – demanding, for example, that the concept of human rights be

applied to women – thereby using the discontinuities in the system to mobilise for their own power.[19]

[. . .]

Undoubtedly, Foucault's analysis of the disciplined body provides some important insights into the way in which individuals are controlled in modern society. However, Foucault slips too easily from describing disciplinary power as a *tendency* within modern forms of social control, to positing disciplinary power as a monolithic and inexorable force which saturates all social relations. This is clearly an over-statement of the efficacy of disciplinary power. It also leads to an impoverished understanding of the individual which cannot encompass experiences, such as those related above, which fall outside the realm of the 'docile' body.

The reduction of individuals to docile bodies not only offers an inadequate account of many women's experiences, but also leads to an underestimation of the significance of the freedoms that women have won in modern society. Modern social relations cannot simply be explained as a manifestation of an all-encompassing 'biopower', but must be understood as the result of an amalgam of different types of power. The lack of differentiation in Foucault's account of power – his failure to conceive of power in any other way than as a constraining form of corporeal control – presents serious limitations in so far as many aspects of experience in modern life remain unexplained. Thus, for example, the development of the prison regime is not considered in relation to legal power and its definitions of the rights of the individual. As Habermas puts it:

> As soon as Foucault takes up the threads of the biopolitical establishment of disciplinary power, he lets drop the threads of the legal organisation of the exercise of power and of the legitimation of the order of domination. Because of this, the ungrounded impression arises that the bourgeois constitutional state is a dysfunctional relic from the period of absolutism.[20]

By positing biopower as the fundamental constitutive principle of the social realm, the history of law, the history of knowledge, the history of all social institutions are reduced to simple effects of an all-pervasive biopower. Thus, in *The History of Sexuality*, Foucault argues that biopower displaces other forms of power, in particular the law, by subsuming it into its own administrative, regulatory functions:

> I do not mean to say that . . . the institutions of justice tend to disappear, but rather that the law operates more and more as a norm, and that the

> judicial institution is increasingly incorporated into a continuum of apparatuses (medical, administrative, and so on) whose functions are for the most part regulatory. A normalizing society is the historical outcome of a technology of power centred on life. We have entered a phase of juridical regression.[21]

There is no theoretical space in Foucault's model for reversing this causal chain and examining the way in which the law may structure and regulate the exercise of power within both penal institutions and society in general. As a result, Foucault underestimates the different types of freedom, legal and otherwise, that have been achieved in modern society. The complicated dialectic characteristic of modern society – that the very means through which (legal) freedom is established are often the means through which freedom is put in jeopardy – is not considered. Legal, social and psychological freedoms are understood, in a one-dimensional fashion, as effects of a ubiquitous form of social control. Whilst not underestimating the discrepancy that often exists between formal and substantive rights, many freedoms have often derived from changes within the law, the most obvious example being the granting of female suffrage. Other legally established rights, such as the possibility for a woman to have an abortion, cannot be dismissed simply as another example of control over the body; rather, it has given women significantly more freedom in the control of their lives.

[...]

The debate on rape illustrates how Foucault fails to appreciate that, although the law may be far from perfect on this issue, the vulnerability of women in respect to sexual crime is at least recognized and some form of legal redress is offered. In a similar fashion, Foucault underestimates the significance of the psychological freedoms gained by women this century. So as we have seen, in *The History of Sexuality* Foucault argues that since the nineteenth century the body has been increasingly subjected to surveillance and discursively invested with neurosis; a self-regulating compulsion to confess is thereby produced in the subject. Psychoanalysis is one of the main practices through which the urge to confess is instilled and through which the production of self-policing individuals is ensured. This account of the regulatory role of psychoanalysis, however, is tendentious in its simplification, particularly in regard to those women who have benefited from a greater understanding of their sexuality and desires. Undoubtedly, the practice of psychoanalysis, in which the practice of confession is enshrined, is overlaid with oppressive power relations. However, much psychoanalytic work has meant a gain in freedom and expressive possibilities for women in regard to their sexuality: 'In the not too distant past there were commands of chastity for women, a production of female frigidity, a double standard for men, the stigmatising of deviant sexual behaviour, as well as all the kinds of degradation of love life about which Freud heard in his treatment room.'[22] By depicting the development of modern power as an increasingly insidious form of domination and by obscuring any lifeworld context which may organize and regulate the exercise of power, Foucault retroactively effaces the specific nature of female subordination and overestimates the normalizing effects of disciplinary power in industrial society.

There is no doubt that Foucault's theory of the body has made a stimulating contribution to feminist analysis of the subordination of women. Whist feminists recognize that an idea of the body is central to explanations of women's oppression, there are theoretical difficulties connected to defining the body. Foucault's thesis that power relations are constitutive of the social realm, and that they operate principally through the human body, provides a way for feminists to show how the construction of gender inequality from anatomical difference is central to the creation and maintenance of social hierarchies. Genealogical analysis of how different discursive practices shape the body circumvents the need to posit an original difference which is represented *a posteriori* in social practices.

Yet despite the potential of Foucault's theory of the body for feminist critique, I have also argued that it is limited in crucial respects. Feminist awareness of these limitations has tended to focus on the lack of attention given to the gendered character of the disciplined body. Foucault's failure, albeit unintentional, to consider issues of gender results in the perpetuation of a 'gender blindness' which predominates in the very forms of orthodox social theory which he claims to attack. Whilst the criticism of gender blindness is not without force, I have argued that it is not necessarily the most serious limitation of Foucault's theory of the body. Rather, following criticisms of Foucault's undifferentiated and unidirectional account of power, I argue that a more serious flaw is the definition of individuals as 'docile' bodies which cannot explain many of the experiences of women in modern society and results in an impoverished and over-stable account of the formation of gender identity. The paradox that Foucault's work presents for feminists is that, by placing so much emphasis on the body as a historically specific entity, he finishes by bypassing any notion of individuality and experience. Thus, whereas feminists have recognized the need to show that women are more than passive victims of domination through the rediscovery and revaluation of their experiences and history, Foucault's understanding of individuals as docile bodies has the effect of pushing women back into this position of passivity and silence.

Notes and References

1 Sandra Lee Bartky, 'Foucault, femininity and the modernisation of patriarchal power', in *Feminism and Foucault*, ed. I. Diamond and L. Quinby (Northeastern University Press, Boston, Mass., 1988), p. 75.
2 Ibid., p. 64.
3 Patricia O'Brien, *The Promise of Punishment* (Princeton University Press, Princeton, N.J., 1982), p. 68.
4 Michel Foucault, *Discipline and Punish*, tr. A. Sheridan (Peregrine, Harmondsworth, 1977), p. 168.
5 Nancy Fraser, 'What's critical about critical theory?', in *Feminism as Critique*, ed. S. Benhabib and D. Cornell (Polity, Cambridge, 1987), p. 44.
6 Bartky, 'Foucault, femininity', pp. 82–3.
7 Pierre Bourdieu, *Distinction* (Routledge and Kegan Paul, London, 1984), pp. 169–225.
8 Denise Riley, *Am I That Name?* (Macmillan, London, 1988), p. 7.
9 Ibid., p. 107.
10 Peter Dews, *Logics of Disintegration* (Verso, London, 1987), p. 188.
11 Michel Foucault, *Power/Knowledge*, ed. C. Gordon (Harvester, Brighton, 1980), p. 142.
12 Michel Foucault, *The History of Sexuality*, tr. R. Hurley (Penguin, Harmondsworth, 1978), p. 33.
13 Ibid., p. 101.
14 Ibid.
15 Ibid., pp. 59–60.
16 Foucault, *Discipline and Punish*, p. 138.
17 Dews, *Logics of Disintegration*, p. 166.
18 Judith Butler, *Gender Trouble* (Routledge, London, 1990), p. 31.
19 Ellen Willis, 'Comment', in *Marxism and the Interpretation of Culture*, ed. L. Grossberg and C. Nelson (Macmillan, London, 1988), p. 118.
20 Jürgen Habermas, *The Philosophical Discourse of Modernity* (Polity, Cambridge, 1987), p. 290.
21 Foucault, *History of Sexuality*, p. 144.
22 C. Honegger, quoted in Habermas, *The Philosophical Discourse of Modernity*, p. 292.

20

The Case of Habermas and Gender

Nancy Fraser

To my mind, no one has yet improved on Marx's 1843 definition of critical theory as "the self-clarification of the struggles and wishes of the age."[1] What is so appealing about this definition is its straightforwardly political character. A critical theory, it says, frames its research in the light of the contemporary social movements with which it has a partisan though not uncritical identification. For example, if struggles contesting the subordination of women figured among the most significant of a given age, then a critical social theory for that time would seek to shed light on the character and bases of such subordination. It would employ categories and explanatory models that revealed rather than occluded relations of male dominance and female subordination. And it would demystify as ideological rival approaches that obfuscated or rationalized those relations. In this situation, then, one of the standards for assessing a critical theory, once it had been subjected to all the usual tests of empirical adequacy, would be: How well does it theorize the situation and prospects of the feminist movement? To what extent does it serve the self-clarification of the struggles and wishes of contemporary women?

In what follows, I am going to presuppose the conception of critical theory that I have just outlined. In addition, I am going to take as the actual situation of our age the scenario I just sketched as hypothetical. On this basis, I shall examine the critical social theory of Jürgen Habermas as elaborated in *The Theory of Communicative Action* and related recent writings.[2] I shall ask: In what proportions does Habermas's theory clarify and/or mystify the bases of male dominance and female subordination in modern societies? In what respects does it challenge and/or replicate prevalent ideological rationalizations of such dominance and subordination? To what extent does it serve the self-clarification of the struggles and wishes of contemporary women's movements? In short, with respect to gender, what is critical and what is not in Habermas's social theory?

[...]

Let me begin by considering two distinctions that are central to Habermas's framework. The first is the distinction between the symbolic reproduction and the material reproduction of societies. On the one hand, claims Habermas, societies must reproduce themselves materially; they must successfully regulate the metabolic exchange of groups of biological individuals with a nonhuman, physical environment and with other social systems. On the other hand, societies must reproduce themselves symbolically; they must maintain and transmit to new members the linguistically elaborated norms and patterns of interpretation that are constitutive of social identities. Habermas claims that material reproduction transpires via "social labor." Symbolic reproduction, on the other hand, involves the socialization of the young, the cementing of group solidarity, and the transmission and extension of cultural traditions. Finally, according to Habermas, in capitalist societies, the activities comprising the sphere of paid work count as material reproduction activities, since they are "social labor" and serve the function of material reproduction. In contrast, the childrearing practices performed without pay by women in the domestic sphere – let us call them "women's unpaid childrearing work" – count as symbolic reproduction activities, since, in his view, they serve socialization and the function of symbolic reproduction.

It is worth noting, I think, that Habermas's distinction between symbolic and material reproduction is susceptible to two different interpretations. The first takes it to demarcate two objectively distinct "natural kinds," implying that childrearing, for example, simply *is* in itself a symbolic reproduction activity. The second interpretation, by contrast, treats the distinction pragmatically and contextually, implying only that it could be useful for certain purposes to consider childrearing practices from the standpoint of symbolic reproduction.

Now I want to argue that the natural kinds interpretation is conceptually inadequate and potentially ideological. I claim that it is not the case that childrearing practices serve symbolic as opposed to material reproduction. Granted, they comprise language-teaching and initiation into social mores, but also feeding, bathing, and protection from physical harm. Granted, they regulate children's interactions with other people, but also their interactions with physical nature. In short, not just the construction of children's social identities but also their biological survival is at stake. And so, therefore, is the biological survival of the societies they belong to. Thus, childrearing is not *per se* symbolic reproduction activity; it is equally and at the same time material reproduction activity. It is a "dual-aspect" activity.

But the same is true of the activities institutionalized in modern capitalist paid work. Granted, the production of food and objects contributes to the biological survival of members of society. But it also and at the same time reproduces social identities. Not just nourishment and shelter *simpliciter* are produced, but culturally elaborated forms of nourishment and shelter. Moreover, such production occurs via symbolically mediated, norm-governed social practices. These serve to form, maintain, and modify the social identities of persons directly involved and indirectly affected. One need only think of an activity like computer programming for a wage in the US pharmaceutical industry to appreciate the thoroughly symbolic character of "social labor." Thus, such labor, like unpaid childrearing work, is a "dual-aspect" activity.

Thus, the distinction between women's unpaid childrearing work and other forms of work cannot be a distinction of natural kinds. Indeed, the classification of childrearing as symbolic reproduction and of other work as material reproduction is potentially ideological. It could be used, for example, to legitimate the institutional separation of childrearing from paid work, a separation that many feminists, including myself, consider a linchpin of modern forms of women's subordination. Whether Habermas uses the distinction in this way will be considered shortly.

The second component of Habermas's framework that I want to examine is his distinction between "socially integrated action contexts" and "system integrated action contexts." Socially integrated action contexts are those in which different agents coordinate their actions with one another by means of an explicit or implicit intersubjective consensus about norms, values, and ends. System-integrated action contexts, on the other hand, are those in which the actions of different agents are coordinated by the functional interlacing of unintended consequences, while each individual action is determined by self-interested, utility-maximizing calculations in the "media" of money and power. Habermas considers the capitalist economic system to be the paradigm case of a system-integrated action context. By contrast, he takes the modern nuclear family to be a socially integrated action context.

Once again, I think it useful to distinguish two possible interpretations of Habermas's position. The first takes the contrast between the two kinds of action contexts as registering an absolute difference. It implies that system-integrated contexts involve absolutely no consensuality or reference to moral norms and values, whereas socially integrated contexts involve absolutely no strategic calculations in the media of money and power. This "absolute differences" interpretation is at odds with a second possibility that takes the contrast, rather, to register a difference in degree.

Now I contend that the absolute differences interpretation is too extreme to be useful for social theory and that, in addition, it is potentially ideological. In few if any human action contexts are actions coordinated absolutely nonconsensually and nonnormatively. In the capitalist marketplace, for example, strategic, utility-maximizing exchanges occur against a horizon of intersubjectively shared meanings and norms; agents normally subscribe to some commonly held notions of reciprocity and to some shared conceptions of the social meanings of objects, including what sorts of things are exchangeable. Similarly, in the capitalist workplace, managers and subordinates, as well as coworkers, normally coordinate their actions to some extent consensually and with some reference to normative assumptions, though the consensus be arrived at unfairly and the norms be incapable of withstanding critical scrutiny. Thus, the capitalist economic system has a moral–cultural dimension.

Similarly, few if any human action contexts are wholly devoid of strategic calculation. Gift rituals in noncapitalist societies, for example, once seen as veritable crucibles of solidarity, are now known to have a significant strategic, calculative dimension, one enacted in the medium of power, if not in that of money. And the modern nuclear family is not devoid of individual, self-interested, strategic calculations in either medium. These action contexts, then, while not officially counted as economic, have a strategic, economic dimension.

Thus, the absolute differences interpretation is not of much use in social theory. It fails to distinguish the capitalist economy – let us call it "the official economy" – from the modern nuclear family. For both of these institutions are *mélanges* of consensuality, normativity, and strategicality. But if this is so, then the classification of the official economy as a system-integrated action context and of the modern family as a socially integrated action context is potentially ideological. It could be used to exaggerate their differences and occlude their similarities, for example, by casting the family as the "negative," the complementary "other," of the (official) economic sphere, a "haven in a heartless world."

Now which of these possible interpretations of the two distinctions are the operative ones in Habermas's social theory? What use does he make of these distinctions? Habermas maps the distinction between action contexts onto the distinction between reproduction functions in order to model the institutional structure of modern societies. He holds that modern societies differ from pre-modern societies in that they split off some material reproduction functions from symbolic ones and hand over the former to two specialized institutions – the (official) economy and the state – which are system integrated. Modern societies also develop two "lifeworld" institutions, which specialize in symbolic reproduction and are socially integrated: the nuclear family, or "private sphere," and the space of political deliberation, or "public sphere." Thus, modern societies "uncouple," or separate, two distinct but previously undifferentiated aspects of society: "lifeworld" and "system."

Now what are the critical insights and blindspots of this model? Consider, first, that Habermas's categorial divide between the "private sphere of the lifeworld" and the "private economic system" faithfully mirrors the institutional separation of family and official economy, household and paid workplace, in male-dominated, capitalist societies. It thus has some prima facie purchase on empirical social reality. But consider, too, that the characterization of the family as a socially integrated, symbolic reproduction domain and of the paid workplace, on the other hand, as a system-integrated material reproduction domain tends to exaggerate the differences and occlude the similarities between them. It directs attention away from the fact that the household, like the paid workplace, is a site of labor, albeit of unremunerated and often unrecognized labor. It obscures the fact that in the paid workplace, as in the household, women are assigned distinctively feminine, service-oriented and often sexualized occupations. And it fails to focalize the fact that in both spheres women are subordinated to men.

Moreover, this characterization casts the male-headed, nuclear family as having only an extrinsic and incidental relation to money and power. These "media" are taken as definitive of interactions in the official economy and the state but as only incidental to intrafamilial ones. But this assumption is counterfactual. Feminists have shown via analyses of contemporary familial decision-making, handling of finances, and wife-battering that families are thoroughly permeated with money and power. They are sites of egocentric, strategic, and instrumental calculation as well as sites of usually exploitative exchanges of services, labor, cash, and sex, not to mention sites, frequently, of coercion and violence. But Habermas's way of contrasting the modern family with the official capitalist economy occludes all this. It overstates the differences between these institutions and blocks the possibility of analyzing families as economic systems – as sites of labor, exchange, calculation, distribution, and exploitation.

[···]

Let me turn now to Habermas's account of late, welfare-state capitalism. Unlike his account of classical capitalism, its critical potential cannot be released simply by reconstructing the gender subtext. Here, the problematical features of his framework inflect the analysis as a whole and diminish its capacity to illuminate the struggles and wishes of contemporary women. In order to show how this is the case, I shall present Habermas's view in the form of six theses.

1 Welfare-state capitalism emerges in response to instabilities inherent in classical capitalism. It realigns the relations between the (official) economy and state, rendering them more deeply intertwined with one another as the state actively engages in "crisis management." It tries to avert or manage economic crises by Keynesian "market replacing" strategies which create a "public sector." And it tries to avert or manage social and political crises by "market compensating" measures, including welfare concessions to trade unions and social movements. Thus welfare-state capitalism partially overcomes the separation of public and private at the level of systems.

2 The realignment of the (official) economy and the state brings changes in the roles linking those systems to the lifeworld. First, there is a major increase in the importance of the consumer role as dissatisfactions related to paid work are compensated by enhanced commodity consumption. Second, there is a major decline in the importance of the citizen role as journalism becomes mass media, political parties are bureaucratized, and participation is reduced to occasional voting. Finally, the relation to the state is increasingly channeled through a new role, the social-welfare client.

3 These developments are "ambivalent." On the one hand, there are gains in freedom with the institution of new social rights limiting the power of capital in the (paid) workplace and of the paterfamilias in the bourgeois family; and social insurance programs represent a clear advance over the paternalism of poor relief. On the other hand, the bureaucratic and monetary means employed to realize these new social rights tend perversely to endanger freedom. As these media structure the entitlements, benefits, and social services of the welfare system, they disempower clients, rendering them dependent on bureaucracies and

therapeutocracies, and pre-empting their capacities to interpret their own needs, experiences and life problems.

4 The most ambivalent welfare measures are those concerned with things like health care, care of the elderly, education, and family law, for when bureaucratic and monetary media structure these things, they intrude upon "core domains" of the lifeworld. They turn over symbolic reproduction functions like socialization and solidarity formation to modes of system integration. But given the inherently symbolic character of these functions, the results *necessarily* are "pathological." Thus, these measures are more ambivalent than, say, reforms of the paid workplace. The latter bear on a domain that is already system integrated and that serves material as opposed to symbolic reproduction functions. So paid workplace reforms, unlike, say, family law reforms, do not necessarily generate "pathological" side-effects.

5 Welfare-state capitalism thus gives rise to an "inner colonization of the lifeworld." Money and power cease to be mere media of exchange *between* system and lifeworld. Instead, they tend increasingly to penetrate the lifeworld's *internal* dynamics. The private and public spheres cease to subordinate (official) economic and administrative systems to the norms, values, and interpretations of everyday life. Rather, the latter are increasingly subordinated to the imperatives of the (official) economy and the administration. The roles of worker and citizen cease to channel the influence of the lifeworld to the systems. Instead, the newly inflated roles of consumer and client channel the influence of the system to the lifeworld. Moreover, the intrusion of system-integration mechanisms into domains inherently requiring social integration gives rise to "reification phenomena." The affected domains are detached not merely from traditional, normatively secured consensus but from "value orientations *per se*." The result is the "desiccation of communicative contexts" and the "depletion of the non-renewable cultural resources" needed to maintain personal and collective identity. Thus, symbolic reproduction is destabilized, identities are threatened, and social crisis tendencies develop.

6 The colonization of the lifeworld sparks new forms of social conflict specific to welfare-state capitalism. "New social movements" emerge in a "new conflict zone" at the "seam of system and lifeworld." They respond to system-induced identity threats by contesting the roles that transmit these. They contest the instrumentalization of professional labor transmitted via the worker role, the commodification of lifestyles transmitted via the inflated consumer role, the bureaucratization of life problems transmitted via the client role, and the rules and routines of interest politics transmitted via the impoverished citizen role. Thus, the

conflicts at the cutting edge of developments in welfare-state capitalism differ both from class struggles and from bourgeois liberation struggles. They respond to crisis tendencies in symbolic, as opposed to material, reproduction; and they contest reification and "the grammar of forms of life" as opposed to distribution or status inequality.

[...]

Now what are the critical insights and blind spots of this account of the dynamics of welfare-state capitalism? To what extent does it serve the self-clarification of the struggles and wishes of contemporary women? I shall take up the six theses one by one.

1 Habermas's first thesis is straightforward and unobjectionable. Clearly, the welfare state does engage in crisis management and does partially overcome the separation of public and private at the level of systems.

2 Habermas's second thesis contains some important insights. Clearly, welfare-state capitalism does inflate the consumer role and deflate the citizen role, reducing the latter essentially to voting – and, we should add, also to soldiering. Moreover, the welfare state does increasingly position its subjects as clients. On the other hand, Habermas again fails to see the gender subtext of these developments. He overlooks that it is overwhelmingly women who are the clients of the welfare state: especially older women, poor women, single women with children. He overlooks, in addition, that many welfare systems are internally gendered. They include two basic kinds of programs: "masculine" ones tied to primary labor force participation and designed to benefit principal breadwinners; and "feminine" ones oriented to "defective" households, that is, to families without a male breadwinner. Clients of feminine programs, virtually exclusively women and their children, are positioned in a distinctive, feminizing fashion as the "negatives of possessive individuals"; they are largely excluded from the market both as workers and as consumers and are often stigmatized, denied rights, subjected to surveillance and administrative harassment. But this means that the rise of the client role in welfare-state capitalism has a more complex meaning than Habermas allows. It is not only a change in the link between system and lifeworld institutions. It is also a change in the character of male dominance, a shift, in Carol Brown's phrase, "from private patriarchy to public patriarchy."[3]

3 This gives a rather different twist to the meaning of Habermas's third thesis. It suggests that he is right about the "ambivalence" of

welfare-state capitalism, but not quite in the way he thought. Welfare measures do have a positive side insofar as they reduce women's dependence on an individual male breadwinner. But they also have a negative side insofar as they substitute dependence on a patriarchal and androcentric state bureaucracy. The benefits provided are, as Habermas says, "system-conforming" ones. But the system they conform to is not simply the system of the official, state-regulated capitalist economy. It is also the system of male dominance, which extends even to the lifeworld. The ambivalence, then, does not only stem, as Habermas implies, from the fact that the role of client carries effects of "reification." It stems also from the fact that this role perpetuates in a new "modernized" form women's subordination. Or so Habermas's third thesis might be rewritten in a feminist critical theory – without, of course, abandoning his insights into the ways in which welfare bureaucracies and therapeutocracies disempower clients by pre-empting their capacities to interpret their own needs, experiences, and life problems.

4 Habermas's fourth thesis, by contrast, is not so easily rewritten. This thesis states that welfare reforms of, for example, the domestic sphere are more ambivalent than reforms of the paid workplace. This is true empirically in the sense I have just described. But it is due to the patriarchal character of welfare systems, not to the inherently symbolic character of lifeworld institutions, as Habermas claims. His claim depends on two assumptions I have already challenged. First, it depends on the natural kinds interpretation of the distinction between symbolic reproduction activities and material reproduction activities, on the false assumption that childrearing is inherently more symbolic and less material than other work. Second, it depends on the absolute differences interpretation of the system-integrated versus socially integrated contexts distinction, on the false assumption that money and power are not already entrenched in the internal dynamics of the family. But once we repudiate these assumptions, then there is no categorial, as opposed to empirical, basis for differentially evaluating the two kinds of reforms. If it is basically progressive that paid workers acquire the means to confront their employers strategically and match power against power, right against right, then it must be just as progressive *in principle* that women acquire similar means to similar ends in the politics of familial and personal life. Likewise, if it is "pathological" that, in the course of achieving a better balance of power in familial and personal life, women become clients of state bureaucracies, then it must be just as "pathological" *in principle* that paid workers, too, become clients – which does not alter the fact that *in actuality* they become two different sorts of clients. But of course the real point is that the term "pathological" is

misused here insofar as it supposes that childrearing differs categorially from other work.

5 This sheds new light as well on Habermas's fifth thesis concerning the "inner colonization of the lifeworld." This thesis depends on three assumptions, two of which have just been rejected: the natural kinds interpretation of the distinction between symbolic and material reproduction activities, and the assumed virginity of the domestic sphere with respect to money and power. The third assumption is that the basic vector of motion in late capitalist society is from state-regulated economy to lifeworld and not vice versa. But the feminine gender subtext of the client role contradicts this assumption. It suggests that even in late capitalism gender norms continue to channel the influence of the lifeworld on to systems. These norms continue to structure the state-regulated economy, as the persistence, indeed exacerbation, of labor-force segmentation according to sex shows. And they also structure state administration, as the gender segmentation of US and European social welfare systems shows. Thus, it is not the case that in late capitalism "system intrusions" detach life contexts from "value orientations *per se*." On the contrary, welfare capitalism simply uses other means to uphold the familiar "normatively secured consensus" concerning male dominance and female subordination. But Habermas's theory overlooks this and so it posits the evil of welfare state capitalism as the evil of a general and indiscriminate reification. It fails to account for the fact that it is disproportionately women who suffer the effects of bureaucratization and monetarization and for the fact that bureaucratization and monetarization are instruments of women's subordination.

6 This entails the revision, as well, of Habermas's sixth thesis concerning new social movements in late capitalist societies. . . . Let me attempt an alternative explanation, at least for women, by invoking the experience of millions of women, especially married women and women with children, who have in the postwar period become paid workers and/or social welfare clients. Granted, this has been an experience of new, acute forms of domination. But it has also been an experience in which many women could, often for the first time, taste the possibility of a measure of relative economic independence, an identity outside the domestic sphere, and expanded political participation. Above all, it has been an experience of conflict and contradiction as women try to juggle the mutually incompatible roles of childrearer and worker, client and citizen. This experience of role conflict has been painful and identity-threatening, but not simply negative. Interpellated simultaneously in contradictory ways, women have become split subjects; and, as a result, the roles themselves, previously shielded in their separate spheres,

have suddenly been opened to contestation. Should we, like Habermas, speak here of a "crisis in symbolic reproduction"? Surely not, if this means the desiccation of meaning and values wrought by the intrusion of money and organizational power into women's lives. Emphatically yes, if it means, rather, an opening on to new possibilities that cannot be realized within the established framework of gendered roles and institutions.

If colonization is not an adequate explanation of contemporary feminism, then decolonization cannot be an adequate conception of an emancipatory solution. The first element of decolonization, the removal of system-integration mechanisms from symbolic reproduction spheres, is conceptually and empirically askew of the real issues. If the real point is the moral superiority of cooperative and egalitarian interactions over strategic and hierarchical ones, then it mystifies matters to single out lifeworld institutions – the point should hold for paid work and political administration as well as for domestic life. Similarly, the third element of decolonization, namely, the reversal of the direction of influence and control from system to lifeworld, needs modification. Since the social meanings of gender still structure late-capitalist official economic and state systems, the question is not *whether* lifeworld norms will be decisive but, rather, *which* lifeworld norms will.

What, then, of the remaining element of decolonization, the replacement of normatively secured contexts of interaction by communicatively achieved ones? Something like this is occurring now as feminists criticize traditional gender norms embedded in legal, government, and corporate policy. It is also occurring as feminists and antifeminists clash over the social meanings of "femininity" and "masculinity," the interpretation of women's needs, and the social construction of women's bodies. In these cases, the political stake is hegemony over what I call the "means of interpretation and communication." Feminists are struggling to redistribute access to and control over these sociocultural discursive resources. We are therefore struggling for women's autonomy in the following special sense: a measure of collective control over the means of interpretation and communication sufficient to permit us to participate on a par with men in all types of social interaction, including political deliberation and decision-making.

Notes and References

1 Karl Marx, "Letter to A. Ruge, September 1843," in *Karl Marx: Early Writings*, tr. Rodney Livingstone and Gregor Benton (Vintage, New York, 1975), p. 209.

2 Jürgen Habermas, *The Theory of Communicative Action*, vol. I, *Reason and the Rationalization of Society*, tr. Thomas McCarthy (Beacon Press, Boston, Mass., 1984); Jürgen Habermas, *Theorie des kommunikativen Handelns*, vol. II, *Zur Kritik der funktionalistischen Vernunft* (Surhkamp, Frankfurt am Main, 1981); both are also published in English by Polity Press.

3 Carol Brown, "Mothers, fathers and children: from private to public patriarchy," in *Women and Revolution*, ed. Lydia Sargent (South End Press, Boston, Mass., 1981).

21

Feminism and Modernism

Janet Wolff

'In or about December, 1910, human character changed.'

Virginia Woolf was, of course, a great champion of the moderns. The quotation is taken from her essay 'Mr Bennett and Mrs Brown' written in 1924, in which she celebrates 'the sound of breaking and falling, crashing, and destruction . . . the prevailing sound of the Georgian age'.[1] She contrasts the old-fashioned, long-winded, and contorted passages of description of the Edwardian novelists, particularly in Arnold Bennett's work, with the promise of the new writers to engage directly with character. James Joyce, T.S. Eliot, D.H. Lawrence, E.M. Forster, Lytton Strachey, and (implicitly) Virginia Woolf herself – the 'Georgians' – recognizing that 'the tools of one generation are useless for the next', began the task of creating a literature to suit the age.

But why December 1910? Virginia Woolf goes on to say that the change was not sudden and definite, adding only 'since one must be arbitrary, let us date it about the year 1910'.[2] The death of King Edward VII and accession of George V in that year is clearly the central symbolic event. But perhaps even more important was the first Post-Impressionist exhibition held in London. This was organized by Virginia Woolf's friend, Roger Fry, and it represented the first serious introduction into Britain of modernist painting from the continent. The date thus conjoins the aesthetic and the political, explaining the real significance of Woolf's literary categories of 'Edwardians' and 'Georgians'.

Virginia Woolf's feminist sympathies are well known, her essays *A Room of One's Own* and *Three Guineas* revived by contemporary feminism as still-topical and illuminating comments on the situation of women in literature, politics, and social life. In some of her literary critical essays, which are less widely read, she addresses the question of women's writing. For her, the 'change in human character' and in literature seemed to offer real possibilities for women to break away from what she describes as 'the sentence made by men' – loose, heavy, pompous. The woman writer, she says, must make her own sentence, 'altering and adapting the current sentence until she writes one that takes the natural shape of her thought without crushing or distorting it'.[3] She identifies such a development in the writing of her contemporary, Dorothy Richardson.

> She has invented, or, if she has not invented, developed and applied to her own use, a sentence which we might call the psychological sentence of the feminine gender. It is of a more elastic fibre than the old, capable of stretching to the extreme, of suspending the frailest particles, of enveloping the vaguest shapes.[4]

Women, unable to articulate their specific experiences and perspective in the world in a language formed and moulded by the dominant group, men, might now have the opportunity of working with the new, barely formulated literary and linguistic tools to speak for themselves.

In this essay I want to look at the relationship between modernism and feminism. Other feminists since Virginia Woolf have suggested that the revolution in the arts around the turn of this century offered exciting opportunities for women writers and artists, and that the death of realism meant the fragmentation of patriarchal culture. Sandra Gilbert and Susan Gubar have argued that modernism can be seen as a product of late nineteenth-century feminism, its texts to be read as a battle of the sexes. Alice Jardine claims that modernism allowed the 'putting of women into discourse'. Julia Kristeva's study of the 'revolution in poetic language' has been taken up by feminists inspired by her suggestion that avant-garde writing in late nineteenth-century France articulates the 'semiotic' (that is, the pre-Symbolic) which pre-dates the child's entry into language and into patriarchy. And in the visual arts, feminist critics have proposed the continuing radical potential for women of a modernist art practice.

I shall come back to some of these arguments later. However, their very diversity should warn against simplistic assertions and alert us to the complexities in this area. One of the issues to be clarified is the concept of 'modernism' itself. Most of those I have just cited date this at the turn of the century; but others are talking about the period of so-called high modernism (post-Second World War), as well as the *continuing* modernist tradition in the arts (those practices in architecture, dance, painting, and so on which resist the eclecticism, populism, and superficiality of the 'postmodern'). Perry Anderson has pointed out that 'a wide variety of very diverse – indeed incompatible – aesthetic practices' are concealed beneath the label 'modernism', including cubism, futurism, symbolism, constructivism, expressionism, surrealism, and others.[5] Noting, too, that the term covers a range of dates and places, and that unlike the terms 'Baroque', 'Romantic', and 'neoclassical' it does not designate a describable object in its own right, he concludes that 'modern*ism* as a notion is the emptiest of all cultural categories'.[6] It will be important, therefore, to clarify the different senses in which the term is used in the debates about feminism and modernism.

It should also be noted that the various arguments for modernism depend on rather different theories – both theories of gender and theories of representation. These range from Kristeva's and Jardine's post-structuralist/psychoanalytic perspectives to the more simplistic reading of literature as direct expression of social reality found in Gilbert and Gubar's work. Nevertheless, I believe it is worthwhile to pursue the question of the congruence of modernism and feminism, and I shall want to argue that modernism (carefully defined) had and continues to have critical and radical potential for women writers and artists.

Books on modernism usually take the period 1890–1930 as covering the major transformations of social and philosophical thought, aesthetic codes and practices, and scientific theory which have constituted our modern consciousness. Some vary by a decade or so, and others trace the early history or prehistory of modernism. The trajectory of modernism after mid-century is more energetically disputed, however, with regard both to its continued aesthetic and political radicalism as against its apparent incorporation into the institutions and values of capitalist society; and to its specific relationship to postmodernism (precursor, moribund parent, ally, competitor, etc.). For the moment I shall confine myself to the period of early modernism, around 1890 to 1930.

Given the great variety of movements, media, locations, and political affiliations involved, how might we define 'modernism'? Eugene Lunn offers a useful set of characteristics as the key features of this phenomenon, understood as a set of 'multiple revolts against traditional realism and romanticism'.[7] These are (i) aesthetic self-consciousness or self-reflexiveness; (ii) simultaneity, juxtaposition, or montage; (iii) paradox, ambiguity, and uncertainty; (iv) 'dehumanization' and the demise of the integrated individual subject or personality.[8] (It might be noted that these features of the 'modern' are strikingly similar to those often identified in the 1980s as the 'postmodern', though the relationship between the two is outside the range of discussion of this essay.) With this cluster of traits identifying a diverse set of anti-realist aesthetic practices, we can consider the proposal that modernism offered particular opportunities for feminist cultural and political interventions.

A glance at the standard histories of modernism is not very

encouraging. Like all histories of art, they are stories about men's achievements, in which women barely figure. H. Stuart Hughes's book, *Consciousness and Society*, which reviews the 'reorientation of European social thought' in the period 1890–1930, discusses the work of social thinkers, philosophers, psychoanalysts, and writers.[9] The book deals with twenty-four men and no women. Alan Bullock, in an essay which traces the origins of modernism, and catalogues its achievements in the arts, sciences, and social thought, lists one hundred and twenty modern innovators, of whom only four are women: one in literature (Gertrude Stein), two in dance (Isadora Duncan and Pavlova), and one in science (Marie Curie).[10] In his study of American writing in the 1920s, Frederick Hoffman includes only seventeen women in the one hundred and thirty-four entries in his biographical appendix.[11] It does not look as though modernism was a movement in which women participated very actively. Most people would find it difficult to think quickly of women modernist writers, for example, apart from (perhaps) Virginia Woolf.

[...]

In the visual arts, feminist historians have already provided us with many texts about the 'hidden heritage' of those women artists whom mainstream art history has obliterated from the record. More recently some of them have turned their attention to women and modernism. As in literature, the orthodox account of the history of modernism consists of a long list of the names of men. The official lineage begins with Manet or Cézanne, moves through Picasso, Mondrian, Man Ray, Dali, and others, and culminates in the institutionalized, mid-twentieth-century modernism of Jackson Pollock. Now we are beginning to know more about late nineteenth-century women painters like Suzanne Valadon, Mary Cassatt, and Berthe Morisot, marginalized in most histories of Impressionism and French painting. Books and exhibitions about Surrealism have reintroduced Leonor Fini, Frida Kahlo, Lee Miller, and Leonora Carrington to their proper place in the history of this movement. In the history of early twentieth-century German painting, Käthe Kollwitz and Paula Modersohn-Becker are better known than they once were. And women involved in painting at the moment of 'high modernism', like Lee Krasner, are beginning to receive the attention so far denied them while their husbands and male associates were exhibited, fêted, and recorded for posterity.

This task of rediscovering women artists in history has always been an essential one for feminist criticism. However, it has two serious limitations. In the first place, it is clear that in important ways it has made very little difference to the major institutions of publishing, exhibiting, criticism, and teaching in so far as they continue to (re)produce a distorted history of modernism. The growing body of knowledge about women is confined to women's studies courses and texts. Moreover, the official culture persists in focusing on the work of men; the important 1981 exhibition of international work at the Royal Academy in London, *A New Spirit in Painting*, showed the work of thirty-six men and no women. Griselda Pollock has demonstrated the dependence of modernism on the notion of the *male* creative artist,[12] and it is clear that the feminist critique of the establishment has more to contend with than a biased history of art. As Andreas Huyssen points out, modernism is always characterized as *masculine* (against the 'feminine' mass culture).[13] In other words, a necessary task will be to dismantle a particular ideology of modernism.

Second, feminist historians must not ignore the fact that art history is not entirely to blame for the marginalization of women. It is equally important to look at the social processes which operated to the disadvantage of women painters in the modern period, and which also explain their relative absence from cultural production. In every period in the history of the arts there have been particular practices and ideologies which have been obstacles to women's participation. By the late nineteenth century, exclusion from the life-class and from membership of the academies was no longer the issue. Nor was participation by writers in the public (male) world of the coffee-house. What were the specific features of cultural life in that period which worked to women's disadvantage?

Shari Benstock suggests that the central themes of modernist writing were bound to marginalize women, whose experience was not encapsulated therein. In particular she identifies the First World War as a major theme, and the postwar psychology of despair as a grounding for the literary movement.[14] But this idea of modernism, as she points out, automatically privileges the masculine experience. Women's different perspective on the war was seen as secondary, since they did not write about the trenches, the activism and involvement, the proximity of death. Nor did they experience the male bonding produced by the war, seen by some writers as central to modernism. So women's writing of the period, much of it at least as innovative as that of men, simply does not *count* as 'modernist', given a particular definition of that category. For modernism is conceived as much in terms of its content as in terms of its literary and formal characteristics. Huyssen, for similar reasons, warns against the over-enthusiastic claiming of modernism for feminism: 'The wholesale theorization of modernist writing as feminine simply ignores the powerful masculinist and misogynist current within the trajectory of modernism.'[15]

In the visual arts it is also possible to identify the central themes of modernism. According to Griselda Pollock, masculine sexuality and in particular its commercial exchange dominate the works seen as the 'founding monuments of modern art'.[16] (Manet's *A Bar at the Folies-Bergère* and *Olympia*, Picasso's *Demoiselles d'Avignon* are examples of an extensive genre.) This is related to the contemporary types of representation of space – the street, the bar, the café. The spaces painted by women, denied equal access to the public sphere with men, were primarily domestic spaces. Again, we could pursue this analysis to try to explain the absence of women from the modernist canon, whose primary subject matter was off limits to them.

But, as this reference to public and private spaces already indicates, we cannot understand gender differentiation around content without relating this back to the social differences in which it occurs. For the issue here is men's and women's very different experiences of 'the modern'. That is not to say that modernism is straightforwardly the art of modernity. Modernism is a particular set of practices and ideologies of representation; modernity is a specific historical experience. Modernism dates from the late nineteenth century; modernity is variously placed at the same date, identified as a sixteenth-century phenomenon, or located somewhere between the two. Baudelaire, undoubtedly the poet of modernity since he writes of the experience of the modern age and the modern city, is not in any definition a 'modernist' writer in aesthetic terms. And yet there is a relationship between the two. Raymond Williams has argued that there are 'decisive links between the practices and ideas of the avant-garde movements of the twentieth century and the specific conditions and relationships of the twentieth-century metropolis'.[17] The city experience, with its antecedents in the nineteenth century, is characterized by alienation and isolation among a crowd of strangers, and by the presence of crime and danger, as well as by the more positive vitality and 'possibilities of unity' offered by the very diversity of city life. Modernism itself developed in these circumstances, though Williams is careful not to identify it with the experience of modernity. 'It is not the general themes of response to the city and its modernity which compose anything that can be properly called Modernism. It is rather the new and specific location of the artists and intellectuals of this movement within the changing cultural milieu of the metropolis.'[18] In other words, describing modernity in art or literature does not constitute modernism. But, as Williams goes on to suggest, the radical transformations *in* the arts were made possible first by the changing social relations and cultural institutions, and second by the dislocations in language effected by immigration and the consequently frequent need for a second language. In such a way it becomes possible to see the relationship between the experience of modernity, its articulation in culture, and the formal innovations in artistic language which constitute modernism.

If modernism is, in this sense, the art of modernity, women's absence from the canon becomes a little clearer, for the subject matter embraced by the new cultural forms is primarily a masculine one. The experience of anonymity in the city, the fleeting, impersonal contacts described by social commentators like Georg Simmel, the possibility of unmolested strolling and observation first seen by Baudelaire and then analysed by Walter Benjamin were entirely the experiences of men. By the late nineteenth century, middle-class women had been more or less consigned (in ideology if not always in reality) to the private sphere. The public world of work, city life, bars, and cafés was barred to the respectable woman.

[...]

Three things are clear. First, the definition of the modern, and the nature of modernism, derived from the experience of men and hence excluded women. Second, women, of course, had their own experience of the modern world, and were engaged in articulating this in literature and painting. And third, there is no doubt that women writers and artists were as much involved in the revolution in literary and visual languages as men. That is why it is both possible and essential to rewrite the history of modernism, showing women's role in it. This means that we need to look again at the classics of modernism, to discover what we can now see as their very particular perspective on 'the modern'. It is not that men did not depict women. But the masculine definition of modernity produced a skewed account, in which the only women visible (apart from at home in the family) were 'marginal' women or women involved in less than respectable occupations.

[...]

Griselda Pollock has suggested that women artists may deploy space in their work in a way which is consonant with their gender-differentiated experience of the world. Looking at French Impressionist painters, and in particular Berthe Morisot and Mary Cassatt, she notes the frequent theme of the balcony, veranda, or embankment in their work, and argues that the balcony demarcates 'the boundary . . . between the spaces of masculinity and femininity inscribed at the level of both what spaces are open to men and women and what relation a man or woman has to that space and its occupants'.[19] The juxtaposition of two spatial systems in the canvas is peculiar to women's paintings, while similar works by men allow apparently free access to the world beyond the window or the balcony.

It is thus possible to undertake the analysis of work by women which does represent or allude to 'the public', and thereby both to understand women's particular relationship to that sphere and to begin to expand our notion of 'modern life' to include the female experience of it. In literature we can reread those stories in which women write about the excursion into the public, or the view of the public from the domestic sphere. Virginia Woolf's short story *Mrs Dalloway in Bond Street*, written in 1922–3, is not only a story about shopping for gloves; it is at the same time an account of a middle-class woman walking through London, observing (and being observed by) others, talking to a male acquaintance she meets, and reflecting on change since the pre-war days.[20] Here modernist strategies (breaking the narrative flow, shifting from the objective to the subjective, following the haphazard movement of the character's mind, switching briefly to the point of view of another person, and so on) facilitate this novel female account. Mrs Dalloway's perceptions, her thoughts, her selective view of what surrounds her are those of a woman, of her age and class, and produce a female account of the modern city. The fat lady in the motor car has 'taken every sort of trouble', but shocks Mrs Dalloway by wearing diamonds and orchids in the morning. Lady Bexborough in her carriage, with a white glove loose at her wrist, looks shabby to her. She notes the motherliness and homeliness of Victoria's statue, and reflects on the present Queen's duties of visiting hospitals and opening bazaars. Walking through Westminster and past the Palace evokes no thoughts about politics or war, except for the memory of the bereaved mother met at last night's party. This is not to stress the superficiality of women's thoughts, or their tendency to export the private into the public, but rather to comment on the ways in which women's perspective transforms the spaces of masculinity.

For the most part, however, women writers and artists did specialize in depicting the domestic sphere, portraying the world they knew best, and to which they had unlimited access. Griselda Pollock argues that here too modernism allowed women to produce new images which dislocated the dominant ideas of femininity and of women's proper role. For example, where men paint women at their toilet or bath in the voyeuristic mode characteristic of Degas or Manet, women paint the same theme with woman as subject rather than body.[21] More interestingly, formal dislocation can stand for social or personal unease. . . .

Now it is also conceivable that male writers and painters can, sometimes unintentionally, portray women's unease in patriarchal culture, including in their prescribed domestic role. Eunice Lipton has analysed Degas's 'uneasy images of women and modern life'.[22] We could see Vuillard's *Girl in an Interior* (1910) as a representation of a young woman hemmed in and trapped by the domestic (the tea things laid, the enclosure of space in which she sits, and so on). We could discuss Joyce's or Henry James's insights into women's experience in the modern world. We might want to say there are limitations on men's understanding of this, or we may praise their ability to see from women's point of view. But the central point is that the literature and art of modernism, as currently defined and categorized, marginalizes or excludes women's experience, gives priority to the public world (with a substantial genre of work showing men's perspective on the private). And it is now possible to question this categorization, and to show how many women artists, experimenting in aesthetic form, were formulating the specifically female experience of modernity. The new literary and visual forms and strategies were invented and deployed to capture and represent the changed situation of women in the modern world, both in the private and in the public arenas.

The fact that women are absent from the modernist canon, therefore, is cause for critically examining that canon rather than for reluctantly accepting that modernism proved inaccessible to women. Its foregrounding of specific key themes and subjects (the war, the public sphere, masculine sexuality, and so on) is not in any way essential to modernism as aesthetic strategy, as the participation of women from Impressionism to Abstract Expressionism testifies. We come back, then, to the question of whether modernism, with its deconstructive, questioning strategies, is particularly well suited to a feminist art practice – whether the new 'feminine sentence' identified by Virginia Woolf is capable, in a way earlier forms of writing were not, of expressing alternatives to patriarchal culture.

There can be no unqualified positive, or for that matter negative, answer to this question. Feminist critics are right to identify the political potential in modernist strategies, and if we look back at the characteristics listed by Eugene Lunn (self-reflexiveness, montage, paradox, 'dehumanization'), it is clear that such destabilizing strategies have the ability to disrupt and interrogate the prevailing modes of viewing and reading, and hence to expose the ideological character of representation, and put into question what has hitherto been taken for granted. This is as true for feminist practice as it is for any other radical cultural politics. Moreover, those strategies first developed in the 1920s are by no means outmoded, as many people have assumed. It is true that modernism as institution has been absorbed into the academy, its politics neutralized, and its techniques denuded of their shock value by their very familiarity in popular culture. But the judicious use of montage, defamiliarization, and other modernist tactics can still achieve that dislocation of thought aimed at by the early political modernists. Two feminist exhibitions in the 1980s have confirmed this: *Beyond the Purloined Image*, curated by Mary Kelly and shown at the Riverside Studios in London in 1983; and *Difference: On Representation and Sexuality*, shown in New York in 1984 and in London in 1985.

Psychoanalytic and semiotic theories also demonstrate that aesthetic strategies that subvert the rule of logic, reason, and realism can release the repressed voice of those who are silenced. Thus Kristeva's analysis of the 'semiotic' character of avant-garde writing has proved extremely suggestive for feminists. Other French feminists, encouraging a writing which comes 'from the body', also speak of the possibility of women's voice finding its expression in the free play of modernist language. Although any lingering essentialism in this account must be firmly resisted, the recognition that entry into language and entry into patriarchal culture are closely connected (though not identical, as some have argued) points to the liberatory potential of a writing or an art which comes from the unconscious (or, in Kristeva's terms, from the semiotic chora).

But there are also some reservations to be made. In the first place, modernism as *institution* had clearly lost its radical potential by the middle of this century. We have also seen how the institutions of modernism (criticism, art history, galleries, publishers) excluded women from their construction of a modernist canon. Nor can we assume that the specific modernist strategies identified by Lunn and others are intrinsically progressive. As Franco Moretti has argued, the politics of irony and ambiguity are by now equally part of the hegemonic culture. 'There is a complicity between modernist irony and indifference to history.'[23] And, as is well known, we are not short of examples of modernist artists and writers whose political affiliations were with the Right or even with fascism.

What we can still insist on, however, is the radical potential of the deconstructive strategies of modernist culture, when founded in an appropriate political and historical analysis. It is in this sense that we may still confidently look forward to the continuing production of modernist work by feminists. In conjunction with the overdue rewriting of the history of modernism, this will ensure that the exciting complementarity of feminist politics and modernist aesthetics is not abandoned because of intimidation in the face of the canon-makers.

Notes and References

1 Virginia Woolf, 'Mr Bennett and Mrs Brown', in *Collected Essays*, vol. 1 (Hogarth Press, London, 1966), p. 334.
2 Ibid., p. 320.
3 Virginia Woolf, 'Women and fiction', in *Virginia Woolf: Women and Writing*, ed. Michèle Barrett (The Women's Press, London, 1979), p. 48.
4 Virginia Woolf, 'Dorothy Richardson', in Barrett, *Virginia Woolf: Women and Writing*, p. 191.
5 Perry Anderson, 'Modernity and Revolution', *New Left Review*, 144 (March–April 1984), pp. 103, 113.
6 Ibid., pp. 102–3, 112.
7 Eugene Lunn, *Marxism and Modernism* (Verso, London, 1985), p. 34.
8 Ibid., pp. 34–7.
9 H. Stuart Hughes, *Consciousness and Society: The Reorientation of European Social Thought 1890–1930* (1959; Paladin, St Albans, 1974).
10 Alan Bullock, 'The double image', in *Modernism, 1890–1930*, ed. M. Bradbury and J. McFarlane (Penguin, Harmondsworth, 1976), pp. 62–7.
11 Frederick J. Hoffman, *The Twenties: American Writing in the Postwar Decade* (Collier, New York, 1962).
12 Griselda Pollock, 'Feminism and modernism', in *Framing Feminism: Art and the Women's Movement 1970–1985*, ed. Rozsika Parker and Griselda Pollock (Pandora, London, 1987), pp. 86, 105.
13 Andreas Huyssen, 'Mass Culture as woman: modernism's other', in *After the Great Divide: Modernism, Mass Culture and Postmodernism* (Macmillan, London, 1988).
14 Shari Benstock, *Women of the Left Bank: Paris 1900–40* (Virago Press, London, 1987), p. 26.
15 Huyssen, 'Mass culture as woman', p. 49.
16 Griselda Pollock, 'Modernity and the spaces of femininity', in her *Vision and Difference: Femininity, Feminism and Histories of Art* (Routledge, London, 1988), p. 54.
17 Raymond Williams, 'The metropolis and the emergence of modernism', in *Unreal City: Urban Experience In Modern European Literature and Art*, ed. Edward Timms and David Kelley (Manchester University Press, Manchester, 1985), p. 13.
18 Ibid., p. 20.
19 Pollock, 'Modernity and the spaces of femininity', p. 62.
20 Virginia Woolf, 'Mrs Dalloway in Bond Street', in *The Complete Shorter Fiction* (Triad Grafton, London, 1987).

21 Pollock, 'Modernity and the spaces of femininity', pp. 80–1.
22 Eunice Lipton, *Looking into Degas: Uneasy Images of Women and Modern Life* (University of California Press, Berkeley, Calif., 1986).
23 Franco Moretti, 'The spell of indecision', in *Marxism and the Interpretation of Culture*, ed. C. Nelson and L. Grossberg (Macmillan, London, 1988), p. 343.

22

Post-postmodernism? Theorizing Gender

Sylvia Walby

Postmodernism in social theory has fragmented the concepts of sex, 'race' and class, denying the pertinence of overarching theories of patriarchy, racism and capitalism. The postmodernist tendency has a double aspect: it is both a mode of theorization and a form of substantive analysis of gendered, ethnic and class phenomena. This reaction to modernist attempts to capture the nature of the social world in spare, elegant formulations is understandable given some of the simplicities and denials of important differences entailed in the old approach. I shall argue in this Reading, however, that the fragmentation has gone too far, resulting in a denial of significant structuring of power, and leading towards mere empiricism.

The fragmentation of macro-analytic concepts in the theorization of 'race', gender and class is a typical part of the postmodernist project. Within each of these fields, there has been a recent move towards arguing that the central category is too internally differentiated to be utilized as a significant unitary concept. Sometimes this has been argued with reference to the other categories, for instance, that women are too divided by ethnicity for the concept of 'women' to be useful. Sometimes the point is made more generally about the number of divisions between women being too great to enable us to utilize the concept of 'patriarchy'. In the field of 'race' and ethnicity it has been suggested that ethnic groups need to be finely differentiated and that the division into black and white hides more than it reveals, since some ethnic minorities do not appear to share the same disadvantages as others. In the debates on class, it has been argued that other divisions – for example, 'consumption cleavages' based on housing – are more important than social class in explaining political behaviour such as voting patterns. Here it has been suggested that divisions over housing tenure, such as owner occupation or tenancy, are better predictors of politics and voting than the 'classic' social divisions over the means of production. The postmodernist aspect of social theory focuses on complexity and denies the coherence of classic analytic concepts such as 'woman', 'class' and 'race'.

There is a substantive as well as a theoretical resonance of postmodernism in social analysis. One instance of this is the argument about a supposed change from organized to disorganized capitalism. Here it is suggested that the social divisions within capitalism are no longer centrally organized in terms of class divisions in the sphere of production, but have become both fragmented and decentralized beyond production into 'consumption'. A related debate is that about the increasing flexibilization of the workforce, where it is argued that monolithic forms of the capital–labour relation are being replaced by flexible utilization of various categories of labour. . . .

A further use of the concept of 'postmodern' in social analysis has been its application to particular cultural forms, especially those of architectural design. I have no quarrel with the distinctions between modernist and postmodernist drawn here, which, for instance, contrast the elegant simplicities of modernist skyscrapers with playful postmodernist pastiches which mix different architectural styles. This is not my concern here, but its usage in this context is not inconsistent with other usages of the concept of 'postmodern'.

I use the concept of 'postmodern' broadly to refer to changes which lead to fragmentation on a number of different levels, from substantive social reality to modes of social analysis. It is my claim that these have common features. I am not arguing that postmodernism simply follows on temporally from modernism. Rather it catches an analytic grouping of themes which are current in contemporary social science, the main aspect of which is fragmentation. The reality of or necessity for fragmentation has been argued empirically, and epistemologically. I shall argue that this tendency has been taken too far.

I shall be arguing that while the social relations involved in gender, 'race' and class have indeed changed, and while the notion of 'new times' does have some purchase on the world and the concept of 'flexibility' has some uses, the postmodernist argument has been taken too far in the attempt to disintegrate the concepts of gender and 'race' and to see capitalism as disorganized. Gender and 'race', or more precisely, patriarchy and racism, remain potent social forces, and capitalism has not withered away despite its new form. Rather than support the idea of the declining significance of 'race' or patriarchy, I shall argue that they remain virulent social divisions. However, I do not wish to argue for a return to the totalizing framework of traditional Marxism, which attempted to tuck all other forms of social inequality under that of class. This extreme modernist metanarrative I reject as well. I am arguing for mutual determination among the three systems of 'race', class and gender. Despite the call for complex accounts of social change, however, most sociologists in practice analyse at best only two out of the three of gender, 'race' and class, and often only one of these.

Finally, I am arguing for an international perspective. Neither class, nor 'race' nor gender can be understood within one country alone. We live in a world system, which is limited only marginally by national sovereignties. However, this world system is one not only of capitalism (as Wallerstein would argue), but also of racism and of patriarchy.

Within feminist analysis there has been a debate about whether the concepts 'woman' and 'patriarchy' necessarily imply a problematic essentialism. The strongest criticism has been reserved for the concept of 'patriarchy' with its implicit theory of gender inequality; but the notion of 'woman' too has come under attack for similar reasons. The concept of 'patriarchy' is criticized for implying that women's oppression is universal and for being unable to handle historical change. Analyses which use the concept of 'patriarchy' are criticized for being unable to deal with the differences between women, especially those based on class and ethnicity. This criticism is not reserved for those radical feminist analyses which use the concept, but has been extended to Marxist feminist and liberal feminist theory more generally. This wider body of feminist work has been criticized for inadequate appreciation of the significance of ethnic differences and inequalities.

Analyses from the perspective of women of colour have raised a number of important issues for theories of gender relations. First, the labour market experience of women of colour is different from that of white women because of racist structures which disadvantage such women in paid work. This means that there are significant differences between women on the basis of ethnicity, which need to be taken into account. Second, ethnic variation and racism mean that the chief sites of oppression of women of colour may be different from those of white women. This is not simply a statement that women of colour face racism which white women do not, but also a suggestion that this may change the basis of gender inequality itself. The best example of this debate is that of the family, which has traditionally been seen by white feminist analysis as a major, if not the major, site of women's oppression by men. Some black feminists, such as Hooks, have argued that since the family is a site of resistance and solidarity against racism for women of colour, it does not hold the central place in accounting for women's subordination that it does for white women. This warns against generalizing from the experience of a limited section of women (white) to that of women as a whole. A third issue is that the intersection of ethnicity and gender may alter ethnic and gender relations. Not only is there the question of recognizing ethnic inequality, and the different sites of oppression for women of different ethnicities, but the particular ways in which ethnic and gender relations have interacted historically change the forms of ethnic and gender relations.

Arguments about the differences between women have been taken a step further in the work of cultural studies' post-structuralist theorists. Some postmodernists argue that not only is the concept of patriarchy essentialist but so also is that of 'women'. These postmodern feminists draw theoretically upon the deconstructionism of Derrida, the discourse analysis of Foucault and the postmodernism of Lyotard. For instance, the project of the journal *m/f* was to argue that not only is there no unity to the category of 'woman', but that analyses based on a dichotomy between 'women' and 'men' necessarily suffer from the flaw of essentialism. Instead, there are considered to be a number of overlapping, cross-cutting discourses of femininities and masculinities which are historically and culturally variable. The notion of 'women' and 'men' is dissolved into shifting, variable social constructs which lack coherence and stability over time.

The project for many feminist post-structuralists is to explore the variety of forms of femininity and masculinity. The substantive focus is usually an investigation of the forms of representation of gender in cultural texts such as film, literature, magazines and pictures. These writers try to catch the nuances of different forms of femininities. Following Derrida and Foucault, these writers make a break with the restrictions of the Freudian tradition and its deep structures of the psyche. As in the Lacanian tradition, there is a focus on language and subjectivity. There are two main types of analysis, one following Derrida with a focus on 'difference', and one Foucault with a focus on 'discourse'. Derrida's concept of difference does not allow much conceptual space for power inequalities, while Foucault's notion of discourse has power through knowledge at its heart. Feminist interventions attempt to criticize and rework rather than simply adopt these approaches.

The deconstructionist emphasis, common in the journal *m/f*, takes as its project the breaking down of the unitary notion of 'woman' because of the essentialism it sees behind such a concept. The intellectual project is to examine how the category women is constructed. . . .

The postmodern critics have made some valuable points about the potential dangers in theorizing gender inequality at an abstract and general level. However, they go too far in their dispersal of identity and power and consequently there are many limitations to their accounts of gender relations. First, they typically neglect the social context of power relations. In so far as power is discussed it is represented as highly dispersed, so dispersed as to preclude the possibility of noting the extent to which one social group is oppressed by another. This dispersal together with a de-emphasis of economic relations makes analyses of gender within a Foucauldian tradition overly free-floating. (Power is not neglected in the analyses by Foucault himself, since for him the knowledge at the base of each of his discourses is also power, but it is very dispersed.)

Second, the postmodern critics go too far in asserting the necessary impossibility and unproductive nature of investigating gender inequality. While gender relations could potentially take an infinite number of forms, in actuality there are some widely repeated features and considerable historical continuity. The signifiers of 'woman' and 'man' have sufficient historical and cross-cultural continuity, despite some variations, to warrant using such terms. It is a contingent question as to whether gender relations do have sufficient continuity of patterning to make generalizations about a century or two and a continent or so useful. While the answer to this cannot be given at a theoretical level, I would argue that in practice such generalization is possible. There are sufficient common features and sufficient routinized interconnections for it to make sense to talk of patriarchy.

The postmodernists are correct to point out that many of the existing grand theories of patriarchy have problems in dealing with historical and cultural variation. But their solution of denying causality itself is unnecessarily defeatist. The problems in many theories of patriarchy are due to a contingent, not necessary, feature in the analyses. Their problem is that they utilize a simple base–superstructure model of causal relations. In a theory in which there is only one causal element it is not surprising that there are difficulties in understanding variation and change. This problem can be solved by theorizing more than one causal base. The solution to this problem is to theorize patriarchy as composed of six structures rather than one and to theorize the different forms of patriarchy which are produced as a consequence of their different articulation. The six main structures which make up a system of patriarchy are: paid work, housework, sexuality, culture, violence and the state. The interrelationships between these create different forms of patriarchy. The ability to theorize different forms of patriarchy is absolutely necessary to avoid the problems of simple reductionism and of essentialism. In private patriarchy the dominant structure is household production, while in the public form it is employment and the state, though in each case the remainder of the six structures is significant. In the private form the dominant mode of expropriation is individual, by the husband or father; in the public it is collective, by men. In the private form the strategy is exclusionary; in the public it is segregationist.

Using such a model for Britain over the last hundred and fifty years, two main forms of patriarchy may be identified: the private based on the household; and the public based on the subordination of women in the public sphere. These forms are found in different periods and among different ethnic groups. There has been a historical shift from public to private. In contemporary Britain, Asian women are more likely to be subordinated within private patriarchy; Afro-Caribbean women by public patriarchy; with white women in between. These are differences in form and are contingently, not necessarily, related to degrees of patriarchy. This point is important in that it enables us to theorize the different forms of patriarchy which are specific to different ethnic groups, without this getting conflated with the question of degree of patriarchy. For instance, the presence of women in the public sphere, especially paid work, may be associated with greater freedoms, but it may not, and may merely indicate a longer working day. I shall come back to this point.

A parallel argument to postmodernist accounts of gender has been advanced in the case of 'race'. It has been argued that the distinction between black and white is too simplistic and does not capture the range of experiences of people of different ethnic minorities. It is suggested that we need to differentiate between, in Britain, Afro-Caribbeans and Asians and, indeed, to subdivide Asians into Hindu and Muslim. (Asians in Britain are from the Indian subcontinent, India, Pakistan and Bangladesh, unlike many Asian-Americans who are of Chinese or Japanese ancestry.) . . .

The argument is similarly about the diversity of experience, in particular that some ethnic minorities are 'successful' in terms of education and employment. The implication of this is that racism should not be treated as the main determinant of the disadvantage of some ethnic groups if others can 'succeed'. Thus again the import of the fragmentation of the ethnic categories is to criticize the more radical writings for their emphasis on discrimination as the most important determinant of the disadvantaged position of ethnic minorities or women. Again this may give rise to the substitution of analyses of difference rather than inequality. A further differentiation within specific ethnic groups is made by some class analysts, who analyse the relative success of some members of an ethnic group and the disadvantage of others. For instance, Wilson analyses the growth of a black middle class and a black underclass of the truly disadvantaged.

There have been two main forms of postmodernist argument in relation to class. First, that class is no longer the main social and political divide because of the growth of internal class divisions. This argument has been advanced particularly in relation to 'consumption cleavages', such as that of housing. For instance, differences in housing tenure, especially the movement into home ownership out of renting from the public sector, have had a significant impact on social and political location.

A second version is the 'new times' thesis, particularly the argument that capitalism has changed from an organized to disorganized form in recent years. The 'new times' writers have argued variously that capitalism has changed from being organized to disorganized; from corporatist to post-corporatist; from Fordist to post-Fordist; that the labour process has become flexibilized; that labour markets have become more segmented; that there has been a decline in the degree of homogeneity of the working class and working-class organizations; that the main focus of politics has changed from production to consumption; and that culture has changed from modernist to postmodernist. These theses have been grouped together to form a composite 'new times'. While there are significant differences between these writers on a number of issues, they share some important themes. They agree that there has been a disintegration of the mid-twentieth-century bargain between capital and labour, which is considered as the origin of the welfare state. They share a belief in an increasing complexity in political and cultural cleavages and that a movement away from the politics of the capital–labour struggle over production is the most important political struggle.

These writers have caught something, but I would argue that their view of the fragmentation of capitalism and their failure to see any overall pattern other than disintegration are results of their insufficiently theorizing gender and ethnicity. If they were to theorize these sufficiently, then they would see not disorganization but rather a new form of organization, which played the elements of gender, ethnicity and class in a slightly different format, but not so dramatically differently as to warrant the term 'disorganization'. Aspects of these new forms of organization are considered more fully in the context of a discussion of the new international division of labour.

Gender and ethnicity are absent from most of these accounts, apart from the occasional footnote, though in a few the arrival of women is seen to herald the breakup of the corporatist bargain. The latter occurs with the reference to the apparently new 'feminization' of the labour force, the development of so-called 'new social movements' such as feminism, and the related apparent decline in the degree of homogeneity of the working class and working-class organizations. However, gender and ethnic divisions within the workforce are not new. Women have always been a disadvantaged minority within the workforce. Ethnic minorities, of different origins, have always been a significant component in the workforces of not only the United States but also Europe (the UK utilized Irish labour before that from the 'Commonwealth'). The leadership of the labour movement has always been drawn from the native white male group; the other groups have always contested this. These divisions are ever present, as are the social and political struggles around them. They do not represent a new, postmodern phenomenon.

[...]

Gender, ethnicity and class cannot be successfully explained within one country; the international dimension is of crucial significance. Most internationalist analyses have taken capital as the dominant force. Following from my discussion in the previous section I argue that this is wrong, and that we need to theorize ethnicity and patriarchy on a world scale as well.

The international dimension is of importance, not only as a form of variation in gender relations in employment, but also for its effect on gendered employment relations in Britain. Most basically, the standard of living in nations such as Britain depends upon the labour of those in the Third World, through unequal exchange relations. Further, the specific forms of industrial restructuring, which have had different effects upon male and female workers in the metropoles such as Britain, the United States and West Germany, have depended upon new international forms of capital. The new international division of labour has an intensely gendered form, although this is not often recognized. A strong case for the interconnectedness of the exploitation of First and Third World women by patriarchal capitalism is made by Mitter and by Mies.

Mitter's book integrates a concern with class, gender and 'race' on an international level.[1] She argues that the new international division of labour has involved new forms of exploitation of workers, and that the labour of black women has been particularly central to this process. Mitter sees the new international division of labour developing as a result of a two-way movement of capital. In the first instance capital moves to the Third World in search of labour cheaper than that in the First World. The labour of women is particularly exploitable because of the conditions of subordination in which women live. Hence one increasing labour pool for capital is that of Third World women. The evidence for this is especially strong in the newly industrializing countries of Asia, in particular Taiwan, South Korea, Singapore and Hong Kong. This exploitation is associated with the repression of trade unions and the militarization of the state. The exploitation of women is not confined to factory work but extends into the sale of their sexuality through organized prostitution and sex-tourism. Here Mitter's account moves beyond the simply economic level into an appreciation of the significance of sexuality as a terrain of women's subordination.

The second instance is in the capitalist heartlands where new forms of 'flexible' working practices involve increases in the exploitation of the labour of certain sectors of the workforce. These forms of economic restructuring are facilitated, though not determined, by new forms of technology. Capital demands a cheap, flexible and disposable workforce, and this need is met by women. Mitter draws particularly on the examples of electronics and clothing workers to illustrate her case. For instance, the branch plants of the electronics industry in the peripheral regions of the UK have particularly recruited married women with little prior experience of factory work. They are preferred for similar reasons to those of capital in the Third World: that they have 'nimble fingers' and are cheap, patient and docile. The employers have the power to define the work as not skilled, despite the dexterity needed. In these new forms of working arrangements there is an increasing tendency to subcontract work away from the main employer, so that the subcontractor rather than the main employer bears the brunt of fluctuations in product demand, and also to ensure a greater degree of control for the main employer. Mitter argues further that racism in Europe makes it difficult for ethnic minorities to obtain employment in the mainstream primary sector of the economy. Hence ethnic minorities are likely to end up in vulnerable positions in the ethnic businesses which are concentrated in precarious niches in the secondary sector of the economy. The most extreme version of this is outworking, in which individuals work at home and are self-employed rather than employees. It is more often women who engage in this form of labour, a practice not discouraged by their men who see it as a way to ensure that the women perform the full range of domestic labour.

In both instances the new forms of capitalist economic organization involve the increased polarization of the workforce and particularly utilize the labour of black women in the newly created 'flexible', casual jobs. Mitter argues that this gives black women across the world a common economic position despite national boundaries, and thus a common political interest. Hence her thesis of the common fate and common bond of women in the newly globalized economy.

Mitter's book represents a tremendous synthesis of a mass of research detail and activists' reports on the new international division of labour and women. Its central thesis that the new international division of labour is as much a strategy about gender as it is about capital is extremely well substantiated by a wealth of detail. Mitter has captured the structure of the changes without losing the nuances of local specificity. However, questions remain. First, the general thesis of the new international division of labour has come under critical scrutiny. Gordon argues that the thesis is massively overstated.[2] While the movements of capital have occurred in some industries, such as the textile industry which is the focus of the work of Froebel et al.,[3] they have not occurred in others. Further, the movements are merely fluctuations which do not necessarily represent long-term trends. Hence, the thesis should not be overstated as a universal feature of contemporary capital. Second, Mitter details the position of women but does not theorize it. We are left unclear as to the structures which determine women's subordination. Is it the result of patriarchy, or simply the outcome of a concatenation of events? Is it structured or is it merely a historical accident? At places Mitter emphasizes the importance of the family and of men's active resistance to women's movement beyond it. In the absence of a theorization of gender inequality we are left with capital as the main motor of change and gender relations as the background. Yet given the foregrounding of women's experiences by Mitter this would not appear to be her intention. Perhaps we should say it is a wonderful account of the changes and how they fit together, but the theorization of gender and its interrelationship with 'race' and class is left undone.

Mies engages in a more explicitly theorized account of women on a global scale.[4] Like Mitter she is concerned with the recent restructuring of capital and with the interconnections between class, gender and 'race' on an international level. An important difference is that Mies seeks to theorize gender relations in terms of patriarchy. Patriarchy, like capitalism, is a world system. Patriarchy is maintained by a series of structures and practices including the family, systematic violence and the expropriation of women's labour. Mies uses the term 'capitalist-patriarchy' to refer to the current system which maintains women's oppression. She argues that we need to go beyond the old usage of the term 'patriarchy' which refers to the rule of the father since, she argues, many other categories of men – for example, male bosses – are involved in the subordination of women. Capitalism, for Mies, is the latest form that patriarchy takes. Thus she reverses the more conventional hierarchy between the two systems and argues that patriarchy pre-dates capitalism and has analytic priority. She resolves the dilemma of dual systems theory, as to how systems of 'patriarchy' and 'capitalism' might interrelate, by theorizing capitalism as an expression of patriarchy.

Mies argues that the dependence of women in the industrialized countries is only possible because of the exploitation of women in non-industrialized countries.

> It is my thesis that these two processes of colonization and housewifization are closely and causally interlinked. Without the ongoing exploitation of external colonies – formerly as direct colonies, today within the new international division of labour – the establishment of the 'internal colony', that is, a nuclear family and a woman maintained by a male 'breadwinner', would not have been possible.[5]

Mies argues that the domestication or, as she calls it, the housewifization of women in the metropolitan capitalist nations is dependent upon the exploitation of the Third World. She argues that the development of this family form was historically specific and was restricted to the rise of imperialism during the nineteenth century. It started with the bourgeoisie and was spread to the working classes. The first stage is the process of forcible colonization and the development of the luxury trade. The second stage is the development of an internal colony, in which women are colonized by men in Europe. The relations within the industrialized countries provide only half the account; the other is that in the colonies and ex-colonies.

Mies argues that there has been a shift in the international division of labour, from the old one in which raw materials were exported from the colonies for processing in the industrialized world and then marketed worldwide, to a new international division of labour. In the new division industrial production is transferred to the developing countries, producing unemployment in the industrialized countries. The general account is not new, but Mies argues that the gender dimension is more important than was previously recognized. It is women who are the new industrial producers in the Third World, and it is women who are the consumers of these items in the First World. Women are the optimal labour force in the Third World since their designation as dependent housewives enables them to be paid low wages. Women in the First World, fired from their jobs as a result of the transfer of industry, are the consumers.

A synthesis of the strengths without the weaknesses of Mies and Mitter would ideally take their impressive grasp of the international interconnectedness of recent economic changes and the significance of the interrelationship of class, gender and ethnicity for understanding this. However, it would need to produce a theorized account of gender and of ethnicity, not only of capital (taking more from Mies than Mitter), and would have a more accurate account of the actual changes in the patterns of women's paid and unpaid work (taking more from Mitter, but as qualified by Gordon). That is, it would produce a theorized notion of capital, patriarchy and racism as analytically autonomous systems of social structures, which are closely interconnected in practice. There is a new international division of labour, though this affects some branches of industry more than others, especially manufacturing rather than services. Women are being increasingly recruited into waged labour by capital, thus changing the nature of the patriarchal relations in which women (and men) are enmeshed. Black women, whether resident in the First or Third World, bear the brunt of the labour to a disproportionate extent, while receiving a disproportionately small part of the rewards.

We are seeing a change in the form of patriarchy in many, though not all, parts of the world: a shift from a relatively privatized form of patriarchy, in which women primarily labour in the home unpaid, to a relatively public form of patriarchy, in which women do waged work. These forms of patriarchy are to be found to differing extents in different ethnic groups.

Notes and References

1 Swasti Mitter, *Common Fate, Common Bond: Women in the Global Economy* (Pluto Press, London, 1986).
2 David M. Gordon, 'The global economy: new edifice or crumbling foundations', *New Left Review*, 168 (1988), pp. 24–64.
3 Folker Froebel, Jürgen Heinreichs and Otto Kreye, *The New International Division of Labour: Structural Unemployment in Industrialised Countries and Industrialisation in Developing Countries* (Cambridge University Press, Cambridge, 1980).
4 Maria Mies, *Patriarchy and Accumulation on a World Scale: Women in the International Division of Labour* (Zed Books, London, 1986).
5 Ibid., p. 110.

23

Feminism and Psychoanalytic Theory

Nancy Chodorow

In this discussion I address two general questions (or objections) posed by feminists and Freudians. . . . Both sets of questions concern a claim put forth by feminist psychoanalytic theory: that femininity, feminism, and Freud are in many ways related and gain meaning one from the other.

What are these two general questions? The feminist asks: what does Freud, or psychoanalysis, have to do with feminism? Does psychoanalysis have anything to do with feminism, or anything meaningful to say about women and "femininity"? The Freudian's question is the obverse. The clinician or psychoanalyst asks, what does feminism have to do with Freud? Does feminism have anything to do with Freud, or with our psychoanalytic understanding of female psychology?

Let us expand the feminist's question. The person who asks what Freud has to do with feminism may have in mind a number of objections. The first and most extreme position holds that women's oppression is political, economic, and social, and that psychology has nothing to do with it.

A second position claims that women are certainly psychologically oppressed, but that we do not need a theory as mystified or complicated – relying on the unconscious and intrapsychic – to explain and understand female socialization and how women turn out the way they do. It has nothing to do with the unconscious but is obvious in daily life. . . . "Society" imposes values on people and they have to behave according to societal expectations. "Society" expects that women will not achieve or be active, so they are not. People respond according to the social situation they are in and the rewards they get. . . .

Third, the feminist argues, Freud's theory was sexist, anti-woman, misogynist. Freud denied women their own orgasms; he thought that women were without as great a sense of justice as men, that they were vain, jealous, full of shame, and had made no contributions to civilization except for weaving. He thought it was obvious that any three-year-old would think the masculine genitalia better than the feminine.

We can also expand the Freudian's question. The person who asks what feminism has to do with Freud may also have several objections in mind. First, according to the Freudian, psychoanalysis is a psychological theory and clinical practice; by contrast, feminism is a political movement, or at most a political theory. Psychoanalysis does not have to do with questions of politics, equality, or inequality.

The Freudian makes a second, related claim, the methodological claim that psychoanalysis is a value-free science, simply recording the truth about human development and human psychological life and not taking sides. Feminism, by contrast, is value-laden, and has an axe to grind.

These are the sorts of questions and considerations I will discuss here.

[...]

To take on the feminist's questions: what does Freud have to do with feminism? Does psychoanalysis have anything meaningful to say about women and "femininity"? Recall the first objection: women's oppression is social and not psychological. It is concerned with wage inequality, job segregation, rape, wife-abuse, the unequal sexual division of labor in the home, men's power over women. Let us develop an answer.

To start, this social and political organization of gender does not exist apart from the fact that we are all sexed and gendered in the first place – that we all have a particular sexual organization and orientation, that we are all either men or women – which is a part of our fundamental identity and being in the world. We cannot understand the social and political organization and history of gender without simultaneously taking people's sexualization and engendering into account. So we are not talking here about external roles, as, for instance, sociologists might want us to do, that people are workers, parents, teachers; that we differentiate occupational from family roles, the mother role from the father role, that people are personifications of economic categories. This is not the case with gender. People do not just play out a gender role that combines with other roles, or that they can step out of. We cannot step out of being sexed and gendered; this is who we are. We do not exist apart from being gendered, or have a separate self apart from our engendering. So, when we are interested in questions of gender and sexuality – even when our questions are in the first instance social, political, or economic questions – there is no easy line between psyche and society. The social organization of gender, and people as sexed and gendered, are an inextricable totality or unity: the social organization of gender is built right into our heads and divides the world into females and males; our being sexed and gendered (our sexuality and our gender identity) is built right into social organization. They are only given meaning one from the other.

Feminist theory must be able to encompass these linkages, this totality. For our purposes here, feminist theory must include the fact that we are psychologically gendered and sexed as part of who we are. The social organization of gender is not an organization of empty places or role categories that anyone can fill, as people have argued about places in the economy or polity. In the social organization of gender, only particular people can fill particular places.

But feminism also wishes to change the social organization and psychology of sex and gender. Its basic argument is that gender and sexuality, whatever the biology that helps to inform these, are created culturally and socially; they are not immutable givens. Therefore, feminism demands a theory of how we become sexed and gendered.

Freud has given us such a theory. He has given us a rich account of the organization and reproduction of sex and gender, of how we are produced as gendered and sexed. Psychoanalytic theory is almost by definition a theory of sexuality and the way sexuality develops in women and men. Freud shows us why we do not exist apart from our particular sexualization and gender identification, even though that sexualization and that gender identification are created. Let me mention a few important elements in Freud's argument.

First, Freud divorced, or liberated, sexuality from gender and procreation. As Freud argues, there is nothing inevitable about the development of sexual object choice, mode, or aim; there is no innate femininity or masculinity. We are all potentially bisexual, active or passive, polymorphous, perverse and not just genital. How any woman or man understands, fantasizes about, symbolizes, internally represents, and feels about her or his physiology is a developmental product, and these feelings and fantasies may be shaped by considerations completely apart from biology. Woman is made, not born, Freud tells us, and he describes quite openly the special difficulty girls have in attaining an expected passive, heterosexual genital adulthood. Freud argued as well that both homosexuality and heterosexuality, for both sexes, are products of development. Neither is innate.

Freud demonstrated that all sex – procreative and non-procreative, genital and non-genital, heterosexual and homosexual, autoerotic and other-oriented, child and adult – is on a continuum and related in manifold ways. There is nothing special about heterosexual coitus for purposes of reproduction, which is just one kind of sex among many. Any organ, almost any object, can have erotic significance.

Freud, secondly, tells us how, in spite of the fact that sexual and gender development as we know them are not inevitable, the development of gender personality and sexual orientation tends to happen in regularized ways for women and for men. We find this in the classic account of the Oedipus complex, which explains the development of masculine identity, the development of female heterosexuality and love for the father, and differential forms of superego formation. We find it in the important, late account of the special nature of the pre-Oedipal mother–daughter relationship and the effect this relationship has on a woman's later life. And we find that Freud is quite candid about the fact that "normal" female development is very costly to women. In a passage in his lecture "Femininity," he says:

> I cannot help mentioning an impression that we are constantly receiving during analytic practice. A man of about thirty strikes us as a youthful, somewhat unformed individual, whom we expect to make powerful use of the possibilities for development opened up to him by analysis. A woman of the same age, however, often frightens us by her psychical rigidity and unchangeability. Her libido has taken up final positions and seems incapable of exchanging them for others. There are no paths open to further development; it is as though the whole process had already run its course and remains thenceforward insusceptible to influence – as though, indeed, the difficult development to femininity had exhausted the possibilities of the person concerned.[1]

In this discussion of how gender personality and sexual orientation develop in regularized ways for women and for men, there are two things of particular note for feminist theory.

First, Freud demonstrates that women's heterosexual attraction to men is very tenuously achieved and even then only partially. In the developmental account, a girl wants a penis from her father, not him for his own sake. Or she wants him as a refuge from mother, and always remains involved with mother, taking the character of her relationship with her mother to her relationships with men. Freud also implies that women only achieve "true" object-love in relation to children, not to men (he never looks to see if women achieve true object-love with women, which would be the logical extension of his theory). Women have no "natural" attraction to men; this attraction must be created.

Second, the theory of the masculine Oedipus complex is a theory of the reproduction of male dominance. Contempt for women, as penisless creatures, and identification with his father in their common masculine superiority, are normal outcomes of the masculine Oedipus complex. The masculine Oedipus complex results in what Freud's follower, Ruth M. Brunswick, calls "what we have come to consider the normal masculine contempt of women."[2] This is the manner by which a boy comes to give up his mother as a love-object and the reason he is willing to do so. Freud does not extend his insight here, but later analysts, like Karen Horney and Grete Bibring, were able to do so, to demonstrate the intertwining of contempt for women, fear of women, and devaluation of women, feminine activities, and ways of being as a developmental product of a boy's first love-object and primary parent being a woman. (Women, also, as a normal outcome of their Oedipus complex, come to devalue their own gender. We become who we are as men and women with a differential valuation of masculinity and femininity.)

Finally, Freud provided perceptive social analyses concerning oppressions of gender and sexuality. Two examples must suffice here. First, in " 'Civilized' sexual morality and modern nervousness," Freud analysed how sexual repression in childhood created conflictual and strained marital relationships which in turn affected the children of these marriages in ways that would reproduce the whole situation in the next generation. A bourgeois woman, Freud argues, brings the sexual repression forced upon her into marriage, along with her dependence on her parents. These together lead her husband to turn elsewhere for sexual satisfaction. As she matures, however, her sexual interests awaken, but by then her husband is no longer around. As a substitute, she sexualizes her relationship to her children, awakening their sexuality, which must then be repressed (helping to create their neuroses). She also feels guilty about the resentment she feels towards her husband because of his marital and sexual failures, and she turns this resentment inward into neurosis, which hurts her, her children, and her marriage. Second, *Studies on Hysteria* gives us the glimmering of an argument for a relationship between constraint on women and neurosis. Here, Freud argues against the view prevalent in his time that hysterics are degenerate and weak, and for the view that the women he treated were especially intelligent, creative, and moral. It was confinement, he suggested, for instance in caring for the sick, that did not allow the expression of a woman's gifts and capacities. Her neurosis was a reaction.

Thus, in answer to the first feminist question, I would suggest that Freud demonstrates the intertwining of psychological and social forms of gender oppression, and especially that he provides an account of the genesis of psychological aspects of gender and sexuality in their social context.

To turn to the second feminist objection: why do we need such a complicated theory, one relying on unconscious mental processes, when it is obvious that society treats women and girls differently and pushes them into certain roles? Two issues are relevant here. First, we need to explain and understand the tenacity of people's commitment to our social organization of gender and sex: the intensity of the taboo on homosexuality; why people often cannot change even when they want to; why a "liberated" man still has difficulty parenting equally or being completely happy about his successful, independent, liberated wife; or why a feminist woman might find it hard to be attracted to a non-macho, non-traditionally masculine man just because he's "nice" and egalitarian or to be unambivalent about choosing not to have children. Psychoanalysis helps here, because it shows us that we also live our past in the present.

[. . .]

Second, role-learning theories and theories of situational reinforcement in fact make people (women in this case) into passive reactors to society. Where can the initiative for change come from in a theory where people only react? Psychoanalysis, by contrast, is a theory founded on people's creativity. People always make something of their situation, even if that something is neurotic. (Neurosis, as we know from Freud's case studies, is highly original and individual.) People appropriate, fantasize, transform, react against, repress, resist, and symbolize their experiences. They create their inner object world and self. The goal of psychoanalysis is to make this individually created unconscious conscious, to move beyond being powered or directed by these active, though not always desirable to the individual, fantasies. Psychoanalysis, then, is a theory of human nature with positive, liberatory implications, a theory of people as active and creative.

Let us turn now to the third feminist objection, that Freud was sexist, and that psychoanalytic theory and practice have been oppressive to women. A few words will have to suffice on this very complex topic. First, we have to acknowledge that this criticism is not entirely wrong; Freud was indeed sexist. He wrote basically from a male norm and ignored women. He repeated cultural ideology in a context where it can be mistaken for scientific findings. He talks, for instance, about women's lesser sense of justice, of their jealousy, shame, vanity, and lack of contribution to civilization as if these were clinical findings, but then claims that these are "character-traits which critics [masculine critics, we may assume] of every epoch have brought up against women."[3] He finds it perfectly natural that girls would find their own genitals inferior, talks of these girls' "genital deficiency" and the "fact [note, not the fantasy] of her being castrated."[4] He recognizes the costs to women of female development, as I mentioned, but he is quite cavalier about it and does not care much. It seems that "Nature" has taken less care of the feminine function than the masculine, but this does not really matter, since the "accomplishment of the aim of biology [i.e. procreation] has been entrusted to man's aggressiveness and left to some extent independent of women's consent."[5] And so forth. Moreover, the evidence seems clear that psychoanalytic theory has been used against women, for instance, when they were labelled frigid because they did not have what turned out to be a non-existent vaginal orgasm, when they were called masculine for wanting careers.

But there is a method to Freud's misogyny, and this method can be used against him. Freud goes wrong, it turns out, when he undercuts his own psychoanalytic methodology and findings. I will give a few examples here. I suggest, however, that this lack of methodological consistency is very widespread.

First, as we have seen, psychoanalysis is founded on Freud's discoveries that there is nothing inevitable about the development of sexual object choice, mode, or aim, and that all sexuality is qualitatively continuous. Freud argues explicitly in the *Three Essays on Sexuality* and the *Introductory Lectures* that nothing inherently distinguishes procreative sex from any other sex. But Freud implicitly has a functionalist, teleological theory that gender differentiation is for the purposes of procreation. And he defines procreative sexuality in a particular way: Procreation is a product of active, genital masculine heterosexuality and passive, genital feminine heterosexuality. The theory becomes coercive, as Freud talks of Oedipal "tasks," and claims that "anatomy is destiny," in a functionalist sense rather than a maturational sense. These tasks, and this destiny, are not at all inevitable biologically, but they "must" happen for nature's requirements to be met.

But, this functionalism is not inherent to psychoanalysis; it comes in as Freud's value system. Similarly, women's passivity is not biologically inevitable, or even necessary to procreation. It is only necessary to male dominant sex, which Freud also takes for granted.

Second, in psychoanalytic theory, traumas need explaining. Psychoanalysis always looks for the history of something conflictual and powerful in previous individual history, except in the case of penis envy. Penis envy is self-evident, and not in need of any explanation: "she sees one and she knows she wants one." If we employ psychoanalytic methodology and look to the history of this powerful conflict, we can learn a lot about the origins of penis envy. We can learn about the pre-Oedipal girl's relation to her mother and early development; about her desire for autonomy and for something that can symbolize that autonomy; about symbols of male supremacy in the culture and in her family.

In addition to the male genitals being self-evidently better than female genitals, penis envy is "necessary" to the creation of female passivity. This is another reason why Freud does not take it as problematic or in need of explanation. In Freud's theory, girls come to want babies as a substitute for the penis (the penis–baby equation). But Freud also admits that girls already may want babies as part of their identification with their mother. This will not do for Freud, however, who has to get the girl's passive heterosexuality and a man into the baby picture. So, he claims, wanting a baby as identification with mother is "not an expression of femininity"! Only when the baby becomes a baby from the father as a substitute for a penis is it a feminine wish. Penis envy here becomes a developmental task, not inevitable or biologically determined but necessary for a girl to achieve her "destiny."

A third example of Freud's undercutting his own methodology is his claim that "woman is made, not born." The little girl is originally a "little man," because she loves her mother with an active sexuality. Both sexes are originally masculine. But there is a peculiar asymmetry in the developmental account here. Either, it would seem, you need to take a biological determinist view, in which case both women and men are born, or a developmental/cultural view, in which case both women and men are made. But if the little girl is a little man, then, seemingly, man is born but woman is made.

I could go on. The point is that unless one thinks that Freud took an extreme "biology of the sexes" position, and he did not (although many psychoanalysts do), his anti-woman statements are not intrinsic to psychoanalytic theory and modes of theorizing or to clinical interpretation, but counter to them. This is why there has been, and has needed to be, such extensive feminist critique and revision of Freud. But because the theory is so useful, this critique and revision have often been rich and provocative.

I now turn briefly to address the questions of the Freudian who wonders what feminism has to do with Freud, who thinks and argues that feminism has nothing to do with Freud. We can use our insights from the previous discussion to address these questions. The first question, or objection, argued that psychoanalysis is only a psychological theory. Clinical practice, interested in psychic structure, mental processes, and the development of sexuality, has nothing to do with politics, equality, or inequality.

My argument for why feminists must incorporate an understanding of Freud into their theory and practice should make the response here obvious. First, Freud made gender and sexuality central to his theory. Psychoanalysis is first and foremost a theory of femininity and masculinity, a theory of gender inequality, and a theory of the development of heterosexuality. Freud did not develop just any theory or clinical practice, but this specific one. Moreover, psychoanalysis makes a feminist argument that women (and men) are made and not born, that biology is not enough to explain sexual orientation or gender personality.

Just as we cannot have a theory of the social organization of gender and sexuality apart from a psychological theory, so we cannot have a psychological theory of sex and gender apart from the social and political. Freud's theory is a social and political theory. The analysis of development that Freud puts forth is not the analysis of any development, but of development in a particular social situation which is intrinsic to the theory. That children develop in a family where women mother or perform primary parenting functions explains the development that Freud found; biology does not explain this development. Psychoanalysis shows that women and men and male dominance are reproduced in each generation as a result of a social division of labor in which women mother (recall the account of men's psychology and ideology of male superiority, of the nature of women's heterosexuality and connections to women and children, of women's self-valuation, of the development of attitudes toward women). That people develop in a society with a heterosexual norm and with parents who are heterosexual is also intrinsic to Freud's theory and explains development, whereas biology does not (otherwise, why should a girl turn from the mother whom she loves? Why should the mother experience her son and daughter differently and treat them differently? Why should father–daughter attraction develop?).

Further, Freud's theory assumes, and is founded on, "politics" in a wide sense. The inequality of child and adult, the child's powerlessness, is central to the explanation of character and neurosis development and of the formation of defenses. The inequality of women and men is central to the theory. Freud does not give us a theory which explains what is necessary for species survival or the survival of any society. He constructs his theory around what is necessary for the perpetuation of a male dominant social organization, for the restriction of women's sexuality to be oriented to men's, for the perpetuation of heterosexual dominance.

What about the second psychoanalytic objection, that psychoanalysis is a value-free science with no axe to grind, that psychoanalysis does not take sides about anything, whereas feminism is value-laden and by definition takes sides. I would give two kinds of answers to this objection. Most generally, I would say, psychoanalysis is not a behavioral or medical science; it cannot be, and should not be, a value-free positivistic description and explanation of behavior. Rather, it is an interpretive theory of mental processes, and with an interpretive theory, we can only say that an interpretation makes better or worse sense, not that it is true or false, right or wrong. Similarly, psychoanalysis is not founded on the objective description of someone out there about someone studied. It comes out of the transference situation, a mutually created interpersonal situation which in its turn reflexively informs the processes of free association, interpretation, and the further working through of the transference. "Observer" and "observed" together create psychoanalytic theory and clinical practice, through their interaction and the interpretation of that interaction.

Notes and References

1 S. Freud, "Femininity," in *New Introductory Lectures on Psychoanalysis, The Standard Edition of the Complete Psychological Works of Sigmund Freud*, ed. James Strachey (The Hogarth Press and the Institute of Psychoanalysis, London) (hereafter *SE*), vol. 22 (1933), pp. 112–35.
2 Ruth Mack Brunswick, "The pre-Oedipal phase of the libido development," in *The Psychoanalytic Reader*, ed. Robert Fliess (International Universities Press, New York, 1940), pp. 231–53.
3 "Some psychical consequences of the anatomical distinction between the sexes," *SE*, vol. 19 (1925), p. 257.
4 *New Introductory Lectures*, *SE*, vol. 22, p. 132, and "Some psychical consequences," p. 253.
5 "Femininity," p. 131.

24

Death of the Subject?

Agnes Heller

Before someone is buried, they need first to be identified. Otherwise, the alleged corpse may resume business right after the funeral. No autopsy has yet been performed on the thing or concept termed 'subject', though its demise is taken as a matter of fact by many students of philosophy. Actually, the concept 'subject' is polysemic to an extent that it lends itself easily to verbal and conceptual manoeuvring. An author can make a case against the subject in one of its interpretations, and then shift the argument in the direction of another, completely different, interpretation, without even noticing the shift. No wonder then that readers and interpreters are often guilty of being a party to mistaken identity.

[···]

The 'end of the subject' thesis is far from being new. Behaviourism preached it half a century ago; one of the greatest philosophical masterpieces of our century, Wittgenstein's *Philosophical Investigations*, can be interpreted as a statement on behalf of this thesis. The contemporary French wave, however, has very little to do with the Anglo-American tradition, in spite of Lyotard's numerous references to Wittgenstein's language-game theorem. In the Anglo-American tradition, the disappearance of the subject is an undramatic affair. Wittgenstein never made the existential dimensions of his philosophy explicit. In the strict behaviourist tradition, the subject is dismissed as a mythological device of pre-scientific thinking. It deserves mention that French structuralism – non-Marxist and Marxist alike – has also played the scientific versus unscientific card. The very assumption that there might be something like an individual 'subject', consciousness or will, was dismissed by structuralism as a fairytale for grown-up children. The structuralists, especially Althusser, convicted the 'philosophy of the subject' as guilty of humanism, i.e. unscientificity, a long time ago.

The prehistory of the contemporary debate deserves a brief glance for obvious reasons. The political and philosophical development of many participants in the new wave took place under the influence of Althusserianism. The 'death of the subject' survived the demise of Marxism, and reappeared in a completely new guise. Now the concept of the 'subject' is rejected not because it is not scientific enough, but for the opposite reason; it is the 'subject' that created the havoc of science and technology. For one reason or another, it is always the subject that has to go.

In contrast to the drabness of behaviourism, the new wave of French ideology reintroduces the good old philosophical custom of presenting the thesis of the subject as a historical fiction. Quite a few philosophical narratives and metanarratives are at present in the air. The speculative strength of these narratives is extremely divergent. I shall refer, very briefly, only to the two most dominant narrative clusters: the neo-Heideggerian and neo (post)-structuralist. Since each participant in the discourse presents his or her own version of the master narratives, I cannot do justice to any of them. I need to add that, even if narratives are fragmented, they remain fictions. Derrida is right that there are nothing but fragments. I would only add that some create the illusion of having presented a whole; though in (post)modern philosophy this rarely happens.

The Heideggerian fiction of the death of the subject unfolds on three levels. The first level is mystico-speculative, the second is meta-philosophical, the third meta-historico-political. Owing to the constant interplay of the three levels, a wide territory is opened up for theoretical speculation. One can speak all in one breath about the forgetfulness of Being, about the Subject of metaphysics and its vicissitudes, and about the doom that has been cast by metaphysics over the modern world in the form of technology (and democracy). The more weighty a philosophy is, the more divergent its interpretations – textual exegesis being, perhaps, the most subjective mode of interpretation. This is not meant as an insult, for 'subjective' can have both positive and negative connotations, at least in my mind, depending on the context. Interpretations (being sometimes textual exegeses of textual exegeses) can appear, among others, in the following composite fictions (I have purposely simplified the language of the fictions):

1 The Subject as the brainchild of metaphysics disappears, whence metaphysics gets deconstructed; metaphysics is now going to be deconstructed, thus the subject disappears.
2 The Subject was the brainchild of metaphysics, modern technology is the ultimate consumption of metaphysics where the forgetfulness of Being comes to pass (albeit technology is also the manifestation of Being). This scenario does not lend much support to the belief in the 'death of the subject', for we are now witnessing the exuberant presence of the 'actualization' of the Subject rather than its final demise.
3 All this plus the deconstruction of the subject of philosophy (metaphysics) (and, maybe, also the presence of works of art) signal the coming end of the subject.

In all these combinations (and they are more complex and more sophisticated than my brief parody suggests) the 'death of the subject' is meant as something 'positive', if I am allowed to use a word from the metaphysical (and everyday) vocabulary. In the post-structuralist scenario, however, the same term refers to something 'dark, unwanted, or negative'. Foucault himself, who played an eminent part in the development of the second scenario, has preserved an aloofness, a playful pretence of mere descriptive objectivity. But this is not the emotional or intellectual experience of the reader who, reading Foucault, forms an opinion about prisons, mental asylums or the discourse of man or sexuality. Thus the negative evaluation of the 'end of the subject' is not a totally false and vulgar conclusion drawn by the uninitiated.

[...]

Whatever is termed 'subject' in contemporary philosophy, it is certainly thought of not as an empirical human universal, but as a real or imaginary entity, feature, attitude, propensity, which happens to belong to occidental history, or just to the modern world. I accept this view as a starting point. Occidental or European history is a modern text that incorporates certain pre-modern traces or testimonies and juxtaposes others as its opposite, its 'alter'. Since we share modern history, we cannot escape being party to the exegesis of the modern text. One can make an attempt at historical transcensus, to challenge the limits of our horizon. In fact, Heidegger attempts just this. I am not joining him, but prefer to clarify our own historical consciousness within the limits of our historical horizon.

There is a novel (and a film) with the title *The World According to Garp*. Neither the novel nor the film interests us here, only the title. There is a person called Garp, so there is also a world according to Garp. If there is a person called Joh Piper, there is also a world according to Joh Piper. There is a world according to every person who dwells here, in modernity. This is what I am going to call *subject.*

The first autobiography was written by Augustine. It was not about the world according to Augustine, but about the representative ascent to Truth. The first 'European' autobiographies were written in the period of the Renaissance. But Cardano did not describe the world according to Cardano, nor Cellini the world according to Cellini – they committed to paper the unusual, unique adventures that were experienced by the man Cardano or by the man Cellini in the world. Rousseau's *Confessions* can be rendered as 'the world according to Rousseau' by us. Yet Rousseau himself would have protested against such an enormous impertinence. His confessions were not the confessions of a contingent person, but the confessions of a representative personality; and the world, too, was meant to be representative, not just a world according to Jean-Jacques.

Let us cast a random glance over recent publications. The book market is swamped with life stories, success stories, failure stories and all else. Schlegel once said that everyone can write at least one good novel, his or her autobiography. I would date the emergence of the subject from this statement rather than from the Cartesian *cogito*. That everyone can write a (good) novel about themselves is questionable if good is understood as high artistic quality. Yet, if it is understood as engaging, or even interesting, reading, Schlegel proved to be a great prophet. If someone was only a little bit known as an actor or an actress, a singer, a director, a criminal, a businessman, a painter, a writer, a boxer, a baseball player, the son or the daughter, the sister or brother of the above, a politician of any renown, or even his secretary or factotum, one expects them to write their autobiography. All of them can expect to be widely read. If they cannot write, their autobiography will be taped and written down by someone else. Can we attribute this thirst for autobiography to mere curiosity, to our irresistible desire for eavesdropping or peeping through the keyhole? The taste for gossip is old, but the general drive to write autobiographies (and biographies) is new. Moreover, autobiographies are read even if one is completely ignorant in the field of the author's celebrity, or if the author is no celebrity at all, just that they happened to write about their life.

In modern autobiographies there is a dual authorship. The person is the *author of the text* (whether written or taped) and he or she is the *author of his or her own life*. To put it more cautiously, he or she is supposed to be the author of his or her own life, as he or she is supposed to be the author of his or her text. The dual authorship guarantees the truth content. The authors are expected to present the reader with a true world, in a dual understanding once again. They are expected to be truthful, that is, to relate a 'real' story (one is not supposed to write fiction as autobiography); and they are also expected to present a world (or rather two worlds, one internal and one external) as they see it, experience it and assess it; this is a world 'according to them'. Even the most pedestrian autobiography full of chunks of stereotyped banalities needs the makebelieve of a world that is the author's own making. To endorse Schlegel, men and women normally succeed beyond all expectations in presenting a world 'according to them'. They happen to present themselves as subjects.

Can we say that the world according to Joh is the subject of Joh? Or can we say that Joh *is* a subject who presents himself in a specific, subject-related interpretation of the world? Or can we say that Joh *as* a subject does the same?

That there is a world according to (Joh) is the subject (of Joh); yet the world according to Joh is not the subject of Joh. The world is not a subject at all, for there is no world according to the world, or, at least, this proposition does not make sense in the framework of my present speculations. In order for there to be a world according to Joh there must be a world first. Joh, like all other human beings, was born into a meaningful human universe. He, like everybody, was also born with the destiny to be related to all other bodies by meaning. He has received the network of meanings from his social universe. They were embedded in, and mediated by, the norms and rules of ordinary language, of the use of objects, and in the customs of his environment. Joh, like all other Johs before him, started his life in making out the meanings of the received meanings, while filling out the received meaning with his personal experience. Objects were given to his inborn drives (like proper food to his hunger), yet he developed a taste of his own. He was taught how and when to manifest his innate affects (like fear), yet he became courageous or a coward. Tasks were given to him (e.g. to cultivate a plot of land) and he did better or worse; his best innate propensities became developed or remained barren. Every Joh became thus a single person different from all others. Before learning the importance of sentences like 'I think' or 'I speak', he certainly learned the importance of the utterance 'I feel'. Every Joh is the navel of his universe.

Had our occidental Joh been born a few hundred years ago (or probably less) he would have received not only the network of meanings but also the general explanation of all of them. He would have learned why everything is as it is and why it should be so; why the stars shine, why people die, and what happens to them after they have died. So he would have received a fairly complete map of the external and internal world. Had our occidental Joh been born a few hundred years ago, there would not have been a world 'according to Joh', for there was no subject.

Let us proceed to the second question. Is Joh himself the subject we talk about? Is there a world 'according to Joh' because Joh (the subject) manifests itself in this world?

Subject can mean 'being subjected to' or 'subjecting something to'. In the modern philosophical vocabulary 'subject' is normally juxtaposed with 'object'. I could even add an unorthodox variation to the theme by rendering the meaning of subject as 'being related to something or someone'. Yet, orthodox or unorthodox, no interpretation of the 'subject' can possibly identify it with Joh or with anyone else.

Joh is, indeed, 'subjected to' several things. *What* he is subjected to is a historical variable (such as God, the sovereign, the constitution, the law of nature, the moral law), and, at least sometimes, open to interpretation and choice. But, whatever Joh is subjected to, he is never identical with his being-subjected-to. If Joh is a slave, he is not identical with himself-as-a-slave – if for no other reason, simply because he also subjects something to himself and is related to something else. Hegel, in the celebrated chapter on Master and Slave in his *Phenomenology of Spirit*,[1] presented the model of this dialectical turn and twist.

Many things are, indeed, subjected to Joh, and so are persons. *What* he subjects to his will is a historical variable, and sometimes open to interpretation and choice. (A Joh subjects the land while tilling it, yet another Joh shares the belief of having subjected nature as such; one Joh subjects his wives and children to his will, yet another Joh in other times will, perhaps, decide not to.) But whatever Joh subjects to his will, he is never identical with the practice of subjecting-to, if for no other reason, simply because he is also subjected to something, and because he also relates to something else.

The same could be said about Joh's 'being related to something'.

Joh as subjecting something, as being subjected to something and as being related to something *taken together* are still *not* Joh. Joh thinks, talks and feels many things in conjunction with these three relations. If two Johs subjected the same things to their will and were also subjected to the same persons and things, they would still remain different persons, and not only in their external appearances. Yet it is not this triviality I wanted to arrive at.

If Joh is not a subject, what *is* he then?

We can answer this question easily: Joh is a human person. This is a correct answer, but an irrelevant one in our quest for the subject. Since we began this quest with the intention of pinning down the subject in 'the world according to Joh', the abstract identity of a person with all the other persons cannot play a role in our enquiry, not even as the exemplification of what the subject is not. Only a theory of a collective Subject (with a capital S) needs to talk about human persons stripped of all their personal and cultural identification marks. And yet the sentence 'Joh is a subject' and the other sentence 'Joh is a human person' are closely linked. More precisely, they are linked *historically*. To this question I will shortly return.

The question still needs to be answered: if Joh is not a subject, what *is* he then?

Space does not allow us to identify our Joh as a Frenchman, as a merchant, and so on, and to show that all such and similar identifications are ultimately irrelevant for our enquiry.

We left our Joh (who had been thrown into a world by the accident of being born just then and there) as he started to cope with this accident, and became such-and-such a single person, different from all other single persons. He *is* a single person, he *is* this-and-this particular unique person. This is what he actually is. But he can be (become) a this-and-this unique person in two different ways. Becoming a unique person in one way or in another does not merely make a difference, it makes *the* difference. For the unique person can remain unique as a particular single being or can become an individual or a personality. Joh is either a particular single being or a unique personality (obviously he can also be some kind of a mixture of both).

Joh is a particular single being and remains one in the process of dual identification. He identifies himself entirely with the world he takes for granted, as he also identifies himself entirely with himself. Put bluntly, he identifies himself with the two *a priori* of his very existence: the genetic *a priori* and the social *a priori*. All his experiences are organized around the two *a priori*: since they are accidental, but he is unaware of their accidental character, he himself becomes entirely accidental. In contrast, the individual unique person (personality) never identifies himself or herself with the world as it is, neither does he or she identify himself or herself entirely with himself or herself. A personality reflects upon the world and upon himself or herself. His or her experiences are synthetic in character for he or she ceases to be accidental and becomes his or her own destiny.

It would be the greatest blunder to identify the individual personality with the subject in any of the latter's current interpretations. Certainly, the historical conditions of modernity, especially of early modernity, favoured the self-development of personalities of this kind. It is also true that the *modus operandi* of modernity does not put as severe a constraint upon personality development as most pre-modern societies did. But all this does not mean that 'the subject' and the individual personality are identical. The referents are different (for Joh *is* a personality, but he *is not* a subject) and there is, in addition, no necessary connection between the two. There were many outstanding individuals in ancient societies, yet one could hardly talk about Oedipus or Moses as 'subjects'. In fact, Hegel and many other thinkers of his time predicted the demise of personalities in the modern world (the time of the subject) and not without foundation. If you wish, you can also associate the birth of the subject with the birth of pettiness. If you agree that Joh's subject is the world according to Joh, then subject can be tied both to a person of unreflected singularity and to a person of individual personality. The lack of reflexivity and complete self-identification as well as total identification with the environment (that is, narcissism and conformity) do not prevent any Joh from conjuring up a world 'according to Joh'; experience teaches rather the opposite.

Having found out what Joh is, and what he can become, it suffices to repeat that he is not a subject. Yet even if this were true, could we still suggest that a person (this time we call her Jill) manifests herself or expresses herself *as* a subject in the world 'according to Jill'?

Mentioning Jill *as* a subject is to presume that Jill *has* certain features, faculties or capacities that can be termed her subject. Spatial thinking normally places this 'subject' of Jill inside the body of Jill.

That our conscious and unconscious 'inside' is not homogeneous is so obvious that one would be unlikely to find primitive cultures that knew it otherwise. Mythologies and other fictions explain this most fascinating and most commonly perceived wonder and many a map of the soul has been drawn and provided by religions and philosophies alike. That our so-called interior is not homogeneous is such an obvious experience that we can compare it only to the experience of seeing or hearing. We actually do not even need to become acquainted with (*erkennen*) this phenomenon given that we know it (*kennen*). What we need to receive, and what we actually do receive from the representative fictions, is *meaning*. Since we are bodies who are connected to all other bodies by meaning, we are surely connected to our own body by meaning. It is from the standpoint of the above (provided) meanings that we understand or interpret our own 'inside'; thus we make sense of our precognitive intuitions.

Jill, our next door neighbour, is in a predicament. Unlike her great-grandmother who understood herself as being composed of a mortal body and an immortal soul, she has no firm solace. Jill is approached and bombarded by at least a dozen entirely different and competing interpretations of her 'interior', and, alas, all of them do make sense of one kind or another, so she cannot figure out for sure what kind of map she is carrying inside. Could we, perhaps, maintain that doing something *as* a subject, or manifesting oneself *as* a subject, amounts to the following two-step procedure: first, one interprets one's own interior by a meaningful world-view and draws the map of one's interior by using an original draft-map of the world-view in question; and, second, one manifests this 'map' in understanding the world. The world according to Jill would then be a world that succeeds in manifesting the map Jill is carrying inside, as interpreted and perceived by Jill herself.

Just as Jill's predicament is modern, so is the subject. There is certainly a connection between Jill's predicament and the emergence of the subject. If there is not one single meaningful world-view or a conglomeration of a few world-views that provide the model-map for understanding the inside of us all, but rather just a marketplace where any world-view is freely exchangeable for any other, then there are no model-maps available for making out the meaning of the world, or anything in the world. There is, indeed, a congruency between the contingency of the internal map and the external map, yet there is no reason to believe that the external map will somehow express or manifest the internal map. The 'world according to Jill', that is, the subject of Jill, can hardly be identified with the direct manifestation of the internal map Jill is carrying inside her body, at least in her own perception.

[. . .]

We know that Jill has not inherited a master map of the soul to guide her self-understanding; neither did she receive from her ancestors a master narrative to guide her understanding of the world. Now we come to know about her third privation, namely that she has not inherited any ideal or real object as the centre of her self and, in this sense, as *hers* by birthright. These three privations together amount to a bunch of open possibilities. The bunch of open (because indeterminate) possibilities equals contingency. Modern men and women are contingent; they are also aware of their contingency. Mere possibilities are empty, yet they can be filled with an infinite variety of contents. Mere possibility is the potential of personal autonomy; it is also the potential of a total loss thereof. Modern men and women are unstable and fragile, yet they seek some solidity; they easily stumble into chaos, so they need at least a fragment of 'cosmos' to make sense of their own lives and, possibly, render meaning to it.

[...]

The subject–object relation is not an epistemological relation, but a historico-ontological one.

Subject is the idiosyncrasy of the interpretation of human world experience and self-experience under the condition of modernity.

Modern men and women manifest their being-in-the-world idiosyncratically. Whether they are (become) unreflected singularities or individual personalities, they all manifest their being-in-the-world as subjects. The world according to a conformist narcissist is a subject no less than the world of a personality. However, the equally idiosyncratic worlds are still different in kind. One Jill chooses herself and thereby also her main involvements (objects). The world according to her will centre around the issues of her involvements. So she gets as close as one ever can to what was once called subject/object identity. The other Jill, who lets others choose for her, will manifest the 'objects' of her self, these fragments of alien meanings, as firm and uncontestable truths whenever they support her narcissism, and as blatant untruths whenever they affront her network of self-identifications. What is idiosyncratic here (the world according to our second Jill) is the ever-changing character of the pendulum movement between unreflected other-identification and unreflected self-identification.

There are many narratives of the 'end of the subject' and all of them are entirely idiosyncratic in the form they happened to be first told by their authors. Sometimes our epoch is compared to Hellenism, with very little justification. Stoicism, Epicureanism, Scepticism and Platonism were professed and practised by thinkers for more than a millennium and beyond. It was the common world that reigned supreme, in philosophy maybe even more than in social and political life. But on our tree of philosophy no two leaves are alike; some leaves do not even resemble others. One sometimes gets the impression that the fury of innovation has completely enchanted what is now termed philosophy; evil tongues talk about fashion, competition and market by way of explanation.

In fact, many a modern philosophy is recycled, though in remarkably idiosyncratic ways. These recycled versions of the old participate in the world of idiosyncratic quasi-monads. Philosophical mini-narratives are quasi-monads only because the sole quality that makes them monads is their idiosyncrasy, their difference. Mini-narratives are not closed but open; they collide with one another, they go into combat, they are even sensitive to social change. This is how philosophy remains the mirror image of our unsocial sociability. Yet the monads are also influence-resistant; their receptivity threshold is extremely high and as a result very little real discourse goes on among them (philosophies of discourse are no exception).

The narratives of the end of the subject are extremely strong statements about both personalities and subjects. In fact, the narratives encapsulate worlds according to those contemporary philosophers. They are subjects; moreover they are *representative subjects*. The less we want them to be representative subjects, the more they become one. Not even philosophers can jump over their own shadows.

Reference

1 G.W.F. Hegel, *Phenomenology of the Spirit (Mind)*, Section B, ch. IV, subsection a.

PART V

Modernity, Democracy, Social Movements

THE SELECTIONS INCLUDED in this part reflect the complex nature of the changes now occurring in modern societies. Scott Lash and John Urry sketch in what they take to be a fundamental transition occurring in the contemporary world (Reading 25). Marx, they point out, had long ago diagnosed the restlessly expanding nature of industrial capitalism. The analysis of modernity which Marx, together with his collaborator Friedrich Engels, developed, holds that modern production unleashes extraordinary transformative powers, which a capitalistic society is poorly equipped to control. In the forthcoming socialist society, Marx believed, human beings would once again be able to direct to their own purposes the forces that they themselves had unleashed.

'Socialism' has developed into two main guises in the twentieth century. On the one hand, the entrepreneurial capitalism of the nineteenth century has largely ceded place to what has often been termed 'welfare capitalism': liberal democracy, with the universal franchise, accompanied by the welfare state. This is 'socialized capitalism'. On the other hand, an apparently more fully fledged version of socialism existed for some seventy years or so in the Soviet Union and later in the other Soviet-type societies of Eastern Europe. These have now, of course, become dissolved, while welfare capitalism has come under increasing attack from those who wish to expand the realm of market forces.

One might interpret this situation as representing a return of the older form of entrepreneurial capitalism, in the face of what now appear to be limitations of socialism in each of its main forms. Lash and Urry suggest a different interpretation. The decline of socialism and the resurgence of 'capitalist individualism' should be understood as part of a movement from an era of 'organized capitalism' to one of 'disorganized capitalism'.

Marx believed that, even prior to a fully fledged socialist revolution, capitalism would become increasingly organized – the 'laws of the market' would become regulated and the anarchy of capitalist production tamed. Max Weber held a similar view, even if he placed more emphasis than Marx did upon the importance of bureaucratic routine in achieving such organization. Yet the process today is actually the reverse – towards fragmentation.

'Disorganized capitalism' has a number of key features. It is directly bound up with globalization, especially the expansion of the global capitalist economy and the international division of labour. As a result of increasing globalization, states and large corporations are less able to regulate the economic conditions that affect them than once they were. Much more emphasis comes to be placed upon the importance of an educated and flexible labour force, while the blue collar working class declines in importance. Such flexibility is closely tied to the 'individualism' of disorganized capitalism, which is not just a reversion to the economic individualism of the nineteenth century. There is an increase in cultural pluralism – a phenomenon emphasized by those who claim that we now live in a postmodern era. For Lash and Urry, the structural characteristics of disorganized capitalism explain a great deal about the cultural changes usually associated with postmodernism.

Globalization is also the theme of the discussion provided by Immanuel Wallerstein (Reading 26). Wallerstein sees current processes of globalization as less distinct from past trends than do Lash and Urry. According to Wallerstein it has long been a mistake to discuss modern societies in separation from one another. Since its early development, industrial capitalism, together with the emerging Third World, have been part of an expanding 'world-system'. 'World-systems analysis', as Wallerstein conceives of it, is highly critical of some of the main orientations of mainstream social theory. The social sciences have become divided into distinct disciplines, such as sociology, anthropology, economics and so forth; yet Wallerstein sees little logic in such a differentiation, which actually prevents us from producing a comprehensive interpretation of modernity. He also argues that social science should incorporate a long-term historical dimension; and that the concept of 'society' should simply be dropped from social analysis. The term 'society' actually refers to the nation-state; and nation-states have from their inception been linked within globalizing orders. The focus of social science should therefore be placed squarely upon the analysis of world-systems. What Lash and Urry label disorganized capitalism is best understood as a phase in the development of a world capitalist economy that is today expanding to cover the whole globe.

Wallerstein is surely right to point to an association between capitalism and the nation-state, and also to emphasize that nation-states have only existed as part of a global nation-state system. However, such a standpoint explains little about why and how nation-states have taken the form they have. It seems probable that in the current era the sovereignty of nation-states is becoming weakened; but in earlier phases of capitalist development one of the most important phenomena to be explained is how it came about that nation-states were able to achieve much greater integration, and control over their subject populations, than was ever possible in the more traditional civilizations.

Christopher Dandeker (Reading 27) interprets the rise of the nation-state using Foucault's notion of 'surveillance'. Nation-states became internally much more centralized and sovereign than traditional states ever were as a result of the intensifying of bureaucratic surveillance in a number of the institutional contexts, including government, industrial organization and the military. In contrast to traditional states, the modern state is no longer segmental in form. In traditional civilizations the political centre was never able to regulate day-to-day life in local communities; such communities retained their own customs, sanctions and forms of authority. Partly as a result of the development of printing, which allowed for much more systematic record-keeping than before, plus the emergence of new techniques of bureaucratic administration, modern states have been able to influence day-to-day life in a much more thorough-going way.

The differentiation of 'state' from 'civil society', characteristic of the modern nation-state, does not separate what is inside the state from what is outside. 'Civil society' was actually *created* by the rise of the modern state: it refers to a politically established division between the public and private realms. Dandeker places considerable emphasis upon the role of war and military power in the formation of modern states. The armed forces became bureaucratized along with other institutions, and as a result military capabilities were vastly increased. The very global expansion of capitalism was in substantial degree dependent upon the consolidation of Western military power.

One of the distinctive features of the modern state, as Dandeker makes clear, is its association with citizenship rights and democracy. In the current period the association between the nation-state and democracy has become almost complete. Virtually all states throughout the world now call themselves 'democracies' – although of course many forms of coercive or authoritarian rule persist.

What is the nature of democracy and what is its likely future? These questions are considered by the Italian social thinker Norberto Bobbio in Reading 28. Democracy, he says, can best be defined as the rule of the majority. It is the system which has a set of rules and procedures connecting the concerns and interests of the mass of the population to politically binding decisions. In a modern society it is impossible for the mass of the population to participate in shaping the policies, or taking decisions, which affect them. Modern democracy is therefore representative democracy. It functions through mechanisms of regular elections and the existence of congressional or parliamentary assemblies. An effective democracy is a 'liberal democracy': democracy can only work reasonably effectively if there is freedom of speech and political association.

Bobbio is critical of those who call for further processes of democratization that go beyond liberal democracy. A basic attribute of democracy is that it only occupies one part of people's lives. Democracy would become oppressive if it were extended too far; in Bobbio's view this is in fact what happened in the Soviet Union and Eastern Europe. Too much democracy, as he puts it, kills off democracy. Soviet-type societies were based upon the ideal of more or less constant political participation; as a result, however, they produced a system of authoritarian rule.

As David Held points out (Reading 29) democracy has been at the centre of debates between Right and Left. For Rightist thinkers effective democracy is only possible if combined with free market enterprise. Equality and freedom are closely tied to economic individualism. Leftist authors, on the other hand, have argued that free market capitalism leads in fact to an unequal society in which the freedom of the 'have nots' is seriously impaired.

These views, Held accepts, are clearly divergent. Yet they share more in common than their various proponents ordinarily recognize. They all seek to maximize the circumstances in which people can develop and express their potentialities. They all agree that there should be protection against the arbitrary use of coercive power and that the 'rule of the majority' in Bobbio's terms is desirable. These joint preoccupations can be summarized in terms of what Held calls a 'principle of autonomy'. This states that individuals should be free and equal in determining the conditions of their own lives. Having established the principle of autonomy as at the core of democracy, Held concludes, we can specify some of the institutional conditions which make possible its realization.

In Reading 30, Held pursues these issues in the context of the international order. Democracy has developed everywhere primarily in relation to the internal constitutions of nation-states. Yet in an increasingly globalized social world, democratization is limited in its implications if it remains confined to the domain of the state. For there are many issues that affect individuals' lives today which are the result of global interconnections.

Against this backdrop, democratic politics today has to be reconstructed. Democracy has to come to terms with three aspects, or consequences, of globalization in particular. These are the reduced ability of the state to control external events which affect it; the influence of movements, and forms of nationalism, that come from 'below', as a response to globalization; and the way in which chains of interlocking global political decisions subvert the democratic mechanisms within the state.

Democracy must become transnational. Here Held speaks of the possible development of a 'cosmopolitan model of democracy' – rights and duties shaped in international law and involving agencies such as the

United Nations. A cosmopolitan global democracy would go well beyond the democracy of the liberal democratic state; but it would still enshrine the principle of autonomy specified in Held's earlier discussion.

Autonomy, in some sense or another, enters into the concerns of virtually all the 'new social movements', regardless of whether or not they are explicitly concerned with questions of democracy. The new social movements, as Boris Frankel points out (Reading 31), are usually associated with the structural changes which many believe are now affecting modern societies – whether these be conceived of as disorganized capitalism, postmodernism, post-industrial society, or something else. Frankel believes, however, that such movements have closer connections to pre-established economic and political problems than is usually thought. Class divisions are still central to modern capitalism and the new social movements will be of little consequence if they do not relate their goals to those of groups and organizations seeking to redress economic injustice and political oppression. There is a 'fundamentalism' within some social movements – such as the Green movement – which rejects all compromise with other agencies. Fundamentalism, however, according to Frankel, is not only dangerous – because it leads to polarization and even violence – but likely to subvert its own aims because it is unable to contemplate the tactical decisions and alliances in which any effective organization must engage.

The selections by Niklas Luhmann, Robert Goodin and Ulrich Beck (Readings 32, 33 and 34) focus particularly upon the Green movement and ecological issues. Luhmann notes how recent is the rise of ecological concerns. The physical environment has long been affected by human intervention. Only over the past two or three decades or so, however, has anxiety over the condition of the environment reached a high pitch. Sociology has been caught unprepared. The social sciences do not have established concepts that allow us readily to deal with ecological questions. The environment has been seen solely as a set of resources making possible the creation of economic wealth, not as a fragile array of organisms and natural systems with which humanity must coexist. 'Nature' was left as the purview of the aptly named 'natural sciences'. In pre-modern cultures, Luhmann points out, nature was regarded with veneration and awe; it was sacralized. With the coming of modernity, however, these attitudes were swept away. Nature came to be seen as wholly secular and was therefore lost as a domain relevant to social reflection or social research. Critical theory, as developed in Marxism and elsewhere, had just as little to say about ecological problems as more orthodox forms of social science.

Environmental issues have come to the fore largely because of the extreme nature of the dangers which global eco-systems now face. Yet it will certainly not do to confine sociological discussion to the question of how environmental threats might be coped with. What is needed is nothing less than a radical change in the sociological world-view. We should understand the 'environment' not as simply an external context for human action, but as an internally defined system which exists alongside the other institutions of the modern social order. The difference between the 'human social order' and the 'environment' has to be understood as itself generated by processes of social evolution.

Goodin seeks to analyse the content of Green political programmes. While, as Luhmann says, such programmes originated first of all in response to threats presented to the environment by modern technological development, the aims of most Green movements go much further than mere damage limitation. Ecological values mean understanding ourselves as part of nature and treating nature as an ally rather than as a subordinate. We return here to Habermas's view of a possible society beyond 'productivism'. A Green political programme, of a radical kind at any rate, is hostile to the present system of open-ended economic growth.

Green political theory might become an energizing medium for rethinking critical social thought. For although socialism now seems largely dead, we cannot suppose that capitalistic economic growth can persist indefinitely upon a worldwide scale. It is not only that the earth's resources are insufficient to sustain such a process; there would also seem to be more desirable and rewarding forms of life than one harnessed to unending economic growth.

This theme is pursued by Ulrich Beck in Reading 34, who questions some of the views suggested by Goodin, however. Ecological movements are concerned with defending nature against the encroachment of human beings. Yet what exactly is 'nature'? 'Nature', meaning a world untouched by human beings, has today almost completely disappeared; the physical environment, including even the climatic conditions of the earth, has been thoroughly transformed by human intervention.

Human beings are part of 'nature' too; again we find the problem of deciding where 'nature' begins and ends. Is it 'natural' to only have a certain number of children, to be a heterosexual, or to develop a muscular body? Humans intervene in their own development just as thoroughly as they do in the material environment. The idea advanced by some ecological movements of bringing about a 'return to nature' thus makes very little sense. The goals of ecological movements, Beck concludes, are actually social and presume ethical values that have to be socially justified.

25

The End of Organized Capitalism

Scott Lash and John Urry

In a sparkling passage in the otherwise maligned *Manifesto of the Communist Party*, Marx and Engels wrote of the

> Constant revolutionising of production, uninterrupted disturbance of all social conditions, everlasting uncertainty and agitation distinguish the bourgeois epoch from all earlier ones. All fixed, fast-frozen relations . . . all swept away, all new-formed ones become antiquated before they can ossify. All that is solid melts into air, all that is holy is profaned. . . .[1]

Bourgeois or capitalist society, then, is one of intense change, particularly in relation to where people live and how their lives are organized over time. According to Marx and Engels, as production is revolutionized in order to bring about massive savings of labour-time, people's relationships to each other across space are transformed since

1. capitalism has 'pitilessly torn asunder the motley feudal ties that bound man to his "natural superiors"';
2. the need for a constantly expanding market 'chases the bourgeoisie over the whole surface of the globe and destroys local and regional markets';
3. the 'immensely facilitated means of communication draws all . . . nations into civilisation' (for 'civilisation' we can read 'modernity');
4. enormous cities are created and this has 'rescued a considerable part of the population from the idiocy of rural life';
5. political centralization is generated as independent, loosely connected provinces 'become lumped together into one nation';
6. masses of labourers 'organised like soldiers' are 'crowded into the factory', the proletariat 'becomes concentrated in greater masses';

7 the development of trade unions is 'helped on by the improved means of communication that are created by modern industry and that place the workers of different localities in contact with one another'.[2]

Marx and Engels in the *Manifesto* are very much the analysts of 'modernity' and indeed see the bourgeoisie as a profoundly revolutionary class, setting in motion an extraordinary train of events, creating more formidable and sophisticated forces of production than all the previous centuries had managed. People's lives are thus controlled by a revolutionary bourgeois class – by a class with vested interest in change, crisis and chaos. The citizen in this modern era must learn not to long nostalgically for the 'fixed, fast-frozen relationships' of the real or fantasized past, but to delight in mobility, to thrive on renewal, to look forward to future developments in their conditions of life. As a world of change, it is a world which swings wildly out of control, menacing and destructive. The bourgeoisie thus moves within a profoundly tragic orbit. It has unleashed tremendous powers, but these powers are destructive as well as constructive, producing as well as resolving conflicts. Within this uncontrollable maelstrom the temporal and spatial structuring of people's lives is continuously transformed.

What Marx and Engels do in the *Manifesto* is thus to presage a massively influential set of social developments which have characterized Western societies roughly from the end of the nineteenth century onwards. What we want to suggest, however, is that this era of 'organized capitalism' that they in part outline has, in certain societies, come to an end, and that there is a set of tremendously significant transformations which have recently been literally 'disorganizing' contemporary capitalist societies – transformations of time and space, of economy and culture – which disrupt and dislocate the patterns that Marx and Engels so brilliantly foresaw.

In this claim that organized capitalism is – if sporadically and unevenly – coming to an end, in our claim that we are moving into an era of '*disorganized* capitalism', we are contravening the conventions, not just of 'orthodoxy', but of a good deal of solid and reasoned social science opinion. We risk offence, not especially to fundamentalists among Marxists and Weberians, but to purveyors of some of the more creative and better thought-out work which draws on these two traditions. In this context both Marxists and Weberians will generally contend that we are living in increasingly *organized* societies. Marxists will speak of 'monopoly capitalism', characterized by the increasing concentration of constant and variable capital complemented by the unidirectional tendency towards centralization of money capital. They will speak of 'finance capitalism', most notably marked by the interpenetration of money capital and productive capital. They may speak of 'state-monopoly capitalism' or 'late capitalism', in which a low-growth and low-profitability phase of capitalist development is counteracted through a combination of state economic subsidies and growth in size of the public sector. Weberians will similarly claim that contemporary society is imbued with increased levels of organization. They will point to the seemingly teleological growth of state bureaucracy in both capitalist and state socialist countries. They will point to an ineluctable rationalization in our whole gamut of institutions – of the school, the police, the civil service, the factory, trade unions and so on. They will view this process of further organization as the obverse side of secularization, in which the dissolution of internal constraints is progressively replaced by normalizing, individuating and ordering external constraints. We risk offence then to some of the best Marxist and Weberian opinion in the contention that contemporary capitalism is undergoing a process of disorganization.

We must begin here by clarifying our terms. The notion of 'organized capitalism' has a considerable pedigree dating back to Hilferding and was particularly developed by Jürgen Kocka and several other contemporary social historians. For these writers organized capitalism begins in most countries in the final decades of the nineteenth century as a consequence of the downward phase of the Kondratieff long wave which began in the mid-1870s. In Kocka's summary formulation, organized capitalism consists of the following interrelated features:[3]

1 the concentration and centralization of industrial, banking and commercial capital – as markets became progressively regulated; in comparison with the preceding epoch of 'liberal capitalism', special growth in producers' goods industries; the increased interconnection of banks and industry; and the proliferation of cartels;
2 the growth of the (famous) separation of ownership from control, with the bureaucratization of control and the elaboration of complex managerial hierarchies;
3 the growth of new sectors of managerial/scientific/technological intelligentsia and of a bureaucratically employed middle class;
4 the growth of collective organizations in the labour market, particularly of regionally and then nationally organized trade unions and of employers' associations, nationally organized professions etc.;
5 the increasing inter-articulation between the state and the large

monopolies; and between collective organizations and the state as the latter increasingly intervenes in social conflicts; development of class-specific welfare-state legislation;

6 the expansion of empires and the control of markets and production overseas;
7 changes in politics and the state, including the increasing number and size of state bureaucracies, the incorporation of various social categories into the national political arena; the increased representation of diverse interests in and through the state; and the transformation of administration from merely 'keeping order' to the attainment of various goals and national objectives;
8 various ideological changes concerning the role of technical rationality and the glorification of science.

We would add to Kocka's enumeration the following further features:

9 the concentration of industrial capitalist relations within relatively few industrial sectors and within a small number of centrally significant nation-states;
10 the development of extractive/manufacturing industry as the dominant sector with a relatively large number of workers employed;
11 the concentration of different industries within different regions, so that there are clearly identifiable regional economies based on a handful of centrally significant extractive/manufacturing industries;
12 the growth of numbers employed in most plants as the economies of scale dictate growth and expansion within each unit of production;
13 the growth and increased importance of very large industrial cities which dominate particular regions through the provision of centralized services (especially commercial and financial);
14 a cultural–ideological configuration which can be termed 'modernism', one aspect of which is Kocka's point (8) above; the other aspect is counterposed to such rationality and scientism and embraces, *inter alia*, aesthetic modernism and nationalism.

Clearly not all of these developments occurred either simultaneously or in the same way in all Western countries. In order to examine the varying developments in Germany, Sweden, Britain, France and the United States, it is necessary to distinguish between organization 'at the top' and organization 'at the bottom'. Organization at the top here includes, for example, the concentration of industry, increasing interarticulation of banks, industry and the state, and cartel formation;

organization 'at the bottom' includes, for example, the development of national trade union bodies, working-class political parties, and the welfare state. In this connection we shall argue that German capitalism was organized early on at both the top and the bottom (1873–95); American capitalism was organized fairly early on at the top but very late on and only briefly at the bottom; Swedish capitalism was only fully organized in the inter-war period at both the top and the bottom; French capitalism was only *fully* organized at top and bottom during and after the Second World War; and Britain was organized only late at the top but rather early at the bottom.

The following are three of the factors which we shall maintain determine the timing when, and the extent to which, the capitalism in each of these countries becomes organized. First is the point in history at which it begins to industrialize. The earlier a country enters into its 'take-off', the less organized *mutatis mutandis* its capitalism will be. This is because countries which are later industrializers need to begin at higher levels of concentration and centralization of capital to compete with those which have already been industrializing for some time. Second, there is the extent to which pre-capitalist organizations survive into the capitalist period. Britain and Germany became more highly organized capitalist societies than France and the United States: this is because the former two nations did not experience a 'bourgeois revolution' and, as a result, guilds, corporate local government, and merchant, professional aristocratic, university and church bodies remained relatively intact. Sweden interestingly occupies a mid-way position, in as much as the high level of state centralization during Swedish feudalism did not allow for the same flourishing development of corporate groups. And the third factor is size of country. For the industry of small countries to compete internationally, resources were channelled into relatively few firms and sectors. Co-ordination between the state and industry was then greatly facilitated, if not necessitated. At the same time there would tend to be higher union densities, more 'organization' of labour, where there were relatively few firms and sectors.

Following the same fourteen points, we will now set out what is meant by 'disorganized capitalism'.

1 The growth of a world market combined with the increasing scale of industrial, banking and commercial enterprises means that national markets have become less regulated by nationally based corporations. From the point of view of national markets there has then been an effective *de*concentration of capital. This tendency has been complemented by the nearly universal decline of cartels. Such

deconcentration has been aided by the general decline of tariffs and the encouragement by states, particularly the United States, to increase the scale of external activity of large corporations. In many countries there is a growing separation of banks from industry.

2 The continued expansion of the number of white collar workers and particularly of a distinctive service class (of managers, professionals, educators, scientists etc.), which is an effect of organized capitalism, becomes an increasingly significant element which then disorganizes modern capitalism. This results both from the development of an educationally based stratification system which fosters individual achievement and mobility and the growth of new 'social movements' (students', anti-nuclear, ecological and women's movements etc.) which increasingly draw energy and personnel away from class politics.
3 Decline in the absolute and relative size of the core working class, that is, of manual workers in manufacturing industry, as economies are de-industrialized.
4 Decline in the importance and effectiveness of national-level collective bargaining procedures in industrial relations and the growth of company and plant-level bargaining. This accompanies an important shift from Taylorist to 'flexible' forms of work organization.
5 Increasing independence of large monopolies from direct control and regulation by individual nation-states; the breakdown of most neo-corporatist forms of state regulation of wage bargaining, planning etc., and increasing contradiction between the state and capital (cf. fiscal crises etc.); development of universalistic welfare-state legislation and subsequent challenges from Left and Right to the centralized welfare state.
6 The spread of capitalism into most Third World countries which has involved increased competition in many of the basic extractive/manufacturing industries (such as steel, coal, oil, heavy industry, automobiles) and the export of the jobs of part of the First World proletariat. This in turn has shifted the industrial/occupational structure of First World economies towards 'service' industry and occupations.
7 The decline of the salience and class character of political parties. There is a very significant decline in the class vote and the more general increase in 'catch-all' parties which reflect the decline in the degree to which national parties simply represent class interests.
8 An increase in cultural fragmentation and pluralism, resulting both from the commodification of leisure and the development of new political/cultural forms since the 1960s. The decodification of some

existing cultural forms. The related reductions in time–space distanciation (cf. the 'global village') likewise undermine the construction of unproblematic national subjects.

9 The considerable expansion in the number of nation-states implicated in capitalist production and the large expansion in the number of sectors organized on the basis of capitalist relations of production.

10 Decline in the absolute and relative numbers employed in extractive/manufacturing industry and in the significance of those sectors for the organization of modern capitalist societies. Increased importance of service industry for the structuring of social relations (smaller plants, a more flexible labour process, increased feminization, a higher 'mental' component etc.).

11 The overlapping effect of new forms of the spatial division of labour has weakened the degree to which industries are concentrated within different regions. To a marked extent there are no longer 'regional economies' in which social and political relations are formed or shaped by a handful of significant central extractive/manufacturing industries.

12 Decline in average plant size because of shifts in industrial structure, substantial labour-saving capital investment, the hiving off of various subcontracted activities, the export of labour-intensive activities to 'world-market factories' in the Third World, and to 'rural' sites in the First World etc.

13 Industrial cites begin to decline in size and in their domination of regions. This is reflected in the industrial and population collapse of so-called 'inner cities', the increase in population of smaller towns and more generally of semi-rural areas, the movement away from older industrial areas etc. Cities also become less centrally implicated in the circuits of capital and become progressively reduced to the status of alternative pools of labour-power.

14 The appearance and mass distribution of a cultural–ideological configuration of 'postmodernism'; this affects high culture, popular culture and the symbols and discourse of everyday life.

[...]

We should also stress that what is meant here by 'disorganized capitalism' is radically different from what other writers have spoken of in terms of 'post-industrial' or 'information' society. Unlike the post-industrial commentators we think that capitalist social relations continue to exist. For us a certain level of capital accumulation is a

Table 25.1 Temporal and spatial changes in liberal, organized and disorganized capitalism

Phase of capitalist development	*Predominant temporal/spatial/ organizational structures*	*Spatial changes within each territory*	*Predominant means of transmitting knowledge and executing surveillance*
Liberal	Large-scale collapsing empires that had been built up around dynastic rulers or world religions; emergence of weak nation-states	Growth of tiny pockets of industry. Importance of substantial commercial cities as well as the expansion of new urban centres in rural areas	Handwriting and word of mouth
Organized	Nation-states within the ten or so major Western economies increasingly dominate large parts of the rest of the world through colonization	Development of distinct regional economies organized around growing urban centres. Major inequalities between new industrial and non-industrial regions and nations	Printing developed through 'print-capitalism'
Disorganized	Development of world economy, an international division of labour, and the wide-spread growth of capitalism in most countries	Decline of distinct regional/national economies and of *industrial* cities. Growth of industry in smaller cities and rural areas, and the development of service industry. Separation of finance and industry	Electronically transmitted information dramatically reduces the time–space distances between people and increases the powers of surveillance

necessary condition of capitalism's disorganized era in which the capitalist class continues to be dominant.

Notes and References

1 K. Marx and F. Engels, *Manifesto of the Communist Party* (Foreign Languages Press, London, 1888), pp. 53–4.
2 Ibid., p. 65.
3 J. Kocka, *Organisierter Kapitalismus*, ed. H. Winckler (Vandenhoeck and Ruprecht, Göttingen, 1974), pp. 20–4.

26

World-systems Analysis

Immanuel Wallerstein

'World-systems analysis' is not a theory about the social world, or about part of it. It is a protest against the ways in which social scientific inquiry was structured for all of us at its inception in the middle of the nineteenth century. This mode of inquiry has come to be a set of often-unquestioned *a priori* assumptions. World-systems analysis maintains that this mode of social scientific inquiry, practised worldwide, has had the effect of closing off rather than opening up many of the most important or the most interesting questions. In wearing the blinkers which the nineteenth century constructed, we are unable to perform the social task we wish to perform and that the rest of the world wishes us to perform, which is to present rationally the real historical alternatives that lie before us. World-systems analysis was born as moral, and in its broadest sense, political, protest. However, it is on the basis of scientific claims, that is, on the basis of claims related to the possibilities of systematic knowledge about social reality, that world-systems analysis challenges the prevailing mode of inquiry.

This is a debate, then, about fundamentals, and such debates are always difficult. First of all, most participants have deep commitments about fundamentals. Second, it is seldom the case that any clear, or at least any simple, empirical test can resolve or even clarify the issues. The empirical debate has to be addressed at a very complex and holistic level. Does the sum of derived theorizing starting from one or another set of premises encompass known descriptions of reality in a more 'satisfactory' manner? This involves us in all sorts of secondary dilemmas. Our known 'descriptions' of reality are to some extent a function of our premises; future 'descriptions' may of course transform our sense of reality. Does the 'theorizing' said today to encompass reality really encompass it? And last but not least, what does it mean to encompass reality 'in a satisfactory manner'? Is the latter criterion anything more than an aesthetic adjunct?

Not only are debates about fundamentals frustrating for all these reasons, but each side has a built-in handicap. The defenders of existing views must 'explain away' the anomalies, hence our present challenge. But the challengers must offer convincing 'data' in a situation where, compared to the hundred and fifty years or so of traditional social scientific inquiry, they have had far less time to accumulate appropriately relevant 'data'. In a subject matter inherently recalcitrant to experimental manipulation, 'data' cannot be accumulated rapidly. So a dispute about fundamentals may be thought of as analogous to a heavyweight championship bout, but without a referee and between two somewhat dyspeptic boxers, each with his left hand tied behind his back. It may be fun to watch, but is it boxing? Is it science?

And who will decide? In some sense, the spectators will decide – and probably not by watching the boxers, but by fighting it out themselves. So why bother? Because the boxers are part of the spectators, who are of course all boxers.

Lest we get lost in analogies, let me return to the discussion of fundamentals. I propose to take three common assumptions of social scientific inquiry and indicate what it is that makes me feel uncomfortable about them. . . .

The social sciences are constituted of a number of 'disciplines' which are intellectually coherent groupings of subject matter distinct from each other.

These disciplines are most frequently listed as anthropology, economics, political science and sociology. There are, to be sure, potential additions to this list, such as geography. Whether history is or is not a social science is a matter of some controversy, and we shall return to this later. There is a similar debate about psychology, or at least about social psychology.

It has been a growing fashion, since at least 1945, to deplore the unnecessary barriers between the 'disciplines' and to endorse the merits of 'interdisciplinary' research and/or teaching. This has been argued on two counts. One is the assertion that the analysis of some 'problem areas' can benefit from an approach combining the perspectives of many disciplines. It is said, for example, that if we wish to study 'labour', pooling the knowledge offered by the disciplines of economics, political science and sociology might be of great advantage. The logic of such an approach leads to multidisciplinary teams, or to a single scholar 'learning several disciplines', at least in so far as they relate to 'labour'.

The second presumed basis for 'interdisciplinary' research is slightly different. As we pursue our collective inquiry it becomes clear, it is argued, that some of our subject matter is 'at the borderline' of two or more disciplines. 'Linguistics', for example, may be located at such a 'border'. The logic of such an approach may lead eventually to the development of a new 'autonomous discipline', which in many ways is what has been happening to the study of linguistics during the last thirty years.

We know that there are multiple disciplines, since there are multiple academic departments in universities around the world, graduate degrees in these disciplines and national and international associations of scholars of these disciplines. That is, we know *politically* that different disciplines exist. They have organizations with boundaries, structures and personnel to defend their collective interests and ensure their collective reproduction. But this tells us nothing about the validity of the *intellectual* claims to separateness, claims which presumably justify the organizational networks.

The lauding of the merits of interdisciplinary work in the social sciences has so far not significantly undermined the strengths of the organizational apparatuses that shield the separate disciplines. Indeed, the contrary may be true: what has enhanced the claim of each discipline to represent a separately coherent level of analysis linked to appropriate methodologies is the constant assertion by practitioners of the various disciplines that each has something to learn from the other which it could not know by pursuing its own level of analysis with its specific methodologies, and that this 'other' knowledge is pertinent and significant to the resolution of the intellectual problems on which each is working. Interdisciplinary work is in no sense an intellectual critique *per se* of the existing compartmentalization of social science, and lacks in any case the political clout to affect the existing institutional structures.

But are the various social science disciplines really 'disciplines'? For a world so widely used, what constitutes a 'discipline' is seldom discussed. There is no entry for this term in the *International Encyclopaedia of the Social Sciences* nor in the *Encyclopaedia of Philosophy* nor in the *Encyclopaedia Britannica*. We do better by going to the *Oxford English Dictionary*, which tells us that

> Etymologically, *discipline*, as pertaining to the disciple or scholar, is antithetical to *doctrine*, the property of the doctor or teacher; hence, in the history of the words, *doctrine* is more concerned with abstract theory, and *discipline* with practice or exercise.

But having reminded us of the term's origins, the *OED* does no better for us in the actual definition than describing it as 'a branch of instruction or education; a department of learning or knowledge; a science or art in its educational aspect'. The emphasis here seems to be on the reproduction of knowledge (or at least its dissemination) and not on its production. But surely the concept, 'discipline', cannot be unrelated to the process of producing knowledge?

The history of the social sciences is quite clear, at least in broad brush strokes. Once, there were no social sciences, or only 'predecessors'. Then slowly but steadily there emerged over the course of the nineteenth century a set of names, and then of departments, degrees and associations, that by 1945 (although sometimes earlier) had crystallized into the categories we use today. There were other 'names' which were discarded and which presumably involved different 'groupings' of 'subject matter'. What is, or was, encompassed by such terms as 'moral economy' or *Staatswissenschaft* is not entirely clear. This is not because their advocates were insufficiently clear-thinking but because a 'discipline' in some real sense defines itself over a long run in its practice. An interrupted practice means an unfulfilled discipline. For example, the famous quadripartite subdivision of anthropology (physical anthropology, social or cultural anthropology, archaeology and linguistics) was (and to some extent still is) a 'practice' rather than a 'doctrine'. It then became a doctrine, taught and justified by doctors or teachers. But did the whole add up to a coherent, defensible level of analysis or mode of analysis, or just to segregated subject matter?

We know where all these divisions of subject matter came from. They derive intellectually from the dominant liberal ideology of the nineteenth century which argued that state and market, politics and economics, were analytically separate (and largely self-contained) domains, each with their particular rules ('logics'). Society was adjured to keep them separate, and scholars studied them separately. Since there seemed to be many realities that apparently were neither in the domain of the market nor in that of the state, these realities were placed in a residual grab-bag which took on as compensation the grand name of sociology. There was a sense in which sociology was thought to explain the seemingly 'irrational' phenomena that economics and political science were unable to account for. Finally, since there were people beyond the realm of the civilized world – remote, and with whom it was difficult to communicate – the study of such peoples encompassed special rules and special training, which took on the somewhat polemical name of anthropology.

We know the historical origins of the fields. We know their intellectual itineraries, which have been complex and variegated, especially since 1945. And we know why they have run into 'boundary' difficulties. As the real world evolved, the contact line between 'primitive' and 'civilized', 'political' and 'economic', blurred. Scholarly poaching became commonplace. The poachers kept moving the fences, without however breaking them down.

The question before us today is whether there are any criteria which can be used to assert in a relatively clear and defensible way boundaries between the four presumed disciplines of anthropology, economics, political science and sociology. World-systems analysis responds with an unequivocal 'no' to this question. All the presumed criteria – level of analysis, subject matter, methods, theoretical assumptions – either are no longer true in practice or, if sustained, are barriers to further knowledge rather than stimuli to its creation.

Or, put another way, the differences between permissible topics, methods, theories or theorizing *within* any of the so-called 'disciplines' are far greater than the differences *among* them. This means in practice that the overlap is substantial and, in terms of the historical evolution of all these fields, is increasing all the time. The time has come to cut through this intellectual morass by saying that these four disciplines are but a single one. This is not to say that all social scientists should be doing identical work. There is every need for, and likelihood of, specialization in 'fields of inquiry'. But let us remember the one significant organizational example we have. Somewhere in the period 1945–55, two hitherto organizationally separate 'disciplines', botany and zoology, merged into a single discipline called biology. Since that time, biology has been a flourishing discipline and has generated many sub-fields, but none of them, as far as I know, bears the name or has the contours of botany or zoology.

The argument of world-systems analysis is straightforward. The three presumed arenas of collective human action – the economic, the political and the social or sociocultural – are not autonomous arenas of social action. They do not have separate 'logics'. More importantly, the intermeshing of constraints, options, decisions, norms and 'rationalities' is such that no useful research model can isolate 'factors' according to the categories of economic, political and social, and treat only one kind of variable, implicitly holding the others constant. We are arguing that there is a single 'set of rules' or a single 'set of constraints' within which these various structures operate.

The case of the virtually total overlap of the presumed domains of sociology and anthropology is even stronger. By what stretch of the imagination can one assert that Elliot Liebow's *Tally Corner* and William F. Whyte's *Streel-Corner Society* – both 'classic' works, one written by an 'anthropologist' and the other by a 'sociologist' – are works in two different 'disciplines'? It would not be hard, as every reader knows, to assemble a long list of such examples.

History is the study of, the explanation of, the particular as it really happened in the past. Social science is the statement of the universal set of rules by which human/social behaviour is explained.

This is the famous distinction between idiographic and nomothetic modes of analysis, which are considered to be antithetical. The 'hard' version of this antithesis is to argue that only one of the modes (which one varies according to one's views) is legitimate or interesting or even 'possible'. This 'hard' version is what the *Methodenstreit* was about. The 'soft' version sees these two modes as two ways of cutting into social reality. Though undertaken separately, differently and for dissimilar (even opposing) purposes, it would be fruitful for the world of scholarship to combine the two modes. This 'soft' view is comparable to arguing the merits of 'interdisciplinary' work in the social sciences. By asserting the merits of combining two approaches, the intellectual legitimacy of viewing them as two separate modes is reinforced.

The strongest arguments of the idiographic and nomothetic schools both seem plausible. The argument of the idiographic school is the ancient doctrine that 'all is flux'. If everything is always changing, then any generalization purporting to apply to two or more presumably comparable phenomena is never true. All that one can do is to understand empathetically a sequence of events. Conversely, the argument of the nomothetic school is that it is manifest that the real world (including the social world) is not a set of random happenings. If so, there must be rules that describe 'regularities', in which case there is a domain for scientific activity.

The strongest critiques of each side about the other are plausible. The nomothetic critique of the idiographic view is that any recounting of 'past happenings' is by definition a selection from reality (as it really happened) and therefore implies criteria of selection and categories of description. These criteria and categories are based on unavowed but none the less real generalizations that are akin to scientific laws. The critique of the nomothetic view is that it neglects those transformational phenomena (due in part to the reflexiveness of social reality) which makes it impossible to 'repeat' structural arrangements.

There are various ways of dealing with these mutual criticisms. One way is the path of 'combining' history and the social sciences. The historian is said to serve the social scientist by providing the latter with wider, deeper sets of data from which to induce his law-like generalizations. The social scientist is said to serve the historian by offering him the results of research, reasonably demonstrated generalizations that offer insight into the explication of a particular sequence of events.

The problem with this neat division of intellectual labour is that it presumes the possibility of isolating 'sequences' subject to 'historical' analysis and small 'universes' subject to 'social scientific' analysis. In practice, however, one person's sequence is another's universe, and the neutral observer is in some quandary as to how to distinguish between the two on purely logical as opposed to, say, stylistic or presentational grounds.

The problem, however, is deeper than that. Is there a meaningful difference between sequence and universe, between history and social science? Are they two activities or one? Synchrony is akin to a geometric dimension. One can describe it logically, but it can be drawn only falsely on paper. In geometry, a point, a line or a plane can be drawn only in three (or four) dimensions. So it is in 'social science'. Synchrony is a conceptual limit, not a socially usable category. All description has time, and the only question is how wide a band is immediately relevant. Similarly, unique sequence is only describable in non-unique categories. All conceptual language presumes comparisons among universes. Just as we cannot literally 'draw' a point, so we cannot literally 'describe' a unique 'event'. The drawing, the description, has thickness or complex generalization.

Since this is an inextricable logical dilemma, the solution must be sought on heuristic grounds. World-systems analysis offers the heuristic value of the *via media* between trans-historical generalizations and particularistic narrations. It argues that, as our format tends toward either extreme, it tends toward an exposition of minimal interest and minimal utility. It argues that the optimal method is to pursue analysis within systemic frameworks, long enough in time and large enough in space to contain governing 'logics' which 'determine' the largest part of sequential reality, while simultaneously recognizing and taking into account that these systemic frameworks have beginnings and ends and are therefore not to be conceived of as 'eternal' phenomena. This implies, then, that at every instant we look both for the framework (the 'cyclical rhythms' of the system), which we describe conceptually, and for the patterns of internal transformation (the 'secular trends' of the system) that will eventually bring about the demise of the system, which we describe sequentially. This implies that the task is singular. There is neither historian nor social scientist, but only a historical social scientist who analyses the general laws of particular systems and the particular sequences through which these systems have gone (the grammatical tense here deliberately not being the so-called ethnographic present). We are then faced with the issue of determining the 'unit of analysis' within which we must work, which brings us to our third premise.

Human beings are organized in entities we may call societies, which constitute the fundamental social frameworks within which human life is lived.

No concept is more pervasive in modern social science than society, and no concept is used more automatically and unreflectively than society, despite the countless pages devoted to its definition. The textbook definitions revolve around the question 'What is society?', whereas the arguments we have just made about the unity of historical social science lead us to ask a different question: 'When and where is a society?'

'Societies' are concrete. Furthermore, society is a term which we might do well to discard because of its conceptual history and hence its virtually ineradicable and profoundly misleading connotations. Society is a term whose current usage in history and the social sciences is coeval with the institutional emergence of modern social science in the nineteenth century. Society is one half of an antithetic tandem in which the other is the state. The French Revolution was a cultural watershed in the ideological history of the modern world-system in that it led to the widespread acceptance of the idea that social change rather than social stasis is normal, both in the normative and in the statistical sense of the word. It thereby posed the intellectual problem of how to regulate, speed up, slow down, or otherwise affect this normal process of change and evolution.

The emergence of social science as an institutionalized social activity was one of the major systemic responses to this intellectual problem. Social science has come to represent the rationalist ideology that if one understands the process (whether idiographically or, more commonly, nomothetically) one can affect it in some morally positive manner. (Even 'conservatives', dedicated to containing change, could broadly assent to this approach.)

The political implications of such an enterprise escaped (and escapes) no one. This is of course why social science has remained to this day 'controversial'. But it is also why in the nineteenth century the concept 'society' was opposed to that of 'state'. The multiple sovereign states that had been and were being constituted were the obvious focuses of political activity. They seemed the locus of effective social control, and therefore the arena in which social change could be affected and effected. The standard nineteenth-century approach to the intellectual–political issue was concerned with the question of how to 'reconcile' society and state. In this formulation, the state could be observed and analysed directly. It operated through formal institutions by way of known (constitutional) rules. The 'society' was taken to mean that tissue of manners and customs that held a group of people together without, despite or against formal rules. In some sense 'society' represented something more enduring and 'deeper' than the state, less manipulable and certainly more elusive.

There has ever since been enormous debate about how society and state relate to each other, which one was or should be subordinate to the other, and which incarnated the higher moral values. In the process we have become accustomed to thinking that the boundaries of a society and of a state are synonymous, or if not should (and eventually would) be made so. Thus, without explicitly asserting this theoretically, historians and social scientists have come to see current sovereign states (projected hypothetically backward in time) as the basic social entities within which social life is conducted. There was some sporadic resistance to this view on the part of anthropologists, but they resisted in the name of a putative earlier political–cultural entity whose importance remained primary, many of them asserted, for large segments of the world's population.

Thus, by the back door, and unanalysed, a whole historiography and a whole theory of the modern world crept in as the substratum of both history and social science. We live in states. There is a society underlying each state. States have histories and therefore traditions. Above all, since change is normal, it is states that normally change or develop. They change their mode of production; they urbanize; they have social problems; they prosper or decline. They have the boundaries, inside of which factors are 'internal' and outside of which they are 'external'. They are 'logically' independent entities such that, for statistical purposes, they can be 'compared'.

This image of social reality was not a fantasy, and so it was possible for both idiographic and nomothetic theorists to proceed with reasonable aplomb using these assumptions about society and state, and to come up with some plausible findings. The only problem was that, as time went on, more and more 'anomalies' seemed to be unexplained within this framework, and more and more lacunae (of uninvestigated zones of human activity) seemed to emerge.

World-systems analysis makes the unit of analysis a subject of debate. Where and when do the entities within which social life occurs exist? It substitutes for the term 'society' the term 'historical system'. Of course, this is a mere semantic substitution. But it rids us of the central connotation that 'society' has acquired, its link to 'state', and therefore of the presupposition about the 'where' and 'when'. Furthermore, 'historical system' as a term underlines the unity of historical social science. The entity is simultaneously systemic and historical.

Having opened up the question of the unit of analysis, there is no simple answer. I myself have put forth the tentative hypothesis that there have been three known forms or varieties of historical systems, which I have called mini-systems, world-empires and world-economies. I have also suggested that it is not unthinkable that we could identify other forms or varieties.

I have argued two things about the varieties of historical systems: one concerns the link of 'logic' and form; the other concerns the history of the coexistence of forms. In terms of form, I have taken as the defining boundaries of a historical system those within which the system and the people within it are regularly reproduced by means of some kind of ongoing division of labour. I argue that empirically there have been three such modes. The 'mini-systems', so-called because they are small in space and probably relatively brief in time (a life-span of about six generations), are highly homogeneous in terms of cultural and governing structures. The basic logic is one of 'reciprocity' in exchanges. The 'world empires' are vast political structures (at least at the apex of the process of expansion and contraction which seems to be their fate) and encompass a wide variety of 'cultural' patterns. The basic logic of the system is the extraction of tribute from otherwise locally self-administered direct producers (mostly rural) that is passed upward to the centre and redistributed to a thin but crucial network of officials. The 'world-economies' are vast uneven chains of integrated production structures dissected by multiple political structures. The basic logic is that the accumulated surplus is distributed unequally in favour of those able to achieve various kinds of temporary monopolies in the market networks. This is a 'capitalist' logic.

The history of the coexistence of forms can be construed as follows. In the pre-agricultural era, there were a multiplicity of mini-systems whose constant death may have been largely a function of ecological mishaps plus the splitting of groups grown too large. Our knowledge is very limited. There was no writing and we are confined to archaeological reconstructions. In the period between, say, 8000 BC and AD 1500, there coexisted on the earth at any one time multiple historical systems of all three varieties. The world-empire was the 'strong' form of that era, since whenever one expanded it destroyed and/or absorbed both mini-systems and world-economies and whenever one contracted it opened up space for the re-creation of mini-systems and world-economies. Most of what we call the 'history' of this period is the history of such world-empires, which is understandable, since they bred the cultural scribes to record what was going on. World-economies were a 'weak' form, individual ones never surviving long. This is because they either disintegrated or were absorbed by or transformed into a world-empire (by the internal expansion of a single political unit).

Around 1500, one such world-economy managed to escape this fate. For reasons that need to be explained, the 'modern world-system' was born out of the consolidation of a world-economy. Hence it had time to achieve its full development as a capitalist system. By *its* inner logic, this capitalist world-economy then expanded to cover the entire globe, absorbing in the process all existing mini-systems and world-empires. Hence by the late nineteenth century, for the first time ever, there existed only one historical system on the globe. We are still in that situation today.

27

Surveillance and Modernity

Christopher Dandeker

The rise of bureaucratic surveillance in modern societies can be viewed in terms of three institutional contexts. Two of these concern the nation-state: they involve the part played by military power in the management of its external relations and the significance of police surveillance in the internal pacification of subject populations.

As Giddens has suggested, sociology and its object of study – society – are in large part the products of modernity. If by society one means a clearly demarcated and internally well-articulated social entity, it is only relatively recently that large human populations have lived under such arrangements; and these have been the administrative achievements of modern nation-states. From a political point of view, the modern world comprises a network of competing nation-states and collectivities aspiring to that status.

Modern nation-states have well-developed bureaucratic systems for the internal policing of their populations as well as for the management of their external relations. Their systems of rule are legitimated in terms of the politics of citizenship and the bonds of national solidarity as expressed in language and customs, although, of course, many nation-states are multi-ethnic or multi-national units. These distinctive features of modern nation-states can be outlined in more detail before focusing more specifically on the impact of war and military organization on the development of their surveillance capacities.

Bendix has argued that 'the central fact of modern nation building is the orderly exercise of a nation wide public authority'.[1] In the West, there were four aspects of this political transformation. First, there was a long-term concentration of political authority. The political structure of absolutism anticipated one of the constitutive features of modern nation-states: 'where all people have rights, where all are subjects of one king; where the king in turn exercises supreme authority over everyone, we get a first intimation of national citizenship and one supreme authority over all public affairs'.[2] With the French revolution, the 'democratic' will of the people replaced monarchy as the agency that wielded nation-wide political authority.

Second, the concentration of political authority was accompanied by a shift from functional to more individualistic systems of political representation with the extension of citizenship rights. In this context, Bendix, Marshall and, more recently, Giddens have discussed three types of citizenship rights: civil rights are those concerned with freedom of association, movement (including the right to sell labour and own property), freedom of speech and the rule of law. Political rights are concerned with the participation of subject populations in the exercise of political power and thus in the supervision of rulers. In contrast, economic rights 'concern the right of everyone within a state to enjoy a certain minimum standard of life, economic welfare and security'.[3]

Bendix argues that in the modern nation-state 'each citizen stands in a direct relation to the sovereign of the country, in contrast with medieval polity'.[4] Although Bendix recognizes the importance of Marshall's discussion of three types of citizenship rights, in his own analysis he focuses mainly on the extension of civil and political rights to the lower classes. This process meant that wider sections of subject populations could speak for their own interests rather than depending on the patronage of their social superiors in whose houses or estates they served.

For Marshall, the emergence of citizenship involved a sequential development of civil, political and social (or what Giddens prefers to call economic) rights. Thus, in the British context, the civil rights realized in the seventeenth and eighteenth centuries provided the basis for an extension of political and economic rights in the nineteenth and twentieth centuries respectively.

Giddens's analysis of citizenship draws on Marshall's discussion but also departs from it in three important respects. Empirically, Giddens suggests that the extension of citizenship rights has been a more complex process than Marshall acknowledges. For instance, in Britain some civil rights were not extended until the twentieth century while yet others have been diminished. In Germany, Bismark's social reforms – the extension of welfare or economic rights – were instituted in order to forestall concessions on the political front.

Second, Giddens prefers to view citizenship rights not simply in terms of phases of social development but rather as recurrent 'arenas of contestation' between rulers and ruled. Each cluster of rights is focused on a particular organizational and thus surveillance context: the police and society (civil rights); the electorate and the political organs of the state (political rights); and the relations between capital and labour within the business enterprise (economic rights). Thus in modern capitalist societies, a crucial area of citizenship rights are 'beyond' the state and anchored in an organization based on private property.

Third, in explaining the rise of modern citizenship, Giddens departs from both Bendix's and Marshall's views. In sharp contrast with Marxist analysis, Bendix relegates class conflict to the periphery of his discussion of political modernization. On the other hand, Marshall views modern citizenship rights as providing a basis of (social democratic) compromise between the main classes of modern capitalism. Although Giddens accepts Marshall's view of some of the consequences of modern citizenship, he prefers to interpret class conflict as a medium for the extension of citizenship rights. This is in contrast to both Marshall's own suggestion that such rights have 'blunted' class divisions and Bendix's marginalization of class in the social analysis of these issues. In the present argument, one qualification of Giddens's analysis will be to suggest that a significant motive for the extension of citizenship has been competition for military and economic power amongst states as well as struggles between classes within states.

The extension of citizenship rights in the modern nation-state has been dependent on the concentration of political authority: the allocation of equal rights to more and more citizens presupposes the development of an agency 'above' those individuals. However, the extension of citizenship rights is connected not only with this process of concentration but also with other features of the modern nation-state. These concern two aspects of modern bureaucracy: as a mode of public administration and as a means of surveillance.

In the modern nation-state, the administrative instruments of power become the property of the public rather than being privately owned by the monarch. The impersonal, public authority of the state is extended in modern polities and this process entails an institutional separation between state and society. The administrative functions of government generally become 'removed from the political struggle in the sense that they cannot be appropriated on a hereditary basis by privileged estates and on this basis parcelled out among competing jurisdictions'.[5] This entails the 'development of a body of officials whose recruitment and policy execution were separated gradually from the previously existing involvement of officials with kinship loyalties, hereditary principles and property interests'. As was observed earlier, this change means that patronage declines as the strategic mechanism in the recruitment to and operation of the administrative structures of the modern nation-state.[6]

The fourth attribute of the modern nation-state concerns its surveillance capacities: these are produced by the use of rational bureaucracy for the administrative penetration of society. As Giddens and Poggi have argued, this development suggests a quite different meaning of separation from the one referred to above as a way of analysing the relationships between the modern state and society.

The modern state is separated from society in respect of the emergence of a public power from pre-existing patrimonial regimes. However, from an administrative point of view, pre-modern states and their rulers were far more separated from their societies than are their modern counterparts. They could not subject their populations to the fine mesh of bureaucratic surveillance evident in modern states.

In the context of the European ancien regime, the rulers of even the most absolutist states found it difficult to supervise and gather information about their populations. The presence availability of rulers was limited by a number of conditions.

A series of technical problems shortened considerably the radii of effective administration from a central point. Poor transport and communications, with roads impassable to wheeled traffic for much of winter, made it difficult to administer subject populations in any detailed way. This remained the case until the end of the eighteenth century.

Demographic considerations were also significant: the population was small compared with those characteristic of modern societies, and widely dispersed in relatively self-sufficient communities. Only a small proportion lived in towns and cities. The limited social division of labour favoured a dispersal of effective administrative control to the localities.

Economic factors reinforced transport and demographic limitations. The economy produced only a limited surplus for the tax system to channel into state coffers. Here was a vicious circle from the standpoint of rulers: limited economic resources made it difficult for rulers to build (expensive) reliable tax and military bureaucracies. In turn, limited bureaucratic development meant that it was difficult to channel those resources that the economy could produce into the hands of the state. Major state functions such as taxation and military force were, in varying degrees, decentralized to private contractors. This process of 'subcontracting', and, in the absence of strategic financial control by the state bureaucracy, the corruption that went with it, constituted important obstacles to the will of the central authorities. However, this line of argument is not to deny the genuine advances made in central government administration during the late seventeenth and eighteenth centuries.

A further limitation on the administrative penetration of society by the central state was that the political aspirations of rulers encountered the jealously guarded prerogatives of local power-holders – in particular, agricultural landlords and city elites. In conjunction with the other limitations, this factor meant that the manner of state penetration depended largely on the form in which local and central powers were articulated.

Two broad patterns can be distinguished: on the one hand, local areas were subordinated politically and monitored by agents of the central authorities. However, for practical as well as political reasons, these arrangements were not accompanied by administrative supervision through rational bureaucracy. Central supervision of what went on in the localities depended upon the co-operation of local power-holders. This was tempered by their connivance at their own subordinates' reluctance to let the rulers divert local resources away from their own hands into those of the central state. Localism existed despite impositions from the centre. Coupled with the tendency towards autocracy, these emergent despotic arrangements were characteristic of absolutist France.

On the other hand, as in England, colonial and post-colonial America, the political and administrative powers of local privileged classes were held relatively independently of the sanction of the central state. The latter was even more delimited in its surveillance capacities and political prerogatives. Its aspirations were confronted by the self-confident independence of the localities. In addition, the central power was more amenable to influence by the middling orders of society than was the case in the more despotic or autocratic regimes. For this reason these arrangements can be defined as a liberal set of institutions.

However, in both patterns, central governments were relatively weak in respect of their surveillance capacities. The real differences between them concerned the degree to which they could monitor and manipulate local power-holders and make themselves susceptible to popular interests. In both cases, the state was relatively separate from society from the point of view of its surveillance capacity. Of course, as Hall has suggested, this may have meant that liberal structures could achieve more in respect of mobilizing resources for war or other collective actions than other more autocratic systems.

The emergence of the modern nation-state can, then, be identified in terms of a combination of four attributes: the concentration of political authority; citizenship as the political basis for the relationships between rulers and ruled; administration by public bureaucracy rather than by patronage; and administration of society through bureaucratic surveillance.

In this overall process, war and military organization were of central importance. First of all, the armed forces constituted the most significant branch of the early modern state in terms of relative size, organizational complexity, consumption of state expenditure, and means of power projection – both internally and externally. Second, war was the most important motive for the establishment of the modern state as a durable and well-articulated social entity. As Paul Kennedy has argued, 'the post 1450 waging of war was intimately connected with the "birth of the Nation state"'.[7] The bureaucratization of military power in the West was connected symbiotically with the development of the capitalist economic system: an expansion of military power depended on the technical, financial and organizational resources of commercial and industrial enterprises; at the same time military power, and especially naval weaponry, aided the global economic expansion of the West overseas in respect of new markets for raw materials and exports. It also provided an important stimulus to capitalist industry and commerce by way of demands for textiles, timber, iron and later steel, chemicals and other goods. All these resources of the capitalist system were channelled into military activities through loans raised by states on the developing financial markets and revenue secured through the tax system.

Bearing in mind this symbiotic relationship between economic and military resources, war was an important motive for the conduct of the state and military organization the most important feature of its administrative structure. Thus, military organization provides a clear example of the association between bureaucratic surveillance and the modern nation-state.

There were distinct phases in the bureaucratization of military power. In the argument defended here, particular attention is paid to the effects of what Roberts has called the 'military revolution' of the late sixteenth and early seventeenth centuries. During this period, the foundations of the modern armed forces as a fusion of professional and bureaucratic principles were laid. This process can be discussed by focusing on changes in the relationships between three groups: the central authorities, the officers' corps, including the important NCO or supervisory class, and the ordinary soldiers and sailors themselves. The state transformed military organization from a system comprising autonomous, largely self-equipped mercenary formations, employed by contracting captains, to one based on professional servants of the state, disciplined in a bureaucratic hierarchy and owing allegiance to the state alone. This process constituted a shift from a system based on petty and competing patrimonialisms to a unified rational–legal order for the administration of military violence. By 1700 the outline of all that is modern about the modern armed forces was visible.

By the eighteenth century,

> the enhanced authority and resources of the state . . . gave to their armed forces a degree of permanence which had often not existed earlier. . . . Power was now national power, whether expressed through the enlightened despotisms of eastern Europe, the parliamentary controls of Britain or the later demagogic forces of revolutionary France.[8]

In the nineteenth century, further developments in the bureaucratization of military discipline can be linked with the impact of the industrial and democratic revolutions. In that context, attention can be focused on the ways in which modern technology and the national citizenship state altered the relationships between military organization and society and increased substantially the capacity of the state to deploy bureaucratized military power.

In the twentieth century, two particular aspects of the bureaucratization of military power stand out: first, the relationships between modern technology and surveillance in military organizations; and second, the impact of the demands of war on the growth of state surveillance beyond the military sphere into the wider society.

During the two world wars and beyond, the seemingly ever-increasing pace of technological change continued to enhance the capacities of the state to mobilize, deploy and control military power. The technical demands of war led not only to an enhancement of the ability of the state to exercise surveillance over its armed forces but also to a tightening of the networks of surveillance over the rest of society. Although this process was rooted in the industrialization of war in the nineteenth century – particularly in the equation linking citizenship and military service – the main connections between war and what is referred to here as the rise of the 'security state' were forged during the two world wars and the subsequent nuclear age. Whilst some of the advanced societies have lessened their dependence on mass conscripted armies, it remains the case that defence and security issues have provided important grounds for supervising the civilian population in time of war or threat of war.

The bureaucratization of military power has, then, been an important aspect of the rise of the modern nation-state. War has been perhaps the most significant motive for the formation of the modern nation-state in the West, and military organization its most crucial arm, particularly of course in the field of external relations. Yet as was pointed out earlier, the institutional differentiation of internal and external relations was itself an achievement of the nation-state. As Giddens has suggested, the process of modernization is accompanied by a decline in the routine use of military power within the territorial boundaries of states and an increased focus on police surveillance as a means of supervising subject populations.

Notes and References

1 R. Bendix, *Nation-Building and Citizenship* (Doubleday Anchor, New York, 1969), p. 22.
2 Ibid., p. 57.
3 A. Giddens, *The Nation-State and Violence* (Polity, Cambridge, 1985), p. 201.
4 Bendix, *Nation-Building*, pp. 89–90.
5 Ibid., pp. 128–9.
6 Ibid., pp. 46–9.
7 P. M. Kennedy, *The Rise and Fall of the Great Powers* (Unwin Hyman, London, 1988), p. 70.
8 Ibid., pp. 75–6.

28

The Future of Democracy

Norberto Bobbio

I have been invited to give a paper on the future of democracy, a subject more fraught with pitfalls than most, and I will cover myself at the outset with two quotations. In his lectures on the philosophy of history at Berlin University, Hegel, faced with a question put to him by a student about whether the United States should be considered the country of the future, replied, patently irritated: 'As a country of the future, America is of no interest to us here, for prophecy is not the business of the philosopher. . . . In philosophy we are concerned with that which *is*, both now and eternally – in short with reason. And that is quite enough to occupy our attention.'[1] In his famous lecture on science as a vocation delivered to students of Munich University at the end of the First World War, Max Weber replied as follows to members of the audience who insisted on asking what his opinion was on the future of Germany: 'The prophet and the demagogue do not belong on the academic platform.'[2]

Even someone who is not inclined to accept the lines of reasoning adopted by Hegel and Weber and who considers them a lame excuse must surely acknowledge that the job of the prophet is a hazardous one. The difficulty of knowing the future also derives from the fact that all of us project our own aspirations and anxieties into it, while history follows its course blithely indifferent to our concerns, a course shaped by millions and millions of little, minute, human acts which no intellect, however powerful, has ever been capable of synthesizing into a synoptic view which is not too abstract to be credible. For this reason the forecasts made by the masters of thought on the course of the world have in the event turned out to be almost always wrong, not least the predictions of the person whom a section of humanity believed and still believes to be the founder of a new and infallible science of society: Karl Marx.

Briefly my opinion is the following: if you ask me whether democracy has a future and, assuming it has one, what it will be, I have no qualms in replying that I do not know. The object of this paper is purely and simply to make some observations on the current state of democratic regimes, and, to echo Hegel, we have our work cut out doing this. If, on the basis of these observations, it were then possible to extrapolate a trend with regard to the progress (or regress) of these regimes, and thus to attempt a cautious prognosis of their future, so much the better.

My premise is that the only way a meaningful discussion of democracy, as distinct from all forms of autocratic government, is possible is to consider it as characterized by a set of rules (primary or basic) which establish *who* is authorized to take collective decisions and which *procedures* are to be applied. Every social group needs to take decisions binding on all members of the group so as to ensure its own survival, both internally and externally. But even group decisions are made by individuals (the group as such does not decide anything). As a result, for a decision taken by individuals (one, several, many, all together) to be accepted as a collective decision, it is necessary for it to be taken on the basis of rules (whether written or customary) which lay down who are the individuals authorized to take the decisions binding on all the members of the group and what procedures are to be used. As for the persons called upon to take (or collaborate in the taking of) collective decisions, a democracy is characterized by conferring this power (which, in so far as it is authorized by the basic law of the constitution, becomes a right) to a large number of members of the group. I realize the phrase 'a large number' is vague. But, apart from the fact that political pronouncements issue forth from the realm of the 'nearly' and 'mostly', it is wrong to say all, because even in the most perfect democratic system, individuals cannot vote until they have reached a certain age. 'Omnicracy', or the rule of everyone, is an ideal upper limit. What number of individuals must have the vote before it is possible to start talking of a democracy cannot be established in terms of an abstract principle, i.e. leaving out of account historical circumstances and the need for a yardstick to make any judgement. All that can be said is that a society in which the ones to have the vote are adult male citizens is more democratic than one in which only property owners have the vote, and less democratic than one in which women also have the vote. The statement that in the last century there occurred in some countries a continuous process of democratization means that the number of those entitled to vote steadily increased.

As for the mode in which decisions are arrived at, the basic rule of democracy is the rule of the majority, in other words the rule according to which decisions are considered collective, and thus binding on the whole group, if they are approved by at least the majority of those entrusted with taking the decision. If a majority decision is valid, a unanimous decision is all the more valid. But unanimity is possible only in a limited or homogeneous group and can be demanded only in two extreme and diametrically opposed cases: either when a very serious decision is involved, so that everyone taking part has the right of veto; or when the decision has negligible implications, so that someone who does not expressly disagree acquiesces (the case of tacit consent). Naturally unanimity is required when only two people are to decide. This provides a clear distinction between a decision based on genuine agreement and one taken according to the law (which usually involves only majority approval).

Moreover, even a minimal definition of democracy, like the one I adopt, requires more than just conferring the right to participate directly or indirectly in the making of collective decisions on a substantial number of citizens, and more than the existence of procedural rules like majority rule (or in extreme cases unanimity). There is a third condition involved, namely that those called upon to take decisions, or to elect those who are to take decisions, must be offered real alternatives and be in a position to choose between these alternatives. For this condition to be realized those called upon to take decisions must be guaranteed the so-called basic rights: freedom of opinion, of expression, of speech, of assembly, of association etc. These are the rights on which the liberal state has been founded since its inception, giving rise to the doctrine of the *Rechtsstaat*, or juridical state, in the full sense of the term, i.e. the state which not only exercises power *sub lege*, but exercises it within limits derived from the constitutional recognition of the so-called 'inviolable' rights of the individual. Whatever may be the philosophical basis of these rights, they are the necessary pre-condition for the mainly procedural mechanisms, which characterize a democratic system, to work properly. The constitutional norms which confer these rights are not rules of the game as such: they are preliminary rules which allow the game to take place.

From this it follows that the liberal state is not only the historical but the legal premise of the democratic state. The liberal state and the democratic state are doubly interdependent: if liberalism provides those liberties necessary for the proper exercise of democratic power, democracy guarantees the existence and persistence of fundamental liberties. In other words: an illiberal state is unlikely to ensure the proper workings of democracy, and conversely an undemocratic state is unlikely to be able to safeguard basic liberties. The historical proof of this interdependence is provided by the fact that when both liberal and democratic states fall they fall together.

Having outlined the basic principles I am now in a position to get down to the subject at issue and offer some observations on the present state of democracy. We are dealing with a topic which is usually debated under the heading 'the transformations of democracy'. A collection of everything that has been written about the transformations of democracy would fill a library. But the word 'transformation' is so vague that it allows radically different assessments. For the Right . . . democracy has been transformed into a semi-anarchic regime which will bring about the 'disintegration' of the state. For the Left . . . parliamentary democracy is progressively turning into an autocratic regime. Rather than concentrate on the notion of transformation, I believe it is more useful for our purposes to reflect on the gap between democratic ideals and 'actually existing democracy' (an expression I am using in the same sense as when people talk of 'actually existing socialism'). Someone in a lecture once drew my attention to the concluding words which Pasternak puts in the mouth of Gordon, the friend of Doctor Zhivago. 'This has happened several times in the course of history. A thing which has been conceived in a lofty, ideal manner is transformed into brute facts. Thus Rome came out of Greece and the Russian Revolution came out of the Russian Enlightenment.'[3] In a similar way, I will add, the liberal and democratic thought of Locke, Rousseau, Tocqueville, Bentham or John Stuart Mill turned into the actions of . . . (you can fill in yourselves any name you see fit – you will easily be able to find more than one). It is precisely these 'brute facts' and not what has been conceived as 'noble and lofty ideals' which are at issue here; or, put another way, what is at issue here is the contrast between what was promised and what has actually come about. I will single out three of these broken promises.

Democracy was born of an individualistic conception of society, at variance with the organic conception which prevailed in classical times and in the intervening period and according to which the whole has primacy over its parts. Instead it conceives every form of society, especially political society, as an artificial product formed by the will of individuals. The emergence of the individualistic conception of society and the state and the decline of the organic conception can be accounted for by the interaction of three events in the history of ideas which are characteristic of social philosophy in the modern age.

1 The contractarian theories of the seventeenth and eighteenth centuries whose initial hypothesis that civil society is preceded by a state of nature in which sovereign power is exercised by free and equal individuals who agree among themselves to bring into existence a communal power entrusted with the function of guaranteeing their life and liberty (as well as their property).
2 The birth of political economy, that is to say, of an analysis of society and of social relations whose subject is once again the individual human being, *homo oeconomicus*, not the *politikon zoon* of traditional thought, who is considered not in his own right but as the member of a community. This individual, according to Adam Smith, 'in pursuing his own interest, often promotes the interests of society more effectively than if he set out to actually promote them'. (Indeed, according to Macpherson's interpretation, the state of nature conceived by Hobbes and Locke is a prefiguration of a market society.)
3 The utilitarian philosophy of Bentham and Mill, for which only one criterion can serve as the basis of an objective ethical system, and hence distinguish good from evil, without resorting to vague concepts such as 'nature' and the like. This criterion takes as its starting point the consideration of essentially personal states of mind, such as pleasure and pain, and thus resolves the traditional problem of the common good by defining it as the sum of individual good, or, in Bentham's formula, as the happiness of the greatest number.

By adopting the hypothesis of the sovereignty of the individual, who, by reaching agreement with other individuals who are equally sovereign, creates political society, democratic doctrine imagined a state without the intermediary bodies which characterize the corporatist society of medieval cities, or the state composed of various ranks and estates which necessarily preceded the institution of absolute monarchies. It envisaged a political society without any subsidiary associations of particular interests intervening between the sovereign people made up of so many individuals (one man one vote) and its representatives. There would be none of the factions so hated by Rousseau, and deprived of legal influence by the law of Le Chapelier (rescinded in France as late as 1887). What has actually happened in democratic states is the exact opposite: increasingly it is less and less the individual who is the most influential factor in politics and more and more it is the group: large organizations, associations of all kinds, trade unions of every conceivable profession, political parties of widely differing ideologies. Groups and not individuals are the protagonists of political life in a democratic society: there is no longer one sovereign power, namely the people or nation, composed of individuals who have acquired the right to participate directly or indirectly in government, the people conceived as an ideal (or mystical) unit. Instead the people are divided into opposing and conflicting groups, all relatively autonomous in relation to central government (an autonomy which individual human beings have lost or have never had, except in an ideal model of government which has always been refuted by the facts).

The ideal model of democratic society was a centripetal society. The reality is a centrifugal society, which has not just one centre of power (the 'general will' envisaged by Rousseau), but a plethora of them, and which deserves the name, as political scientists agree, of polycentric society or polyarchy (or, put more strongly but not altogether incorrectly, a 'polycracy'). The model of the democratic state, based on popular sovereignty, was conceived in the image of, and as analogous to, the sovereignty of the prince, and hence was a monist model of society. The real society underlying democratic government is pluralist.

This primary transformation of democracy (primary in the sense that it concerns the distribution of power) gives rise to the second which concerns the nature of representation. Modern democracy, which came into being as representative democracy, was meant, in contrast to the democracy of classical times, to be epitomized by a system of political representation, i.e. a form of representation in which the representative who is called on to pursue the interests of the nation cannot be subject to a binding mandate. The principle on which political representation is based is the exact antithesis of the one underlying the representation of particular interests, where the representative, having to support the cause of the person represented, is subject to a binding mandate (a feature of private law which makes provisions for the contract being revoked in cases where the mandate has been exceeded). One of the most famous and historically significant debates held in the French Constituent Assembly, which gave birth to the Constitution of 1791, witnessed the victory of those who maintained that the deputy, once elected, became the representative of the nation and no longer of the electorate: as such he was no longer bound by any mandate. The unrestricted mandate had previously been a prerogative of the king who, on convening the *états généraux*, had claimed that the delegates of the estates had not been sent to the assembly with *pouvoirs restrictifs*. As an overt expression of sovereignty, unrestricted mandate was transferred from the sovereignty of the king to the sovereignty of the assembly elected by the people. Ever since then, the veto on binding mandates has become an axiomatic rule in all constitutions based on democratic representation, and where democracy has had to fight for survival it has always found convinced supporters in those who defended representative democracy against attempts to replace it by, or integrate it with, representation of particular interests.

No constitutional norm has ever been more violated than the veto on binding mandates. No principle has been more disregarded than that of political representation. But in a society composed of relatively autonomous groups competing to gain supremacy, to assert their own interests over those of other groups, could such a norm, such a principle, ever be realized in practice? Apart from the fact that every group tends to identify the national interest with its own, is there any general criterion which would enable us to distinguish the common interest from the particular interest of this or that group, or from the combination of particular interests of groups which come to an arrangement among themselves at the expense of others? Whoever represents particular interests always has a binding mandate. And where can we find a representative who does not represent particular interests? Certainly not in trade unions, for the drawing up of wage agreements depends on them as do national agreements concerning the organization and cost of labour, all of which have an enormous political impact. In parliament? But what does party discipline signify if not an open violation of the veto on restricted mandates? Every now and then some deputies take advantage of the secret ballot to give party discipline the slip, but are they not branded in Italy as 'snipers', that is, as renegades to be singled out for public disapproval? The veto on restricted mandates, when all is said and done, is a rule without any sanctions attached. On the contrary, the only sanction feared by the deputy, whose re-election depends on the continued support of his party, is the one applied if he transgresses the opposite principle of toeing the official line, thus obliging him to consider himself bound by the mandate given to him by his party.

Confirmation of the victory – I would dare to say a definitive one – of the representation of interests over impartial political representation is provided by the type of relationship, which is coming to be the norm in most democratic states in Europe, between opposed interest groups (representatives of industrialists and workers respectively) and parliament. This relationship has brought about a new type of social system which is called, rightly or wrongly, 'neo-corporatism', and is characterized by a triangular arrangement in which the government, ideally the representative of national interests, intervenes only as a mediator between the two sides and at most can act as guarantor (generally an impotent one) to ensure that any agreement reached is honoured. Those who some ten years ago thought out this model, which is now at the centre of the debate on the 'transformations' of democracy, defined a neo-corporatist society as offering a solution to social conflicts involving a procedure, that of agreement between large organizations, which has nothing to do with political representation but instead is the typical expression of the representation of particular interests.

The third unfulfilled promise of democracy concerns its failure to put an end to oligarchical power. I have no need to dwell on this point because the subject has been extensively dealt with and is uncontroversial, at least since the end of the last century when Gaetano Mosca propounded his theory of the political class which, due to Pareto's influence, came to be known as the theory of elites. The guiding principle of democratic thought has always been liberty, understood in the sense of autonomy, that is, the ability to be governed by one's own laws (according to Rousseau's famous definition). This should lead to the perfect identification between the person who lays down a rule of conduct and the one who submits to it, and hence to the elimination of the traditional distinction, which is the basis of all political thinking, between the governed and those who govern. Representative democracy, which is after all the only form of democracy which actually exists and is operative, is by its very nature a renunciation of the principle of liberty as autonomy. The hypothesis that the future 'computer-ocracy', as it has been called, might make direct democracy possible, by giving all citizens the possibility of transmitting their votes to an electronic brain, is puerile. To judge by the number of laws which are tabled every year in Italy, responsible citizens would have to be called upon to cast their vote at least once a day. Such an excess of participation, which produces the phenomenon which Dahrendorf has pejoratively called that of the 'total citizen', only results in the political satiety and increasing apathy of the electorate. The price which has to be paid for the commitment of the few is often the indifference of the many. Nothing risks killing off democracy more effectively than an excess of democracy.

Naturally the fact that elites are present in the power structure does not eliminate the difference between democratic and autocratic regimes. Even Mosca realized this, though he was a conservative who professed to be a liberal but not a democrat, and who worked out a complex typology of forms of government with a view to demonstrating that, while oligarchies will always be found in power, distinctions can be made between different forms of government on the basis of the different ways they are formed and organized. As my starting point was a largely procedural definition of democracy, it should not be forgotten that one of the advocates of this interpretation, Joseph Schumpeter, struck the nail on the head when he argued that the defining characteristic of a democratic regime is not the absence of elites but the presence of several elites in competition with each other for the votes of the public. In C. B. Macpherson's book, *The Life and Times of Liberal Democracy*, four phases are identified in the development of democracy from the last century to the present: the current phase, which he defines as 'democracy of equilibrium', corresponds to Schumpeter's definition. An Italian elitist who is an expert on Mosca and Pareto made a concise but, in my view, telling distinction between elites which *impose* themselves and elites which *propose* themselves.

Notes and References

1 G. W. F. Hegel, *Lectures on the Philosophy of World History*, tr. H. B. Nibet (Cambridge University Press, Cambridge, 1975), p. 171.
2 H. H. Gerth and C. Wright Mills (eds), *From Max Weber* (Routledge and Kegan Paul, London, 1970), p. 146.
3 Boris L. Pasternak, *Doctor Zhivago*, tr. M. Hayward and M. Harari (Collins and Harvill, London, 1958), p. 460.

29

What Should Democracy Mean Today?

David Held

The New Right thinkers have in general tied the goals of liberty and equality to individualist political, economic and ethical doctrines. The individual is, in essence, sacrosanct, and is free and equal only to the extent that he or she can pursue and attempt to realize self-chosen ends and personal interests. Equal justice can be sustained between individuals if, above all, individuals' entitlement to certain rights or liberties is respected and all citizens are treated equally before the law. In this account, the modern state should provide the necessary conditions to enable citizens to pursue their own interests; it should uphold the rule of law in order to protect and nurture individuals' liberty, a state of affairs in which no one is entitled to impose their vision of the 'good life' upon others. This has been, of course, a central tenet of liberalism since Locke: the state exists to safeguard the rights and liberties of citizens who are ultimately the best judge of their own interests; the state is the burden individuals have to bear to secure their own ends; and the state must be restricted in scope and restrained in practice to ensure the maximum possible freedom of every citizen. Liberalism has been and is preoccupied with the creation and defence of a world in which 'free and equal' individuals can flourish with minimum political impediment.

By contrast, New Left thinkers have defended the desirability of certain social or collective means and goals. For them, to take equality and liberty seriously is to challenge the view that these values can be realized by individuals left, in practice, to their own devices in a 'free-market' economy and a minimal state. Equality, liberty and justice – recognized by them as 'great universal ideals' – cannot be achieved in a world dominated by private ownership of property and the capitalist economy. These ideals, according to them, can be realized only through struggles to ensure that society, as well as the state, is democratized, i.e. subject to procedures that ensure maximum accountability. Only the latter can ultimately guarantee the reduction of all forms of coercive power so that human beings can develop as 'free and equal'. While New Left thinkers differ in many respects from traditional Marxist writers, they share a concern to uncover the conditions whereby the 'free development of each' is compatible with the 'free development of all'. This is a fundamental common goal.

The views of the New Right and New Left are, of course, radically different. The key elements of their theories are fundamentally at odds. It is therefore somewhat paradoxical to note that they share a vision of reducing arbitrary power and regulatory capacity to its lowest possible extent. Both the New Right and the New Left fear the extension of networks of intrusive power into society, 'choking', to borrow a phrase from Marx, 'all its pores'. They both have ways of criticizing the bureaucratic, inequitable and often repressive character of much state action. In addition, they are both concerned with the political, social and economic conditions for the development of people's capacities, desires and interests. Put in this general and very abstract manner, there appears to be a convergence of emphasis on ascertaining the circumstances under which people can develop as 'free and equal'.

To put the point another way, the aspiration of these traditions to a world characterized by free and equal relations among mature adults reflects a concern to ensure

1 the creation of the best circumstances for all humans to develop their nature and express their diverse qualities (involving an assumption of respect for individuals' diverse capacities, their ability to learn and enhance their potentialities);
2 protection from the arbitrary use of political authority and coercive power (involving an assumption of respect for privacy in all matters which are not the basis of potential and demonstrable 'harm' to others);
3 the involvement of citizens in the determination of the conditions of their association (involving an assumption of respect for the authentic and reasoned nature of individuals' judgements);
4 the expansion of economic opportunity to maximize the availability of resources (involving an assumption that when individuals are free from the burdens of unmet physical need they are best able to realize their ends).

There is, in other words, a set of general aspirations that 'legal' and 'participatory' theorists have in common. Moreover, these aspirations have been shared by thinkers as diverse as J. S. Mill and Marx, and by most of those eighteenth- and nineteenth-century theorists who have sought to clarify the relation between the 'sovereign state' and 'sovereign people'.

The concept of 'autonomy' or 'independence' links together these aspirations and helps explain why they have been shared so widely. 'Autonomy' connotes the capacity of human beings to reason self-consciously, to be self-reflective and to be self-determining. It involves the ability to deliberate, judge, choose and act upon different possible courses of action in private as well as public life. Clearly, the idea of an 'autonomous' person could not develop while political rights, obligations and duties were closely tied, as they were in the medieval world-view, to property rights and religious tradition. But with the changes that wrought a fundamental transformation of medieval notions, there emerged a new preoccupation in European, political thought with the nature and limits of political authority, law, rights and duty.

Liberalism advanced the challenging view that individuals were 'free and equal', capable of determining and justifying their own actions, capable of entering into self-chosen obligations. The development of autonomous spheres of action, in social, political and economic affairs, became a (if not *the*) central mark of what it was to enjoy freedom and equality. While liberals failed frequently to explore the actual circumstances in which individuals lived – how people were integrally connected to one another through complex networks of relations and institutions – they nonetheless generated the strong belief that a defensible political order must be one in which people are able to develop their nature and interests free from the arbitrary use of political authority and coercive power. And although many liberals stopped far short of proclaiming that for individuals to be 'free and equal' they must themselves be sovereign, their work was preoccupied with, and affirmed the overwhelming importance of, uncovering the conditions under which individuals can determine and regulate the structure of their own association – a preoccupation they shared with figures such as Rousseau and Marx, although both the latter dissented, of course, from liberal interpretations of this central issue.

The aspirations that make up a concern with autonomy can be recast in the form of a general principle – what I call the 'principle of autonomy'. The principle can be stated as follows:

> individuals should be free and equal in the determination of the conditions of their own lives; that is, they should enjoy equal rights (and, accordingly, equal obligations) in the specification of the framework which

generates and limits the opportunities available to them, so long as they do not deploy this framework to negate the rights of others.

The qualification – that individual rights require explicit protection – represents the familiar call of liberals from Locke to Hayek for *constitutional* government. Hayek's distinction between 'sources of power' and 'limitations on power' restates the traditional liberal position, as does Nozick's claim that liberty means that people should not be able to impose themselves on others. Liberals have always argued that 'the liberty of the strong' must be restrained, although they have not, of course, always agreed about who constitutes 'the strong'. For some 'the strong' has included those with special access to certain kinds of resources (political, material and cultural), but for others 'the strong' has been elements of the *demos* itself. But whatever the precise conception of the proper nature and scope of individual liberty, liberals have been committed to a conception of the individual as 'free and equal' and to the necessity of creating institutional arrangements to protect their position, i.e. they have been committed to a version of the principle of autonomy.

Could Marxists (orthodox or otherwise) and the New Left theorists subscribe to the principle of autonomy? There is a fundamental sense in which the answer to this question is 'no'. They have not thought it necessary to establish a theory of the 'frontiers of freedom' (rights, cultural ends, objective interests or whatever we choose to call them) which 'nobody should be permitted to cross' in a post-capitalist political order. This is precisely the sense in which the Left does not have an adequate account of the state and, in particular, of democratic government as it exists and as it might be. Its dominant view of the future has always been that its 'music' could not and should not be composed in advance. To the extent that theories have been developed about existing or possible 'governing processes', they are wanting in many respects. However, matters ought not to be left here; for there is another sense in which this position is misleading. Marx's attempt to unpack the broad conditions of a non-exploitative society – an order arranged 'according to need' which maximizes 'freedom for all' – presupposes that such a society will be able to protect itself rigorously against all those who would seek to subject productive property and the power to make decisions once again to private appropriation. In the account offered by New Left thinkers, a similar presupposition is also clearly crucial; in fact, in many passages of their work it is quite explicit. But the ideas in these vital passages remain, unfortunately, undeveloped. Participatory democracy requires a detailed theory of the 'frontiers of freedom', and a detailed account of the institutional arrangements necessary to protect them, if it is to be defended adequately. A conception of the principle of autonomy is, thus, an unavoidable presupposition of radical democratic models.

What is the status of the principle of autonomy? The principle of autonomy ought to be regarded as an essential premise of liberalism and Marxism, and of their various contemporary offshoots. It ought to be considered one of their central elements, a basic and inescapable aspect of their rationale. All these traditions have given, and continue to give, priority to the development of 'autonomy' or 'independence'. But to state this – and to try to articulate its meaning in a fundamental but highly abstract principle – is not yet, it must be stressed, to say very much. For the full meaning of a principle cannot be specified independently of the conditions of its enactment. Liberalism and Marxism may give priority to 'autonomy', but they differ radically over how to secure it and, hence, over how to interpret it.

The specification of a principle's 'conditions of enactment' is a vital matter; for if a theory of the most desirable form of democracy is to be at all plausible, it must be concerned with both theoretical and practical issues, with philosophical as well as organizational and institutional questions. Without this double focus, an arbitrary choice of principles, and seemingly endless abstract debates about them, are encouraged. A consideration of principles, without an examination of the conditions for their realization, may preserve a sense of virtue, but it will leave the actual meaning of such principles barely spelt out at all. A consideration of social institutions and political arrangements without reflecting upon the proper principles of their ordering might, by contrast, lead to an understanding of their functioning, but it will barely help us come to a judgement as to their appropriateness and desirability.

Bearing this double focus in mind, I shall contend that both the liberal and the Marxist traditions – and contemporary variants of them – can contribute to the development of a proper understanding of the conditions of enactment of the principle of autonomy. Further justification of the principle alone will not be attempted here: first, because the reasons for its overriding significance have already been set out: it ought to be thought of as a fundamental axiom of key strands of modern Western political thought. And, second, because its further justification depends on a satisfactory elucidation of its meaning in relation to the conditions for its realization. For simplicity, the discussion below will focus, in the first instance, on broad issues in liberalism and Marxism. The complexities introduced into democratic theory by elitism, pluralism, neo-pluralism and so on do not alter the basic structure of the argument given here, although they do contribute important insights. In short, the conditions of enactment of the principle of autonomy can be specified adequately only if one (*a*) draws upon aspects of both liberalism and Marxism and (*b*) appreciates the limitations of both overall positions.

A starting point for reflection is provided by table 29.1, which sums up (albeit in rather stark form) some of the central positions of liberalism and Marxism. There are good grounds for taking seriously some of the central arguments and, thus, some of the central prescriptions of *both* liberalism and Marxism. The principle of autonomy can only be conceived adequately if we adopt this (somewhat eclectic) approach. It is important to appreciate, above all, the complementarity of liberalism's scepticism about political power and Marxism's scepticism about economic power. To focus exclusively on the former or the latter is to negate the possibility of realizing the principle of autonomy.

Liberalism's thrust to create a sovereign democratic state, a diversity of power centres and a world marked by openness, controversy and plurality is radically compromised by the reality of the so-called 'free market', the structure and imperatives of the system of private capital accumulation. If liberalism's central failure is to see markets as 'powerless' mechanisms of co-ordination and thus to neglect – as neo-pluralists, among others, point out – the distorting nature of economic power in relation to democracy, Marxism's central failure is the reduction of political power to economic power and thus to neglect – as participatory democrats, among others, point out – the dangers of centralized political power and the problems of political accountability. Marxism's embodiment in East European societies today is marked by the growth of the centralized bureaucratic state; its claim to represent the forces of progressive politics is tarnished by socialism's relation in practice, in the East and also in the West, with bureaucracy, surveillance, hierarchy and state control. Accordingly, liberalism's account of the nature of markets and economic power must be rejected while Marxism's account of the nature of democracy must be severely questioned.

It is important to take note, furthermore, of some of the limitations shared by liberalism and Marxism. Generally, these two political traditions have failed to explore the impediments to full participation in democratic life other than those imposed, however important these may be, by state and economic power. The roots of the difficulty lie in narrow conceptions of 'the political'. In the liberal tradition the political is equated with the world of government or governments alone. Where this equation is made and where politics is regarded as a sphere apart

Table 29.1 Justified prescriptions of liberalism and Marxism

	Liberalism		*Marxism*
1	Hostility to and scepticism about state power, and emphasis on the importance of a diversity of power centres	1	Hostility to and scepticism about concentration of economic power in private ownership of the means of production
2	Separation of state from civil society as an essential prerequisite of a democratic order	2	Restructuring of civil society, i.e. transformation of capitalist relations of production, as a prerequisite of a flourishing democracy
3	The desirable form of the state is an impersonal (legally circumscribed) structure of power	3	The 'impersonality' or 'neutrality' of the state can only be achieved when its autonomy is no longer compromised by capitalism
4	Centrality of constitutionalism to guarantee formal equality (before the law) and formal freedom (from arbitrary treatment) in the form of civil and political liberties or rights essential to representative democracy: above all, those of free speech, expression, association, belief and (for liberal democrats) one-person one-vote and party pluralism	4	The transformation of the rigid social and technical division of labour is essential if people are to develop their capacities and involve themselves fully in the democratic regulation of political as well as economic and social life
5	Protected space enshrined in law for individual autonomy and initiative	5	The equally legitimate claims of all citizens to autonomy are the foundation of any freedom that is worth the name
6	Importance of markets as mechanisms for co-ordinating diverse activities of producers and consumers	6	Unless there is public planning of investment, production will remain geared to profit, not to need in general

from economy or culture, that is, as governmental activity and institutions, a vast domain of politics is excluded from view: above all, the spheres of productive and reproductive relations. The Marxist conception of politics raises related matters. Although the Marxist critique of liberalism is of great significance, its value is ultimately limited because of the direct connection it postulates (even within the framework of the 'relative autonomy' of the state) between the political and the economic. By reducing political to economic and class power, and by championing 'the end of politics', Marxism itself tends to marginalize or exclude certain types of issue from politics. This is true of all those issues which cannot, in the last analysis, be reduced to class-related matters – the development of power in organizations, for instance.

The narrow conception of 'the political' in both liberalism and Marxism has meant that key conditions for the realization of the principle of autonomy have been eclipsed from view: conditions concerning, for example, the necessary limits on private possession of the means of production, if democratic outcomes are not to be skewed systematically to the advantage of the economically powerful (insufficiently examined by liberalism); and the necessary changes in the organization of the household and childrearing, among other things, if women are to enjoy 'free and equal' conditions (insufficiently examined by both liberalism and Marxism). (This is not to say, of course, that no liberal or Marxist has been concerned with these things; this would clearly be untrue. Rather, it is to argue that their perspectives or frameworks of analysis cannot adequately encompass them.) In order to grasp the diverse conditions necessary for the adequate institutionalization of the principle of autonomy, we require a broader conception of 'the political' than is found in either of these traditions.

In my view, politics is about power; that is, it is about the *capacity* of social agents, agencies and institution to maintain or transform their environment, social or physical. It is about the resources that underpin this capacity and about the forces that shape and influence its exercise. Accordingly, politics is a phenomenon found in and between all groups, institutions (formal and informal) and societies, cutting across public and private life. It is expressed in all the activities of co-operation, negotiation and struggle over the use and distribution of resources. It is involved in all the relations, institutions and structures which are implicated in the activities of production and reproduction in the life of societies. Politics creates and conditions all aspects of our lives and it is at the core of the development of problems in society and the collective modes of their resolution. While politics, thus understood, raises a number of complicated issues – above all, about whether a concept of the private is compatible with it (a matter returned to later) – it usefully highlights the nature of politics as a universal dimension of human life, unrelated to any specific 'site' or set of institutions.

If politics is conceived in this way, then the specification of the conditions of enactment of the principle of autonomy amounts to the specification of the conditions for the participation of citizens in decisions about issues which are important to them (i.e. us). Thus, it is necessary to strive towards a state of affairs in which political life – democratically organized – is, in principle, a central part of all people's lives.

30

Democracy: From City-states to a Cosmopolitan Order?

David Held

There is a striking paradox to note about the contemporary era: from Africa to Eastern Europe, Asia to Latin America, more and more nations and groups are championing the idea of 'the rule of the people'; but they are doing so at just that moment when the very efficacy of democracy as a national form of political organization appears open to question. As substantial areas of human activity are progressively organized on a global level, the fate of democracy, and of the independent democratic nation-state in particular, is fraught with difficulty.

It could be objected that there is nothing particularly new about global interconnections, and that the significance of global interconnections for politics has, in principle, been plain for people to see for a long time. Such an objection could be elaborated by emphasizing that a dense pattern of global interconnections began to emerge with the initial expansion of the world-economy and the rise of the modern state from the late sixteenth century. Further, it could be suggested that domestic and international politics have been interwoven throughout the modern era: domestic politics has always to be understood against the background of international politics, and the former is often the source of the latter. However, it is one thing to claim that there are elements of continuity in the formation and structure of modern states, economies and societies, quite another to claim that there is nothing new about aspects of their form and dynamics. For there is a fundamental difference between, on the one hand, the development of particular trade routes, or select military and naval operations which have an impact on certain towns, rural centres and territories, and, on the other hand, an international order involving the emergence of a global economic system which stretches beyond the control of any single state (even of dominant states); the expansion of networks of transnational relations and communications over which particular states have limited influence; the enormous growth in international organizations and regimes which can limit the scope for action of the most powerful states; the development of a global military order, and the build-up of the means of 'total' warfare as an enduring feature of the contemporary world, which can reduce the range of policies available to governments and their citizens. While trade routes and military expeditions can link distant populations together in long loops of cause and effect, contemporary developments in the international order link peoples through multiple networks of transaction and co-ordination, reordering the very notion of distance itself.

It needs to be emphasized that processes of globalization do not necessarily lead to growing global integration; that is, to a world order marked by the progressive development of a homogeneous or unified society and politics. For globalization can generate forces of both fragmentation and unification. Fragmentation or disintegrative trends are possible for several reasons. The growth of dense patterns of interconnectedness among states and societies can increase the range of developments affecting people in particular locations. By creating new patterns of transformation and change, globalization can weaken old political and economic structures without necessarily leading to the establishment of new systems of regulation. Further, the impact of global and regional processes is likely to vary under different international and national conditions – for instance, a nation's location in the international economy, its place in particular power blocs, its position with respect to the international legal system. In addition, globalization can engender an awareness of political difference as much as an awareness of common identity; enhanced international communications can highlight conflicts of interest and ideology, and not merely remove obstacles to mutual understanding.

In positive terms, globalization implies at least two distinct phenomena. First, it suggests that political, economic and social activity is becoming worldwide in scope. And, second, it suggests that there has been an intensification of levels of interaction and interconnectedness within and among states and societies. What is new about the modern global system is the spread of globalization through new dimensions of activity – technological, organizational, administrative and legal, among others – each with their own logic and dynamics of change; and the chronic intensification of patterns of interconnectedness mediated by such phenomena as the modern communications industry and new information technology. Politics unfolds today, with all its customary uncertainty and indeterminateness, against the background of a world shaped and permeated by the movement of goods and capital, the flow of communication, the interchange of cultures and the passage of people.

In this context, the meaning and place of democratic politics, and of the contending models of democracy, have to be rethought in relation to a series of overlapping local, regional and global processes and structures. It is essential to recognize at least three elements of globalization: first, the way processes of economic, political, legal and military interconnectedness are changing the nature, scope and capacity of the sovereign state from above, as its 'regulatory' ability is challenged and reduced in some spheres; second, the way in which local groups, movements and nationalisms are questioning the nation-state from below as a representative and accountable power system; and, third, the way global interconnectedness creates chains of interlocking political decisions and outcomes among states and their citizens, altering the nature and dynamics of national political systems themselves. Democracy has to come to terms with all three of these developments and their implications for national and international power centres. If it fails to do so, it is likely to become ever less effective in determining the shape and limits of political activity. The international form and structure of politics and civil society has, accordingly, to be built into the foundations of democratic thought and practice.

Three distinct requirements arise: first, that the territorial boundaries of systems of accountability be recast so that those issues which escape the control of a nation-state – aspects of monetary management, environmental questions, elements of security, new forms of communication – can be brought under better democratic control. Second, that the role and place of regional and global regulatory and functional agencies be rethought so that they might provide a more coherent and useful focal point in public affairs. Third, that the articulation of political institutions with the key groups, agencies, associations and organizations of international civil society be reconsidered to allow the latter to become part of a democratic process – adopting, within their very *modus operandi*, a structure of rules and principles compatible with those of democracy.

How might this approach to democracy be developed? What are its essential characteristics? Addressing these questions requires conceiving democracy as a double-sided process, while reappraising the proper domain for the application of this process. For if the above arguments are correct, democracy has to become a transnational affair if it is to be possible both within a restricted geographic domain and within the wider international community. The possibility of democracy today must, in short, be linked to an expanding framework of democratic institutions and agencies. I refer to such a framework as 'the cosmopolitan model of democracy'. The framework can be elaborated by focusing initially on some of its institutional requirements.

In the first instance, the 'cosmopolitan model of democracy' presupposes the creation of regional parliaments (for example, in Latin America and Africa) and the enhancement of the role of such bodies where they already exist (the European Parliament) in order that their decisions become recognized, in principle, as legitimate independent sources of regional and international law. Alongside such developments, the model anticipates the possibility of general referendums, cutting across nations and nation-states, with constituencies defined according to the nature and scope of controversial transnational issues. In addition, the opening of international governmental organizations to public scrutiny and the democratization of international 'functional' bodies (on the basis perhaps of the creation of elected supervisory boards which are in part statistically representative of their constituencies) would be significant.

Hand in hand with these changes the cosmopolitan model of democracy assumes the entrenchment of a cluster of rights, including civil, political, economic and social rights, in order to provide shape and limits to democratic decision-making. This requires that they be enshrined within the constitutions of parliaments and assemblies (at the national and international level); and that the influence of international courts is extended so that groups and individuals have an effective means of suing political authorities for the enactment and enforcement of key rights, both within and beyond political associations.

In the final analysis, the formation of an authoritative assembly of all democratic states and societies – a re-formed UN, or a complement to it – would be an objective. The UN combines two contradictory principles of representation: the equality of all countries (one country, one vote in the General Assembly) and deference to geopolitical strength (special veto power in the Security Council to those with current or former superpower status). An authoritative assembly of all democratic states and societies would seek unreservedly to place principles of democratic representation above those of superpower politics. Moreover, unlike the UN General Assembly, it would not, to begin with at least, be an assembly of all nations; for it would be an assembly of democratic nations which would draw in others over time, perhaps by the sheer necessity of being a member if their systems of governance are to enjoy legitimacy in the eyes of their own populations. As such, the new Assembly in its early stages can best be thought of as a complement to the UN, which it would either replace over time or accept in a modified form as a 'second chamber' – a necessary meeting place for all states irrespective of the nature of their regimes.

Of course, the idea of a new democratic international Assembly is open to a battery of objections commonly put to similar schemes. Would it have any teeth to implement decisions? How would democratic international law be enforced? Would there be a centralized police and military force? And so forth. These concerns are significant, but many of them can be met and countered. For instance, it needs to be stressed that any global legislative institution should be conceived above all as a 'standard-setting' institution. Although a distinction ought to be made between legal instruments which would have the status of law independently of any further negotiation or action on the part of a region or state or local government, and instruments which would require further discussion with them, implementation of the detail of a broad range of recommendations would be a matter for non-global levels of governance. In addition, the question of law enforcement at a regional and global level is not beyond resolution in principle: a proportion of a nation-state's police and military (perhaps a growing proportion over time) could be 'seconded' to the new international authorities and placed at their disposal on a routine basis. To this end, avenues could be established to meet the concern that 'covenants, without the sword, are but words'.

Equally, only to the extent that the new forms of 'policing' are locked into an international democratic framework would there be good grounds for thinking that a new settlement could be created between coercive power and accountability. If such a settlement seems like a fantasy, it should be emphasized that it is a fantasy to imagine that one can advocate democracy today without confronting the range of issues elaborated here. If the emerging international order is to be democratic, these issues have to be considered, even though their details are, of course, open to further specification.

The implications for international civil society of all this are in part clear. A democratic network of states and civil societies is incompatible with the existence of powerful sets of social relations and organizations which, by virtue of the very bases of their operations, can systematically distort democratic conditions and processes. At stake are, among other things, the curtailment of the power of corporations to constrain and influence the *political* agenda (through such diverse measures as the public funding of elections, the use of 'golden shares' and citizen directors), and the restriction of the activities of powerful transnational interest groups to pursue their interest unchecked (through, for example, the regulation of bargaining procedures to minimize the use of 'coercive tactics' within and between public and private associations, and the enactment of rules limiting the sponsorship of political representatives by sectional interests, whether these be particular industries or trade unions).

If individuals and peoples are to be free and equal in determining the conditions of their own existence there must be an array of social spheres – for instance, privately and co-operatively owned enterprises, independent communications media, and autonomously run cultural centres – which allow their members control of the resources at their disposal without direct interference from political agencies or other third parties. At issue here is a civil society that is neither simply planned nor merely market oriented but, rather, open to organizations, associations and agencies pursuing their own projects, subject to the constraints of democratic processes and a common structure of action.

The key features of this model are set out in table 30.1. The cosmopolitan model of democracy presents a programme of possible transformations with short- and long-term political implications. It does not present an all-or-nothing choice, but rather lays down a direction of possible change with clear points of orientation (see appendix I).

Would a cosmopolitan framework of democracy, assuming its details could be adequately fleshed out, have the organizational resources – procedural, legal, institutional and military – to alter the dynamics of resource production and distribution, and of rule creation and enforcement, in the contemporary era? It would be deeply misleading to suggest that it would initially have these capabilities. Nevertheless, its commitment to the extension and deepening of mechanisms of democratic accountability across major regions and international structures would help to regulate resources and forces which are already beyond the reach of national democratic mechanisms and movements. Moreover, its commitment to the protection and strengthening of human rights, and to the further development of a regional and international court system, would aid the process whereby individuals and groups could sue their governments for the enactment of key human rights.

In addition, the establishment of regional authorities as major independent voices in world politics might contribute further to the erosion of the old division of the world by the United States and the former USSR. Likewise, the new institutional focus at the global level on major transnational issues would go some way towards eradicating sectarian approaches to these questions, and to countering 'hierarchy' and some of the major asymmetries in life chances. Finally, new sets of regional and global rules and procedures might help prevent public affairs from

Table 30.1 The cosmopolitan model of democracy

1. The global order consists of multiple and overlapping networks of power including the political, social and economic.
2. All groups and associations are attributed rights of self-determination specified by a commitment to individual autonomy and a specific cluster of rights. The cluster is composed of rights within and across each network of power. Together, these rights constitute the basis of an empowering legal order – a 'democratic international law'.
3. Law-making and law-enforcement can be developed within this framework at a variety of locations and levels, along with an expansion of the influence of regional and international courts to monitor and check political and social authority.
4. Legal principles are adopted which delimit the form and scope of individual and collective action within the organizations and associations of state *and* civil society. Certain standards are specified for the treatment of all, which no political regime or civil association can legitimately violate.
5. As a consequence, the principle of non-coercive relations governs the settlement of disputes, though the use of force remains a collective option in the last resort in the face of tyrannical attacks to eradicate democratic international law.
6. The defence of self-determination, the creation of a common structure of action and the preservation of the democratic good are the overall collective priorities.
7. Determinate principles of social justice follow: the *modus operandi* of the production, distribution and the exploitation of resources must be compatible with the democratic process and a common framework of action.

becoming a quagmire of infighting among nations wholly unable to settle pressing collective issues.

Of course, there would be new possible dangers – no political scheme is free from such risks. But what would be at issue would be the beginning of the creation of a new international democratic culture and spirit – one set off from the partisan claims of the nation-state. Such developments might take years, if not decades, to become entrenched. But 1989–91 has shown that political change can take place at an extraordinary speed, itself no doubt partially a result of the process of globalization.

Appendix I
Objectives of the Cosmopolitan Model of Democracy: Illustrative Issues

	Short-term		*Long-term*
	Polity/governance		
1	Reform of UN Security Council (to give the Third World a significant voice)	1	Global Parliament (with limited revenue-raising capacity) connected to regions, nations and localities
2	Creation of a UN second chamber (on the model of the EC?)	2	New Charter of Rights and Duties locked into different domains of power
3	Enhanced political regionalization (EC and beyond)	3	Separation of political and economic interests; public funding of electoral processes
4	Compulsory jurisdiction before the International Court. New International Criminal Court and New Human Rights Court for the pursuit of rights	4	Interconnected global legal system
5	Establishment of a small but effective, accountable, international, military force	5	Permanent 'secondment' of a growing proportion of a nation-state's coercive capability to regional and global institutions. Aim: demilitarization and transcendence of war system
	Civil Society		
1	Enhancement of non-state, non-market solutions in the organization of civil society	1	Creation of a diversity of self-regulating associations and groups in civil society
2	Introduction of limits to private ownership of key 'public-shaping' institutions: media, information etc.	2	Systematic experimentation with different democratic organizational forms in civil society
3	Provision of resources to those in the most vulnerable social positions to defend and articulate their interests	3	Multi-sectoral economy and pluralization of patterns of ownership and possession

31

Class, Environmental and Social Movements

Boris Frankel

In recent years it has become highly fashionable to replace class theory with the theory of new social movements. Writers such as Touraine, Cohen, Eder and many others have focused on Solidarity, the peace movement, the Greens, and the women's movement as examples of a new politics which reflects the obsolescence of class struggle. But, despite the many valuable insights which these theorists offer us in relation to the nature and practice of these movements, their work provides endless typologies and descriptive contrasts between the old and new political movements yet little on the ability of social movements to replace the existing structural differentiation and institutionalization of political decision-making in state and private organizations and apparatuses. It is one thing to propose new social movements as the agents of the transition from industrial to post-industrial society; it is quite another matter to concentrate on the political struggle at the expense of evaluating whether the end goals of these struggles are feasible. That is, new social movements are generally conceived to be reactions against bureaucratization, statism, corporatism and 'the colonization of the life-world' or technocratic interference in all aspects of civic life and physical existence. Moreover, the struggle between social movements and traditional political processes is erroneously depicted as the struggle of 'civil society against the state'. This is because new social movement theorists do not adequately differentiate between 'the state' in the narrow sense of political administration (that is, government by freely elected ministers, one-party dictators or military–bureaucratic regimes) and state institutions in the larger sense as part of what is called 'civil society', for example, the vital educational, social welfare, transport, media and other national and local services, not to mention nationalized industries in telecommunications, electricity, manufacturing and so forth. Hence, social movements exist both *inside* the larger state (for example, Solidarity or student movements in state-run universities), and outside state institutions, just as workers and their unions exist both within private businesses and also in state institutions.

At one level it is clear, for example, that many environmentalist or feminist organizations are directly opposing government policies, practices and potential legislation. But at another level, social movements have no more 'natural' coherence or existence than pure classes. That is, women, environmentalists, peace activists, gays etc. do not have a ready-formed identity as a social movement any more than workers have an innate class consciousness. Rather, individuals become active within particular organizations or support in a looser manner (via protest marches or lifestyle practices) some or all of the demands made by particular organizations or coalitions. There are just as many political divisions within new social movements – divisions between revolutionaries, reformists, fundamentalists and pragmatists – as there are within labour movements. Claus Offe points out that social movements are often unable to make compromises in the way that political parties or unions can because they articulate non-negotiable values, for example less nuclear power is just as unacceptable as full reliance upon nuclear power generation. While Offe and other new social movement theorists note all the tensions and divisions within social movements, they do not emphasize that a social movement cannot function as an organization or as an actor who enters into negotiations with other organizations or forms alliances. For example, particular groups of women (not the 'feminist movement') enter into negotiations or struggles. This theoretical distinction is important as a great deal of the literature on social movements is so unsatisfactory. In treating social movements as historical actors, there is a real danger of succumbing to a new form of substitutionalism. That is, new social movements are substituted for the proletarian class as the subject of historical change. This misconception repeats all the old problems associated with treating classes as coherent social actors.

The major divisions within the West German Green movement are a good illustration of the limits of new social movement theory and practice. At the practical level, Bahro represents all those fundamentalists in the Green movement who reject compromise with the system, who oppose 'limits' on armaments or animal experiments and want to do away with them completely. Bahro's fundamentalism is qualitatively distinct from the old division between revolutionaries and reformists. Whereas revolutionaries attacked reformists for working in the system, they did not necessarily believe that parliamentary tactics were bad, and argued that strategic alliances were at times necessary with non-working-class organizations. But the Green fundamentalists oppose the 'realists', not because of their methods, but because of the impending 'eco-catastrophe' which 'limited reforms' will delay but not avert. If Bahro and his supporters believe that the whole industrial system is doomed, and that compromise with this system is a replay or renewal of conventional politics, all contact with state institutions is self-defeating unless this contact is one of fundamental opposition. But how is a transitional politics to be exercised by social movements who play an all-or-nothing game? Leninists believe in the need for a vanguard party which grows in size until dual power results in the bourgeois state being overthrown. But believers in new social movements must either hope for the system to weaken and wither away, or come into major confrontation with state power.

If one does not believe in either violence or compromise, as Bahro does, there can be no transitional politics, but only collapse of the old and replacement by the new. Life in a social movement must then become increasingly oriented to consciousness-raising, messianic prophecy about the impending *catastrophe* (nuclear war or ecological devastation) and withdrawal into a micro-politics of small face-to-face relations, or quasi-religious, sect-like activities. Bahro actually sees spiritualist and religious orders of the past as examples for the present generation. But the history of humanity reveals no examples of societies reverting to much simpler and less complex organizational forms of life save after a natural or social catastrophe (usually war). Religious groups have long preached the renunciation of worldly possessions without much success. Mass mobilization of earlier generations of peasants or workers was possible through the promise of a richer material life and greater freedom, rather than a dismantling of the whole production system.

I must agree with Bahro: the orthodox Marxist belief that socialists can utilize the means of production developed by capitalists is not only profoundly conservative but totally incompatible with the construction of a post-industrial socialist society. But while I support the dismantling of military–industrial complexes and other anti-human means of production, this is not equivalent to support for total 'industrial disarmament'. If Bahro is correct about the industrial system (and there is great merit in many of his warnings), then the political conclusions must be profoundly pessimistic – given his opting out of conventional politics. For if millions of workers cannot be assured of alternative jobs, social welfare etc. in the peaceful transition from eco-doomed industrialism to eco-pacifist post-industrialism – and there is no indication whatsoever that Bahro wants or is able to address and resolve this massive problem

– then the end result, if we subscribe to Bahro's analysis, must be the end of the world.

I do not believe that things are as bad as Bahro makes them out to be, although I can fully agree with many specific examples of environmental damage which alarm Bahro and all other sensitive people. More importantly, even though I agree with many of the critiques from feminists, environmentalists, gays and other new social activists, there is a vast difference between those who wish to extend and democratize existing undemocratic and bureaucratic public institutions, and the other members of new movements who reject any form of state institution and seek a radically decentralized and diffused stateless society. New social movement organizations have tried to implement, with mixed success, a 'new politics'. But they are also plagued by 'old politics' problems: bureaucratic tendencies, tension between the rank-and-file and the leaders or media 'stars', intolerance of dissenters or ideological divisions, funding crises, and co-option into neo-corporatist policy-making processes. These problems often arise from having to oppose the system, while at the same time trying to gain concessions or new policies by using whatever resources or institutions are available.

Most organizations in new social movements actually accept to a lesser or greater extent the prevailing public and private political processes, rather than advocate a total dismantling of the whole state institutional system. Others have a naive disregard or ignorance of the massive repressive state apparatuses and private corporate resources which can be (and often are) deployed against critics of prevailing socio-political orders. But those members of new social movements who advocate a radical anti-statism and the end of the 'welfare state' appear to ignore important members of their own diverse constituency. Sociologically, many members of new social movements are drawn from what Offe calls 'decommodified' groups: students, retired persons, middle-class housewives and unemployed or marginalized people who are not engaged in the labour market, as well as many public sector workers (for example, teachers, social workers) whom conservatives call 'the new class'.[1] Consider, then, a transition to post-industrial society in which new social movement organizations dismantle the very 'social wage' services that keep 'new class' members employed, or the revenue structures which provide pensions, student allowances and dole payments for the 'decommodified' groups. Such a process is bound to promote a rightwing post-industrialism – or, somewhat less plausibly, a stateless society without mass support in either the labour movement or the 'decommodified' groups.

If we assume that contemporary Western societies are based upon complex relations between a dominant private sector and a broad range of local and national state institutions (which perform the contradictory roles of assisting and preserving capitalist enterprise as well as maintaining legitimacy and crisis managing), then social movement theorists have to be able to show that class relations, and hence the relationship between class power and state power, are much less decisive than the relationship between social movements and state power. If we still live in a capitalist society, what has happened to class domination and exploitation? Social movements are made up of members who come from more than one class; yet there is little to suggest (as is implied in social movement theory) that new social movements have replaced classes as the sociological basis of contemporary societies. If a post-industrial society is to be a classless society, it would have to be shown how the political organizations (which express new social movement values and interests) can overthrow or negate the power of ruling capitalist classes.

[...]

Despite all the important issues raised and struggles waged by new social organizations, the post-industrial theorists have failed to address adequately the vital issue of state power, as well as the related strategic issue of how class-dominated and bureaucratized state institutions can be transformed into their post-industrial opposites. While policies and practices developed by feminists, environmentalists and other movements can never all be reduced back to class politics, the post-industrial theorists conspicuously fail to explain how working-class organizations fit into their transitional scenarios. It is also asserted, but not clearly shown, that workers will benefit from the microelectronic revolution, 'industrial disarmament', 'prosuming', 'electronic cottages' and other such potential changes. Wage workers constitute the vast majority of all existing populations in capitalist countries, yet the post-industrial theorists are either openly hostile to workers' organizations or regard them as irrelevant to the shaping of the future. Such short-sightedness or antagonism is both unjustified and self-defeating.

Reference

1 C. Offe, 'New social movements: challenging the boundaries of institutional politics', *Social Research*, 52 (4) (1985), pp. 833–4.

32

Ecological Communication

Niklas Luhmann

Compared to the history of reflection on humanity and society this theme – ecology – is not very old. Only in the last twenty years has one seen a rapidly increasing discussion of the ecological conditions of social life and the connection between the social system and its environment. Contemporary society feels itself affected in many different ways by the changes that it has produced in its own environment. This is clearly shown by a number of these: the increasingly rapid consumption of non-replaceable resources and (even if this would prove beneficial) the increasing dependence on self-produced substitutes, a reduction in the variety of species forming the basis of further biological evolution, the ever-possible development of uncontrollable viruses resistant to medicine, the familiar problem of environmental pollution and not least of all over-population. Today these are all themes for social communication. Society has thus become alarmed as never before without possessing, however, the cognitive means for predicting and directing action because it not only changes its environment but also undermines the conditions for its own continued existence. This is by no means a new problem. It appeared in earlier stages of social development too. But only today has it reached an intensity that obtrudes as a 'noise' distorting human communication that can no longer be ignored.

As far as sociology is concerned, this discussion began – like so many others – unexpectedly and caught it, as it were, unprepared theoretically. Originally, sociology had been concerned with the internal aspects of society. It entangled itself in ideologies of the correct social order and then tried to extricate itself from them. All this was done under the assumption that its theme was society or its parts. The history of the foundations of this discipline had already predisposed it in this direction. Nature, on the other hand, could and indeed had to be left to the natural sciences. What the new discipline called sociology could discover and claim as its own field of study was either society or, if this concept was unsatisfactory, social facts, for example *faits sociaux* in Durkheim's sense, or social forms and relations in the sense of Simmel and von Wiese, or social action in Weber's sense. Thus the delimitation of the discipline had to be interpreted as a demarcation of a section of reality.

But in addition to 'grand theory', research in the domain of the most diverse *social problems* is also attuned to the social origins of these problems. This is precisely what forms the basis of the researcher's hopes of being able to contribute something to a better solution of the problem. The problematic is reduced to structures of the social system or its subsystems, and if these cannot be changed then at least one can blame the circumstances. The external sources of the problems are not even considered. And although every problem of the system is ultimately reducible to the difference between system and environment, this is not even considered.

Even for the earlier theory of *societas civilis* this was no different, and the same is true for practical philosophy: what is social was viewed as *civitas*, as *communitas perfecta* or as political society, even if this included all of humanity. According to the Stoic as well as the Christian theory, non-human nature was to be used by everyone. *Dominium terrae* thereby became a concept by which the sacralization of all of nature was prevented and the specification of what was religious was secured. Nature in this sense, so ecologically important today, was de-sacralized nature. The ever present counter-opinions were never strong enough to present the developing natural sciences with a problem. Then in the eighteenth century the problem experienced a dramatic reversal. The counter-concept (which, as is so often the case, suggests the real interest) was changed. Civilization took the place of the sacred (whose specifically monotheistic version was retained) as the counter-concept to nature. Thereby nature became, on one hand, an irretrievably lost history and, on the other, society's field of research.

But even this version was not enough to determine the difference between nature and civilization. It does, however, offer the first chance at an awareness of the environment (for example, as the consequence of the ancient doctrine that God is to be worshipped in his creations). The eighteenth century discovered the meaning of milieu, i.e. of being situated concretely, for example, as the connection between climate and culture. Stimulated by progress in agricultural technology, the early French economists (physiocrats) saw property as a legal institution that is both economically and ecologically ideal because it guarantees the proper treatment of natural resources while it guarantees the proper treatment of natural resources while it reconciles them with human interests. It is noteworthy that at that time the *internalization* of the consequences of actions and their inclusion in rational calculation were viewed as a function of property. Today the converse is the case: the consequences of actions are discussed in terms of *externalization* and property is criticized for lacking in responsibility for these consequences.

At first nothing resulted from all this. The French Revolution led to an ideologizing of social debates linked to social position and political goals, and the descriptions of social relations occurred entirely within society. This is most clearly visible in the way in which Darwin was carried over into the social sciences. Instead of accepting the idea that the environment selectively decides how society can develop, an ideologically tainted Social Darwinism came into being that promised individuals, economies and nations the right to success through the survival of the fittest. But after a few years this too became bogged down in the mire of a new social morality, and even today the theory of evolution in the social sciences has not freed itself completely from this disaster.

Even where sociology presented itself as opposition or as 'critical theory' all that it considered was society and humane principles that did not correspond to the society, or at least not at that time. This found expression as insufficient freedom, equality, justice or reason – in any event, all bourgeois themes. The part that sociology played within this social discussion was the *self-critique* of society *vis-à-vis determinate ideals*, not *frustration* regarding *uncertain hopes and fears*. But it was simply too easy to reject this critique because ideals have a fatal tendency to transform themselves into illusions. The theoretical background for this discussion has long since disappeared even though the 'simultaneity of the non-simultaneous' still had to be reckoned with for a long time. In this state of alarm the only question must be how justified specific hopes or fears are. Or, from the perspective of a disinterested observer, which factors determine the readiness to accept risks and how are they distributed in society?

Totally absorbed in its own object, sociology did not even notice that a reorientation had already started among the natural sciences, begun by the law of entropy. If this law that declares the tendency to the loss of heat and organization is valid then it becomes even more important to explain why the natural order does not seem to obey it and evolves in opposition to it. The answer lies in the capacity of thermodynamically open systems – those related to their environments through inputs and outputs – to enter into relations of exchange, i.e. environmental dependence, and nevertheless to guarantee their autonomy through structural regulation. Ludwig von Bertalanffy appropriated this idea and used it as the basis for what today is called 'general systems theory'.

It would be unfair, however, to say that sociology did not take account of this at all because there are some programmatic similarities. For example, research in the sociology of organizations, emphasizing the environmental reference of organizations, has been successful. But here the environment always means something internal to the society, for example markets or technological innovations, in other words only society itself.

This preoccupation with society itself can be avoided only through a change in the theoretical focus of the paradigm. Such a manoeuvre, however, has consequences that reach all the way into the ramification of sociological thought. This means that radical incisions have to be made, and only after such an operation – if it is not refused to begin with – does one learn to proceed again slowly.

The surprising appearance of a new ecological consciousness has left little time for theoretical consideration. Initially, therefore, the new theme was considered within the context of the old theory. Accordingly, if society endangers itself through its effects on the environment then it has to suffer the consequences. The guilty should be found out, restrained and, if necessary, opposed and punished. Moral right, then, is on the side of those who intervene against the self-destruction of society. In this way the theoretical discussion surreptitiously becomes a moral question and any of its possible theoretical shortcomings are offset by moral zeal. In other words, the intention to demonstrate good intentions determines the formulation of the problem. So, by accident as it were, a new *environmental* ethics enters the discussion without ever analysing the all-important system structures.

Whoever proposes a new ethics brings the question of blame into historical view at the same time. It has been advocated, for instance, that the Christian West was disposed to deal with nature in a crude and insensitive way, if not simply to exploit it, while on the other hand it was also argued that Christians always loved and respected animals and paid homage to the Creator through His creation. When the question is put in such a simple and naive way both of these arguments are valid. This historical perspective serves only to provide contrast and does not concern itself at all with the actual course of events. It merely helps to bring the new ethics into view without raising the difficult question of whether and how it is possible as such.

Despite this, it has become obvious that as scientific research progressed respect for 'natural balances' increased, whether this was in ecological relations, foreign cultures or even today in developing countries and their traditions. But at the same time, one's own society was exposed to an incisive critique that was replete with demands for intervention, *as if it was not a system at all.* Obviously this reveals a negative ethnocentrism, and it is possible that a significant aversion to 'systems theory' has had something to do with the critical restraint this theory has directed against its own society.

At the very least this summary discussion lacks an understanding of the theoretical structure of the ecological question, above all of its fundamental paradox – that it has to treat all facts in terms of unity *and* difference, i.e. in terms of the unity of the ecological interconnection and the difference of system and environment that breaks this interconnection down. As far as the ecological question is concerned, the theme becomes the unity of the difference of system and environment, not the unity of an encompassing system.

Therefore the systems-theoretical difference of system and environment formulates the radical change in world-view. This is where the break with tradition is to be found, not in the question of a crude and insensitive exploitation of nature. Indeed, historical investigations of the concepts of *periechon*, *continens*, *ambiens*, *ambiente* and medium can show that what is today called environment was viewed by the Greek and even the medieval tradition as an encompassing body, if not as a living cosmos that assigned the proper place to everything in it. These traditions had in mind the relation of a containment of little bodies within a larger one. Delimitation was not viewed as the restriction of possibilities and freedom but instead as the bestowal of form, support and protection. This view was reversed only by a theoretical turn that began in the nineteenth century when the terms '*Umwelt*' and '*environment*' were invented and which has reached its culmination today: systems define their own boundaries. They differentiate themselves and thereby constitute the environment as whatever lies outside the boundary. In this sense, then, the environment is not a system of its own, not even a unified effect. As the totality of external circumstances, it is whatever restricts the randomness of the morphogenesis of the system and exposes it to evolutionary selection. The 'unity' of the environment is nothing more than a correlate of the unity of the system since everything that is a unity for the system is defined by it as a unity.

The consequences of this interpretation for a theory of the system of society (and indeed for a system of society that communicates about ecological questions) can be reduced to two points.

1 The theory must change its direction from the *unity* of the social whole as a smaller unity within a larger one (the world) to the

difference of the system of society and environment, i.e. from unity to difference as the theoretical point of departure. More exactly, the theme of sociological investigation is not the system of society, but instead the *unity of the difference of the system of society and its environment.* In other words, the theme is the world as a whole, seen through the system reference of the system of society, i.e. with the help of distinctions by which the system of society differentiates itself from an environment. After all, difference is not only a means of separating but also, and above all, a means of reflecting the system by distinguishing it.

2 The idea of system elements must be changed from substances (individuals) to self-referential operations that can be produced only within the system and with the help of a network of the same operations (autopoiesis). For social systems in general and the system of society in particular the operation of (self-referential) communication seems to be the most appropriate candidate.

If these two points are accepted then 'society' signifies the all-encompassing social system of mutually referring communications. It originates through communicative acts alone and differentiates itself from an environment of other kinds of systems through the continual reproduction of communication by communication. In this way complexity is constituted through evolution.

I propose this theory, not in order to provide a solution to the problem of the ecological adaptation of the system of society, but instead to see what contours the problem takes on when it is formulated with the help of this theory.

33

The Green Political Programme

Robert Goodin

Principles of 'ecological wisdom' are preeminent among the 'key values' contained in Green political programmes worldwide. Green politics, thus understood, is first and foremost a matter of finding answers to questions like: How can we operate human societies with the understanding that we are part of nature, not on top of it? How can we live within the ecological and resource limits of the planet . . .? . . . How can we further biocentric wisdom in all spheres of life?

The diagnosis of the central problem that we find contained in the German Greens' 1983 election manifesto would be common currency among Greens worldwide. There they say:

> The global ecological crisis is becoming daily more acute: raw materials are getting scarce, one poison scandal follows another, animal species are being exterminated, plant species becoming extinct. Rivers and oceans are turned into sewers, human beings are threatened with mental and spiritual atrophy in the midst of a late-industrial and consumer society, and we are burdening future generations with a deadly inheritance. The destruction of the very basis of life and work, and the demolition of democratic rights, have reached such a threatening scale as to make necessary a fundamental alternative in economics, politics and society.[1]

Even if only as a matter of purely self-interested prudence, humanity must learn nature's lessons, for 'human life . . . is enmeshed in the circuits of the ecosystem: we intervene in it by our actions and this reacts back on us. We must not destroy the stability of the ecosystem. . . . [U]nlimited growth is [simply] impossible in a limited system.'[2]

The general terms of the prescribed cure follow fairly straightforwardly from that diagnosis of the problem. 'Proceeding from the laws of nature . . . an ecological policy means understanding ourselves and our environment as part of nature. . . . Our policy is a policy of active partnership [between] nature and human beings. . . . The supreme commandment must be the smallest possible change in natural processes.'[3]

Somewhat more concretely, 'an ecological policy implies all-round rejection of an economy based on exploitation and the uncontrolled pillage of natural wealth and raw materials, as well as refraining from destructive intervention in the circuits of the natural ecosystem.' Greens say that 'we stand for an economic system oriented to the necessities of human life today and for future generations, to the preservation of nature and a careful management of natural resources'.[4]

More concretely still, there are certain things that Greens say that they simply 'will not accept'. Included among those intolerable outcomes are: 'the irresponsible treatment of soil, water and air like a disposable consumer good'; 'the ever increasing number of animal and plant species that are exterminated . . . due to the destruction of their habitats'; and 'the occurrence of climatic deterioration, soil erosion and . . . deforestation. . .'.[5]

The policy measures that Greens propose along these lines are fairly unsurprising. They include:

1 the immediate application of the principle that the causer of pollution must pay its costs;
2 the maintenance and extension of forests, especially for the biological cleaning of air, the safety of water supply and for recreation;
3 production processes which do not produce toxic refuse;
4 in principle, all 'waste' should be discharged in such a way that it is reusable as raw material;
5 the quantity of refuse should be reduced by replacing one-way packaging and short-lived consumer goods by standardized packaging and durable products.

In the area of air and water quality Greens recommend that 'production processes and products should . . . produce only a minimum of ecologically bearable effluents'. They envisage that being done through 'closed circuit water systems in industry' and through reducing airborne emissions from industry, power stations, public and private heating equipment and refuse incinerators and, most especially, motor vehicles. Greens insist that reduced limits on air and waterborne emissions should be strictly enforced, and charges should be levied on those that are still permitted. They say that certain emissions should be banned altogether on account of the environmental damage that they do; among these are phosphates in washing powder, phosphates in fertilizers, carcinogens of all sorts, and fluorohydrocarbons as propellants in aerosols. As the threat of ozone depletion has come to loom ever larger, the latter sort of proposal has come to occupy an increasingly central role in Green policy discussions – just as the increasing threat of climate change has moved proposals for a certain sort of pollution tax (the carbon tax) to the forefront of Green policy thinking.

Greens urge protection of the countryside and town planning based on open spaces, public transport and reduction of private automobile traffic. They inveigh against agricultural policies based on artificial fertilizers and pesticides, and they commend instead organic farming ('healthy foodstuffs can only be produced on healthy soil') and mixed farming. They commend a forestry policy based on 'mixed foliage, mainly with native types of wood' and 'individual selective felling' instead of complete deforestation of particular areas. While Greens are often prepared to tolerate the raising of farm animals for human consumption, they say that animals nonetheless have rights and they urge protection of animals from cruelty both on the farm and in research laboratories.

What especially worries Greens, though, is the survival of non-human species threatened with extinction. The burning question is not so much 'how can we ensure the rights of individual animals?' but, rather, 'how can we guarantee rights of non-human species' as a whole?[6] Towards that end, Greens commend a fishery policy based on the 'immediate reduction of catch quotas of endangered species to allow stocks to recover' and 'an immediate ban on catching and hunting of any species of whale' in particular.[7] Greens oppose the 'industrialization of agriculture', precisely because it is 'one of the main reasons for the disappearing of more and more plant species'.[8] And they urge measures to protect plant and animal species under threat of extinction, more generally.

There are many legitimate reasons why we might worry about the preservation of species. Some are purely pragmatic. Having a great deal of variety in nature (especially in the gene pool) is instrumental in various ways for various human purposes. Others are essentially aesthetic. We enjoy looking at more complex and variable scenes. Still others point to the intrinsic (non-anthropocentric) value of the species which are being destroyed.

It is admittedly anomalous that Greens should be so little concerned about the demise of any particular animal and so disproportionately more concerned about the demise of the species as a whole. What is it about a species as such that makes the whole so much more valuable than the sum of its parts? The Green response is, I think, best seen as being rooted in their respect for nature as such – combined with the fact that destroying a whole 'type' (a whole species) constitutes so much more of a violation of the natural order than does destroying a mere 'token' (a particular animal of that species).

It follows from much of what Greens say about environmental despoliation that they regard modern technology as very much a mixed blessing. They regard chemical fertilizers and pesticides as 'agricultural poisons'; and they are particularly wary of biotechnology and of 'genetically manipulated organisms', whose 'ecological risks are unknown'. They bemoan the way in which 'monotony, mental stress and lack of communication have all become worse due to the introduction of new technologies' into the workplace. They complain about the way in which the pharmaceutical industry 'constantly throw[s] new medicines onto the market, with negative side-effects which frequently outweigh their healing powers'. Greens save their very special anger, though, for one particular modern technology: nuclear-powered electricity generating plants. 'Nuclear power is', quite simply, 'not safe': 'the operation of nuclear plants leads to creeping contamination by radioactivity, the potential for catastrophe presents an irresponsible risk, and nuclear waste still cannot be got rid of.'[9]

It would be a mistake to infer from all that rhetoric that Greens are unqualified Luddites, though. Sensitive though they are to all the various ways in which modern technology has made life worse, they are also alive to the possibility that it might also make life better. In particular, they welcome the fact that, 'with the use of modern technologies, productivity has in many cases reached a level which would . . . make it possible to reduce the working week while maintaining full pay'.[10]

The issue, then, is not how to do away with modern technologies altogether but rather how to choose in a discriminating way between them. 'How can we judge whether new technologies are socially useful – and use those judgments to shape our society? . . . How can we develop new economic activities and institutions that will allow us to use our new technologies in ways that are humane, freeing, ecological, and accountable and responsive to communities?'[11]

[. . .]

Green technology policy calls for the use of 'appropriate technology' to use in guiding our communities more generally. 'Appropriate' here runs the risk of serving as an all-purpose term of approbation, devoid of any particular meaning. But it is best understood as referring, in this context, to the fit between the technology and the end-uses to which it will be put, the purposes for which it will be employed, the goals we are trying to achieve through its use. The best example, perhaps, comes once again in connection with discussions of energy policy. In the masterly study of 'soft energy paths' to which the 1983 German Green manifesto refers, Amory Lovins stresses that such schemes are more appropriate forms of technology because they are better matched (both in terms of scale and geographical distribution and in terms of energy quality) to 'end-use needs'.[12]

The latter is a particularly telling point. Electricity, in particular, is an especially 'high-quality' form of energy. There are certain purposes for which electricity, and electricity alone, will suffice. Among them are 'lighting, electronics, telecommunications, electrometallurgy, electrochemistry, arc welding, [and running] electric motors'. But those applications account for only about 8 per cent of all US energy use. Mostly, energy requirements – in the United States and elsewhere in the First World – are for home heating and cooking and driving mechanical motors, and for those purposes forms of energy of much lower quality would suffice. As Lovins puts it,

> Plainly we are using premium fuels and electricity for many tasks for which their high energy quality is superfluous, wasteful and expensive. . . . Where we want only to create temperature differences of tens of degrees, we should meet the need with sources whose potential is tens or hundreds of degrees, not with a flame temperature of thousands or a nuclear reaction temperature equivalent to trillions. . . .

That, in Lovins's telling phrase, is rather like 'cutting butter with a chainsaw'.[13]

That is just one particularly telling example, though. Notions of appropriate technology have application in organizing social production more generally. Taking a leaf from Gandhi, E. F. Schumacher insists that 'the poor of the world cannot be helped by mass production' but 'only by production by the masses'. Elaborating on that theme, he writes,

> The system of *mass production*, based on sophisticated, highly capital-intensive, high energy-input dependent, and human labour-saving technology, presupposes that you are already rich, for a great deal of capital investment is needed to establish one single workplace. . . . [It] is inherently violent, ecologically damaging, self-defeating in terms of non-renewable resources, and stultifying for the human person. The technology of *production by the masses* . . . is conducive to decentralization, compatible with the laws of ecology, gentle in its use of scarce resources, and designed to serve the human person instead of making him the servant of machines.

Schumacher suggests that this technology might, equally well, be called 'intermediate technology', on the grounds that it is 'vastly superior to the primitive technology of bygone ages but . . . much simpler, cheaper and freer than the super-technology of the rich'. It could also be called a 'self-help . . . democratic . . . people's technology', on the grounds that it 'is not reserved to those already rich and powerful'.[14]

That is the sort of technology that Greens would favour. Instead of tyrannizing over humanity and over nature, such technology harmonizes with them. It puts people more in control of their own lives. It permits people to live and work in more human-sized communities. It is more in tune with both human purposes and the natural order.

The Green environmental programme depends on a reorientation of the present economic system every bit as much as on a renunciation of high technology. As the German Greens put it in the preamble to their 1983 election manifesto, 'We do not accept that the present economy of waste promotes happiness or a fulfilling life. On the contrary.' It leads to 'a real impoverishment, in spite of increased incomes. . . . Only if we free ourselves from over-valuing the material standard of living . . . will our creative forces also be freed for reshaping life on an ecological basis.'[15]

'A radical reorganization of our short-sighted economic rationality is', Greens say, 'essential.'[16] They call for 'shifting economic priorities [away] from consumption [and] to conservation'. And part and parcel of that is shifting 'away from . . . self-defeating economic growth . . . and towards sustainable regional economies'.[17]

The central question for Greens is 'how can we make the quality of life, rather than open-ended economic growth, the focus of future thinking?'[18] Green economic policy 'thoroughly repudiates a way of thinking oriented to output and hierarchy and governed by lethal competition'.[19] It would involve an 'all-round rejection of an economy based on exploitation and the uncontrolled pillage of natural wealth and raw materials'. In its place, Greens would advocate 'an economic system oriented to the necessities of human life today and for future generations, to the preservation of nature and a careful management of natural resources'.[20]

Accordingly, Greens place heavy emphasis in their political programmes on their vision of a Green economy. In so doing, they are in many respects merely picking up on some by now fairly well-established critiques of economic theory. Economists themselves are the first to acknowledge the uncounted 'costs of economic growth', in the sense of 'external costs' that have not been properly captured in ordinary growth statistics. Making producers bear the full costs of their activities, through for example pollution taxes of the sort that Greens recommend, would be required if we are to maximize growth in *real* economic well-being, properly calculated. And at least some economists are sensitive to the need, keenly felt among Greens, for 'sustainable' development – for a steady-state economy reliably yielding a tolerable standard of living rather than a boom–bust economy whose highs (and even average yield) might be higher but whose lows are much lower as well.

Beyond picking up on those familiar points within established and semi-established economic theory, Greens also take on board some more radical critiques of neoclassical economics. Greens would have the economy produce what people really need rather than what, through advertising, they have been artificially made to desire; and, indeed, they would radically restrict the sort of advertising that would be allowed at all. Greens are sensitive to the ways in which 'instruments' shape rather than just serve our desires; they would take advantage of that fact, reshaping our desires in more modest directions. They would restrict counterproductive competition in 'status goods', which lose their value to you once everyone else has them as well. There are, furthermore, more radical possibilities – so far largely unexplored among Greens – within Georgescu-Roegen's reformulation of economic theory around the Second Law of Thermodynamics.[21] That, properly understood, might provide the strongest theoretical warrant yet for the Greens' natural inclination towards keeping our interventions into the natural order as modest as possible.

All of that operates on the plane of high theory, though. In more concrete terms, Green economic proposals essentially revolve around notions of localism. The goal is production for use, rather than production for profit. The aim is to produce for own consumption rather than for gains from trade. The Green economy 'would be based, above all, on the most elemental and most elegant principle of the natural world, that of self-sufficiency. Just as Nature does not depend on trade, so the bioregion would find all its needed resources – for energy, food, shelter, clothing, craft, manufacture, luxury – within its own environment.'[22]

Of course, much turns on what one supposes is 'needed'. The more narrowly needs are defined, the more possible it is to satisfy them all purely locally. But Greens advocating economic decentralization are anxious to insist that, while small communities 'cannot possibly supply all the gadgets and geegaws and gimcrackery that is to be found in our stores today', neither would life in such communities be at a bare subsistence standard either. 'Using current standards', it is observed, a community of one 'thousand people could operate one plant in each of the thirteen basic manufacturing categories.'[23]

So, arguably, 'a small town can without much difficulty provide for virtually *all* material needs on a household or community level – and make the goods more affordable, more durable, more aesthetic, more repairable, and more harmless, too.' It can do this, Greens would say, in various ways:

1 by sharing, . . .
2 by recycling and repairing, . . .
3 by depending on handicrafts rather than manufactures, . . .
4 by developing and using local products and raw materials instead of depending on imported ones, . . .
5 by local ingenuity, . . .
6 by using general instead of specialized machines, . . .
7 by . . . use of multipurpose factories, . . .
8 by adapting plants to the community level, . . .
9 by networking, where necessary, with other communities, . . . and
10 finally, and simplest, by doing without what is not needed.

[· · ·]

Greens are, at root, egalitarian. They are greatly exercised by the gross imbalances in the distribution of income and wealth, both within societies and across the world. They 'are committed to a radical sharing of wealth – between continents and between generations, not only between classes'.[24] This egalitarianism manifests itself, internationally, as a concern that peoples of the Third World should 'receive a fair price for their work and products'.[25] It manifests itself, in domestic economic policy, primarily as a concern to minimize unemployment through a variety of measures (ranging from job retraining to early retirement and shorter work weeks).

[· · ·]

Greens are egalitarian not only on distributional questions but on social issues more generally. They strive for a society in which 'the oppression of one person by another is abolished'. They oppose discrimination in all its forms – against women, the old, immigrants, Romanies and 'sexual outsiders'.[26] The 'solidarity' the Greens propose is, at one and the same time, 'with the earth, with the poor and with . . . future generations'.[27] They do so primarily on the grounds, often regarded as too obvious to be stated, that any such social divisions are 'unnatural'. Social discrimination is an artificial artefact of deformed human culture, and it is opposed by Greens for precisely that reason.

The policies which Greens propose to remedy discrimination against the presently disadvantaged may not seem particularly radical. They are familiar enough from the academic literature, it is true. Still, they are rare indeed on the statute books. In that sense, they would mark a genuinely radical change from present policies.

Putting the point in terms of non-discrimination might seem to suggest that Greens are simply advocating tolerance of deviant minorities. That would give a completely false impression of their programme. In truth, they positively embrace pluralism. They count 'respect for diversity' as one of their 'key values', and they cherish diversity in its social every bit as much as in its biological form. They bemoan the effects of the 'dominant monoculture' and want to encourage instead the flourishing of a multiplicity of cultures, both within a single region and especially across regions.

Greens suppose that discrimination and social oppression are largely responsible for the 'instabilities' of existing society. Merely eliminating it would, they say, do much to alleviate problems of 'crime, higher suicide rates, drug consumption and alcoholism'. But Greens would not stop at eliminating those evils. They would also strive, more positively, for a 'nonviolent' society. They want to find ways to 'resolve interpersonal and intergroup conflicts without just turning them over to lawyers and judges'. They seek to 'use nonviolent methods to oppose practices and policies with which we disagree and in the process reduce the atmosphere of polarization and selfishness that is itself a source of violence'.[28]

[. . .]

All this is no more than the briefest indication of how Greens see the main issues of our day. Still, even this brief sketch should be enough to show (or if not to show, anyway to suggest) several things.

1 One is that the Greens are no single-issue movement. They take stands on a wide range of contemporary social and political problems.
2 A second is that there is an interestingly different intellectual centre of gravity in the Green political programme, compared with that of the programmes of other more mainstream parties.
3 A third is that the Green agenda is organized around, and justified by, the distinctively 'Green theory of value'; and that the Green theory of value both underpins and bolsters the Green cause, politically.

Notes and References

1 Die Grünen, *Bundesprogramm* (1983), p. 7.
2 Ibid.
3 Ibid., p. 30.
4 Ibid., p. 7.
5 Ibid., p. 30.
6 Green Committees of Correspondence (CoC), *Ten Key Values* (Kansas City, Mo., 1986, item 1).
7 Die Grünen, *Bundesprogramm*, p. 20.
8 European Greens, *Common Statement of the European Greens for the 1989 Elections to the European Parliament* (European Greens, Brussels, 1989), sec. 7.
9 Die Grünen, *Bundesprogramm*, pp. 15–16.
10 Ibid., p. 12.
11 Green CoC, *Ten Key Values*, items 10 and 6.
12 A. Lovins, *Soft Energy Paths* (Penguin, Harmondsworth, 1977), p. 39.
13 Ibid., pp. 39–40.
14 E.F. Schumacher, *Small is Beautiful* (Blond and Briggs, London, 1973), pp. 153–4.
15 Die Grünen, *Bundesprogramm*, p. 7.
16 Ibid., p. 6.
17 European Greens, *Common Statement*, sec. 1.
18 Green CoC, *Ten Key Values*, item 10.
19 Die Grünen, *Bundesprogramm*, p. 7.
20 Ibid.
21 N. Georgescu-Roegen, *The Entropy law and the Economic Process* (Harvard University Press, Cambridge, Mass., 1971).
22 K. Sale, 'Bioregionalism', *The Ecologist*, 14 (1984), p. 169.
23 K. Sale, *Human Scale* (Coward, Cann and Geoghegan, New York, 1980), pp. 404, 398.
24 European Greens, *Common Statement*, sec. 1.
25 Die Grünen, *Bundesprogramm*, p. 24.
26 Ibid., pp. 33–49.
27 European Greens, *Common Statement*, sec. 12.
28 Green CoC, *Ten Key Values*, items 3 and 4.

34

The Naturalistic Fallacy of the Ecological Movement

Ulrich Beck

Whoever utters the word 'nature' deserves to be needled by the question, 'which nature?': Naturally fertilized cabbage? Nature as it is, i.e. industrially lacerated? Country life during the 1950s (as it is represented in retrospect today, or as it represented itself in days gone by to countryfolk, or to those who dreamed of country life, or whoever)? The solitude of the mountains before publication of the book, *Wandern in den einsamen Bergen* ('To wander in the lonely mountains')? Nature as conceived by natural science? Nature without chemicals? The polished ecological models of interconnectedness? Nature as depicted in gardening books? Such Nature as one yearns for (peace, a mountain stream, profound contemplation)? As it is praised and priced in the supermarkets of world solitude? Nature as a sight for sore eyes? The beauty of a Tuscan landscape – in other words, a highly cultivated art of nature? Or nature in the wild? The volcano before it erupts? The nature of early cultures, invested with demonic power, subjectivity, and the living gods of religion? The primeval forest? Nature conceived as a zoo without cages? As it roars and rages in the cigarette adverts of the city's cinemas?

Every human being is a part of nature too. Yet where does nature begin? When a babe is first suckled? Or as soon as a woman goes off the pill? In intercourse (where and how)? Of the homosexual or heterosexual variety? Polygamously, perhaps, in selective diversity? Or in extramarital fidelity to permanent change?

Of course, the physique of the Central European adult on two legs is no longer that of nature pure and simple: beer, the 40-hour-per-week desk job, norms of dress and of undress, the clothing industries, job security in the cosmetics industry, and the idea that a human being must create himself in the image of others' expectations, have left a few historical traces. Chest hairs, sometimes, though only in the male, recall a natural past and awaken dreams of natural possibilities which – in view of the bloatedness of the formerly natural human body, or the high muscular definition available to citizens in the nautilus gyms of the economic wonderland – make the cry of 'back to nature' thoroughly understandable.

The 'natural blend' with which we have to deal today, a remoulded nature devoid of nature, is the socially internalized furniture of the civilized world: work, production, government, and science at once reconstruct it and furnish it with the norms by whose yardsticks it is adjudged to be endangered and damaged. The process of interaction with nature has consumed, abolished, and transformed it into a civilizing meta-reality which can no longer rid itself of the attributes of human (co-)creation. In this age of battery farms, plant, animal, and human genetics, parks, development programmes, and the 're-naturalization' of towns, one is dealing with variants of an artificial nature: projections of nature, wish-fulfilment natures, nature utopias, all roughly as natural as a big-screen advertisement replete with roaring, turbulent rivers in the bustle of Tokyo city.

This irreversible artificiality of nature is additionally, albeit involuntarily, confirmed precisely by its conservation through ecological intervention: thus centrally administered museums of real nature appear, constructed according to ecological principles – 'arks of civilization' for dying natural species. In the mixed forest of administered nature that emerges here, dying species of songbirds and plants are offered an appropriate breeding ground for their civilization.

Another index of nature's transformation into society is the degree to which disasters, natural disasters of the 'classical type' – landslides, floods, dying forests and so forth – are now interpreted and treated as disasters to which policy is answerable. That provides a measure not only of the social integration of nature, but also of social perception of this basic fact.

To put it paradoxically, the social 'consumption' of nature renders philosophically invalid all those concepts and theories that conceive of nature as the counter-image of human activity and power, to which it must be subjugated. At the same time, there is a vindication and revival of those which do not model nature as a world of dead objects (with God as the 'supreme mathematician'), but comprehend nature as living, intelligent, and active, such as Schelling's philosophy of nature.

Thus even nature is not nature, but rather a concept, norm, memory, utopia, counter-image. Today more than ever, now that it no longer exists, nature is being rediscovered, mollycoddled. The ecology movement has fallen prey to a fallacious, naturalistic conception of itself. It reacts to a global fusion, rife with contradictions, of nature and society; this fusion has sublated the two concepts into a blend of reciprocal interconnections and injuries of which we have as yet not the faintest idea, let alone a concept. The high esteem which attaches to it corresponds to the devastation, to the loss, and draws from memory a nature that is anything but natural. This does not merely tie in with epistemological questions: opportunities for political action, arising from the despoliation of 'nature' as a domestic social phenomenon, are lost.

The very word 'nature' still seems to have a green flavour. The concept of nature is a self-negating human invention: with his internalized conception of nature, man abolishes, rescinds his own role of creator, discoverer, ruler, destroyer – more still, man cultivates it in opposition to his role of creator and destroyer, upholding it as the extreme of non-alienation, of non-civilization. Recourse to the concept of nature gives the appearance of an outer limit, prescribed from within, to humanity's perceived subjection to increasing hazards and self-destructiveness. The concept of nature does not betray the model its utterer associates with it – neither to himself/herself, nor to the addressee – in any event, not at first glance. It is, as it were, language that appears to retract its utterance, a concept that apparently 'leaps into the eye' of the beholder, veritably 'growing out at him (or her)'. Its significance is that the concept of nature enables the speaker, by recourse to the outer world, to bring forth that which is inwardly, profoundly oppressive. The concept of nature achieves a kind of self-expropriation in which, as it were, the image becomes independent of the subject that it mirrors, and – in reflecting – provides the mirage of a reality for itself, apparently uninvolved in all the mirroring; a given, by whose means the mirrored subject can orient himself or herself. The effect is internal, as are the model and the conditions for triggering it off. But the operation proceeds via an outer world that pretends to an utterly tautologous self-identity.

'Nature' is a kind of anchor by whose means the ship of civilization, sailing over the open seas, conjures up, cultivates, its contrary: dry land, the harbour, the approaching reef. In the process it negotiates the conditions under which it may continue to voyage, to drift.

Upon close inspection, all who talk of 'nature' in the sense the word pretends to, namely that which is untouched, free of human creation and destruction, have always refuted themselves. To speak thus presupposes amnesia – of the fact that talk of nature conjures up the whole split, the history of nature's subjugation, cultivation, and destruction, the history of concepts of nature – and it also begs the question of the sense in which the word 'nature' is used, when the subject under discussion is the shaping of life in society and the provision of social norms. The concept of nature dissimulates naivety, allowing its utterer to lay claim to a naivety of the given, of the prior given, immutable and good, which becomes the more significant and enticing as doubt is cast on all unquestioned assumptions. 'Nature' seems capable, if not of hacking apart the Gordian knot of civilization in which one feels bound up, entangled, then at least of helping one loosen and shake it off. It is, as it were, the bolt-hole of antimodernism, keeping open to its dissidents (those weary of modernism and convinced antimodernists alike) the option of modernism as a variant of itself.

The theme first secreted into the concept of an external 'nature', which, however, breaks forth ever more openly and directly, is that of self-delimitation: the self-guidance and self-determination of a modernity that has always yielded its claims of shaping reality to the flat necessity of a manufactured determinism of progress.

There are manifold reminders of the fact that the meanings of 'nature' do not grow on trees, but must be constructed. . . . All scientific representations of nature as governed by laws are also projections. They may be true or false, but they are not of a nature that has, as it were, recovered itself in human consciousness. Nature does not speak to us even in experiments; rather, scientific questions are (more or less) answered. If the experiment says 'no' – thus apparently expressing nature's veto – then the interpretations and consequences of this 'reply' still remain to be decided entirely by the researcher.

Even ecology, this spokesperson for nature conceived as a network, is a variant of natural science, not nature's own articulation of itself. Moreover, it is a variant which was sickly for a long while (ever since Ernst Haeckel coined the term in 1868), and is now attempting to compensate for its century-long slumber by a kind of surprise attack which bears all the hallmarks of a cybernetic hyperscientism. To put it another way, ecology is on the verge of placing itself at the greatest possible distance from that 'naturalness' to which it sometimes appears disposed to give expression. Yet the attractiveness of ecology surely derives from awareness of the repercussions of economically programmed, highly specialized, professional natural science and technology. Not least by averting their gaze from the connections that they destroy, these disciplines have become the motor of self-jeopardization of the 'nature–society relationship' that is our concern. But the allure of ecology thereby answers precisely to a modern experience, which seeks for its articulation counter-images developed and jettisoned in the historic process

– i.e. ecology. All the same, this is a variant of human conceptions of nature which, because it thinks in relational concepts and norms, sensitizes one to the devastation to which the natural science intoxication with technology blinds one.

Ecology is guilty of forgetting about society, just as social science and social theory are predicated on the forgetting of ecology. The terrain has been staked out by the concepts both of system and of environment. The proponents of each disdain the other, without noticing that it is public awareness that preselects ecological questions via a historical blend of society and nature, in which so-called 'ecological hazards' are always systemic hazards.

PART VI
Modernity and Postmodernity

ZYGMUNT BAUMAN (READING 35) accepts that we are living in a post-modern order and endeavours to chart some of the implications of this fact. The 'end of historical metanarratives' might seem to produce a situation of universal permissiveness, in which 'anything goes'. If, as Habermas might say, there are no justifying criteria of reason, what is to prevent the world from relapsing into pure chaos? The decline of universalizing criteria, however, Bauman argues, is not inherently crippling. Postmodernity means coming to terms with ambivalence, with the ambiguity of meanings and with the indeterminacy of the future; yet acceptance of ambivalence can be life-enhancing, especially when contrasted to the driven world of certitudes that modernity used to foster.

A celebration of difference and contingency, for Bauman, is not at all the same thing as abandoning systematic social reflection or moral standards. Postmodernism promotes tolerance and diversity, although it demands in return a life lived without guarantees. Postmodern tolerance may degenerate into selfishness on the part of those who are affluent, compared with those who are poor, both within nations and across the world. For tolerance of difference can also become, precisely, indifference: injustice is simply accepted as part of a natural order of things, much as it was in the pre-modern world. Yet in Bauman's view the news is certainly not all bad. For the universalizing tendencies of modernity have in the past often promoted totalitarian power.

As described by Bauman, and also by Jean Baudrillard (Reading 36), the postmodern order is one that privileges consumption rather than production. The consumer society is one of rapidly changing fashion, the constant creation and obsolescence of goods, and a society 'without history'. The objects with which consumers are surrounded are not grounded in historical tradition and have no particular relation to the past. 'Profusion', as Baudrillard puts it, is the most characteristic feature of the consumer society. Shops crammed with goods, usually drawn from all parts of the world, offer themselves to the buyer. The consumer is 'surrounded by objects' rather than by persons; the accumulation of wealth has as its object the expansion of purchasing power. Objects gain their desirability from their position in the mosaic of other commodities. Action in the consumer society, according to Baudrillard, has become more or less completely separate from external contexts: it is internally self-sufficient. Thus a multipurpose drug store, or a shopping mall, contains a complete kaleidoscope of possible purchases.

Like Baudrillard, Gianni Vattimo (Reading 37) also sees the mass media as pivotal to the contemporary social order. For him, as for Bauman, the term 'postmodern' has a definite meaning: it refers to a society of 'generalized communication', carried through the electronic media. Modernity, according to Vattimo, was ideological in a very important sense. For the characteristic views associated with modernity, including especially the idea of historical progress, helped justify the domination of the West over the rest of the world. Like Bauman, Vattimo sees the advent of postmodernity in a positive vein. The mass media today introduce us to a dizzying variety of images, cultures and voices. They produce a sort of 'chaos', as everything becomes visible or 'transparent'; yet this chaos is itself a potential means of enlightenment. In this newly emerging order we can still sustain the ideal of emancipation. Emancipation today, however, does not consist in having a knowledge of reality and conforming to it. Rather, we make our own 'realities' in the plural worlds which we invent.

Alex Callinicos (Reading 38) has emerged as one of the most forceful critics of all versions of postmodernity or postmodernism. For him, in contra-distinction to Vattimo, these concepts are incoherent. All of the features of art and literature supposed to be characteristic of postmodernism were already to be found in the 'modernism' of the earlier part of the century. Postmodernity signals a series of changes in the nature of modern capitalism, but is certainly not a distinct type of social condition.

Surveying the various interpretations of the postmodern offered by different authors, Callinicos finds them mutually contradictory. The terms postmodernism and postmodernity are substitutes for proper analysis rather than a helpful guide to it.

The controversies about modernity, postmodernism and postmodernity might seem to be largely intellectual froth. In the final section of the book (Reading 39) Bauman shows that such is far from the case. The Holocaust – the destruction of millions of Jews in Nazi Germany during the Second World War – was not just an aberration of German history. It actually exemplified certain distinctive traits of modernity. For Bauman the Holocaust stands at a point of connection, yet also disjunction, between modernity and postmodernity. The Holocaust was made possible by distinctively modern social conditions, including the development of centralized administrative power, control of communications and the consolidation of military power. In this sense the Holocaust expressed intrinsic possibilities of modernity. Yet at the same time we see clearly that modern social development by no means inevitably tends towards 'progress'. The totalitarian potential of modernity can best be avoided precisely by promoting the more pluralistic and decentred framework of the postmodern.

35

Modernity and Ambivalence

Zygmunt Bauman

The collapse of 'grand narratives' (as Lyotard put it) – the dissipation of trust in supra-individual and supra-communal courts of appeal – has been eyed by many observers with fear, as an invitation to the 'everything goes' situation, to universal permissiveness and hence, in the end, to the demise of all moral, and thus social, order. Mindful of Dostoyevsky's dictum 'If there is no God, everything is permitted', and of Durkheim's identification of asocial behaviour with the weakening of collective consensus, we have grown to believe that unless an awesome and incontestable authority – sacred or secular, political or philosophical – hangs over each and every human individual, then anarchy and universal carnage are likely to follow. This belief supported well the modern determination to install an artificial order: a project that made all spontaneity suspect until proven innocent, that proscribed everything not explicitly prescribed and identified ambivalence with chaos, with 'the end of civilization' as we know it and as it could be imagined. Perhaps the fear emanated from the suppressed knowledge that the project was doomed from the start; perhaps it was cultivated deliberately, since it served a useful role as an emotional bulwark against dissension; perhaps it was just a side-effect, an intellectual afterthought born of the socio-political practice of cultural crusade and enforced assimilation. One way or the other, modernity bent on the bulldozing of all unauthorized difference and all wayward life patterns could not but gestate the horror of deviation and render deviation synonymous with diversity. As Adorno and Horkheimer commented, the lasting intellectual and emotional scar left by the philosophical project and political practice of modernity was the fear of the void; and the void was the absence of a universally binding, unambiguous and enforceable standard.

Of the popular fear of the void, of the anxiety born of the absence of clear instruction that leaves nothing to the harrowing necessity of choice, we know from the worried accounts narrated by intellectuals, the appointed or self-appointed interpreters of social experience. The narrators are never absent from their narration, though, and it is a hopeless task to try to sift out their presence from their stories. It may well be that at all times there was life outside philosophy, and that such life did not share the worries of the narrators; that it did quite well without being regimented by rationally proved and philosophically approved universal standards of truth, goodness and beauty. It may well be even that much of that life was liveable, orderly and moral *because* it was *not* tinkered with, manipulated and corrupted by the self-acclaimed agents of the 'universal ought'. There is hardly any doubt, however, that one form of life can fare but badly without the prop of universally binding and apodictically valid standards: the form of life of the narrators themselves (more precisely, such form of life as contains the stories those narrators were telling through most of modern history).

It was that form of life first and foremost that lost its foundation once social powers abandoned their ecumenical ambitions, and felt therefore more than anyone else threatened by the fading out of universalistic expectations. As long as modern powers clung resolutely to their intention of constructing a better, reason-guided, and thus ultimately universal order, intellectuals had little difficulty in articulating their own claim to the crucial role in the process: universality was their domain and their field of expertise. As long as the modern powers insisted on the elimination of ambivalence as the measure of social improvement, intellectuals could consider their own work – the promotion of universally valid rationality – as a major vehicle and driving force of progress. As long as the modern powers continued to decry and banish and evict the Other, the different, the ambivalent – intellectuals could rely on mighty support for their authority of passing judgement and sorting out truth from falsity, knowledge from mere opinion. Like the adolescent hero of Cocteau's *Orphée*, convinced that the sun would not rise without his guitar and serenade, the intellectuals grew convinced that the fate of morality, civilized life and social order hangs on their solution of the problem of universality: on their clinching and final proof that the human 'ought' is unambiguous, and that its non-ambiguity has unshakeable and totally reliable foundations.

This conviction translated into two complementary beliefs: that there will be no good in the world *unless* its necessity has been proven; and that proving such a necessity, if and when accomplished, will have a similar effect on the world as that imputed to the legislative acts of a ruler: it will replace chaos with order and make the opaque transparent.

Husserl was perhaps the last great philosopher of the modern era spurred into action by those twin beliefs. Appalled by the idea that whatever we see as truth may be founded but in beliefs, that our knowledge has merely a psychological grounding, that we might have adopted logic as a secure guide to correct thinking simply because this is how people happen on the whole to think, Husserl (like Descartes, Kant and other recognized giants of modern thought before him) made a gigantic effort to cut reason free from its worldly habitat (or was it prison?): to return it to where it belonged – a *transcendental*, out-worldly region, towering above the daily human bustle at a height at which it cannot be reached – neither glimpsed nor tarnished – from the lowly world of common daily experience. The latter could not be the domicile of reason, as it was precisely the world of the common and the ordinary and the spontaneous that was to be remade and reformed and transformed by the verdicts of reason. Only the few, capable of the formidable effort of transcendental reduction (an experience not unlike the shaman's trances, or forty days of desert meditation), can travel to those esoteric places where truth comes into view. For the time of their journey, they must forget – suspend and bracket out – the 'mere existing', so that they may become one with the transcendental subject – that thinking subject that thinks the truth because it does not think anything else, because it is free from its worldly interests and the common errors of the worldly way.

The world which Husserl left behind while embarking on his solitary expedition to the sources of certainty and truth took little note. This was a world of evil on the loose, of concentration camps and of growing stockpiles of bombs and poison gas. The most spectacular and lasting effect of absolute truth's last stand was not so much its *inconclusiveness*, stemming as some would say from the errors of design, but its utter *irrelevance* to the worldly fate of truth and goodness. The latter fate was decided far away from philosophers' desks, down in the world of daily life where struggles for political freedom raged and the limits of the state ambition to legislate social order, to define, to segregate, to organize, to constrain and to suppress were pushed forward and rolled backwards.

It seems that the more advanced is the cause of freedom at home the less demand there is for the services of explorers of distant lands where absolute truth is reputed to reside. When one's own truth seems secure and the truth of the other does not seem to be a challenge or a threat, truth can live well without sycophants assuring it of being 'the truest of them all' and the warlords determined to make sure that no one disagrees. Once the difference ceases to be a crime, it may be enjoyed at peace, and enjoyed for what it is, rather than for what it represents or what it is destined to become. Once the politicians abandon their search for empires, there is little demand for the philosophers' search for universality. Empires of unconfined and unchallenged sovereignty, and the truth of unlimited and uncontested universality were the two arms with which modernity wished to remould the world according to the design of perfect order. Once the intention is no more, both arms find themselves without use.

In all probability the diversity of truths, standards of goodness and beauty does not grow once the intention is gone; neither does it become more resilient and stubborn than before; it only looks less alarming. It was, after all, the modern intention that made difference into an offence: *the* offence, the most mortal and least forgivable sin, to be precise. The pre-modern eye viewed difference with equanimity; as if it was in the pre-ordained order of things that they are and should remain different. Being unemotional, difference was also safely out of the cognitive focus. After a few centuries during which human diversity lived in hiding (a concealment enforced by the threat of exile) and it learned to be embarrassed about its stigma of iniquity, the postmodern eye (that is, the modern eye liberated from modern fears and inhibitions) views difference with zest and glee: difference is beautiful and no less good for that.

The appearance of sequence is, to be sure, itself an effect of the modern knack for neat divisions, clean breaks and pure substances. The postmodern celebration of difference and contingency has not displaced the modern lust for uniformity and certainty. Moreover, it is unlikely ever to do it; it has no capacity of doing so. Being what it is, postmodern mentality and practice cannot displace or eliminate or even marginalize anything. As it is always the case with the notoriously ambivalent (multi-final: opening more than one option, pointing to more than one line of future change) human condition, the gains of postmodernity are simultaneously its losses; what gives it its strength and attraction is also the source of its weakness and vulnerability.

There is no clean break or unambiguous sequence. Postmodernity is weak on exclusion. Having declared limits off limits, it cannot but include and incorporate modernity into the very diversity that is its distinctive mark. It cannot refuse admission lest it should lose its identity. (Paradoxically, refusal would be equivalent to the ceding of the whole real estate to the rejected applicant.) It cannot but admit the rights of a legitimate resident even to such a lodger as denies its right to admit residents and the right of other residents to share its accommodation. Modern mentality is a born litigant and an old hand in lawsuits.

Postmodernity cannot defend its case in court, as there is no court whose authority it would recognize. It might be forced instead to follow the Christian injunction of offering another cheek to the assailant's blows. It certainly is doomed to a long and hard life of cohabitation with its sworn enemy as a room-mate.

To the modern determination to seek or enforce consensus, postmodern mentality may only respond with its habitual tolerance of dissent. This makes the antagonists' chances unequal, with the odds heavily on the side of the resolute and strong-willed. Tolerance is too wan a defence against wilfulness and lack of scruples. By itself, tolerance remains a sitting target – an easy prey for the unscrupulous. It can repulse assaults only when reforged into solidarity: into the universal recognition that difference is one universality that is not open to negotiation and that attack against the universal right to be different is the only departure from universality that none of the solidarity agents, however different, may tolerate otherwise than at its own, and all the other agents', peril.

And so the transformation of the *fate* into a *destiny*, of tolerance into solidarity, is not just a matter of moral perfection, but a condition of survival. Tolerance as 'mere tolerance' is moribund; it can survive only in the form of solidarity. It just would not do to rest satisfied that the other's difference does not confine or harm my own – as some differences, of some others, are most evidently bent on constraining and damaging. Survival in the world of contingency and diversity is possible only if each difference recognizes another difference as the necessary condition of the preservation of its own. Solidarity, unlike tolerance, its weaker version, means readiness to fight; and joining the battle for the sake of the other's difference, not one's own. Tolerance is ego-centred and contemplative; solidarity is socially oriented and militant.

Like all other human conditions, postmodern tolerance and diversity has its dangers and its fears. Its survival is not guaranteed – not by God's design, universal reason, laws of history, or any other suprahuman force. In this respect, of course, the postmodern condition does not differ at all from all other conditions; it differs only by knowing about it, by its knowledge of living without guarantee, of being on its own. This makes it exceedingly anxiety-prone. And this also gives it a chance.

Postmodernity is a chance of modernity. Tolerance is a chance of postmodernity. Solidarity is the chance of tolerance. Solidarity is a third-degree chance. This does not sound reassuring for one wishing solidarity well. Solidarity cannot draw its confidence from anything remotely as solid and thereby as comforting as social structures, laws of history or the destination of nations and races from which modern projects derived their optimism, self-confidence and determination.

The bridge leading from the postmodern condition to solidarity is not built of necessities. It is not even certain whether there is such a bridge at all. Emancipated from modern hubris, the postmodern mind has less need for cruelty and humiliating the Other; it can afford Richard Rorty's 'kindness'. But kindness may be, and often is, superior, lofty and detached – frequently it feels more like a snub than sympathy. On its own, kindness would not beget solidarity – much as solidarity is not the only possible outcome (not even the most probable outcome) of the collapse of the modern romance with 'designer society'.

More than from anything else, modern designs of global perfection drew their animus from the horror of difference and impatience with otherness. And yet they also offered a chance for genuine concern with the plight of the wretched and miserable (it was this chance that attracted to the modern promise the spokesmen for the underdog). The modern conviction that society need not be as it happens to be, that it might be made better than it was, made each case of individual and group unhappiness into a challenge and a task. As long as the decent life of everybody was, by common consent, a feasible proposition, the administrators of social order felt the need to apologize for their sloth or ineptitude in bringing about a decent life for everybody.

It is not that the likes of Mayhew or Booth or Riis are not with us any more; there are in all probability more of them now than at any other time. The real difference is between the explosive effect that the revelation of human misery once had – and the equanimity with which it is received today. Today the news of human poverty and distress comes as more colourful accounts among the many images of the many ways people choose or are fated (by their history, by their religion, by their culture) to live. For a mentality trained to treat society as an unfinished project for the managers to complete, poverty was an abomination; its life expectation depended solely on the managerial resolve. For mentality repelled by global visions and wary of all prospects of societal engineering, that poverty is but an element in the infinite variety of existence. Once more, as in pre-modern times convinced of the inscrutable and timeless wisdom of divine order, one can live with daily sights of hunger, homelessness, life without future and dignity; live happily, enjoy the day and sleep quietly at night.

At the height of the modern dream of the perfect society round the corner and of the determination to turn that corner as soon as resources allowed, a tacit agreement had been reached between the managers and the managed as to the priorities to be observed on the way to global happiness. Last time, says J. K. Galbraith, such an agreement – a kind of unwritten 'social contract' (we would rather speak of a promise taken up and trusted) – came into being in Britain under Lloyd George and was agreed in the United States under Roosevelt. But, Galbraith says, 'In the 1980s this understanding was, at a minimum, put in abeyance.' That those who cannot avail themselves of the glittering prizes of rampant consumerism deserve our care and have the right to compensation is no more a matter of silent consent.

> Our poor in the US have remained poor, and the number so classified has substantially increased, as has, more markedly, the share of income going to the very rich. The conditions of life in the centres of our large cities is – the word is carefully chosen – appalling. Housing is bad and getting worse. Many of our citizens are without even the barest element of shelter, their income at near starvation levels. Schools are also bad, and young and old, sustained often by crime, contrive a temporary escape from despair with drugs.[1]

That things are bad is not news; for a great many people things used to be bad at the best of times. What is truly new is that things that are bad for some people are seldom a worry for those for whom things are good. The latter have accepted and declared that little they can do may improve the lot of the others. And they even managed to convince themselves that, since social engineering has been proved rotten at the core, whatever they decide to do may only make things worse still. The promise has not just been broken. It has been withdrawn.

Kindness may be an opposite of cruelty. Both are, however, sentiments of the interested and the involved; attitudes of *concerned* people – of people who not only look but see, and who worry about what they have seen. Alternatives of kindness and cruelty both serve the engagement with the Other; they remain on this side of the mutual bond. Outside such an engagement, as the '*otherwise than engagement*', the otherwise than both kindness and cruelty, stands the attitude of *indifference-fed callousness*: a sort of tolerance which to its objects looks more like a life sentence than a hope of freedom.

It is only too easy for postmodern tolerance to degenerate into the selfishness of the rich and resourceful. Such selfishness is indeed its most immediate and daily manifestation. There seems to be a direct relation between exuberant and expanding freedom of the 'competent consumer' and the remorseless shrinking of the world inhabited by the disqualified one. The postmodern condition has split society into the happy seduced and unhappy oppressed halves – with postmodern mentality celebrated by the first half of the division while adding to the misery of the second. The first half may abandon itself to the carefree celebration only because it has satisfied itself that the misery of the second half is their rightful *choice*, or at least a legitimate part of the world's exhilarating diversity. For the first half, misery is the 'form of life' the second half has selected – if only through carrying on a happy-go-lucky style of existence and neglecting the duty of selection.

There is no shortage of postmodern formulae meant to make the conscience of the seduced spotless. Disciples of the Hayeks and Friedmans are around in growing numbers, ready to prove that the rich must be given ever greater prizes so that they may wish to be rich, while for the poor rich rewards are only an encouragement to wallow in poverty; and that enriching themselves ('creating material wealth') is the only service the rich may render to the poor (that is, if service is to be rendered). There are economists, political scientists, sociologists and of course politicians to reassure the rich that the poverty of the poor is their – the poor's – problem, while the resistance of the poor against poverty is the problem for the organs of law and order. There are 'photo opportunities' obligingly provided by the police to inform the public about the bottomless depravity and iniquity of the drug-infested poor. (One cannot help recalling Goebbels's cameramen avidly recording the filthy ugliness of lice-infested ghetto Jews.) With bated breath, residents of the theft-proof, fortified homes glue themselves to their TV screens for the spectacle of brutality that is the mark of the brutalized. And there are also boffins and moral preachers to remind the shocked voyeurs that there is a 'problem' of how to prevent single mothers from breeding football hooligans, and that scientific studies once conducted by the expert racial hygienists may perhaps – who knows? – tell us something about its rational solution.

A long and tortuous way led historically from cruelty to kindness, but there is just a small step to be taken on the return trip. The postmodern world of joyful messiness is carefully guarded at the borders by mercenaries no less cruel than those hired by the managers of the now abandoned global order. Smiling banks beam only at their present and prospective customers. The playgrounds of happy shoppers are surrounded by thick walls, electronic spies and sharp-toothed guard-dogs. Polite tolerance applies only to those allowed inside. And thus drawing the line between the inside and the outside seems to have lost nothing of its violence and genocidal potency. If anything, the potency has grown, as no missionary, proselytizing prospects salvage the outsiders from total and final condemnation. Indeed, it is not clear any more why the useless and troublesome outsiders, whose bodies no one needs and whose souls no one wants to win or convert (as they are no longer the 'reserve army of labour', nor the prospective objects of exploitation or cannon-fodder), should not be removed by force ('repatriated') if there is a place to which they can be removed, or barred from propagating if the graveyard is the only place to which they can be moved.

In *Modernity and the Holocaust* I suggested that the unprecedented condensation of cruelty which marked the twentieth-century genocides could be the result of the application of modern management and technology to the unresolved pre-modern tensions and conflicts. A similar dialectic encounter is not to be ruled out lightly under emerging postmodern circumstances. The unfinished business of modern social engineering may well erupt in a new outburst of savage misanthropy, assisted rather than impeded by the newly legalized postmodern self-centredness and indifference. The protective wall of playful unconcern that the postmodern style offers was precisely what the perpetrators of modern mass cruelties missed, and what they had to replace with custom-made artifices by stretching their cunning and ingenuity to the utmost. Since then unconcern has made tremendous advances – the other people's misery having been dissolved in the incessant flow of mildly worrying and mildly amusing (amusing *because* mildly worrying) spectacles, and become indistinguishable from other Baudrillardian simulacra; while the mental technique through which life is cut into a series of cases each to be dealt with separately 'as it deserves' radically removed 'the need of the other' (not to mention such abstract and by now largely discredited notions as 'the responsibility for the other') from relevant 'factors of the case'. For most pursuers of a better world, the vision of a universal paradise has been reduced to the attempts to dump the vexing aspects of life (a silo for toxic waste, an air-polluting plant, a noxious bypass or a noisy airport) in other people's backyards.

Thorough, adamant and uncompromising *privatization* of all concerns has been the main factor that has rendered postmodern society so spectacularly immune to systemic critique and radical social dissent with revolutionary potential. It is not necessarily the case that the denizens of postmodern– privatized and commodified – society enjoy the sum total of greater happiness (one would still wish to know how to measure happiness objectively and compare it), and that they experience their worries as less serious and painful; what does truly matter is that it would not occur to them to lay the blame for such troubles they may suffer at the door of the state, and even less to expect the remedies to be handed over through that door. Postmodern society proved to be a well-nigh perfect translating machine – one that interprets any extant and prospective *social* issue as *private* concern (as if in a direct defiance of C. Wright Mills's very modern, very pre-postmodern description of, simultaneously, good democracy and good social science). It is not the 'ownership of the means of production' that has been privatized (its 'private' character, to be sure, is ever more in doubt at the age of the mergers and the multinationals). The most seminal of privatizations was that of human problems and of the responsibility for their resolution. The politics that reduced its acknowledged responsibilities to the matters of public safety and otherwise declared its retreat from the tasks of social management, effectively desocialized the ills of society and translated social injustice as individual ineptitude or neglect. Such politics is insufficiently attractive to awaken the *citizen* in a *consumer*; its stakes are not impressive enough to make it an object of the kind of anger that would be amenable to collectivization. In the postmodern society of consumers, failure rebounds in guilt and *shame*, not in political *protest*. Frustration breeds embarrassment, not dissent. Perhaps it triggers off all the familiar behavioural symptoms of Nietzsche–Scheler's *ressentiment*, but politically it disarms and gestates apathy.

The systemic consequence of the privatization of ambivalence is a dependence that does not need either coercion-supported dictatorship or ideological indoctrination; a dependence that is sustained, reproduced and reinforced by mostly DIY methods, that is embraced willingly and is not felt as dependence at all – one may even say: that is experienced as freedom and a triumph of individual autonomy. The coveted freedom of the consumer is, after all, the right to choose 'of one's own will' life purpose and life methodology that the supra-individual market mechanics has already defined and determined for the consumer. Consumer freedom means orientation of life towards market-approved commodities and thereby precludes one crucial freedom: freedom from the market, freedom that means anything else but the choice between standard commercial products. Above all, consumer freedom successfully deflects aspirations of human liberty from communal affairs and the management of collective life.

All possible dissent is therefore depoliticized beforehand; it is dissolved into yet more personal anxieties and concerns and thus deflected from the centres of societal power to private suppliers of consumer goods. The gap between desirable and achieved states of happiness results in the increased fascination with the allurements of the market and the appropriation of commodities; the wheels of the self-perpetuating mechanism of the consumer-oriented economy are thereby lubricated, while political and social structures emerge unscathed and intact. With the definitions and particularly the avenues and mechanisms of social mobility privatized, all potentially explosive troubles like frustrated personal ambitions, humiliating refusals of the public confirmation of self-definitions, clogged channels of advancement, even eviction from the sphere in which job-ascribed, publicly recognized meanings and identities are distributed, lead at best to a still more feverish search for market-supplied prescriptions, skills and tools of self- or image-improvement, or finish up in the disconsolate resignation of the welfare recipient – that socially confirmed paragon of personal incompetence and impotence. In neither case are the outcomes invested with political meanings. Privatized ambitions predefine frustration as an equally private matter, singularly unfit to be reforged into a collective grievance.

There is no solidarity without the tolerance for the otherness of the other. But tolerance is not solidarity's sufficient condition. Nor is solidarity tolerance's predetermined consequence. True, one cannot conceive of cruelty perpetrated *in the name* of tolerance; but there is a lot of cruelty that tolerance, through the lofty unconcern it feeds, makes *easier to commit.* Postmodernity is a site of opportunity and a site of danger; and it is both for the same set of reasons.

Reference

1 John Kenneth Galbraith, 'Assault on ideology in the last decade hit not only East but also West', *The Guardian*, 16–17 December 1989, p. 17.

36

The Consumer Society

Jean Baudrillard

Today, we are everywhere surrounded by the remarkable conspicuousness of consumption and affluence, established by the multiplication of objects, services, and material goods. This now constitutes a fundamental mutation in the ecology of the human species. Strictly speaking, men of wealth are no longer surrounded by other human beings, as they have been in the past, but by *objects*. Their daily exchange is no longer with their fellows, but rather, statistically as a function of some ascending curve, with the acquisition and manipulation of goods and messages: from the rather complex domestic organization with its dozens of technical slaves to the "urban estate" with all the material machinery of communication and professional activity, and the permanent festive celebration of objects in advertising with the hundreds of daily mass media messages; from the proliferation of somewhat obsessional objects to the symbolic psychodrama which fuels the nocturnal objects that come to haunt us even in our dreams. The concepts of "environment" and "ambiance" have undoubtedly become fashionable only since we have come to live in less proximity to other human beings, in their presence and discourse, and more under the silent gaze of deceptive and obedient objects which continuously repeat the same discourse, that of our stupefied (*medusée*) power, of our potential affluence and of our absence from one another.

As the wolf-child becomes wolf by living among them, so are we becoming functional. We are living the period of the objects: that is, we live by their rhythm, according to their incessant cycles. Today, it is we who are observing their birth, fulfillment, and death; whereas in all previous civilizations, it was the object, instrument, and perennial monument that survived the generations of men.

While objects are neither flora nor fauna, they give the impression of being a proliferating vegetation; a jungle where the new savage of modern times has trouble finding the reflexes of civilization. These fauna and flora, which people have produced, have come to encircle and invest them, like a bad science fiction novel. We must quickly describe them as we see and experience them, while not forgetting, even in periods of scarcity or profusion, that they are in actuality the *products of human activity*, and are controlled, not by natural ecological laws, but by the law of exchange value.

> The busiest streets of London are crowded with shops whose show cases display all the riches of the world: Indian shawls, American revolvers, Chinese porcelain, Parisian corsets, furs from Russia and spices from the tropics; but all of these worldly things bear odious white paper labels with Arabic numerals and then laconic symbols £SD. This is how commodities are presented in circulation.

Accumulation, or *profusion*, is evidently the most striking descriptive feature. Large department stores, with their luxuriant abundance of canned goods, foods, and clothing, are like the primary landscape and the geometrical locus of affluence. Streets with overcrowded and glittering store windows (lighting being the least rare commodity, without which merchandise would merely be what it is), the displays of delicacies, and all the scenes of alimentary and vestimentary festivity, stimulate a magical salivation. Accumulation is more than the sum of its products: the conspicuousness of surplus, the final and magical negation of scarcity, and the maternal and luxurious presumptions of the land of milk and honey. Our markets, our shopping avenues and malls mimic a new-found nature of prodigious fecundity. Those are our Valleys of Canaan where flows, instead of milk and honey, streams of neon on ketchup and plastic – but no matter! There exists an anxious anticipation, not that there may not be enough, but that there is too much, and too much for everyone: by purchasing a portion one in effect appropriates a whole crumbling pyramid of oysters, meats, pears or canned asparagus. One purchases the part for the whole. And this repetitive and metonymic discourse of the consumable, and of commodities, is represented, through collective metaphor and as a product of its own surplus, in the image of the *gift*, and of the inexhaustible and spectacular prodigality of the *feast*.

In addition to the stack, which is the most rudimentary yet effective form of accumulation, objects are organized in *displays*, or in *collections*. Almost every clothing store or appliance store presents a gamut of differentiated objects, which call upon, respond to, and refute each other. The display window of the antique store is the aristocratic, luxurious version of this model. The display no longer exhibits an overabundance of wealth but a *range* of select and complementary objects which are offered for the choosing. But this arrangement also invokes a psychological chain reaction in the consumer who peruses it, inventories it, and grasps it as a total category. Few objects today are offered *alone*, without a context of objects to speak for them. And the relation of the consumer to the object has consequently changed: the object is no longer referred to in relation to a specific utility, but as a collection of objects in their total meaning. Washing machine, refrigerator, dishwasher, have different meanings when grouped together than each one has alone, as a piece of equipment (*ustensile*). The display window, the advertisement, the manufacturer, and the *brand name* here play an essential role in imposing a coherent and collective vision, like an almost inseparable totality. Like a chain that connects not ordinary objects but *signifieds*, each object can signify the other in a more complex super-object, and lead the consumer to a series of more complex choices. We can observe that objects are never offered for consumption in an absolute disarray. In certain cases they can *mimic* disorder to better seduce, but they are always arranged to trace out directive paths. The arrangement directs the purchasing impulse towards *networks* of objects in order to seduce it and elicit, in accordance with its own logic, a maximal investment, reaching the limits of economic potential. Clothing, appliances, and toiletries thus constitute object *paths*, which establish inertial constraints on the consumer who will proceed *logically* from one object to the next. The consumer will be caught up in a *calculus* of objects, which is quite different from the frenzy of purchasing and possession which arises from the simple profusion of commodities.

The drugstore is the synthesis of profusion and calculation. The drugstore (or the new shopping malls) makes possible the synthesis of all consumer activities, not least of which are shopping, flirting with objects, idle wandering, and all the permutations of these. In this way, the drugstore is more appropriately representative of modern consumption than the large department store where quantitative centralization leaves little margin for idle exploration. The arrangement of departments and products here imposes a more utilitarian approach to consumption. It retains something of the period of the emergence of department stores, when large numbers of people were beginning to get access to *everyday* consumables. The drugstore has an altogether different function. It does not juxtapose categories of commodities, but practices an *amalgamation of signs* where all categories of goods are considered a partial field in a general consumerism of signs. The cultural center becomes, then, an integral part of the shopping mall. This is not to say that culture is here "prostituted"; that is too simple. It is *culturalized*. Consequently, the commodity (clothing, food, restaurant, etc.) is also culturalized, since it is transformed into a distinctive and idle substance, a luxury, and an item, among others, in the general display of consumables.

> A new art of living, a new way of living, claims advertising (and fashionable magazines): a pleasant shopping experience, in a single air-conditioned location; one is able to purchase food, products for the apartment or summer home, clothing, flowers, the latest novel, or the latest gadget in a single trip, while husband and children watch a film; and then later you can all dine together on the spot.

Cafe, cinema, book store, auditorium, trinkets, clothing, and many other things can be found in these shopping centers. The drugstore recaptures it all in a kaleidoscopic mode. Whereas the large department store provides a marketplace pageantry for merchandise, the drugstore offers the subtle recital of consumption, where, in fact, the "art" consists in playing on the ambiguity of the object's sign, and sublimating their status and utility as commodity in a play of "ambiance."

The drugstore is neo-culture universalized, where there is no longer any difference between a fine gourmet shop and a gallery of paintings, between *Playboy* and a *Treatise on Paleontology*. The drugstore will be modernized to the point of offering a bit of "gray matter":

> Just selling products does not interest us, we would like to supply a little gray matter. . . . Three stories, a bar, a dance floor, and shops; trinkets, records, paperbacks, intellectual books, a bit of everything. But we are not looking to flatter the customer. We are actually offering them "something": a language lab on the second floor; records and books where you find the great trends that move our society; music for research; works that explain an epoch. Products accompanied by "gray matter", this is the drugstore, but in a new style, with something more, perhaps a bit of intelligence and human warmth.

A drugstore can become a whole city: such as Parly 2, with its giant shopping center, where "art and leisure mingle with everyday life"; where each residential group encircles a pool club (the center of attraction), a circular church, tennis courts ("the least of things"), elegant boutiques, and a library. Even the smallest ski resort is organized on the "universalist" model of the drugstore, one where all activities are summarized, systematically combined and centered around the fundamental concept of "ambiance." Thus Idleness-on-the-Wasteful simultaneously offers you a complete, polymorphic and combinatorial existence:

> Our Mt Blanc, our Norway spruce forest; our Olympic runs, our "park" for children; our architecture, carved, trimmed, and polished like a work of art; the purity of the air we breathe; the refined ambiance of our Forum, modeled after Mediterranean cities where, upon return from the ski slopes, life flourishes. Cafes, restaurants, boutiques, skating rinks, night clubs, cinemas, and centers of culture and amusement are all located in the Forum to offer you a life off the slopes that is particularly rich and varied. There is our closed-circuit TV; and our future on a human scale (soon, we will be classified as a work of art by the department of cultural affairs).

We have reached the point where "consumption" has grasped the whole of life; where all activities are sequenced in the same combinatorial mode; where the schedule of gratification is outlined in advance, one hour at a time; and where the "environment" is complete, completely climatized, furnished, and culturalized. In the phenomenology of consumption, the general climatization of life, of goods, objects, services, behaviors, and social relations represents the perfected, "consummated," stage of evolution which, through articulated networks of objects, ascends from pure and simple abundance to a complete conditioning of action and time, and finally to the systematic organization of ambiance, which is characteristic of the drugstores, the shopping malls, or the modern airports in our futuristic cities.

37

The Postmodern: A Transparent Society?

Gianni Vattimo

Much is said about postmodernity nowadays. So much, in fact, that it has become almost obligatory to distance oneself from the notion, to see it as a fad and to insist on its having been overcome. It is my belief, however, that the term 'postmodern' has a meaning, and that this meaning is linked to the fact that the society in which we live is a society of generalized communication. It is the society of the mass media.

In the first place, we speak of the postmodern because we feel that, in some essential way, modernity is over. To understand what is meant by saying that modernity is over, one must first understand what is meant by modernity. Amongst the many definitions, there is one that may be generally agreed upon: modernity is the epoch in which simply being modern became a decisive value in itself.... I believe that it is still an insult to call someone a 'reactionary', that is, attached to values from the past, to tradition, to forms of thought that have been 'overcome'. Broadly speaking, this eulogy to being modern is what, in my view, characterizes the whole of modern culture. It is an attitude that did not really come to the fore until the end of the fifteenth century (the 'official' beginning of the modern age), at which point the artist came to be thought of as a creative genius and an increasingly intense cult of the new and original emerged that had not existed before (in previous ages the imitation of models was in fact of the utmost importance). As the centuries passed, it became more and more clear that the cult of the new and original in art was linked to a more general perspective according to which, as in the Enlightenment, human history is seen as an ongoing process of emancipation, as if it were the perfection of the human ideal (the essay 'On the education of the human race' by Lessing is typical in this respect). If history is progressive in this sense, greater value will clearly be attached to that which is more 'advanced', that which is nearer to the conclusion and the end of the process. However, a conception of history as the progressive realization of what is genuinely human requires that it be seen as unilinear. Only if there is History can one speak of progress.

According to the hypothesis I am putting forward, modernity ends when – for a number of reasons – it no longer seems possible to regard history as unilinear. Such a view requires the existence of a centre around which events are gathered and ordered. We think of history as ordered around the year zero of the birth of Christ, and more specifically as a serial train of events in the life of peoples from the 'centre', the West, the place of civilization, outside of which are the 'primitives' and the 'developing' countries. In the nineteenth and twentieth centuries philosophy has launched a radical critique of the idea of unilinear history, exposing the *ideological* character of these views. Thus, in a short essay from 1938 ('Theses on the philosophy of history'), Walter Benjamin maintained that unilinear history is a representation of the past constructed by dominant groups and social classes. Indeed, what is passed on from the past? Not everything that took place, but only that which seems *relevant.* For example, at school we studied the dates of battles, peace treaties and even revolutions, but they never told us of radical changes in forms of nutrition, or in sexual attitudes, or things of that kind. History speaks only of events involving those who count, the nobles, the sovereigns, or the middle classes once they became powerful. The poor, and those aspects of life considered 'base', do not 'make history'.

If observations such as these are developed further (along a path cleared before Benjamin by Marx and Nietzsche), the idea of unilinear history ends up being dissolved. There is no single history, only images of the past projected from different points of view. It is illusory to think that there exists a supreme or comprehensive viewpoint capable of unifying all others (such as 'History', encompassing the histories of art, of literature, of wars, of sexuality, etc.).

With the crisis in the idea of history comes a second crisis in the idea of progress: if human events do not make up a unilinear continuum, then one cannot regard them as proceeding towards an end, realizing a rational programme of improvement, education and emancipation. Moreover, the end that modernity took to be giving direction to the course of events was itself drawn according to a certain ideal of man. More or less all Enlightenment thinkers, Hegel, Marx, positivists, historians of every type, considered the meaning of history to be the realization of civilization, that is, of the form of Western European man. Just as history may be thought as unilinear only from the point of view of one placed at the centre (whether this be the coming of Christ or the Holy Roman Empire), so the conception of progress requires a certain ideal of man as its criterion. In modernity, however, the criterion has always been that of modern European man – as if to say: we Europeans are the best form of humanity and the entire course of history is directed towards the more or less complete realization of this ideal.

Bearing this in mind, one appreciates that the present crisis in the unilinear conception of history and consequently the crisis in the idea of progress and the end of modernity are not determined by transformations in theory alone – by the critiques undergone by nineteenth-century historicism (idealist, positivist, Marxist, etc.) at the level of ideas. What has happened is something quite different and of far greater magnitude: the so-called 'primitive' peoples colonized by Europeans in the good and rightful name of 'superior' and more evolved civilization have rebelled, making a unilinear and centralized history *de facto* problematic. The European ideal of humanity has been revealed as one ideal amongst others, not necessarily worse, but unable, without violence, to obtain as the true essence of man, of all men.

Along with the end of colonialism and imperialism, another decisive factor in both the dissolution of the idea of history and the end of modernity is the advent of the society of communication. Here I come to my second point, which concerns the 'transparent society'. It will not have gone unnoticed that the expression 'transparent society' has been introduced here with a question mark. What I am proposing is (i) that the mass media play a decisive role in the birth of a postmodern society; (ii) that they do not make this postmodern society more 'transparent', but more complex, even chaotic; and finally (iii) that it is in precisely this relative 'chaos' that our hopes for emancipation lie.

The impossibility of thinking history as unilinear – an impossibility that, according to the thesis put forward here, lays the basis for the end of modernity – does not derive solely from the crisis in European colonialism and imperialism. It is also, and perhaps above all, the result of the birth of means of mass communication. These means – newspapers, radio, television, what is now called telematics – have been decisive in bringing about the dissolution of centralized perspectives, of what the French philosopher Jean-François Lyotard calls the 'grand narratives'. . . . This giddy proliferation of communication as more and more subcultures 'have their say' is the most obvious effect of the mass media. Together with the end, or at least radical transformation, of European imperialism, it is also the key to our society's shift towards postmodernity. The West is living through an explosive situation, not only with regard to other cultural universes (such as the Third World), but internally as well, as an apparently irresistible pluralization renders any unilinear view of the world and history impossible.

This is why the society of the mass media should be contrasted sharply with a more enlightened, more 'educated', society (in the sense intended by Lessing, or Hegel, or even Comte or Marx). The mass media, which in theory offer information in 'real time' about everything happening in the world, could in effect be seen as a kind of concrete realization of Hegel's Absolute Spirit: the perfect self-consciousness of the whole of humanity, the coincidence between what happens, history and human knowledge. On close inspection, Hegelian and Marxist critics such as Adorno work with this model in mind, and their pessimism is based on the fact that it is not realized as it might have been (owing to the market, ultimately), or is realized only in a perverse and caricatural form (as in the sanctioned world of 'Big Brother', which may even be 'happy', thanks to the manipulation of desires). But the freedom given by the mass media to so many cultures and *Weltanschauungen* has belied the very ideal of a transparent society. What could freedom of information, or even the existence of more than one radio or TV channel, mean in a world where the norm is the exact reproduction of reality, perfect objectivity, the complete identity of map and territory? In actual fact, the increase in possible information on the myriad forms of reality makes it increasingly difficult to conceive of a *single* reality. It may be that in the world of the mass media a 'prophecy' of Nietzsche's is fulfilled: in the end the true world becomes a fable. If we, in late modernity, have an idea of reality, it cannot be understood as the objective given lying beneath, or beyond, the images we receive of it from the media. How and where could we arrive at such a reality 'in itself'? For us, reality is rather the result of the intersection and 'contamination' (in the Latin sense) of a multiplicity of images, interpretations and reconstructions circulated by the media in competition with one another and without any 'central' co-ordination.

The view I want to put forward is that, in the media society, the ideal of emancipation modelled on lucid self-consciousness, on the perfect knowledge of one who knows how things stand (compare Hegel's Absolute Spirit or Marx's conception of man freed from ideology), is replaced by an ideal of emancipation based on oscillation, plurality and, ultimately, the erosion of the very 'principle of reality'. Humanity today can finally become aware that perfect freedom is not that described by Spinoza, and does not lie in having a perfect knowledge of the necessary structure of reality and conforming to it – as metaphysics has always dreamt. This is where the philosophical lessons learnt from Nietzsche and Heidegger are most important. For they have provided us with the means to understand the emancipatory significance of the end of modernity and of its idea of history. Nietzsche showed the image of reality as a well-founded rational order (the perennial metaphysical image of the world) to be only the 'reassuring' myth of a still primitive and barbaric humanity. Metaphysics is a violent response to a situation that is itself fraught with danger and violence. It seeks to master reality at a stroke, grasping (or so it thinks) the first principle on which all things depend (and thus giving itself an empty guarantee of power over events). Following Nietzsche in this respect, Heidegger showed that to think of being as foundation, and reality as a rational system of causes and effects, is simply to extend the model of 'scientific' objectivity to the totality of being. All things are reduced to the level of pure presences that can be measured, manipulated, replaced and therefore easily dominated and organized – and in the end man, his interiority and historicity are all reduced to the same level.

If the proliferation of images of the world entails that we lose our 'sense of reality', as the saying goes, perhaps it's not such a great loss after all. By a perverse kind of internal logic, the world of objects measured and manipulated by techno-science (the world of the *real,* according to metaphysics) has become the world of merchandise and images, the phantasmagoria of the mass media. Should we counterpose to this world the nostalgia for a solid, unitary, stable and 'authoritative' reality? In its effort to reconstruct the world of our infancy, where familial authority was both a threat and a comfort, such nostalgia is in continual danger of turning into neurosis.

But what exactly might this loss of reality, this genuine erosion of the principle of reality, mean for emancipation and liberation? Emancipation, here, consists in *disorientation*, which is at the same time also the liberation of differences, of local elements, of what could generally be called dialect. With the demise of the idea of a central rationality of history, the world of generalized communication explodes like a multiplicity of 'local' rationalities – ethnic, sexual, religious, cultural or aesthetic minorities – that finally speak up for themselves. They are no longer repressed and cowed into silence by the idea of a single true form of humanity that must be realized irrespective of particularity and individual finitude, transience and contingency. Incidentally, the liberation of differences does not necessarily mean the surrender of every rule or the manifestation of brute immediacy. Dialects have grammar and syntax too, and indeed only discover them when they become visible and acquire a dignity of their own. With the liberation of diversity, they 'find their voice', present themselves and so 'get into shape' for recognition; this is anything but a manifestation of brute immediacy.

The emancipatory effect of the liberation of local rationalities is not confined to guaranteeing everyone the possibility of greater recognition and 'authenticity', as if emancipation meant finally showing what everyone – black, woman, homosexual, Protestant, etc. – 'really' is (to use terms that are still metaphysical, Spinozan).

The emancipatory significance of the liberation of differences and dialects consists rather in the general *disorientation* accompanying their initial identification. If, in a world of dialects, I speak my own dialect, I shall be conscious that it is not the only 'language', but that it is precisely one amongst many. If, in this multicultural world, I set out my system of religious, aesthetic, political and ethnic values, I shall be acutely conscious of the historicity, contingency and finiteness of these systems, starting with my own.

38

Against Postmodernism

Alex Callinicos

Compare these two passages:

> In the multidimensional and slippery space of Postmodernism anything goes with anything, like a game without rules. Floating images such as those we see in the painting of David Salle maintain no relationship with anything at all, and meaning becomes detachable like the keys on a key ring. Dissociated and decontextualized, they slide past one another failing to link up into a coherent sequence. Their fluctuating but not reciprocal interactions are unable to fix meaning.[1]

> [T]he nature of our epoch is multiplicity and indeterminacy. It can only rest on *das Gleitende* [the moving, the slipping, the sliding], and is aware that what other generations believed to be firm is in fact *das Gleitende*.[2]

The first passage comes from a talk given by the art critic Suzy Gablik in Los Angeles in 1987, the second was written by the poet Hugo von Hofmannsthal in 1905. Both depict the world as plural and polysemic, but for Gablik such a view is distinctive to postmodern art. A conception of reality of ultimately Nietzschean provenance which was fairly widespread among the intelligentsia of *Mitteleuropa* at the end of the last century and which is often present in the work of major modernist figures such as Hofmannsthal is presented as peculiarly *post*modernist.

But this kind of appropriation of modernist motifs is absolutely typical of accounts of postmodernist art. The force of this point can only be established by considering first the nature of modernism itself. Eugene Lunn offers an excellent definition:

'1 *Aesthetic Self-Consciousness or Self-Reflexiveness.*' The process of producing the work of art becomes the focus of the work itself:

Proust, of course, provided the definitive example in *A la recherche du temps perdu*.

'2 *Simultaneity, Juxtaposition, or "Montage".*' The work loses its organic form and becomes an assemblage of fragments, often drawn from different discourses or cultural media. Cubist and Surrealist collages come to mind, along with the practice of cinematic montage developed by Eisenstein, Vertov and other revolutionary Russian film-makers.

'3 *Paradox, Ambiguity, and Uncertainty.*' The world itself ceases to have a coherent, rationally ascertainable structure, and becomes, as Hofmannsthal says, multiple and indeterminate. Klimt's great paintings 'Philosophy', 'Medicine' and 'Jurisprudence', commissioned for the University of Vienna but rejected because of the scandal their dark and ambiguous images represented to Enlightenment thought, exemplify this vision.

'4 *"Dehumanization" and the Demise of the Integrated Individual Subject or Personality.*' Rimbaud's famous declaration '*JE est un autre*' ('*I* am another') finds its echoes in the literary explorations of the unconscious inaugurated by Joyce and pursued by the Surrealists.[3]

Oddly enough, the authors of two of the most interesting recent discussions of modernism, Perry Anderson and Franco Moretti, both deny that there is any relatively unified set of artistic practices which can be captured by a definition such as Lunn's. Anderson writes: 'Modern*ism* as a notion is the emptiest of cultural categories. Unlike Gothic, Renaissance, Baroque, Mannerist, Romantic, or Neoclassical, it designates no describable object in its own right at all; it is completely lacking in positive content.'[4] Anderson perhaps places excessive faith in the traditional categories of art history, terms whose origins are often arbitrary and use uncertain and shifting. Moretti is rather more concrete in the way he expresses his scepticism about the label 'modernism':

> 'Modernism' is a portmanteau word that perhaps should not be used too often. But I don't think I would classify Brecht as a modernist. . . . I just cannot think of a meaningful category that could include, say, surrealism, *Ulysses*, and something by Brecht. I can't think what the common attributes of such a concept could be. The objects are too dissimilar.[5]

But in fact Brecht's plays can be seen quite plausibly to fall under the 'common attributes' of Lunn's definition: the alienation (*Verfremdung*) effect is intended precisely to make the audience realize that they are in a theatre and not eavesdropping on real life; Brecht explicitly gives montage as a defining feature of his epic theatre; the plays are constructed in part to deny the spectator the satisfaction of an unequivocal meaning; and the narratives they unfold no longer treat the individual subject as the sovereign and coherent author of events. This is not to deny the considerable variations within modernism: one of the merits of Lunn's account is the contrast it draws between the confident rationalism of cubism in France before 1914, and, on the one hand, the 'languorous aestheticism' of Vienna, and, on the other, the 'nervous, agitated and suffering' art produced by German Expressionism.[6] Nor is it to ignore the very important differences within modernism concerning the status of art itself. Nevertheless, Lunn's definition does, in my view, capture the distinctive features of the art which emerged across Europe at the end of the nineteenth century.

The advantages of having some such conception of modernism become plain when one considers the definitions offered of postmodernism, for example by Charles Jencks: 'To this day I would define Postmodernism as . . . *double-coding: the combination of Modern techniques with something else (usually traditional building) in order for architecture to communicate with the public and a concerned minority, usually other architects*.'[7] This definition gets its purchase from the attempts by architects over the last couple of decades to get away from the elongated slabs characteristic of the International Style, with which architectural modernism is identified. But if (as it is intended to be) it is taken as a *general* characterization of postmodern art, then it is hopelessly inadequate. 'Double-coding' – what Lunn calls 'Simultaneity, Juxtaposition, or "Montage" ' – is a defining feature of modernism. Thus Peter Ackroyd writes of *The Waste Land*:

> Eliot found his own voice by first reproducing that of others – as if it was only through his reading of, and response to, literature that he could find anything to hold onto, anything 'real'. That is why *Ulysses* struck him so forcibly, in a way no other novel ever did. Joyce had created a world which exists only in, and through, the multiple uses of language – through voices, through parodies of style. . . . Joyce had a historical consciousness of language and thus of the relativity of any one 'style'. The whole course of Eliot's development would lead him to share such a consciousness. . . . In the closing sequence of *The Waste Land* itself he creates a montage of lines from Dante, Kyd, Gérard de Nerval, the *Pervigilium Veneris* and Sanskrit. . . . There is no 'truth' to be found, only a number of styles and interpretations – one laid upon another in an endless and apparently meaningless process.[8]

Eliot is a particularly relevant example to take in the light of Jenck's claim that postmodernism represents a 'return to the larger Western tradition' after modernism's 'fetish of discontinuity'.[9] For one of Eliot's main preoccupations – expressed, for example, in 'Tradition and the individual talent' – was the relationship of both continuity and discontinuity between his own work and the broader European tradition:

> the historical sense compels a man to write not merely with his own generation in his bones, but with a feeling that the whole literature of Europe from Homer and within it the whole literature of his own country has a simultaneous existence and composes a simultaneous order. This historical sense, which is a sense of the timeless as well as of the temporal and of the timeless and the temporal together, is what makes a writer traditional. And it is at the same time what makes a writer most acutely conscious of his place in time, of his own contemporaneity.[10]

Eliot is in no sense exceptional among the major modernists in this concern for placing himself with respect to 'the larger Western tradition', as any acquaintance with the work, say, of Joyce or Schönberg or Picasso will confirm. It is therefore difficult to be persuaded by Linda Hutcheon's claim that 'postmodernism goes beyond self-reflexivity to situate discourse in a broader context'.[11] She uses what she calls 'historiographic metafiction', a number of contemporary novels, in order to illustrate this thesis, but the examples she gives – Salman Rushdie's *Midnight's Children*, John Fowles's *The French Lieutenant's Woman*, Julian Barnes's *Flaubert's Parrot* and E. L. Doctorow's *Ragtime* among others – seem fairly heterogeneous, and united chiefly by their use, for various ends and in different modes, of the modernist fictional devices pioneered by Conrad, Proust, Joyce, Woolf and others at the beginning of the century.

Hutcheon's argument is one among a number of manoeuvres used to deal with the embarrassing fact that both the definitions given and the examples cited of postmodern art place it most plausibly as a continuation of and not a break from the *fin-de-siècle* modernist revolution. Another popular move is to treat modernism as essentially elitist. Thus Hutcheon talks of '[t]he obscurity and hermeticism of modernism',[12] while even Andreas Huyssen (who is usually above such things) tells us that 'the most significant trends within postmodernism have challenged modernism's relentless hostility to mass culture.'[13] Taken as claims about the internal construction of modernist art these are far too strong. Even the forbiddingly mandarin Eliot loved the London music hall and sought to integrate its rhythms into some of his poetry, especially *Sweeney Agonistes*. Stravinsky wrote not only *Le Sacre du printemps* but also *L'Histoire du soldat*, which draws heavily on ragtime. If directed at the great modernists' aestheticism, their tendency to view art as refuge from 'the immense panorama of futility and anarchy that is contemporary history', the accusation of elitism does strike home, but even here those committed to the idea of a radically novel postmodern art must confront the development of avant-garde movements such as Dadaism, Constructivism and Surrealism which deployed modernist techniques to overcome the separation between art and life as part of a broader struggle to revolutionize society itself. The arguments presented so far seem to me sufficient to cast doubt on the claims made for the novelty of postmodern art.

There are nevertheless considerably more subtle attempts to establish the existence of a distinctively postmodern art than any considered so far. These conceive postmodernism as a tendency within modernism itself. Such an approach clearly involves a retreat from or the rejection of the idea that modernism and postmodernism can be correlated in any very strong sense with distinctive stages of social development – say, respectively, industrial and post-industrial society.

Confusingly enough Lyotard, who helped to get the hare of a new, postmodern epoch running in the first place, also argues that treating the ' "post-" in the term "postmodernist" . . . in the sense of a simple succession, of a diachrony of periods, each of them clearly identifiable' is 'totally modern. . . . Since we are beginning something completely new, we have to re-set the hands of the clock at zero.' But the idea of a total break with tradition 'is, rather, a manner of forgetting or repressing the past. That's to say of repeating it. Not overcoming it.'[14]

If postmodernism isn't a movement beyond modernism, what is it? 'It is undoubtedly a part of the modern', Lyotard replies.[15] To develop his point he draws here on Kant's conception, elaborated in the *Critique of Judgement* as part of his aesthetics, of the sublime, which 'is to be found in an object even devoid of form, so far as it immediately involves, or its presence provokes, a representation of *limitlessness*, yet a superadded thought of its totality'. The particular philosophical significance of the sublime is that it offers us an experience of nature 'in its chaos, or in its wildest and most irregular disorder and desolation', which, 'provided it gives signs of magnitude and power', leads us to formulate ideas of pure reason, in particular that of the physical world as a unified and purposive order, which, according to Kant, cannot be found in sense-experience. The feeling, therefore, of the sublime is a form of aesthetic experience which breaks the boundaries of the sensuous. And, 'though the imagination, no doubt, finds nothing beyond the sensible world to which it can lay hold, still this thrusting aside of the sensible barriers gives it a feeling of being unbounded and this removal is thus a presentation of the infinite.' Kant suggests that there may be 'no more sublime passage' than the Mosaic ban on graven images.[16]

The essential for Lyotard is less the religio-metaphysical connotations of the sublime for Kant but rather 'the incommensurability of reality to concept which is implied in the Kantian philosophy of the sublime'. He emphasizes, not the 'superadded thought of . . . totality' which Kant says is inherent in the feeling of the sublime, but rather our inability to experience this totality. Lyotard distinguishes between two different attitudes towards 'the sublime relation between the presentable and the conceivable', the modern and the postmodern:

> modern aesthetics is an aesthetic of the sublime, though a nostalgic one. It allows the unpresentable to be put forward only as the missing contents; but the form, because of its recognizable consistency, continues to offer to the reader or viewer matter for solace or pleasure. . . . The postmodern would be that which, in the modern, puts forward the unpresentable in presentation itself; that which denies itself the solace of good forms, the consensus of a good taste which would make it possible to share collectively the nostalgia for the unattainable; that which searches for new presentations, not in order to enjoy them but in order to impart a stronger sense of the unpresentable.[17]

Postmodern art therefore differs from modernism in the attitude it takes up towards our inability to experience the world as a coherent and harmonious whole. Modernism reacts to 'the immense panorama of futility and anarchy that is contemporary history' by looking back nostalgically to a time before our sense of totality was lost, as Eliot does when he claims that in the Metaphysical poets of the seventeenth century there was 'a direct sensuous apprehension of thought, or a recreation of thought into feeling', which disappeared after the 'dissociation of sensibility' already evident in Milton and Dryden.[18] Postmodernism, by contrast, ceases to look back. If focuses instead 'on the power of the faculty to conceive, on its "inhumanity" so to speak (it was the quality Apollinaire demanded of modern artists)' and 'on the increase of being and jubilation which result from the invention of new rules of the game, be it pictorial, artistic, or any other'.[19]

This conception of postmodernism effectively abandons the attempt to ascribe to it structural characteristics such as 'double-coding' in order to differentiate it from modernism. Indeed, as Frederic Jameson observes, Lyotard's argument has 'something of the celebration of modernism as its first ideologues projected it – a constant and ever more dynamic revolution in the languages, forms and tastes of art'.[20] Similarly

Jencks complains that 'Lyotard continues in his writings to confuse Post-Modernism with the latest avant-gardism, that is Late Modernism'.[21] Jencks has in mind in particular some of the Minimalist art of the 1960s and 1970s, and indeed it does seem that Lyotard is inclined to favour such work, as is suggested by the exhibition, *Les Immatériaux*, which he organized at the Pompidou Centre. The main thrust of Lyotard's argument, however, involves the claim that postmodernism is a tendency within modernism characterized by its refusal to mourn, and indeed its willingness to celebrate our inability to experience reality as an ordered and integrated totality. Minimalist art may fall under this definition, but a perhaps more interesting question concerns the exemplars of postmodernism during the heroic era of modernism at the beginning of the century.

Lyotard offers one rather unconvincing example. He argues that Proust's work is plainly modernist, since, although 'the hero is no longer a character but the inner consciousness of time, . . . the unity of the book, the odyssey of that consciousness, even if it is deferred from chapter to chapter, is not seriously challenged'. By contrast 'Joyce allows the unpresentable to become perceptible in his writing itself, in the signifier. The whole range of available narrative and even stylistic operators is put into play without concern for the unity of the whole, and new operators are tried.'[22] But surely, despite the variety of styles and voices present in *Ulysses*, an implicit coherence is achieved through Joyce's use of myth? And is not this order even more evidently at work in *Finnegans Wake* in the cyclical pattern traced by both the book and history?

Joyce is placed firmly in the modernist camp by Jameson in his brilliant study of Wyndham Lewis, the most sustained attempt to show postmodernist impulses at work within modernism. Lewis's significance for Jameson lies in his rejection of the 'impressionistic aesthetic' characteristic of 'Anglo-American modernism'. Pound, Eliot, Joyce, Lawrence and Yeats all pursued 'strategies of inwardness, which set out to reappropriate an alienated universe by transforming it into personal styles and private languages'. Nothing could be more different than 'the prodigious force with which Wyndham Lewis propagates his bristling mechanical sentences and hammers the world into a forbidding cubist surface', the relentless externality of his style, in which the human, the physical and the mechanical are shattered and assimilated to each other. In a daring and imaginative move for a Marxist to take, Jameson argues that the writing of Lewis – fascist, sexist, racist, elitist – must be seen, precisely because of its distinctive formal 'expressionism', as a particularly powerful 'protest against the reified experience of an alienated social life, in which, against its own will, it remains formally and ideologically locked'.[23]

The difficulty lies not so much with Jameson's reading of Lewis, which is essentially a particularly bold example of what Frank Kermode calls the 'discrepancy theory', in accord with which Marxist criticism seeks to uncover in texts an unconscious meaning often at odds with their author's intentions, but with the picture of mainstream modernism which he contrasts with Lewis's writing. Modernism on this account is especially concerned with the time of private, subjective experience, what Bergson called *durée*, time as the individual person lives it, at once fragmented and operating at quite different rhythms from the homogeneous and linear 'objective' time of modern society. Perhaps this will do when applied to Proust, but it fits Lewis's great English-speaking contemporaries rather badly. To take (yet again) the case of Eliot, we saw above that he conceived the entire European tradition as composing 'a simultaneous order' with his own writing. Indeed, it has been argued more generally that literary modernism is characterized precisely by the *spatialization* of writing, the juxtaposition of fragmentary images torn out of any temporal sequence. In 'Tradition and the individual talent' Eliot also makes the celebrated claim that '[p]oetry is not a turning loose of emotion, but an escape from emotion; it is not the expression of personality, but an escape from personality.'[24] Such statements seem to fit poems like *The Waste Land* better than the claim that they represent a 'strategy of inwardness', a retreat into the 'inner consciousness of time'. Eliot approvingly described *Ulysses* as a return to Classicism that uses the materials provided by modern life rather than relying on a sterile academicism; interestingly Lewis claimed that the 'Men of 1914', by which he meant Eliot, Pound, Joyce and himself, represented 'an attempt to get away from romantic into classical art' comparable to Picasso's revolution in painting.[25]

Jameson, the author after all of a book called *The Political Unconscious*, might argue that such professions by Eliot and others of a commitment to an impersonal, spatialized art very different from the 'impressionist aesthetic' which he ascribes to them are less important than what is revealed by the formal construction of their work. But without entering into such a formal analysis, it is worth observing how much less plausible Jameson's interpretation becomes when applied to the broader currents of modernism beyond the English-speaking world. Where, for example, does Expressionism fit in – a highly subjective kind of art which nevertheless *externalized* inner anguish, projecting it on to and thereby distorting the objective environment of the personality? Or cubism, which systematically dismantled the objects of common-sense experience, spreading out before the viewer their internal structure and external relationships? Or the *Neue Sachlichkeit* of Weimar Germany, which reacted against the extravagances of Expressionism in favour of cool, matter-of-fact (*sachlich*), sometimes avowedly neoclassical art, but combined this with a critical, if not revolutionary attitude towards existing society – an art whose greatest achievement was perhaps Brecht's 'theatre for a scientific age'?

More generally, Jameson's attempt to counterpose Lewis's 'expressionism' with the 'impressionistic aesthetic' supposedly typical of modernism occludes what is best understood as a dialectical relationship between interiority and exteriority. The exploration of the peculiar rhythms of subjective experience is undoubtedly one of the major themes of modernist writing: think of Proust, Woolf, Joyce. The paradox is that the deeper one probes beyond even fragmentary inner consciousness into the unconscious, the more one threatens to crack the subject open, and to confront the external forces which traverse and constitute the ego. This is the trajectory taken by Freud: the unravelling of unconscious desires led him face to face with history – not simply the history of the individual subject, but the historical processes which produced the social institutions, above all the family, subtending the odyssey of the self. Deleuze and Guattari argue that Freud's fault was that he did not take the process far enough, relying instead on the mythologized history which rendered the bourgeois family eternal. However that may be, the point stands that the logic of depth psychology, the exploration of inner consciousness, is to disintegrate the subject, and display its fragments as directly related to the social and natural environment supposedly external to the self. One can see this logic at work, for example, in two of the great figures of Viennese modernism, Klimt and Kokoschka. Klimt's paintings are suffused with an inner unease and pervasive eroticism which are still held in control in a harmonious, indeed stylized relationship of the parts to the whole; in Kokoschka the tensions which Klimt was still able more or less to manage have exploded, distorting and disorganizing the subjects of his paintings, which are traversed by an anarchic psychic energy.

One might argue that postmodernism is nothing but the outcome of this dialectic of interiority and exteriority, an art of the surface, the depthless, even the immediate. Thus Scott Lash proposes that we see postmodernism as 'a figural, as distinct from discursive, regime of signification. To signify via figures rather than words is to signify iconically. Images or other figures which signify iconically do so through their resemblance to the referent.' Consequently postmodern art involves 'de-differentiation', so that, on the one hand, the signified (meaning) tends 'to wither away and the signifier to function as a referent', and, on the other hand, 'the referent functions as a signifier'. Contemporary film (*Blue Velvet*) and criticism (Susan Sontag's attack on interpretation) provide Lash with examples of this essentially Imagist art, but, like Lyotard, he sees postmodernism as immanent within modernism, particularly in the shape of Surrealism, which 'understood reality to be composed of signifying elements. Thus Naville enthused that we should get pleasure from the streets of the city in which kiosks, autos and lights were in a sense already representations, and Breton spoke of the world itself as "automatic writing".'[26]

One obvious difficulty with this analysis is that it offers no account of how postmodernism thus understood differs from those arts – for example, painting and cinema – which are necessarily iconic. John Berger has claimed recently that painting is distinguished by the way it 'offers palpable, instantaneous, unswerving, continuous, physical presence. It is the most immediately sensuous of the arts.'[27] It is at least arguable that one of the main thrusts of modernist painting is to release this immediate sensuous charge inherent in painting from both aesthetic ideologies of form and representation and broader social ideologies subordinating art to organized religion and the state. One can see the resulting sense of liberation at work, for example, in Matisse's paintings. The attempt to achieve something like the same effect in poetry was a crucial impulse in the modernist literary revolution: Pound called Imagism the 'sort of poetry where painting or sculpture seems as if it were "just coming over into speech"'.[28] If the figural is the defining characteristic of postmodernism, then the latter is a far more pervasive feature of modernism than Lash appears to believe.

Matters are not much improved if we focus on Surrealism, as Lash does. It is quite true that the Surrealists had a magical conception of reality according to which chance events in the daily life of the city offered occasions of what Walter Benjamin called 'profane illumination'. In this sense reality did indeed function for them as a signifier. But by the mid-1920s what had originally been a primarily aestheticist project intended to realize Rimbaud's injunction that '[t]he poet makes himself a *seer* by a long, prodigious and rational *disordering of all the senses*' had developed into a broader political commitment to social revolution which led most leading Surrealists to join the Communist Party (in most cases rather briefly) and Breton to a life-long involvement in the anti-Stalinist Left. '"Transform the world", Marx said; "change life", Rimbaud said – these two watchwords are for us one and the same', Breton told the Congress of Writers for the Defence of Culture in 1935.[29]

This conjoining of political and aesthetic revolution makes it difficult to see the Surrealists as precursors of postmodernism. For most accounts of postmodern art tend to emphasize its rejection of revolutionary political change. Lyotard associates 'the nostalgia of the whole and one, ... the reconciliation of the concept and the sensible, of the transparent and the communicable experience' with 'terror, ... the fantasy to seize reality'.[30] The thought is presumably the traditional liberal one that any attempt at total social change will lead straight to the Gulag. One consideration behind the frequent claims made for postmodern 'wit' and 'irony' seems to be that the collapse of belief in the possibility or desirability of global political transformation leaves us with nothing better to do than playfully to parody what we can no longer take seriously. Parody, however, is so pervasively present in the great modernists – Eliot and Joyce, for example – that any attempt to claim it exclusively for postmodernism just seems implausible. Jameson suggests that matters have gone a stage further – that while modernist parody retains some conception of a norm from which one is deviating, postmodernism is distinguished by pastiche, the 'neutral practice of mimicry, without any of parody's ulterior motives, amputated of the satiric impulse, devoid of laughter and of any conviction that alongside the abnormal tongue you have momentarily borrowed, some healthy linguistic normality still exists'.[31]

How can Surrealism, which united Rimbaldian artistic experimentation with Marxist revolutionary socialism, be plausibly regarded as a precursor of postmodernism, which sees revolution as, at best a joke, at worst a disaster? Lash doesn't help matters by drawing on Benjamin's discussion of post-auratic art. Benjamin used the term 'aura' in order to capture the properties of uniqueness and unapproachability which he argues are characteristic of the traditional work of art. '[T]he unique value of the "authentic" work of art has its basis in ritual,' he claims, 'the location of its original use value.' The aura preserves this 'ritual function' even after the decline of organized religion in the shape of the 'secular cult of beauty, developed during the Renaissance' and the 'negative theology' of art involved in nineteenth-century aestheticism (*l'art pour l'art*). The contemporary development of the mass reproduction of art by mechanical means reaching its climax in cinema, however, causes the aura to decay, both by destroying the uniqueness of images and by altering their mode of consumption – the reception of the work of art is no longer a matter of individual absorption in the image, but – above all in the film theatre – is 'consummated by a collectivity in a state of distraction'.[32]

Now Lash claims that modernism is typically auratic, postmodernism post-auratic, the latter shattering the organic unity of the work of art 'through pastiche, collage, allegory and so on'.[33] Lash doesn't explain how postmodernism's use of collage and the like distinguishes it from a paradigmatically modernist movement like cubism. More to the point, his argument involves a serious misunderstanding of Benjamin's account of post-auratic art. Benjamin argued that decay of the aura achieved by mass media such as cinema was the explicit objective of avant-garde movements such as Dada. 'What they intended and achieved was a relentless destruction of the aura of their creations. . . . Dadaistic activities actually assured a rather vehement distraction by making works of art the centre of scandal.' But the kinds of shock effects sought by the Dadaists with their meaningless poems and assaults on their audiences are achieved on a much larger scale by film, whose rapid succession of shots interrupts the spectator's consciousness, preventing her from sinking into a state of absorbed contemplation.[34]

[. . .]

The abiding impression left by the various claims made for postmodern art surveyed in the preceding pages is their contradictory character. Postmodernism corresponds to a new historical stage of social development (Lyotard) or it doesn't (Lyotard again). Postmodern art is a continuation of (Lyotard) or a break from (Jencks) modernism. Joyce is a modernist (Jameson) or a postmodernist (Lyotard). Postmodernism turns its back on social revolution, but then practitioners and advocates of a revolutionary art like Breton and Benjamin are claimed as precursors. No wonder that Kermode calls postmodernism 'another of those period descriptions that help you to take a view of the past suitable to whatever it is you want to do'.[35]

What runs through all the various – mutually and often internally inconsistent – accounts of postmodernism is the idea that recent aesthetic changes (however characterized) are symptomatic of a broader, radical novelty, a sea-change in Western civilization. A little before the postmodern boom got into full swing Daniel Bell noted the widespread 'sense of an ending' among the Western intelligentsia 'symbolized . . . in the widespread use of the word *post* . . . to define, as a combined form, the age into which we are moving'. Bell illustrated this proliferation of 'posts-' by listing the following examples: post-capitalist, post-bourgeois, post-modern, post-civilized, post-collectivist, post-Puritan, post-Protestant, post-Christian, post-literature, post-traditional, post-historical, post-market society, post-organization society, post-economic, post-scarcity, post-welfare, post-liberal, post-industrial. . . .[36]

For postmodernists the decisive break is usually with the Enlightenment, with which modernism tends to be identified. Sometimes this involves the most astonishing claims, such as the following: 'Modernism in philosophy goes back a long way: Bacon, Galileo, Descartes – pillars of the modernist conception of the fashionable, the new and the innovative'[37] – a statement so ignorant as almost to invite one's admiration. How can thinkers committed to a representational epistemology most fully articulated by Locke in which the sensory qualities of objects are signs of their rationally ascertainable inner structure be assimilated in an artistic movement whose products affronted common-sense expectations often in the belief that the scientific knowledge of reality was neither possible or even desirable? The point of such assertions seems to be less their factual content, which is slight, than the attempt to establish the novelty of postmodernism, usually characterized in terms borrowed from modernism, by treating the latter as merely the latest exemplar of Western rationalism.

Notes and References

1 S. Gablik, 'The aesthetics of duplicity', *Art and Design*, 3 (7/8) (1987), p. 36.
2 Quoted in C. Schorske, *Fin-de-siècle Vienna* (Cambridge University Press, Cambridge, 1981), p. 19.
3 E. Lunn, *Marxism and Modernism* (Verso, London, 1985), pp. 34–7.
4 P. Anderson, 'Modernity and revolution', in *Marxism and the Interpretation of Culture*, ed. C. Nelson and L. Grossberg (Macmillan, London, 1988), p. 332.
5 F. Moretti, 'The spell of indecision' (discussion), in *Marxism and the Interpretation of Culture*, ed. C. Nelson and L. Grossberg (Macmillan, London, 1988), p. 346.
6 Lunn, *Marxism*, p. 58.
7 C. Jenks, *What is Postmodernism?* (Academy Editions, London, 1986), p. 14.
8 P. Ackroyd, *T.S. Eliot* (Abacus, London, 1985), pp. 118–19.
9 Jenks, *Postmodernism?*, p. 43.
10 T.S. Eliot, *Selected Prose*, ed. F. Kermode (Faber, London, 1975), p. 38.
11 L. Hutcheon, *A Poetics of Postmodernism* (Routledge, London, 1988), p. 41.
12 Ibid., p. 32.
13 A. Huyssen, 'Mapping the postmodern', *New German Critique*, 33 (1984), p. 16.
14 J.F. Lyotard, 'Defining the postmodern', *ICA Documents*, 4 (1985), p. 6.
15 J.F. Lyotard, *The Postmodern Condition* (University of Minnesota Press, Minneapolis, Minn., 1984), p. 79.
16 I. Kant, *Critique of Judgement* (Clarendon, Oxford, 1973), vol. I, pp. 90, 92, 127.

17 Lyotard, *Postmodern Condition*, pp. 79, 81.
18 Eliot, *Selected Prose*, pp. 63–4.
19 Lyotard, *Postmodern Condition*, pp. 79–80.
20 F. Jameson, Foreword to Lyotard, *Postmodern Condition*, p. xvi.
21 Jenks, *Postmodernism?*, p. 42.
22 Lyotard, *Postmodern Condition*, p. 80.
23 F. Jameson, *Fables of Aggression* (California University Press, Berkeley, Calif., 1979), pp. 2, 81, 2, 14.
24 Eliot, *Selected Prose*, p. 43.
25 Ibid., pp. 176–7; W. Lewis, *Blasting & Bombardiering* (Calder and Boyars, London, 1967), p. 250.
26 S. Lash, 'Discourse or figure?', *Theory, Culture and Society*, 5 (2/3) (1988), pp. 320, 331–2.
27 J. Berger, 'Defending Picasso's late work', *International Socialism*, 2 (40) (1988), p. 113.
28 Quoted in N. Zach, 'Imagism and vorticism', in *Modernism 1890–1930*, ed. M. Bradbury and J. McFarlane (Penguin, Harmondsworth, 1976), p. 234.
29 M. Nadeau, *A History of Surrealism* (Penguin, Harmondsworth, 1973), p. 212, n. 5.
30 Lyotard, *Postmodern Condition*, p. 82.
31 F. Jameson, 'Postmodernism, or the cultural logic of late capitalism', *New Left Review*, 146 (1984), p. 45.
32 W. Benjamin, *Illuminations* (Fontana, London, 1970), pp. 226, 241.
33 S. Lash and J. Urry, *The End of Organized Capitalism* (Polity, Cambridge, 1987), pp. 286–7.
34 Benjamin, *Illuminations,* pp. 239–40.
35 F. Kermode, *History and Value* (Clarendon, Oxford, 1988), p. 132.
36 D. Bell, *The Coming of Post-Industrial Society* (Heinemann Educational, London, 1974), pp. 51–4.
37 J. Silverman and D. Welton, editors' introduction to *Postmodernism and Continental Philosophy* (SUNY Press, Albany, N.Y., 1988), p. 2.

39

Modernity and the Holocaust

Zygmunt Bauman

There are two ways to belittle, misjudge, or shrug off the significance of the Holocaust for sociology as the theory of civilization, of modernity, of modern civilization.

One way is to present the Holocaust as something that happened to the Jews; as an event in *Jewish* history. This makes the Holocaust unique, comfortably uncharacteristic and sociologically inconsequential. The most common example of such a way is the presentation of the Holocaust as the culmination point of European-Christian antisemitism – in itself a unique phenomenon with nothing to compare it with in the large and dense inventory of ethnic or religious prejudices and aggressions. Among all other cases of collective antagonisms, antisemitism stands alone for its unprecedented systematicity, for its ideological intensity, for its supranational and supra-territorial spread, for its unique mix of local and ecumenical sources and tributaries. In so far as it is defined as, so to speak, the continuation of antisemitism through other means, the Holocaust appears to be a 'one item set', a one-off episode, which perhaps sheds some light on the *pathology* of the society in which it occurred, but hardly adds anything to our understanding of this society's *normal* state. Less still does it call for any significant revision of the orthodox understanding of the historical tendency of modernity, of the civilizing process, of the constitutive topics of sociological inquiry.

Another way – apparently pointing in an opposite direction, yet leading in practice to the same destination – is to present the Holocaust as an extreme case of a wide and familiar category of social phenomena; a category surely loathsome and repellent, yet one we can (and must) live with. We must live with it because of its resilience and ubiquity, but above all because modern society has been all along, is and will remain, an organization designed to roll it back, and perhaps even to stamp it out altogether. Thus the Holocaust is classified as another item (however prominent) in a wide class that embraces many 'similar' cases of conflict, or prejudice, or aggression. At worst, the Holocaust is referred to a primeval and culturally inextinguishable, 'natural' predisposition of the human species – Lorenz's instinctual aggression or Arthur Koestler's failure of the neo-cortex to control the ancient, emotion-ridden part of the brain. As pre-social and immune to cultural manipulation, factors responsible for the Holocaust are effectively removed from the area of sociological interest. At best, the Holocaust is cast inside the most awesome and sinister – yet still theoretically assimilable category – of genocide; or else simply dissolved in the broad, all-too-familiar class of ethnic, cultural or racial oppression and persecution.

Whichever of the two ways is taken, the effects are very much the same. The Holocaust is shunted into the familiar stream of history:

> When viewed in this fashion, and accompanied with the proper citation of other historical horrors (the religious crusades, the slaughter of Albigensian heretics, the Turkish decimation of the Armenians, and even the British invention of concentration camps during the Boer War), it becomes all too convenient to see the Holocaust as 'unique' – but normal, after all.[1]

[. . .]

When compared with the awesome amount of work accomplished by the historians, and the volume of soul-searching among both Christian and Jewish theologians, the contributions of professional sociologists to Holocaust studies seem marginal and negligible. Such sociological studies as have been completed so far show beyond reasonable doubt that . . . the real point at issue is not; 'What can we, the sociologists, say about the Holocaust?', but, rather, 'What has the Holocaust to say about us, the sociologists, and our practice?'

While the necessity to ask this question seems both a most urgent and a most ignobly neglected part of the Holocaust legacy, its consequences must be carefully considered. It is only too easy to over-react to the apparent bankruptcy of established sociological visions. Once the hope to contain the Holocaust experience in the theoretical framework of malfunction (modernity incapable of suppressing the essentially alien factors of irrationality, civilizing pressures failing to subdue emotional and violent drives, socialization going awry and hence unable to produce the needed volume of moral motivations) has been dashed, one can be easily tempted to try the 'obvious' exit from the theoretical impasse; to proclaim the Holocaust a 'paradigm' of modern civilization, its 'natural', 'normal' (who knows – perhaps also *common*) product, its 'historical tendency'. In this version, the Holocaust would be promoted to the status of *truth* of modernity (rather than recognized as a *possibility* that modernity contains) – the truth only superficially concealed by the ideological formula imposed by those who benefit from the 'big lie'. In a perverse fashion, this view, having allegedly elevated the historical and theoretical significance of the Holocaust, can only belittle its importance, as the horrors of genocide will have become virtually indistinguishable from other sufferings that modern society does undoubtedly generate daily – and in abundance.

A few years ago a journalist of *Le Monde* interviewed a sample of former hijack victims. One of the most interesting things he found was an abnormally high incidence of divorce among the couples who went jointly through the agony of hostage experience. Intrigued, he probed the divorcees for the reasons for their decision. Most interviewees told him that they had never contemplated a divorce before the hijack. During the horrifying episode, however, 'their eyes opened', and 'they saw their partners in a new light'. Ordinary good husbands 'proved to be' selfish creatures, caring only for their own stomachs; daring businessmen displayed disgusting cowardice; resourceful 'men of the world' fell to pieces and did little except bewail their imminent perdition. The journalist asked himself a question: which of the two incarnations each of these Januses was clearly capable of was the true face, and which was the mask? He concluded that the question was wrongly put. Neither was 'truer' than the other. Both were possibilities that the character of the victims contained all along – they simply surfaced at different times and in different circumstances. The 'good' face seemed normal only because normal conditions favoured it above the other. Yet the other was always present, though normally invisible. The most fascinating aspect of this finding was, however, that were it not for the hijackers' venture, the 'other face' would probably have remained hidden forever. The partners would have continued to enjoy their marriage, unaware of the unprepossessing qualities some unexpected and extraordinary circumstances might still uncover in persons they seemed to know, liking what they knew. . . .

One of the most powerfully (and convincingly) argued conclusions of the study was the impossibility of 'spotting in advance' the signs, or symptoms, or indicators, of individual readiness for sacrifice, or of cowardice in the face of adversity; that is, to decide, outside the context that calls them into being or just 'wakes them up', the probability of their later manifestation.

John R. Roth brings the same issue of potentiality versus reality (the first being a yet-undisclosed mode of the second, and the second being an already-realized – and thus empirically accessible – mode of the first) in a direct contact with our problem:

> Had Nazi Power prevailed, authority to determine what ought to be would have found that no natural laws were broken and no crimes against God and humanity were committed in the Holocaust. It would have been a question, though, whether the slave labour operations should continue, expand, or go out of business. Those decisions would have been made on rational grounds.[2]

The unspoken terror permeating our collective memory of the Holocaust (and more than contingently related to the overwhelming desire not to look the memory in its face) is the gnawing suspicion that the Holocaust could be more than an aberration, more than a deviation from an otherwise straight path of progress, more than a cancerous growth on the otherwise healthy body of the civilized society; that, in short, the Holocaust was not an antithesis of modern civilization and everything (or so we like to think) it stands for. We suspect (even if we refuse to admit it) that the Holocaust could merely have uncovered another face of the same modern society whose other, more familiar, face we so admire. And that the two faces are perfectly comfortably attached to the same body. What we perhaps fear most is that each of the two faces can no more exist without the other than can the two sides of a coin.

Often we stop just at the threshold of the awesome truth. And so Henry Feingold insists that the episode of the Holocaust was indeed a new development in a long, and on the whole blameless, history of modern society; a development we had no way to expect and predict, like an appearance of a new malign strain of an allegedly tamed virus:

> The Final Solution marked the juncture where the European industrial system went awry; instead of enhancing life, which was the original hope of the Enlightenment, it began to consume itself. It was by dint of that industrial system and the ethos attached to it that Europe was able to dominate the world.

As if the skills needed and deployed in the service of world domination were qualitatively different from those which secured the effectiveness of the Final Solution. And yet Feingold is staring the truth in the face:

> [Auschwitz] was also a mundane extension of the modern factory system. Rather than producing goods, the raw material was human beings and the

end-product was death, so many units per day marked carefully on the manager's production charts. The chimneys, the very symbol of the modern factory system, poured forth acrid smoke produced by burning human flesh. The brilliantly organized railroad grid of modern Europe carried a new kind of raw material to the factories. It did so in the same manner as with other cargo. In the gas chambers the victims inhaled noxious gas generated by prussic acid pellets, which were produced by the advanced chemical industry of Germany. Engineers designed the crematoria; managers designed the system of bureaucracy that worked with a zest and efficiency more backward nations would envy. Even the overall plan itself was a reflection of the modern scientific spirit gone awry. What we witnessed was nothing less than a massive scheme of social engineering. . . .[3]

The truth is that every 'ingredient' of the Holocaust – all those many things that rendered it possible – was normal; 'normal' not in the sense of the familiar, of one more specimen in a large class of phenomena long ago described in full, explained and accommodated (on the contrary, the experience of the Holocaust was new and unfamiliar), but in the sense of being fully in keeping with everything we know about our civilization, its guiding spirit, its priorities, its immanent vision of the world – and of the proper ways to pursue human happiness together with a perfect society. In the words of Stillman and Pfaff,

There is more than a wholly fortuitous connection between the applied technology of the mass production line, with its vision of universal material abundance, and the applied technology of the concentration camp, with its vision of a profusion of death. We may wish to deny the connection, but Buchenwald was of our West as much as Detroit's River Rouge – we cannot deny Buchenwald as a casual aberration of a Western world essentially sane.[4]

Let us also recall the conclusion Raoul Hilberg has reached at the end of his unsurpassed, magisterial study of the Holocaust's accomplishment: 'The machinery of destruction, then, was structurally no different from organized German society as a whole. The machinery of destruction *was* the organized community in one of its special roles.'[5]

Richard L. Rubenstein has drawn what seems to me the ultimate lesson of the Holocaust. 'It bears', he wrote, 'witness to the *advance of civilization*.' It was an advance, let us add, in a double sense. In the Final Solution, the industrial potential and technological know-how boasted by our civilization has scaled new heights in coping successfully with a task of unprecedented magnitude. And in the same Final Solution our society has disclosed to us its heretofore unsuspected capacity.

Taught to respect and admire technical efficiency and good design, we cannot but admit that, in the praise of material progress which our civilization has brought, we have sorely underestimated its true potential.

> The world of the death camps and the society it engenders reveals the progressively intensifying night side of Judeo-Christian civilization. Civilization means slavery, wars, exploitation, and death camps. It also means medical hygiene, elevated religious ideas, beautiful art, and exquisite music. It is an error to imagine that civilization and savage cruelty are antithesis. . . . In our times the cruelties, like most other aspects of our world, have become far more effectively administered than ever before. They have not and will not cease to exist. Both creation and destruction are inseparable aspects of what we call civilization.[6]

[. . .]

As a profession, sociologists have succeeded in all but forgetting it, or shelving it away into the 'specialist interests' area, from where it stands no chance of reaching the mainstream of the discipline. If at all discussed in sociological texts, the Holocaust is at best offered as a sad example of what an untamed innate human aggressiveness may do, and then used as a pretext to exhort the virtues of taming it through an increase in the civilizing pressure and another flurry of expert problem-solving. At worst, it is remembered as a private experience of the Jews, as a matter between the Jews and their haters (a 'privatization' to which many spokesmen of the State of Israel, guided by other than eschatological concerns, have contributed more than a minor share).

This state of affairs is worrying not only, and not at all primarily, for the professional reasons – however detrimental it may be for the cognitive powers and societal relevance of sociology. What makes this situation much more disturbing is the awareness that if 'it could happen on such a massive scale elsewhere, then it can happen anywhere; it is all within the range of human possibility, and like it or not, Auschwitz expands the universe of consciousness no less than landing on the moon'.[7] The anxiety can hardly abate in view of the fact that none of the societal conditions that made Auschwitz possible has truly disappeared, and no effective measures have been undertaken to prevent such possibilities and principles from generating Auschwitz-like catastrophes; as Leo Kuper has recently found out, 'the sovereign territorial state claims, as an integral part of its sovereignty, the right to commit genocide, or engage in genocidal massacres, against people under its rule, and . . . the UN, for all practical purposes, defends this right.'[8]

One posthumous service the Holocaust can render is to provide an insight into the otherwise unnoticed 'other aspects' of the societal principles enshrined by modern history. I propose that the experience of the Holocaust, now thoroughly researched by the historians, should be looked upon as, so to speak, a sociological 'laboratory'. The Holocaust has exposed and examined such attributes of our society as are not revealed, and hence are not empirically accessible, in 'non-laboratory' conditions. In other words, *I propose to treat the Holocaust as a rare, yet significant and reliable, test of the hidden possibilities of modern society.*

Notes and References

1 George M. Kren and Leon Rappoport, *The Holocaust and the Crisis of Human Behaviour* (Holmes and Meier, New York, 1980), p. 2.
2 John K. Roth, 'Holocaust business', *Annals of AAPSS*, 450 (July 1980), p. 70.
3 Henry L. Feingold, 'How unique is the Holocaust?', in *Genocide: Critical Issues of the Holocaust*, ed. Alex Grobman and Daniel Landes (The Simon Wiesenthal Centre, Los Angeles, Calif., 1983), pp. 399–400.
4 Edmund Stillman and William Pfaff, *The Politics of Hysteria* (Harper and Row, New York, 1964), pp. 30–1.
5 Raoul Hilberg, *The Destruction of the European Jews* (Holmes and Meier, New York, 1983), vol. III, p. 994.
6 Richard L. Rubenstein, *The Cunning of History* (Harper, New York, 1978), pp. 91, 195.
7 Kren and Rappoport, *The Holocaust and the Crisis*, pp. 126, 143.
8 Leo Kuper, *Genocide: Its Political Use in the Twentieth Century* (Yale University Press, New Haven, Conn., 1981), p. 161.

Index